The Rise of Regions

The Rise of Regions

Conflict and Cooperation

Edited by
Ronald L. Tammen and Jacek Kugler

ROWMAN & LITTLEFIELD
Lanham • Boulder • New York • London

Published by Rowman & Littlefield
An imprint of The Rowman & Littlefield Publishing Group, Inc.
4501 Forbes Boulevard, Suite 200, Lanham, Maryland 20706
www.rowman.com

6 Tinworth Street, London SE11 5AL, United Kingdom

British Library Cataloguing in Publication Information Available

Library of Congress Cataloging-in-Publication Data

Names: | Tammen, Ronald L., 1943– editor. | Kugler, Jacek, editor.
Title: The rise of regions : conflict and cooperation / edited by Ronald L. Tammen and
  Jacek Kugler.
Description: Lanham, Maryland : Rowman & Littlefield, 2020. | Includes bibliographical
  references and index.
Identifiers: LCCN 2019048703 (print) | LCCN 2019048704 (ebook) | ISBN
  9781538131879 (cloth) | ISBN 9781538131886 (epub)
  ISBN 9781538171158 (pbk)
Subjects: LCSH: Regionalism—Case studies. | International cooperation—Case studies. |
  World politics—21st century—Case studies.
Classification: LCC JF197 .R57 2020 (print) | LCC JF197 (ebook) | DDC 327.1/7—
  dc23
LC record available at https://lccn.loc.gov/2019048703
LC ebook record available at https://lccn.loc.gov/2019048704

Contents

Figures and Tables

FIGURES

TABLES

Abbreviations and Acronyms

AfD	Alternative für Deutschland
AIDS	acquired immunodeficiency syndrome
AIIB	Asian Infrastructure Investment Bank
ANC	African National Congress
ARF	Alliance for a Responsible Future
ASEAN	Association of Southeast Asian Nations
AU	African Union
BBC	British Broadcasting Company
BJP	Bharatiya Janata Party
BMD	ballistic missile defense
CAR	Central African Republic
CELAC	Community of Latin American and Caribbean States
CFSP	Common Foreign and Security Policy
CINC	Composite Indicators of National Capabilities
COF	Commission on Overseas Filipino
DA	Democratic Alliance
DEW	Distant Early Warning
EFF	economic freedom fighters
EMU	economic and monetary union
ESCB	European System of Central Banks
EU	European Union
FTA	Free Trade Agreement
GDP	gross domestic product
GNA	government of national accord
HIV	human immunodeficiency virus
IAEA	International Atomic Energy Agency
IMF	International Monetary Fund
ISIS	Islamic State of Iraq and Syria
ITRA	Inter-American Treaty of Reciprocal Assistance
JDP	Justice and Development Party
LAFTA	Latin American Free Trade Association

LNA	Libyan National Army
MAD	mutually assured destruction
MI	Mérida Initiative
MILF	Moro Islamic Liberation Front
MOS	Memorandum of Security
NAFTA	North American Free Trade Agreement
NATO	North Atlantic Treaty Organization
NDA	Niger Delta Avengers
NORAD	North American Aerospace Defense Command
OAS	Organization of American States
PA	Pacific Alliance
PFR	Popular Front for Recovery
PKK	Partiya Karkeren Kurdistan
PNG	Papua New Guinea
POW	prisoner(s) of war
PPP	purchasing power parity
PRC	People's Republic of China
PTT	power transition theory
RPE	relative political extraction
SCO	Shanghai Cooperation Organization
SDF	Syrian Democratic Forces
SPLA	Sudan People's Liberation Army
SPLA-M	Sudan People's Liberation Army-Militia
SPP	Security and Prosperity Partnership
THAAD	Terminal High Altitude Area Defense
TPP	Trans-Pacific Partnership
UAE	United Arab Emirates
UKIP	United Kingdom Independence Party
UN	United Nations
UNSC	United Nations Security Council
USAN	Union of South American Nations
USMCA	United States–Mexico–Canada Agreement
USSR	Union of Soviet Socialist Republics
WTO	World Trade Organization

Acknowledgments

The editors understand that this book would not have been possible without the enthusiastic contributions of the membership of the TransResearch-Consortium (TRC). TRC was created by schools at three universities: Claremont Graduate University, La Sierra University, and Portland State University. TRC subsequently metamorphosed into an official nonprofit educational entity with a worldwide membership.

We say enthusiastic support because it is very rare in the academic world for scholars to cooperate for a long period of time, let alone the sixty years that the power transition research team has been testing, challenging, and expanding the horizons of this academic tradition.

Except for the classical literature, modern academic theories seldom last much beyond the life of the founder of the concept—in this case A. F. K. Organski at the University of Michigan. The reason for this is obvious. There no longer is a trail of students going into the discipline carrying on and extending research into new dimensions. But in the case of power transition theory, there have been five generations of researchers captivated by the empirical findings of the theory and the commonsense policy prescriptions they have produced. It is pretentious but accurate to indicate that power transition has replaced theoretically and empirically the older internally flawed balance of power perspective.

While we stipulate that intellectual stimulation and curiosity is critical to this longevity, no less important is a sense of loyalty, responsibility, commitment, and friendship—all characteristics that seem to be escapees from other social science literatures.

We give evidence of this research continuum with a power transition timeline following these acknowledgments, and we invite scholars from around the world to join us.

This book and its various authors and editors owe a significant debt to Professor Douglas Lemke at Penn State University. It was his intellectual breakthrough in 2002, with the publication of *Regions of War and Peace,* that subsequently made it possible to produce a policy-oriented book at the regional level based on the tenets of power transition theory.

For this current volume, fifth in our primary book line, we thank in particular Rowman & Littlefield's senior executive acquisitions editor, Susan McEachern, for her keen sense of judgment about academic work and what might be particularly promising. Plus her tolerance for dealing with an edited/ multi-authored work. We also greatly appreciate the excellent grammatical review conducted by Sabrina Petra Ramet. And thanks to assistant editor Katelyn Turner for her organizational competence.

We recognize that academic work does not exist in a vacuum. It must have executive leadership to thrive, let alone survive. We have found this kind of environment at the Mark O. Hatfield School of Government at Portland State University, where Birol Yesilada is director, and at the College of Urban and Public Affairs, where Steve Percy is dean; the Department of International Studies at Claremont Graduate University, where Professors Jacek Kugler, Yi Feng, and Mark Abdollahian provide support; and at the School of Business at La Sierra University led by Dean John Thomas.

The production of a multi-authored, edited book requires more than the usual support mechanisms. For this in particular we appreciate the high-quality contributions of Kristina Khederlarian, our executive editor; Nicholas Stowell, our footnote detective; and Zeyad Kelani and Manish Ranjan Shrivastav, our technical advisors.

In addition to the contributors to this book, we have benefitted by the participation and organizational capabilities of many students, faculty, and staff at our various institutions, including Jonathan Thomas and Eduardo Brugman at La Sierra University; Sarah Orizaga, Osman Tanrikulu, and Kierrah Byrd at Portland State University; and Lauren Copeland, Eliana Leon, Kristine Webster, Norvell Thomas, Glenn-Iain Steinback, Simon Tang, and Daniel Rose at the Claremont Graduate University.

Our hope is that this work will motivate colleagues to move beyond the great powers and explore the implications of power transition within regional hierarchies to account for civil and international conflicts but above all to seek paths to peace.

THE POWER TRANSITION TIMELINE

1958 Organski *World Politics*

Organski *Population and World Power* **1961**

1965 Organski *The Stages of Political Development*

Organski *World Politics (revised)* **1968**

1977 Organski and Kugler "The Costs of Major War: The Phoenix Factor," *APSR*

Kugler "Terror without Deterrence?" **1984** *JCR*

1984 Organski, Kugler and Cohen *Birth, Death and Taxes*

Organski and Kugler *War Ledger* **1980**

1986 Kugler and Domke "Comparing the Strength of Nations," *CPS*

Houweling and Siccama "Power **1988** Transitions as a Cause of War," *JCR*

1989 Arbetman and Kugler "Choosing Among Measures of Power," *World Politics*

Kim "Power Transitions and Great **1992** Power War from Westphalia to Waterloo," *World Politics*

1996 Kugler and Lemke *Parity and War*

Benson and Kugler "Power Parity, **1998** Democracy, and the Severity of Internal Violence," *JCR*

1999 DiCicco and Levy "Power Shifts and Problem Shifts," *JRC*

Feng, Kugler and Zak "The Politics **2000** of Fertility and Economic Development," *ISQ*

2000 Kugler and Lemke *The Power Transition Research Program in Modelarski Handbook of War Studies II*

Tammen et al. *Power Transitions* **2000** (translated into Chinese and Arabic)

2002 Lemke *Regions of War and Peace*

Efrid, Genna, and Kugler "From War 2003
to Integration: Generalizing Power
Transition Theory," *International
Interactions*

2006 Tammen and Kugler "Power
Transitions and China-US Conflicts,"
*The Chinese Journal of International
Politics*

Tammen "The Impact of Asia on 2006
World Politics: China and India
Options for the United States," *ISR*

2007 Benson editor "Extending the Bounds
of Power Transition Theory,"
International Interactions

Kugler editor "The Organski Legacy 2008
on Power Transition," *International
Interactions*

2008 Alsharabati and Kugler "War
Initiation in a Changing World,"
International Interactions

Abdollahian and Kang "In Search of 2008
Structure," *International Interactions*

2008 Tammen and Kugler "Implications
of Asia's Rise to Global Status" *in
Systemic Transitions: Past, Present, and
Future* edited by Thompson

Tammen "The Organski Legacy: A 2008
Fifty-Year Research Program,"
International Interactions

2010 Tammen and Wahedi "Challenging the
Argument that China will become the
Next Dominant Power" *in Power
Transitions: Theory and Applications* (in
Chinese)

**T. Kugler, Kang, J. Kugler, Arbetman, 2013
and Thomas** "Demographic and
Economic Consequences of Conflict," *ISQ*

2015 Kim and Gates "Power Transition
theory and the Rise of China," *IAS*

Kugler and Tammen *Performance of 2017
Nations*

2018 Thompson *Empirical International
Relations Theory, Foundations of PTT V:
2:19-64, PTT V:1:112, 722, 2:153, 3:138*

Tammen and Kugler *The Rise of 2020
Regions*

2020 T. Kugler *Political Consequences
of Population Dynamics)*

Kugler and Kang *Conditional 2021
Deterrence (Forthcoming)*

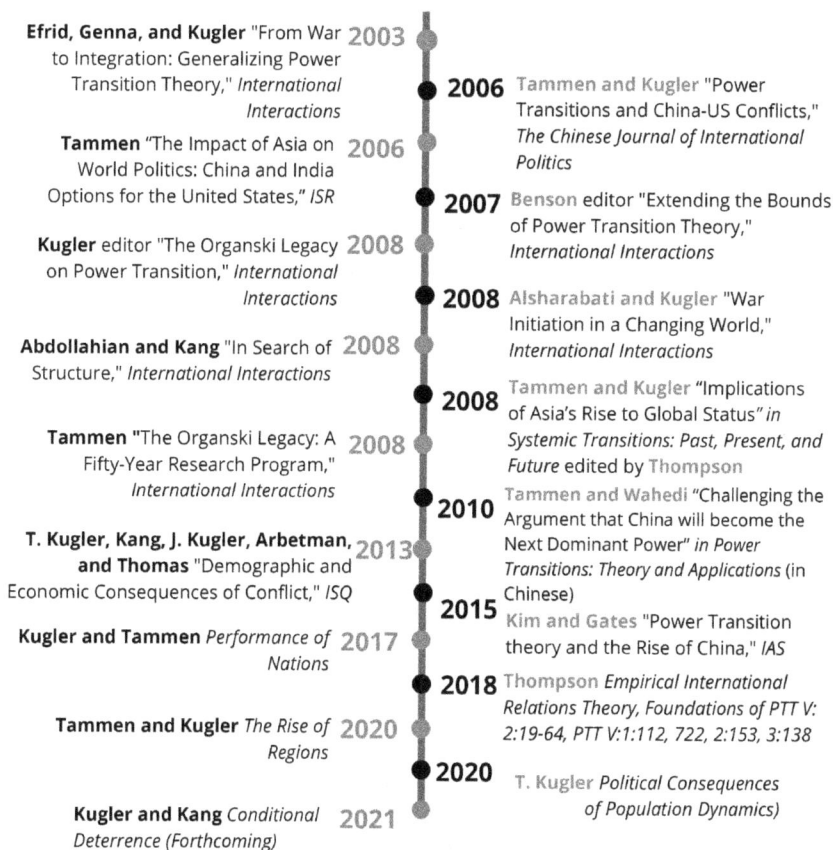

*This Time Line represents only a preliminary and thus incomplete list of primary power transition books
and articles. We welcome all other scholars who have participated directly or indirectly in this research
agenda to contact the two editors of this book and be listed in this evolving history, which will be
updated on our website at transresearchconsortium.com.*

Chapter One

The Rise of Regions

Ronald L. Tammen and Jacek Kugler

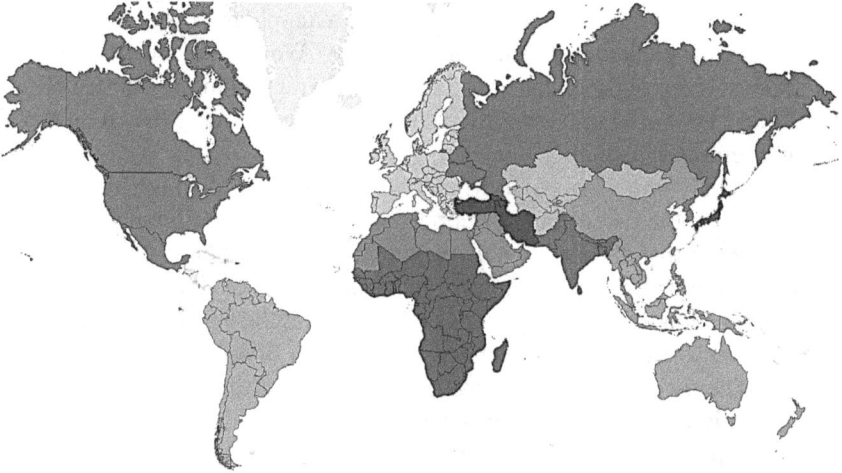

Global Regions

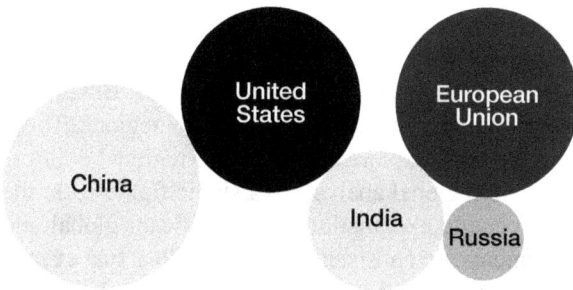

7,000 ▭▬▬▬ 60,000
Shading denotes GDPPC in PPP Constant
2005 USD & Size denotes GDP PPP
Constant 2005 USD

Global Hierarchies

The world has changed dramatically since the widely unanticipated fall of the Soviet Union on a cold winter day in December 1991.[1] One-half of the so-called bipolar world disappeared, and not in warfare or civil war, but in a proclamation. Warsaw bloc trucks and tanks turned east and ran until fuel gave out, forcing soldiers to walk home to Mother Russia. Seldom have words meant so much for world politics.

Behind the startling fall of the Soviet empire was an equally unanticipated failure of the supportive intellectual architecture that sustained stability during the Cold War. What would rise to replace the "security" resting on the logic of mutual deterrence? Would a unipolar power distribution lead to war or preserve systemic global peace? Would the new asymmetric structure release regional tensions previously wrapped in the bounds of the Cold War? Or would both conditions prevail—peace among the Great Powers and regional instability?

And equally important, what would the new rules of the international system be? With the rise of the developing world, would conflict emerge from regions rather than the traditional superpower confrontations? Would politics move down to the regions in a new fundamental shift of power?

This book answers these questions by looking at the various regions of the world in a systematic manner under the umbrella of a grand strategy architecture. The theory of power transition is not new, although it has grown in sophistication and application. It is the only power distribution survivor of the Cold War period that accurately accounts for peace and war in the last three centuries.[2] Unlike prevailing realist Cold War theories, it does not require contorted explanations to account for one of the most dramatic events of the twentieth century—the collapse of the Union of Soviet Socialist Republics (USSR) and subsequent absence of global war.[3]

That noted, the Western superpower era is drawing to a close. We are witnessing the rise of the developing nations. China, India, Indonesia, Brazil, and a resurgent Africa are all creating new sets of politics in their regions. These are the focus for this book—the underexplored dynamics of regional politics.

By linking grand strategy and regional analysis to a single framework, the authors lay out historically accurate explanations for significant global and regional trends. These assessments are consistent not only with actual events, but with a theory that provides intellectual structure to what otherwise would be informed speculation and overuse of the "it depends" equivocation.

The underlying structure of this book is based on modern power transition theory (PTT).[4] It is modern in the sense that, without betraying its core, PTT has metamorphosed over time into a policy relevant construct. It has expanded into explaining the initiation and intensity of regional conflicts. It has moved beyond nation-states to regional questions of integration, migration, and recovery from war.[5] It is a probabilistic theory that does not purport to answer every question or detail every development but rather sets the necessary preconditions for war and peace. PTT provides the structure, the architecture by which analysts can unfold and relate events of significance to policy choices. This book expands on that base with a systematic review of regional politics.

THEORETICAL FOUNDATIONS

More than fifty years ago, to the dismay and fierce criticism of many scholars, A. F. K. Organski stood the balance of power theory on its head.[6] There was little security in the distribution of power equally among leading nations, only a threat of war, he argued. On the contrary, he wrote, a preponderance of power preserves the peace. Heresy, preposterous! cried the balance-of-power community, which even then was becoming the bulwark of Cold War thinking and the source of classical deterrence that insisted that peace was assured only by deterrence based on the threat of mutually assured destruction (MAD). On the other hand, PTT stated that conventional or nuclear balance was a precondition for massive war, whereas nuclear deterrence was tenuous and subject to failure both at parity and most extreme asymmetry.

Today, many scholars, directly and indirectly, with and without attribution, have adopted the heart of the arguments put forth by Organski.[7] Power transitions among the Western Great Powers led to the severe world wars that shook the international system in the twentieth century—and may do so again when the Asian giants overtake the United States. Or they can be peaceful transitions depending on the degree of satisfaction of the challenging and preeminent nations excluded from the dominant coalition.

Although Organski did not explore regional confrontations, subsequent research by Lemke and others has shown that the same conditions of parity and dissatisfaction also prompt regional confrontations and are directly associated with intense civil wars.[8] This opens the door for a new way to understand regional politics. And in combination with techniques to measure the political capacity of nations, regions, and provinces, regional conflict and civil war can now be predicted with some confidence.

PTT rests on three novel and fundamental observations. The first is that power parity is a precondition for major conflict. This insight directly challenges the notion that a balance of power ensures peace and instead argues that parity creates the preconditions that favor war if dissatisfaction is present.

Related and central to this argument is the realization that national power is derived from internal development. Recognizing that economic development occurs at different rates, the theory indicates that the national product along with the capacity to mobilize resources and increase military capabilities will rise and fall relative to that of proximate competitors. This rise is driven in part by population changes, in part by investment and technological innovation, and in part by the political performance of governments. This realization that the international system and various regional systems are dynamic shifts the analytical focus from a static cross-sectional to a dynamic cross-temporal perspective.

The third fundamental element of PTT is that the norms of the international system are shaped by a dominant, preeminent nation temporarily on top of the international hierarchy. Stability emerges as the group of nations satisfied with the existing norms established by the preeminent nation, seeking security and economic opportunities, coalesce into an overwhelming alliance that supports the status quo. The dominant power is not a hegemon and considers its allies in drafting the norms that rule the international system because it needs support from the other important international members to succeed.

This book demonstrates that these three elements also apply at the regional and subregional level of analysis. There are regional dominant powers, and as in the global environment, regional hierarchies are constantly changing as national power grows or wanes. This dynamic is responsible for conflict or peace, development or stagnation, at the regional level.

History shows that no global or regionally preeminent nation can maintain a hegemonic position in perpetuity.[9] Regions demonstrate this observation more vividly than the global picture because, simply, there are more examples.

Regional power transitions occur when a rising challenger overtakes the preeminent regional power.[10] If the challenger is dissatisfied with its regional standing and objects to the leadership values or style of the leading regional power, then the probability of war increases dramatically. Conversely if the challenging nation has reached an accord with the leading regional power and shares the same values in a trusting environment, then, despite a change in relative power, peace will be maintained.[11]

The policy implications of this perspective are important for understanding whether regions will be in conflict or cooperation. Consistent with global-level dynamics, regional asymmetry led by a satisfied dominant nation ensures peace; parity and dissatisfaction set the preconditions for conflict. Stability is assured not by fear and confrontation but by strong alliances and further enhanced by regional integration. Shifts in relative power are far more frequent at the regional than at the global level because of the vast differences in levels of development among smaller entities. The current of change is both more observable and more malleable at the regional level where policy opportunities abound.

THE LINK BETWEEN GLOBAL AND REGIONAL ANALYSIS

Certain distinct conditions account for confrontation, competition, and cooperation among nations. This is true both at global and regional levels.

The fundamental element that determines the type of engagement among nations is their standing in the power hierarchy, coupled with their level of satisfaction. This establishes their status quo behavior.[12] The original power transition formulation focused on global interactions.[13] Power is defined as the capacity of one nation to advance policy goals by altering the policy of another through persuasion or coercion. The status quo reflects the commitment by participants to existing international rules and norms. Although these concepts are transparent, their measurement is not.

Acknowledging the varying commitments among nations to the status quo allows one to divide the world into satisfied nations that grant broad acceptance of and support for the prevailing existing structures and dissatisfied nations that challenge existing rules. Actions are constrained by the power of the participants. Figure 1.1 shows the interaction between globally powerful and less powerful states and two select regions. The likelihood of cooperation or conflict within each hierarchy derives from the degree of support for the status quo.

The international system is divided into global and regional hierarchies. Within each hierarchy, a dominant or preeminent nation and a challenger compete for preponderance. This book focuses on an extension of global assessments to regional hierarchies. Following Lemke, we postulate that key members of regional hierarchies follow the same pattern as those in the

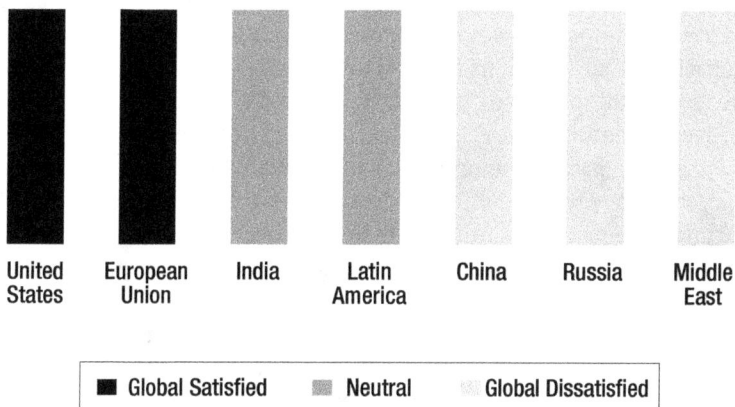

Figure 1.1. Global and Regional Hierarchies

global hierarchy. Regional interactions are directly or indirectly affected by the global actors but the converse does not hold.

THE GLOBAL HIERARCHY

Based on the current distribution of power shown, the United States is the globally dominant nation, followed closely by China. India is a potential Great Power whose influence is expected to rise substantially after 2050.[14] The hybrid European Union (EU) community will be a bit weaker after the anticipated departure of Britain at Brexit. But the larger nations—Germany, France, and Italy—remain formidable in combination with other European nations. Russia is a declining state that increasingly will be influenced by China.

At the global level, the United States and the EU, supported by Great Britain, Japan, South Korea, Canada, Australia, and New Zealand, comprise the satisfied Western coalition. China and Russia are the dissatisfied challengers joined in a not-yet-firmly established coalition. India is not officially tied to either grouping and, thus, becomes the prize by mid-century.

PTT stipulates that the relative power of the competing Great Powers, which is approximated by gross domestic product (GDP) and reflects the number of people who can work and fight, defines the core global hierarchy. As argued in this volume, actual power emerges from the interaction between population and productivity.[15] National wealth is fungible and can be allocated to fulfill military or economic priorities depending on the level of satisfaction on the part of national leaders.[16] GDP is a useful proxy for power, particularly when combined with political capacity, because it can be disaggregated to regions or within states. It can be used to analyze past events while also serving as a forecasting tool up to fifty years into the future.

The key to improving the accuracy of GDP as a predictive tool lies in political capacity.[17] Extrapolations that exclude political performance consistently underestimate the power of developing mobilized societies, like Vietnam, while overestimating the performance of oil-rich societies like Saudi Arabia.[18] When comparing countries at similar levels of development, political capacity may have reduced effects. Most regions of concern in this book have approximately equal levels of internal development. But there are exceptions. To be consistent across all regions, no controls for political performance are imposed in this volume.

There is a dynamic connection between power and changes in the status quo, and both are associated with conflict and cooperation. Power transition postulates that the distributions of power set the preconditions, and changing satisfaction levels provide the conditions for war and peace. The critical triggering mechanism differentiating periods of war and peace is captured by commitment to the status quo. Figure 1.2 outlines three conditions based on power and the relative commitment to the status quo.

Status Quo

| Cooperation | Competition | Confrontation |

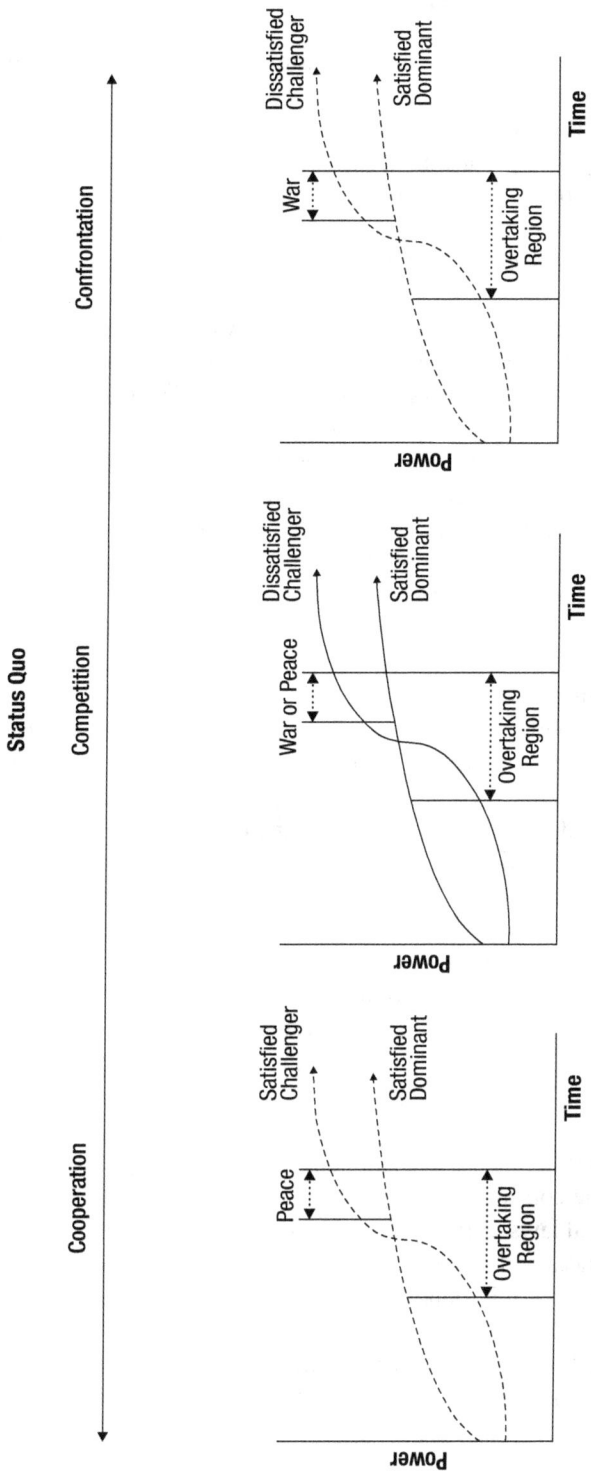

Figure 1.2.   Power Transition: Conflict or Cooperation

The first condition is in which two dissatisfied leading states hold roughly equal shares of power. This situation presents the most likely conditions for conflict. The reason is that dissatisfied nations reject the status quo and are restrained only by the cost of war. In the absence of a dominant state supporting the status quo, both challenger and defender have only war as an instrument to resolve serious disputes. War is likely within such a discordant global or regional hierarchy because contenders with different interests and incentives attempt to impose their influence on others.

The second condition generally prevails in world politics. The dominant side is satisfied, but the challenger is not. The satisfied dominant nation does not initiate conflict because satisfied allies supporting the dominant nation seek to maintain the status quo designed to advance the goals of the satisfied coalition. Interactions between a dominant satisfied and dissatisfied challenger result in mixed outcomes. Either cooperation or confrontation is possible. Power parity conditions produce severe wars only when a dissatisfied risk-prone challenger seeks to overtake the defender.

Peaceful interactions emerge when the dissatisfied challenger is persuaded to accept or join an evolving status quo. The rare preconditions for severe war are present, but so is the possibility of accommodation. Dissatisfied Germany entered conflicts in World Wars I and II when there was parity with the United Kingdom, but policy differences could not be resolved. However, when the United States overtook Britain after 1870, the result was a lasting alliance, and, when Germany overtook France and Great Britain in the 1960s, this passed unnoticed because all parties remained satisfied.

A final, rare condition leads to peace.[19] This is the situation in which the challenger and defender are both satisfied. This circumstance leads to institutionalized alliances, free-trade zones, and ultimately, to integration and even the creation of new states.

Peaceful competitive interactions represent the majority of international exchanges. Nations generally seek to preserve their identity and interests but are open to trade, movement, and normal activities with other nations. Competitive states follow international rules and contracts but do not establish new institutional structures to secure them. These nations depend on market forces to determine the quality and quantity of economic and social transactions within the confines of loosely defined international rules and nonbinding international laws. Before 1898, this described the United States, a nation avoiding alliances and foreign entanglements but willing to support freedom of the seas by forcefully opposing piracy when it interfered with freedom of navigation and commerce.

War and conflict command our attention even though they are not the prevailing conditions globally or regionally. Competitive interactions become confrontational, and severe wars can be waged between contenders when the challengers (or the hegemons) attempt to change the rules in their favor. Evidence shows that severe wars are waged at power parity when the dissatisfied challenger attempts to alter the status quo.[20]

As China overtakes the United States, the structure of global politics inevitably will be altered as seen in figure 1.3.[21] The Western alliance of the United States and the EU can sustain dominance of the global hierarchy even if China and Russia, no longer a contender for global dominance, fully cooperate and generate an alliance like the North Atlantic Treaty Organization (NATO). The rise of India may have a major impact on global structures. An alliance with the West would create a preponderant coalition preserving much of the current global structure. On the other hand, a potential alliance between China and India supported by the weaker Russia could create a powerful bloc of developing nations that could challenge the Western alliance and restructure the norms of the global hierarchy.

During the Cold War, arguments advancing a balance of power notwithstanding, global stability has been maintained by the clear preponderance of the United States over the USSR and the undisputed supremacy of NATO over the Warsaw Pact. Parity in nuclear capabilities did not provide the USSR, and does not now allow a much weaker Russia, the capability to

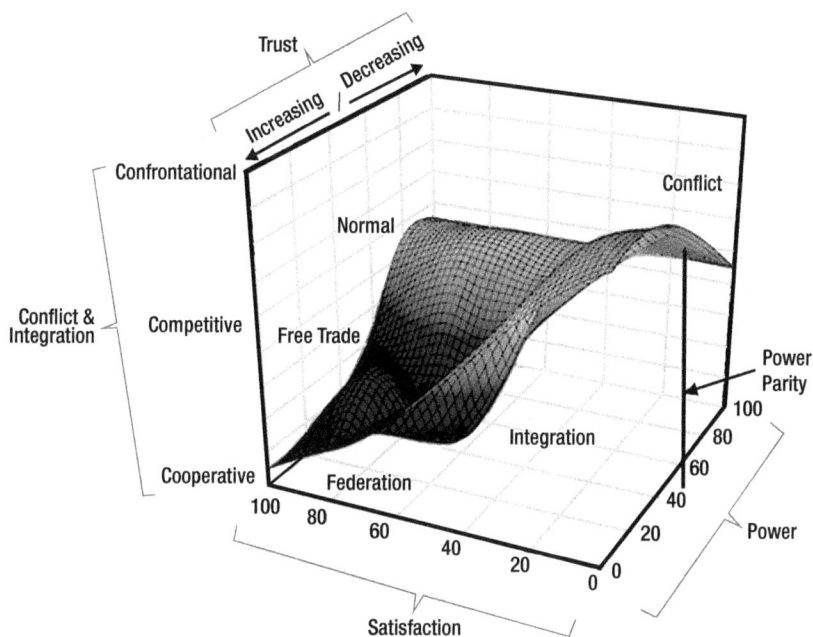

Figure 1.3. **Power Projections of World Global Powers**

challenge the EU or the United States—and certainly not the NATO alliance. Due to its size, any severe international confrontation in the next half-century would have to directly involve a dissatisfied China.

This book uses the power transition perspective to analyze regions because the empirical record connecting power transitions to global conflict has been extensively documented.[22] A transition is a necessary but not sufficient prerequisite for conflict. When the rare transition condition is met, war is waged to resolve severe disputes in more than half of all transitions. Based on the pioneering work by Angus Maddison, figure 1.4 shows recent results that generally support power transition insights.[23]

Conflicts among members of the global hierarchy have been extensively studied. Using well-established criteria for major powers, figure 1.4 displays the most severe conflicts, historically located in Europe, waged for control of the global hierarchy. The most severe conflicts were clearly waged at parity between groups of dissatisfied states seeking to redress grievances. The one clear outlier is Japan's decision to bomb Pearl Harbor. This brought the United States into the most massive global conflict on record and also determined the outcome of World War II. Even though some have attributed this attack to a

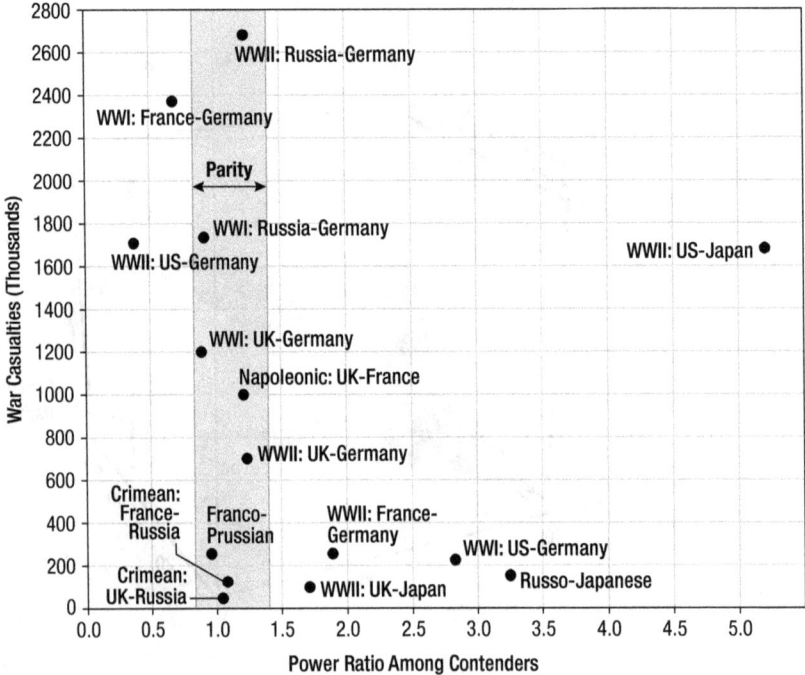

Figure 1.4. Power Transition and Global War

transition, we find no evidence supporting this claim.[24] Adding dissatisfaction to power parity accounts for more than 80 percent of severe wars.[25]

Lemke has shown that the same conditions of parity and dissatisfaction also prompt regional confrontations, and Benson and Kugler show that similar conditions are directly associated with civil wars. Finally, conflict is not the only or even the prevailing condition of world politics. As Yesilada et al. demonstrate, the formation of the EU may encourage federation and other forms of integration outside Europe.[26]

THE ASCENT OF REGIONALISM

This book provides analytical tools with which to anticipate these fundamental changes in politics at the regional level. These tools could provide decision makers with regional early warning systems.

This review is particularly pertinent now because of the tectonic changes in the distribution of global power that are taking place. For the first time since the early 1900s, the dominance of the United States is directly challenged by China and likely to be followed by a challenge from India.[27] As this process evolves, American dominance, originally made possible by the collapse and disintegration of the USSR, will erode. By mid-century, global power will be equally distributed between the developed and developing world. For the first time since the Treaty of Westphalia in 1648, the relatively less-affluent developing societies, holding the majority of the world's population, will match or supersede the output of the most developed nations.[28] The opportunity for dissatisfaction and disagreement is large.

Further, massive shifts in population are underway. Although an approximate constant 70 percent of total output continues to be produced by populations in the great global powers (EU, China, the United States, and India), these societies now are home to almost 50 percent of the global population. This will not last. From a high of 75 percent at the start of the Industrial Revolution in 1820, these countries are expected to decline sharply to less than 30 percent by century's end. Major population imbalances are imminent because a vast majority of the global population soon will reside in small developing states.[29]

If current trends continue, for a period of time the regions of the world, rather than superpowers, will be the generators of war and peace. Border disputes; water shortages; access to oil, gas, and minerals; and ideological, religious, and cultural frictions, when coupled with a change in the hierarchy of regions, will be the new triggers of stability and instability. For a while, regions will drive world politics.

We are about to live in a new world. A world where the "have-nots" suddenly hold far more of the reins of power. The commonly held explanations about how the old world worked have proven to be, at best, questionable. But we are not without guidance moving forward, as this book will detail.

DEFINING REGIONS

Defining regions is part art and part specialized knowledge. Scholars and foreign policy practitioners disagree frequently over the names and even over which countries belong in each region. A globe from the 1950s provides substantial evidence of fluidity over time at the regional level. For this book, the classic taxonomic debate between lumpers and splitters is reviewed, which applies well to the current topic. Unlike most regional scholars, our chapters do not focus on geography, religion, water, form of government, history, trade, ethnic composition, oil, commerce, or any of a dozen other variables that distinguish each country from its neighbors, close and distant. In our view, these variables are important but can lead to "uniqueism," the form of scholarship that states, "my country is unique and therefore must be understood as a standalone single entity."

Because our definition of regions focused on conflict and cooperation along a scale ranging from war to integration, we have sympathy with the lumpers. Our purpose is to operationalize findings from the global level of analysis dealing with conflict and cooperation and apply those lessons at the regional level. Countries are lumped together where there is evidence that they influence each other in their neighborhood, positively or negatively, on a routine basis. That said, we confess that we are influenced by Lemke's brilliant work measuring whether or not the principles of the global power transition theory could be applied regionally.[30]

His scheme follows:

South America

Northern Tier		*Pacific Coast*
Atlantic Coast		*Central*

Middle East

Arab-Israeli
Northern Rim
Arab Peninsula

Far East

South Asia	*Asian Archipelago*
Southeast Asia	*Overlapping Dyadic Local Hierarchies*
East Asia	

Africa

Maghreb	*Central Highlands*
West Africa	*South Atlantic Coast*
Gulf of Guinea	*Indian Ocean*
Central Lowlands	*Southern Africa*
Horn of Africa	

Our second line of authority is the categorization used by the US Department of State (USDS), which, it notes, is based on political and economic criteria:

African Affairs
East Asian and Pacific Affairs
European Affairs
Near Eastern Affairs
New Independent States of the Former USSR
South Asian Affairs
Western Hemisphere Affairs

Our third authority, and a comprehensive lumper, is the unified commands of the US Department of Defense (USDOD):

NORTHCOM	US Northern Command
SOUTHCOM	US Southern Command
AFRICOM	US Africa Command
CENTCOM	US Central Command
EUCOM	US European Command
INDOPACOM	US Indo-Pacific Command

While appreciating such expert guidance, in figure 1.5 we deviate from one or more of the three options by constructing our own regions in the following way.

North Africa	Central Asia
Sub-Saharan Africa	Eurasia
South America	East Asia
North America	South Asia
Europe	Southeast Asia
Middle East	Northeast Asia

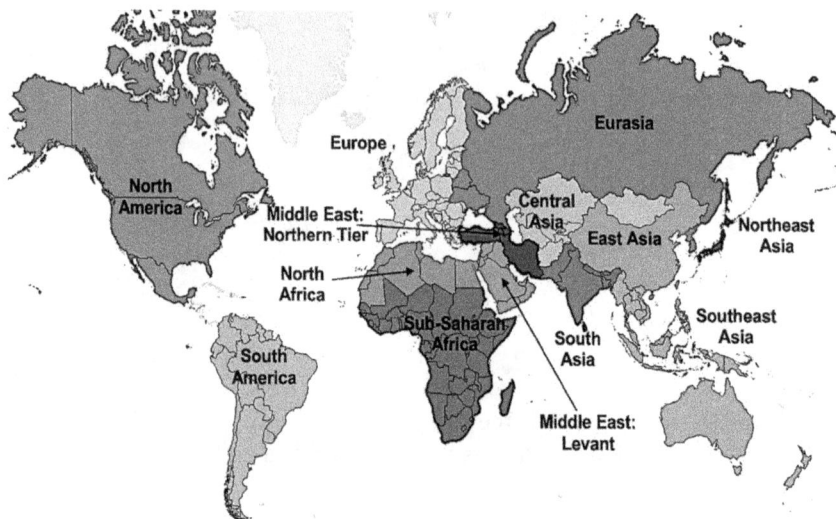

Figure 1.5.   Regions

Note that individual states such as Russia, China, and India are listed at the head of hierarchies in their geographic arenas. Each of these has a halo effect of different intensity. Some of these hierarchies overlap, some are expanding, and some have collapsed.

For our purposes and understanding the role of internal rather than external conflict there, we look at Africa as having two regions—a Maghreb to include Mauritania and Egypt and a sub-Saharan African complex. We expect this to change over time as Africa finds ways to compete with the emerging world and put to work what will be a huge population.

Somewhat similar is the picture in South America, where we view the continent as one region. We understand the Northern Tier's potential for conflict but trust our analysis, which continues to find Brazil the unparalleled but reluctant dominant power.

There are many maps of the Middle East. Our Middle East runs from Turkey to Yemen and the Red Sea to Afghanistan. Yes, we understand that Egypt has one foot in Africa and one in the Middle East, and it is so treated in this book.

As for Central Asia, we believe it is long past time to recognize this as a real region and not just as the area comprising the former provinces of the USSR. The nations of Central Asia may be "caught in the middle," but increasingly Central Asia is acting like a new region.

Southeast Asia has reasons to be viewed as a whole, which we do, recognizing that it is bounded by China and India, the two rising giants. As lumpers we also include Australia, which always has kept a wary eye on Indonesia, and companion-in-arms New Zealand, although both could claim ownership of a spot in North America if they asked.

Our Northeast Asia includes Japan and North and South Korea, with halo effects from the United States, Russia, and China.

We are not performing analyses on the Caribbean or Central America because although interesting, these countries cannot influence even the smallest of the major and Great Powers that surround them. Cuba has a modest but important historical claim to the contrary. Similarly, there are interesting developments in the Arctic regions with potential disputes over transit and mineral/oil resources at stake. We do not cover these because, essentially, they are multiparty disputes.

These regional "borders" are not fixed. They are porous, permeable. The rise of China, India, and Indonesia, for example, will see their influence spill over to nearby areas. Already we are seeing Chinese influence snaking across the South Asia region toward Africa, the Middle East, and beyond, including Italy.

For a very few decades, regions will dictate to the world. But the day will soon come when the twin giants arise and reorder the international system. This book outlines what this intervening period will look like.

NOTES

1. Global Map shows region contours. The hierarchy map shows the relative size of the top contenders in this region. World Bank, "World Development Indicators," last modified March 27, 2016, http://documents.worldbank.org/curated/en/805371467990952829/World-development-indicators-2016.

2. Douglas Lemke, "The Continuation of History: Power Transition Theory and the End of the Cold War," *Journal of Peace Research* 34, no. 1 (1997): 23–36.

3. Ronald L. Tammen, Jacek Kugler, Douglas Lemke, Allan Stam, Carole Alsharabati, Mark Abdollahian, Brian Efird, and A. F. K. Organski, *Power Transitions: Strategies for the 21st Century* (New York: Chatham House, 2000).

4. Jacek Kugler and Ronald L. Tammen, eds., *The Performance of Nations* (Lanham, MD: Rowman & Littlefield, 2012).

5. Ronald L. Tammen, Jacek Kugler, and Doug Lemke, *The Oxford Encyclopedia of Empirical International Relations Theory* (Oxford: Oxford University Press, 2018); Birol Yesilada, Jacek Kugler, Gaspare Genna, and Osman Tanrikulu, *Global Power Transition and the Future of the European Union* (London: Routledge, 2018); Tadeusz Kugler, Kyungkook Kang, Marina Arbetman, Jacek Kugler, and John Thomas, "Demographic and Economic Consequences of Conflict," *International Studies Quarterly* 57, no. 1 (2013): 1–12.

6. A. F. K. Organski, *World Politics* (New York: Alfred A. Knopf Inc., 1958).

7. Jonathan DiCircco, "Power Transition Theory and the Essence of Revisionism" in William Thompson, ed., *Oxford Research Encyclopedia of Politics* (online publication, Sept. 2017).

8. Douglas Lemke, *Regions of War and Peace* (Cambridge: Cambridge University Press, 2002); Michelle Benson and Jacek Kugler, "Power Parity, Democracy and the Severity of Internal Violence," *The Journal of Conflict Resolution* 42, no. 2 (1998): 196–209.

9. Paul Kennedy, *The Rise and Fall of the Great Powers* (New York: Random House, 1988).

10. Douglas Lemke, "Dimensions of Hard Power: Regional Leadership and Material Capabilities," in Daniel Flemes, ed., *Regional Leadership in the Global System: Ideas, Interests and Strategies of Regional Powers* (London: Routledge, 2010): 31–50.

11. Lemke, *Regions of War and Peace.*

12. Tammen et al., *Power Transitions*; Tammen and Kugler, *The Performance of Nations.*

13. Lemke, *Regions of War and Peace.*

14. See chapter 16.

15. The original measure proposed was gross product, which roughly reflects the size and productivity of a population: Power = GDP/Capita × Population. For an assessment of limitations and advantages of this measure see A. F. K. Organski and Jacek Kugler, *The War Ledger* (Chicago: University of Chicago Press, 1980); Marina Arbetman and Jacek Kugler, "Choosing among Measures of Power: A Review of the Empirical Record," in Michael Ward and Richard Stoll, eds., *Power in World Politics* (Boulder: Lynne Rienner Publishers, 1989); Angus Maddison, *Dynamic Forces in Capitalist Development: A Long-Run Comparative View* (Oxford: Oxford University Press, 1991).

16. An alternative frequently used by scholars in related analysis is the Composite Indicator of National Capabilities (CINC), which aggregates and weights equally six indicators: military expenditures, military personnel, energy consumption, iron and steel production, urban population, and total population. The advantage of CINC is its availability and common use, which secures easy replication. The main drawbacks are: first, the difficulty in effectively assessing societies over time because the number of actors affects the relative size of societies; second, the difficulty in forecasting power over time because components vary and even change over time; third, the excessive impact of military capabilities on the overall measure is notable—the USSR was dominant during the Cold War. $CINC = \sum_{(k=1-6)}^{n} K/6$, where the k indicators are ratios of each country n's total population, urban population, iron and steel production, primary energy consumption, military expenditure, and military personnel over the corresponding world total. National leaders can choose to allocate different portions of domestic product to security, growth, health, education, infrastructure, or other priorities as needed. Moreover, in confrontational conditions depending on the level of threat perceived by the ruling elite, military expenditures can rise and fall dramatically. The overall correlation between gross domestic product (GDP) and the CINC measures that include military, demographic, and economic indicators is high for developed societies. The difference between GDP and power emerges when comparisons are made between developed and developing nations, but results are similar among nations at equivalent levels

of development. Organski and Kugler, *The War Ledger*; Kugler and Arbetman, "Choosing among Measures of Power."

17. Kugler and Tammen, *The Performance of Nations.*

18. The new formulation is Power = GDP × RPE, where RPE is the relative ability of a government to extract resources from the population. The computation can be extended to include foreign aid; see Organski and Kugler, *The War Ledger*, chapter 3.

19. This condition *cannot* be deduced from realism or neorealism because it assumes anarchy. Despite the overwhelming evidence, the possibility of integration among nations is excluded because a nation-state needs to give up sovereignty to gain economic, security, and political rewards. Commitment to common status quo goals and trust is needed for such an accommodation. Brexit suggests—as we empirically show—that Britain is satisfied with the security arrangements and seeks a common trade zone but is unwilling for any responsibility for labor mobility, immigration, and monetary matters to defer to Brussels.

20. A. F. K. Organski, *World Politics* (New York: Knopf, 1958); Organski and Kugler, *The War Ledger*; Jacek Kugler and Douglas Lemke, *Parity and War* (Ann Arbor: University of Michigan Press, 1996); and Tammen et al., *Power Transitions*. In the long term, the size of population, which heavily favors Asian societies, as shown in figure 1.6, will determine the dominant power in global politics.

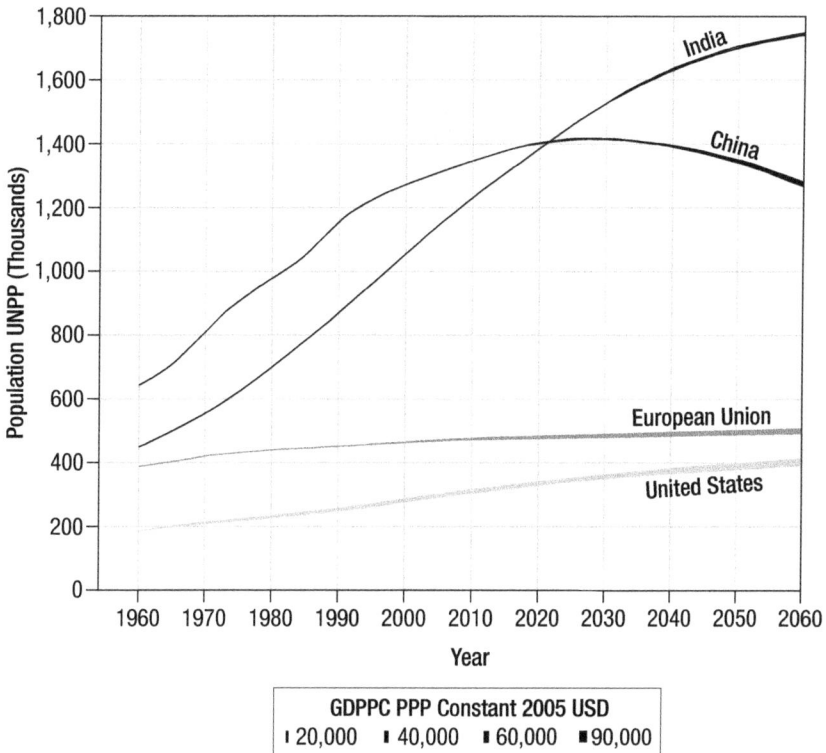

Figure 1.6. Population of Major Contenders

21. Figure 1.3 source: Birol Yesilada, Jacek Kugler, Gaspare Genna, and Osman Tanrikulu, *Global Power Transition and the Future of the European Union* (London: Routledge, 2018).

22. Mark Abdollahian et al., "The Mosaic of International Power: Reflections on General Trends," in Bouds Estemad, Jean Batou, and Thomas David, eds., *Towards an International Economic and Social History* (Genève: Editions Passé present, 1995).

23. Allison Hamlin and Jacek Kugler, "The Ukraine Crisis: Peaceful or Conflictual Transition," paper presented at the International Studies Association, 2016. Figure 1.4 source: Data from Maddison Project Database, version 2013. J. Bolt and J. L. van Zanden (2014). The Maddison Project: Collaborative Research on Historical National Accounts. *The Economic History Review*, 67 (3): 627–651, working paper, available at https://www.rug.nl/ggdc/historicaldevelopment/maddison/releases/maddison-project-database-2013.

24. Graham Allison, *Destined for War: Can America and China Escape Thucydides's Trap?* (London: Scribe Publications, 2017).

25. Suzanne Werner and Jacek Kugler, *Power Transitions and Military Buildups: Resolving the Relationship between Arms Buildups and War in Parity and War: Evaluations and Extensions of The War Ledger* (Ann Arbor: University of Michigan Press, 1996).

26. Birol Yeşilada et al., *Global Power Transition*.

27. United Nations, "2030 Demographic Challenges and Opportunities for Sustainable Development Planning," last modified 2015, http://www.un.org/en/development/desa/population/publications/pdf/trends/Population2030.pdf.

28. World Bank, "The World Bank, Population, total (2017)," last modified 2019, https://data.worldbank.org/indicator/sp.pop.totl.

29. United Nations, "Population 2030."

30. Lemke, *Regions of War and Peace*.

Chapter Two

East Asia

China on the Move

Ronald L. Tammen and Ayesha Umar Wahedi

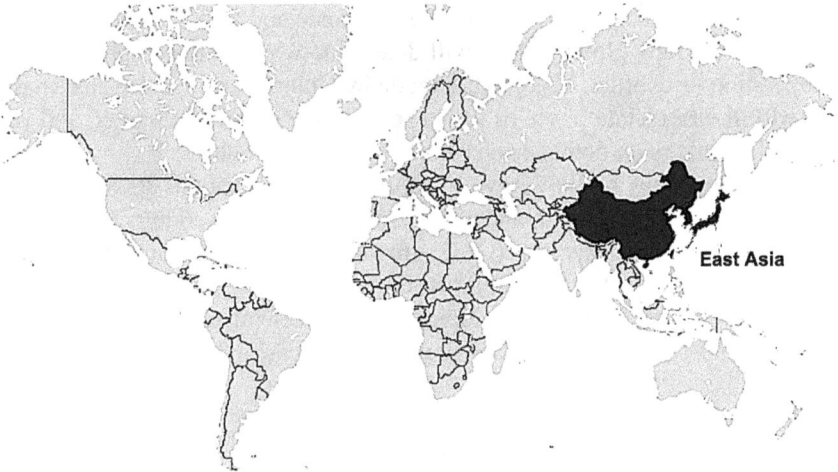

East Asia

East Asia–China Region

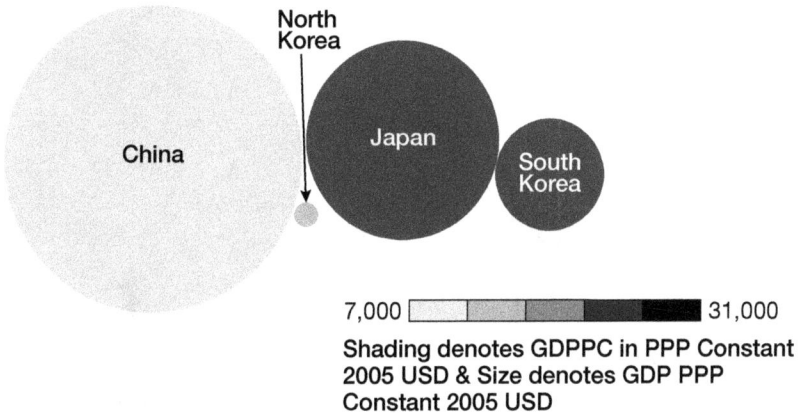

North
Korea

China

Japan

South
Korea

7,000 □□□□□■■■■ 31,000

Shading denotes GDPPC in PPP Constant
2005 USD & Size denotes GDP PPP
Constant 2005 USD

East Asia–China Hierarchy

THE BENEFITS OF FAST GROWTH

China has entered the middle of the fast-growth curve period, an era character-ized by national exuberance. In the decades following the end of the Great Pro-letarian Cultural Revolution, China has experienced steep growth, accompa-nied by heightened nationalism, a flexing of newfound power, expansionism, and some degree of arrogance. There has been a testing of the boundaries of power amid expectations that the country enjoys a manifest destiny. This pe-riod will not last forever. It will come to an end when China's aging population begins to curtail its growth rate. But for now, this is the time of greatest danger to the global community as China recognizes and tests its newfound power.[1]

How China manages this period of exuberance and how the United States adjusts to the new global reality will determine whether the emphasis is on cooperation or conflict. The choices made by Chinese and US decision mak-ers will in turn dictate peace or war. The stakes could not be higher, and yet strategic thinkers on both sides have not broken the code.

The endogenous growth curve in figure 2.1 describes the developmental path for both a slow-growth and a successful fast-growth country.[2]

This overlapping generation (OLG) growth model was introduced by Samu-elson[3] and expanded by Diamond.[4] It tells us that over time, nations' econo-mies converge because the developing group accelerates, while at the same time, the most advanced societies slow down. Lucas[5] extended this argument

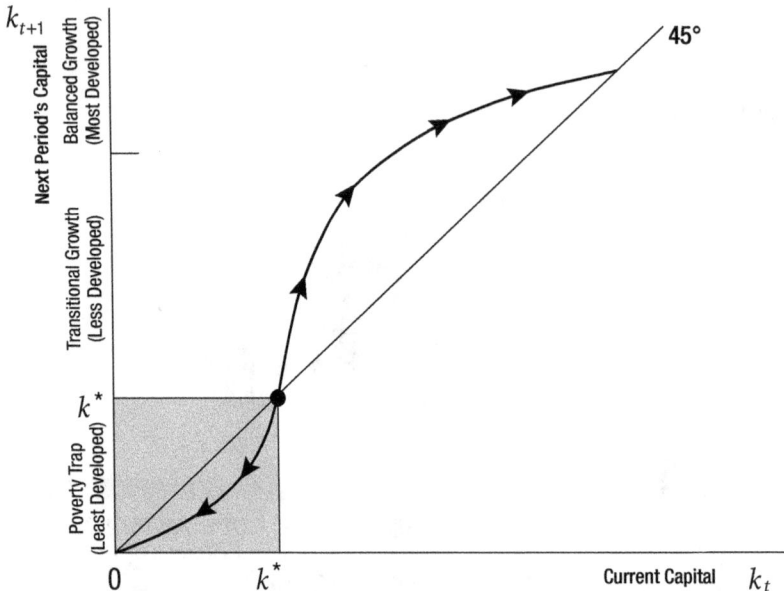

Figure 2.1.   Endogenous Growth Path

to build an OLG growth model with a general equilibrium condition in which all market demand equals supply. Finally, Feng, Kugler, and Zak incorporate in their expanded politics of fertility and economic development (POFED) model the effects of economic, political, and demographic factors that substantially improve the explanatory power of the OLG growth model.[6]

China is a perfect exemplar of a country that escaped the boundaries of the poverty trap cycle, located at the bottom left of this graph. Under the regime of Mao Zedong, population growth continued to eat away at productivity. But after China's economy was liberalized, output per capita took off and the country's wealth increased. When China broke through the poverty population barrier, its society then benefitted from the advantages of a large population rather than suffering from its drag effects. Figure 2.2 shows that the results, anticipated in figure 2.1, are more than impressive.[7]

This describes the current situation in which China finds itself. It has already enjoyed more than thirty years of high growth and finds itself slowing

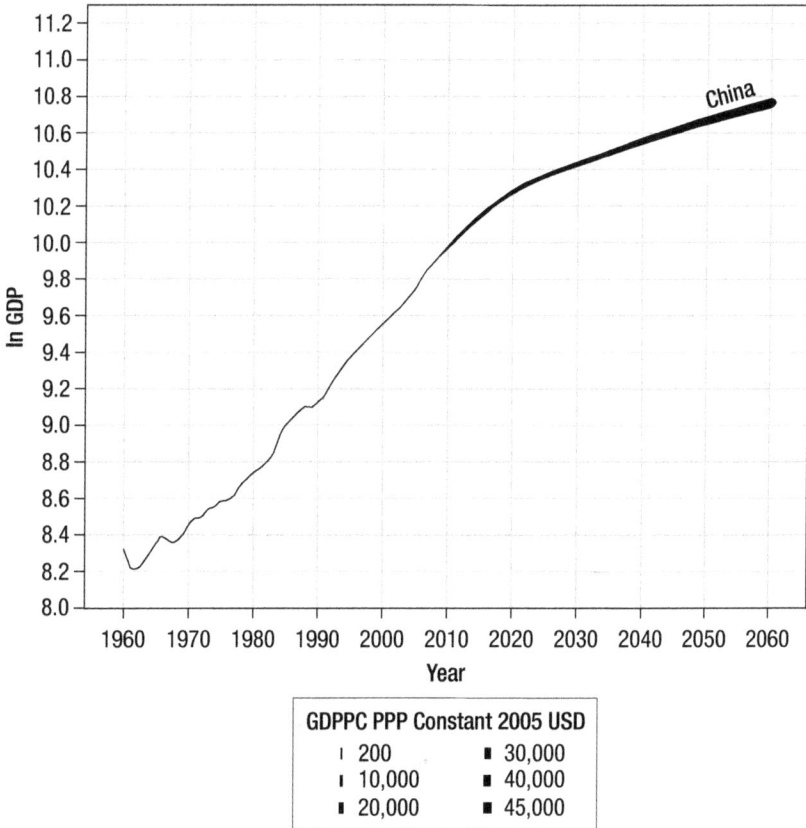

GDPPC PPP Constant 2005 USD	
ı 200	∎ 30,000
ı 10,000	∎ 40,000
∎ 20,000	∎ 45,000

Figure 2.2.   China Growth Trajectory (1960–2060)

down after accumulating wealth that can be expressed as realized power. The question for the world community is how to adjust to the new China, and the question for the new China is how it may peacefully exploit its new condition.

Successful fast-growth countries share some common characteristics. In the early phases, such countries understand that they are vulnerable and must protect the painful early successes they have achieved. They take care not to endanger their limited gains. In the early stages they protect these gains by exercising caution and restraint in their foreign policies, seeking to protect their fundamental achievement, and adopting new technologies. In the case of China, the adoption of new technologies fueled the revolution.

This is followed by a period of single-minded commitment to rapid internal development. When the fruits of this rapid growth make it possible to act more assertively, there will no longer be any need to mask its position of preeminence regionally or hide aspirations globally.[8] One can follow these cascading developments in China through the lens of sloganeering.

China's foreign policy in the modern era has been characterized by a series of slogans. These slogans are a device used by the Chinese government to signal the line or policy that officials should follow. These slogans do not provide specific policy directives, but they set the tone, the direction, and the boundaries of the debate. And they are malleable. China can and does violate its own rules of the road when that serves its interests.

Consider the evolution of China's policy slogans. In the 1990s, there was Peaceful Rising, defined as "observe calmly, secure our position; cope with our affairs calmly; hide our capacities and bide our time; be good at maintaining a low profile, and never claim leadership."

And the three no's: "no challenge (don't challenge the US), no exclusion (don't be excluded from your legitimate place at the table), and no confrontation (don't deliberately generate a confrontation)."

In 1997, China reasserted the famous five principles, originally but unsuccessfully advanced in 1954.[9] Each of the following has a double edge:

Mutual respect for sovereignty and territorial integrity
Mutual nonaggression
Noninterference
Equality and mutual benefit
Peaceful coexistence

The double edge refers to the fact that in Chinese thought these principles apply both to Chinese foreign policy abroad and equally to the foreign policy of other countries toward China.

In the 2000s came the period of "Strategic Opportunity"—twenty years of relative peace given over to economic growth. This metamorphosed into "peaceful rising," which signaled a shift in direction—a global vector replaced internal development. This is the most important and underappreciated of Chinese foreign policy statements because it created a launch pad into the future.

China now seeks to become a global power, directly in competition with the United States.[10] When China's neighbors and the United States became concerned over the implications of the peaceful rising slogan, it mutated into "Peaceful Development." This was an attempt to modulate the rhetoric and reassure neighbors of China's peaceful intent.

By 2006 China entered a phase of multilateralism and aggressive outreach to nations in its neighborhood. The policy was motivated partly out of a desire to reassure, partly to further joint economic interests, and partly for reasons of security. Some scholars believe that this was the threshold of a new China, an engaged China, a resurgent China. Policy changes toward Japan and in the China Sea generated considerable attention. At about the same time came the concept of *Harmonious World*, a confidence building or reassurance strategy. We want to live in a harmonious world, Chinese leaders stated, and we will play a role in the creation of that harmony.

In 2017, President Xi Jinping ushered in rapid changes emphasizing a global presence. China is now pressing efforts to engage neighboring states with a new purpose: to translate economic relationships into political and military ties. China has moved openly toward an equal relationship with the United States. Chinese leaders have called for a new type of Great Power relationship requiring more respect from the United States and no toleration of US interference. China is pushing initiatives for open trade and economic corridors—a new silk road in Central Asia; a maritime silk road in the Southeast; and an economic corridor through India, Burma, and Pakistan (see Chapter 3).

All of this created enough confidence that China supported the Russian annexation of Crimea in direct violation of previous 1997 commitments to defend "mutual respect for the sovereignty and territorial integrity" of smaller nations. China is demonstrating that it can play the Russian card. In short, we now see the structural blocks of a more globally oriented China—the foundation of a global superpower.[11]

There is a strong strain of nationalism and populism in President Xi's speeches, even a nostalgia for the Mao era. Part of this seems to come from his personal history, but the themes aim to secure the loyalty of the People's Liberation Army (PLA) and consolidate ideological conservatives. In a relatively short period of time, this classic securing-your-base move enabled Xi to acquire overwhelming authority and dominance within the Communist Party, the military establishment, and the government. He has also generated a mass appeal via populist themes, such as his "we have arrived" congratulatory statement and his flirting with Maoism.

President Xi has added his own slogan—the Chinese Dream of National Rejuvenation.[12] On another occasion he added his "Strong Army Dream." These dream phrases could have been taken from US literature (the American Dream) or some other traditional Chinese source. According to President Xi, they mean the dream of being "rich and strong," which sounds familiar to US elites.

Note that in each case, there is room for interpretation as to the meaning and application of these slogans. This offers a tactical advantage to the leadership. Without specific directions, it is easy to run afoul of the party line in scope, direction, or magnitude. This means that local leaders must check higher in the leadership hierarchy before taking any bold steps on their own. This consideration reinforces party discipline.

Despite the move toward a single leader dictatorship, Chinese leaders must pay attention to important interest groups. Most prominent are the economic development specialists on one side and the PLA on the other. So foreign policy gets pushed and pulled. With the ascendance of Xi, foreign policy is more pushed downward than pulled apart. Some scholars suggest that China has the same realpolitik strategies as any other large powerful country, whereas others argue that China has a hidden foreign policy. In fact, consistent with the power transition theory (PTT) logic, China is simply following the opportunities opened by its S-curve benefits.[13]

How China responds to its increasing economic, diplomatic, and military power is the most important question facing the world. It is far too easy for policy makers to be distracted by events in Syria, Pakistan, Iran, or North Korea. Short-term myopia is galvanizing. But a true strategist understands that China should be the long-term focus of the world's attention. The Chinese already know this, but the West is still in denial. The Chinese have anticipated this time, planned for this event, set the stage with language and action, and now they are seizing the moment. China is on the cusp of what they quietly assess will be a Chinese century beginning in mid-century.[14] This is the central element of their long-range strategic vision.

CHINESE STRATEGIC THINKING

Analyzing Chinese strategic thinking is extraordinarily challenging. Their foreign policy is a mixture of historical references, slogans, and biases colored by more recent events. The same is true for current US strategic thinking in some ways—but the tea leaves in the US cup are clearer. That noted, the following elements can be identified in various articles published in China on strategic planning and from conversations with government leaders.

Which domestic events have conditioned the world view of Chinese strategic elites? In the precommunist period, interventions by Western powers—among these the aftermath of the Opium Wars, the Boxer Rebellion, and Japan's invasion during World War II—are still seen as the root of all evil.

In the modern era, senior party, government, and military elites have personal or family stories about the Great Leap Forward when from 1958 to 1960, 700 million people were placed in communes. Moreover, the nationwide construction of backyard furnaces with the goal of matching US steel output by 1988 is also remembered. These were significant disastrous events that impacted a substantial percentage of the population, as did the Red Guard period from 1966 to 1976 during the Cultural Revolution, which touched almost every family. One of the authors of this chapter has had more than one senior officer in the PLA recount their personal mistreatment and that of their families during these times (for a camouflaged history of one senior leader, see the appendix in this chapter). No one wants these times repeated, but they live in the national consciousness and permeate local perceptions of international interactions.

In addition to prior events now seen as shameful, Chinese strategic leaders have had their thinking conditioned by significant regional events. This is easily verifiable with a visit to the Guilin Military History Museum. Photographs of Guilin military officers hang on the many walls of this museum in tribute to those who died defending China and its vital interests. Each wall and date provides a story about China's fight for independence and expansion:

Tibet 1951
Korea 1950–1953
Vietnam 1959–1975
India 1962
Soviet Union 1969
Vietnamese border war 1979

A country-specific perspective offers even sharper images. When Chinese strategists looks north, they see another nuclear power in Russia. To the west, there are border countries with populations susceptible to religious indoctrination and expansion. Looking south, they see two nuclear powers, India and Pakistan, plus a not-so-friendly Vietnam that at least once fought China to a standstill. Looking east, they see the twin floating Western aircraft carriers—Taiwan and Japan.

Chinese strategists might well ask their counterparts in the United States: How would you react if Canada and Mexico were hostile and had nuclear weapons? Or if British Columbia were an independent country with nuclear weapons run by an unpredictable leader?

Chinese strategists must also consider internal phenomena. Dissent at the borders is widespread. There is periodic unrest in Tibet and in adjoining Chinese provinces. There are demonstrations, stabbings, mass arrests, and incarcerations in Xinjiang province and relatively porous borders with suspect neighbors Kazakhstan, Kyrgyzstan, Tajikistan, and Pakistan.

There are any number of scapegoats to blame for domestic and regional unrest—including meddling by foreign entities—the Dalai Lama, Turkish tribal associations, radical Islamists, Western religions, cults, the Internet, and Western concepts of the law and human rights. Most Chinese strategists view these "infections" as cancers that must be destroyed or at least isolated and contained.

Chinese strategists also understand the threat of the 150-million-strong mainly rural, masculine floating work force that must be kept employed at all costs. This drives the need for 6–8 percent annual growth,[15] which is becoming more difficult to maintain. Chinese decision makers worry about the future. As China approaches the top of the S curve, the annual growth rate will decline concurrently with the increasing costs of supporting a massive retiring population. This confluence will likely cause domestic pressure on employment and a possible internal threat if the young workforce is not fully integrated into society.

When international conditions become tense, Chinese strategists can and do look to history for lessons to whip up public support, for example, the two Opium Wars of 1839–1842 and 1856–1860, resulting in the Unequal Treaties, the loss of Hong Kong, and a recognition that weakness resulted in national humiliation. The same can be said of the Boxer Rebellion of 1900, which brought further Western interventions and concessions. It was a long period of "swallowing bitterness," an important phrase that occurs from time to time in strategic tomes.

History also provides memories of the unspeakable: the Japanese invasion of Manchuria in 1931, the Rape of Nanking in 1937, the Japanese military unit 37 that practiced vivisection on Chinese prisoners, and experiments using chemical weapons, biological weapons, and torture, as well as medical experiments on Chinese prisoners of war (POW). There is enough emotional history here to push passions to a fever pitch, and this has happened several times in the past.

If the government wants to stir up discontent against the United States, it can revisit the great patriotic civil war and recall how the Americans sided with the Kuomintang before the war and afterward, as well as during the Korean War when Chinese warnings were disregarded, not to mention Taiwan and Tibet. China has already achieved sufficient power not to have to swallow bitterness again, but all the historical elements are present to allow the Chinese government and its strategists to manipulate domestic public opinion during a crisis.

These are the dark memories, terrible events that Chinese scholars and strategists understand but do not want to relive. The dark side is balanced by the positive recognition of inevitable progress, a middle class turning into a modern educated base, changes in the international arena that weaken relative US and EU power, and China's increased global status. Justifying failure will not be difficult, but sustaining growth and achieving a peaceful integration into the global economy will be more challenging than the Chinese realize.

The next section of this chapter will explore how the global community should respond to the new Chinese reality and how China should manage its own behavior to avoid conflict such as has sometimes arisen in fast-developing countries enjoying the exuberance of power. Dealing with long-term Chinese strategists will be exceedingly difficult for the United States because our political leaders respond effectively only to immediate crises and the demands of the two-, four-, and six-year election cycles.

MANAGING EXUBERANCE: A LOOK INTO THE FUTURE

China is not rising; it *has* risen. Figure 2.3 shows that China has the largest economy in the world based on purchasing power parity (PPP).[16] This has not been a totally peaceful rise. Tibet, border skirmishes, threats over the South China Sea, ultimata about Taiwan, and anti-Japanese riots have proliferated. But none of this has sparked the severe conflict that could have happened. China understands that, as a Great Power, it has a world role.

It has tried to acknowledge its new role with reassuring slogans, but being forced onto the world stage creates dilemmas and contradictions for its foreign policy. Its economic interests, which, like ours, are national security interests, put China in awkward situations. As interests overlap, China may be forced to be more interventionist; it may be forced to interfere more often to protect its interests; and it may well be forced to choose allies—such as Russia—that do not respect China's noninterventionist postures. There is already evidence of this. The Chinese are going to be more aggressive, more assertive, and more

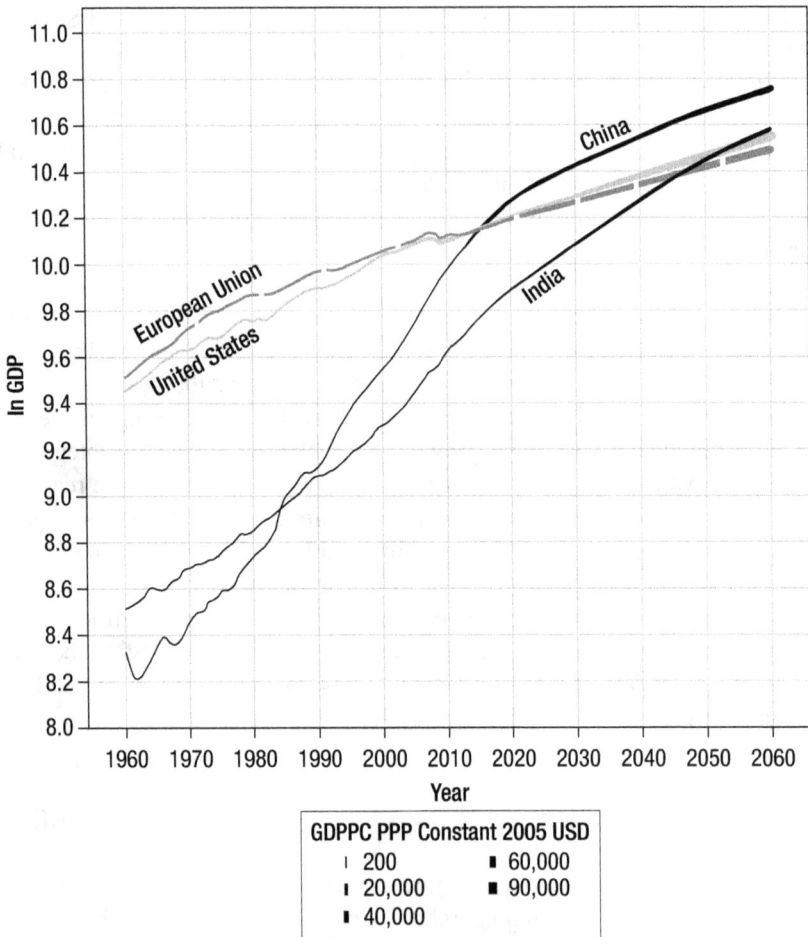

Figure 2.3.   China, United States, India, and European Union Power Trajectory

demanding under the cloak of the demand for respect. Nations in Asia are going to have to pick an allegiance. Nations, maybe even in the Middle East, Latin America, and Africa, will have to do so as well.

The next twenty-five years will be uncomfortable for US leaders as they respond to China's new role with a judicious mix of encouragement and resistance, cooperation, and policy conflict, and as both countries test out new strategies.

Here are some of the tools and concepts for the United States and China that could be used to secure a peaceful transition into a dominant but satisfied role in world politics.

US OPTIONS

In the Chinese perspective, there is a thin line between constructive advice from friends and meddling. Recognizing this, US leaders need to appreciate the subtleties of indirection and third-party utility. Chinese leaders reject Western lectures on topics ranging from human rights to religious practices to free courts. At the same time, at home US leaders must be careful not to be called out for appeasement or economic blackmail.

The middle ground rests with the US business community. There are few Chinese domestic organizations that can be influenced by the West. Effectively there is no governing role for nonprofits, interest groups, and single-issue organizations. But there is a prominent role for business activity.

Encouraging Western business practices and the legal structures that surround them is the best indirect approach to influence China domestically. The objective in this case is to build trust, reliability, and most important, satisfaction among China's leadership, the emerging business elites there, and Western business allies. Suggestions for internal reforms such as creating a fair system of legal protections for the business community are best put forward by partnerships in China rather than lecturing from abroad.

Conducted with some degree of sophistication, this approach will create "golden handcuffs" that regulate business practices for mutual self-interest while avoiding the appearance of interventions from abroad. Trade wars will not produce effective solutions. The more effective alternative is negotiating agreements that generate new norms and rules applied to benefit both sides. This would be similar to the US role during the creation of the European Union (EU), which led to cooperative interactions.

The importance of this tool rests with the generation of satisfaction, a key element of PTT, and specifically satisfaction in the form of acceptance of the status quo globally and regionally.[17] This cannot be achieved if US leadership finds ways to generate mistrust and uncertainty in its relationship with China. If this occurs, then as China becomes an obvious superpower by mid-century, it will be inclined to go it alone. Instead of accepting the agreed-on norms of the international system, China will attempt to redesign that system in ways the West will find most uncomfortable.

Although the West has limited tools for influencing Chinese policies, there are strategic calculations that should be made and executed now. The most important is quiet coalition building. The target of this confidence-building and satisfaction-spreading effort should be India. While lagging behind China economically, India nonetheless is a potential superpower destined eventually to have the largest population of any country with a vibrant economy now unleashed from its socialist bounds. India is a natural partner of the West and a potential stabilizing influence in Asia. This partnership should not exclude the possibility of placing China in the mix. An economic-security alliance among the United States, China, India, and the EU could ensure long-term global stability. But it sounds utopian. This long-term option is not viable today, but in the nuclear age, it may well be the most important, though challenging, goal.[18]

CHINESE OPPORTUNITIES AND CONSTRAINTS

China has developed strategies to help manage the economic imperatives that drive its foreign and domestic policy. The first imperative is the development of sources of energy supply. China has been busy quietly establishing relationships with the petroleum-exporting nations in the Middle East, Africa, and most recently, Latin America.[19] This simultaneously creates political allies. China reinforces purchase rights with a basket of other economic benefits, such as roadbuilding and dam building. All of this is designed to increase China's influence in the region in the long run. Using Chinese labor has its own benefits.

The key to this first imperative is understanding the network of relationships that arises. Once sources of energy are established, these must be protected with political relationships, and then the political relationships must be protected with military power.

Also, the route home to China must be protected with a blue-water navy. Keeping sea-lanes open has both a global focus and a near-home component. The global focus means the deployment abroad of large warships and submarines with staying power. This suggests that China will continue to negotiate for ports in friendly energy-rich states.

The near-home threat focuses on the Straits of Malacca. China obtains 75 percent of its oil from the Middle East. One-quarter of the world's annually traded goods are carried by 60,000 vessels through the straits. The straits are 1.5 nautical miles wide at one choke point near Singapore and relatively shallow. The straits are surrounded by Indonesia, Malaysia, and Singapore, and ships must ply waters close to the Philippines and Vietnam. Virtually any one of these countries, or the United States, could blockade the straits.

Looking at this strategic picture, it is possible to see the outline of a future China even more deeply tied to the current international system. A more interdependent China could emerge. It is even possible to visualize a powerful China constrained by regional multilateral ties in Asia, for example, with the Association of Southeast Asian Nations (ASEAN), or the Alliance for a Responsible Future (ARF), and the East Asia Summit, plus the various global international organizations such as the United Nations (UN) and the World Trade Organization (WTO). To some degree this limits Chinese actions, producing an active, potentially satisfied China.

But it is equally plausible that these constraints will melt away under the pressure of hypernationalism and xenophobic behavior. Such behavior would be consistent with other nations passing through a period of exuberance on the S curve of growth, but the consequences in the nuclear age would be far more devastating than those suffered by the Great Powers in the twentieth century.

FUTURE COOPERATION AND CONFLICT

As already mentioned, China is not rising; it has risen. China understands that, as a Great Power, it has a world role. Its economic interests, like those of other global powers, are driven by both economic and national security interests. As its economic interests expand, China may become more interventionist and may seek new allies, like Russia or India, that can help assure its global dominance. There already is evidence of this. China is more aggressive, more assertive, and more demanding. Faced with this new reality, nations in Asia, the Middle East, Africa, and even South America or Europe may have to choose between the current status quo and that offered by China. For that reason, the next US leaders will have to respond to a judicious mix of cooperative and confrontational China policies. As these giants test out new strategies, satisfaction with an emerging status quo may evolve, but the oft-trodden path of escalating demands and aggravation is also likely to be taken, and that could lead to conflict.

Which path to follow is a choice that any nation faces in the high-growth period. There is little doubt that the rapid accumulation of wealth, power, and standing offers many temptations to rising societies such as China. There are many examples of countries in this category becoming adventurous and exploitative.[20] The alternative is to seek a satisfactory resolution of differences that rewards contenders and ensures global stability.

The first challenge to China is to avoid temptations to rearrange the region to its liking, as Russia attempted to do. At the top of that list is the need to resist the urge to reabsorb Taiwan. China has played the waiting game on Taiwan effectively, but overwhelming power stokes long-suppressed grievances; hence, this is a trigger point for Chinese strategists. Here persuasion is the better part of valor. Actions in Hong Kong provide a preview and will no doubt influence, and perhaps even determine, the willingness of Taiwan to join peacefully with the mainland. A balanced strategy that allows effective amalgamation is critical to the future prominence of China and the safety of the Asia continent.

The second challenge is also an opportunity. China could establish the pattern of offering its good offices to resolve or temper regional disputes. Instead of reinforcing disputes in the South China Sea, the much larger and preponderant China could seek to share the potential economic bounty of this region and open lines of transit. This could help to reassure not only Japan but also other neighboring countries seeking a more prosperous future, including Vietnam, the Philippines, Indonesia, and by extension, Australia and even the United States. Such actions, telegraphed in the same way as when China emerged from the dark period of Mao's rule, would help to bind China to the international community.

The third challenge is to resist border disputes with India. These two giants, rising in contingent regions, represent a classic recipe for transition and conflict if there is shared dissatisfaction over borders. Yet, both societies may share a desire to develop and join the advanced nations, thus providing opportunities for their populations to prosper. A satisfactory resolution of this arms-length relationship provides enormous opportunities. A coalition of China and India would produce the real first hegemon since 1945. Adding the United States and the EU to this mix would ensure stability in the global hierarchy. This outcome may seem quite unlikely today, but immense payoffs can drive coalitions to develop rapidly in the face of mutual benefits.

Assessing future options is difficult when going through a temporary and fast-moving period. Global structures are evolving rapidly. The bipolar world changed, following the collapse of the Soviet Union, into a unipolar world with a single dominant nation, and it is evolving once more because of the rise of China. Now a challenge from India is on the horizon. For a period of time, as global structures solidify, regional politics will dominate international politics. What role China plays in this interregnum period will not only determine future regional stability but will also have the same impact on global interactions.

The posture the West takes toward China will no doubt shape future options. China is on the move and so is India.[21] Russia, Japan, and Britain, following Brexit, can no longer play their previous roles. The United States is retrenching its political and leadership role in Asia. A twenty-five-year period of uncertainty is underway. A path to peace is open, but a second path, fraught with the danger of another global confrontation, cannot be ignored. It is in the hands of today's decision makers in China, the United States, the EU, and India to choose between these two paths. Who among these will have the instinct to overcome the past and look strategically into the future?

APPENDIX
CAMOUFLAGED CHINESE SENIOR OFFICIAL HISTORY

You were born in the early 1940s. You have few direct memories of World War II, but your family handed down to you vivid reflections about that war. You lost several family members fighting against the Japanese and the Nationalists. One part of your family suffered at the hands of the Japanese occupation in Manchuria six years before your birth. Your father took part in the 1938 Long March. He was considered a third-tier leader in the military.

In 1958 when you were about fifteen, your family was forced into an agricultural commune along with 700 million others as part of Mao's Great Leap Forward. You were strong, but work was extraordinarily difficult. Without tools you used your hands in the fields. You were given production goals for your family unit. When the family could not meet the goals, you were beaten and called a bourgeois reactionary. Some in the commune were tortured. You heard their cries at night.

By 1960, when you were about seventeen, the commune was hit by starvation. Two members of your extended family died of starvation. You survived by eating roots from the ground where you worked. Between 10 and 45 million others perished in the great starvation. You do not ever talk about this time. You have suppressed it.

When you were twenty-three, your remaining extended family was caught up in the Cultural Revolution. Your family had moved to a larger village. Then one day the student Red Guards marched into the village, seized the village elder, tied his hands, and made him crawl the length of the village while being beaten with sticks. They seized your house, leaving your family to sleep in the fields. Soon another Red Guard group came to the village and the competing two Red Guard brigades fought each other. Virtually all government officials were purged during this time. One and a half million "officials" were killed.

In 1976, with the Gang of Four displaced by the military, a period of relative political stability allowed you to go to school. First, you attended the party school at the provincial level where you received nonstop indoctrination in Marxist-Leninist theory—no give and take with the lecturers—just transmit and receive in hard-backed seats. But you do remember learning about the Time of Troubles and the Opium Wars when China, because of its weakness, had to swallow bitterness at the hands of Britain, France, Russia, and the United States.

You were a good student, you repeated doctrine precisely without interpretation or variation. You were picked to go to school in Russia. It was a new world in Moscow. You were watched closely by your minders and, again, studied Marxist-Leninist philosophy, and you met your first non-Chinese. You found them strange looking, racially biased, and yet interesting. When you came back home you were privileged to attend college at Tsinghua University—China's best. There you were exposed to international foreign policy concepts.

After college you rose rapidly up the ranks of the party in a province remote from Beijing. Soon you were transferred to another province, closer to Beijing, to broaden your experience. You operated within a bureaucratic system with certain unwritten rules. You attached yourself to cautious leaders moving up with good reputations. You did not join in factional groups.

You learned how signals would be given by Beijing leaders. You were smart enough to identify these signals and respond to them quickly. You thought of this as governance by slogan and you excelled at it: "Hide your Strength—Keep a Low Profile" or "First Strong Economy, then Strong Army." Or "Peaceful Rising," or "Striving for Achievement." With this, you were noticed even more.

You were lucky. You followed in the footsteps of a provincial leader as he moved up the ladder of power in Beijing. He trusted you and gave you sensitive missions. In turn you supported him and his family politically and financially.

By the time you turned fifty-five, you were handpicked by your old friend to serve in a key foreign policy position for the politburo. Despite the troubles of your family, you remain a patriot and a true believer in the role of the party. In fact, because of your family, you are keenly patriotic.

But what you think privately remains your own domain.

NOTES

1. Global Map shows region contours. The hierarchy map shows the relative size of the top contenders in this region. Data are from World Bank, "World Development Indicators," last modified March 27, 2016, http://documents.worldbank.org/curated/en/805371467990952829/World-development-indicators-2016

2. Figure 2.1 source: Tadeusz Kugler, Kyungkook Kang, Jacek Kugler, Marina Arbetman-Rabinowitz, and John Thomas, "Demographic and Economic Consequences of Conflict," *International Studies Quarterly* 57, no. 1 (March 2013): 1–12.

3. Paul A. Samuelson, "An Exact Consumption-Loan Model of Interest with or without the Social Contrivance of Money," *The Journal of Political Economy* 66, no. 6 (December 1958): 467–482.

4. Peter A. Diamond, "National Debt in a Neoclassical Growth Model," *The American Economic Review* 55, no. 5, part 1 (December 1965): 1126–1150.

5. Robert E. Lucas, "Econometric Policy Evaluation: A Critique," *Carnegie-Rochester Conference Series on Public Policy* 1 (1976): 19–46.

6. Yi Feng, Jacek Kugler, and Paul J. Zak, "The Politics of Fertility and Economic Development," *International Studies Quarterly* 44, no. 4 (December 2000): 667–693, and Yi Feng, Jacek Kugler, Siddharth Swaminathan, and Paul J. Zak, "The Path to Prosperity: The Dynamics of Freedom and Economic Development," *International Interactions* 34, no. 4 (2008): 423–441.

7. Figure 2.2 source: World Bank, "The World in 2050," last modified 2016, https://www.pwc.com/gx/en/issues/economy/the-world-in-2050.html.

8. The United States after 1870 demonstrated a pattern very similar to that of China today: Non-intervention in other countries' politics but concerted efforts to expand economic ties that can accelerate internal development.

9. United Nations, "Treaties and International Agreements Registered or Filed and Recorded with the Secretariat of the United Nations," United Nations Treaty Collection, last modified on May 1958, https://treaties.un.org/doc/Publication/UNTS/Volume%20299/v299.pdf.

10. Jacek Kugler and Ronald L. Tammen, "Implications of Asia's Rise to Global Status," in William R. Thompson, ed., *Systemic Transitions: Past, Present, and Future* (New York: Palgrave Macmillan, 2009).

11. Ronald L. Tammen and Jacek Kugler, "Power Transition and China–US Conflicts," *The Chinese Journal of International Politics* 1, no. 1 (Summer 2006): 35–55.

12. Zheng Wang, "The Chinese Dream: Concept and Context," *Journal of Chinese Political Science* 19, no. 1 (March 2014): 1–13.

13. Kugler and Tammen, "Implications of Asia's Rise."

14. A. F. K. Organski and Jacek Kugler, *The War Ledger* (Chicago: University of Chicago Press, 1980).

15. World Bank, "The World Bank in China," last modified April 8, 2019, https://www.worldbank.org/en/country/china/overview.

16. Figure 2.3 source: World Bank, "PPP conversion factor, GDP (LCU per international $)," last modified 2019, https://data.worldbank.org/indicator/pa.nus.ppp.

17. Ronald L. Tammen, Jacek Kugler, and Douglas Lemke, "Foundations of Power Transition Theory," in William Thompson, ed., *Oxford Research Encyclopedias* (Oxford: Oxford University Press, 2017).

18. Japan, Russia, and the United Kingdom are no longer included in this assessment simply because their base capabilities will in the immediate future no longer be sufficient to alter global interactions.

19. Gustavo Flores-Macias and Sarah Kreps, "The Foreign Policy Consequences of Trade: China's Commercial Relations with Africa and Latin America, 1992–2006," *The Journal of Politics* 75, no. 2 (April 2013): 357–371.

20. Ronald L. Tammen, Jacek Kugler, Douglas Lemke, Allan Stam, Carole Alsharabati, Mark Abdollahian, Brian Efird, and A. F. K. Organski, *Power Transitions: Strategies for the 21st Century* (New York: Chatham House, 2000).

21. Kugler and Tammen, "Implications of Asia's Rise."

Chapter Three

East Asia

China's Campaign to Become a New World Leader

Yi Feng, Zhijun Gao, and Zining Yang

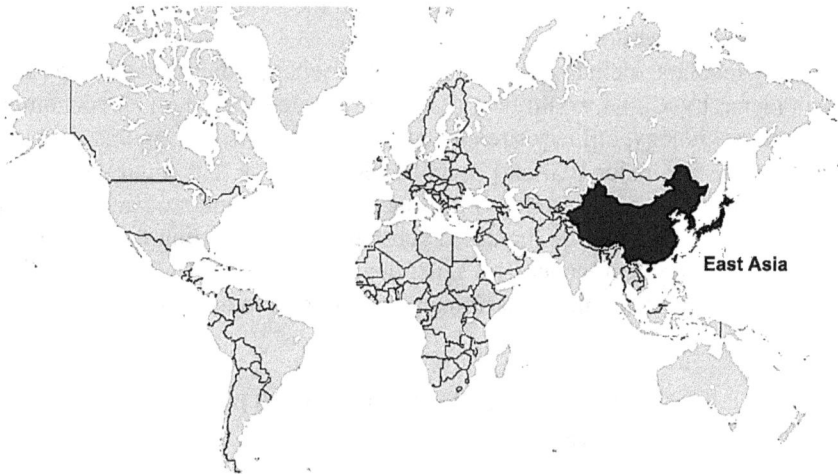

East Asia

East Asia–China Region

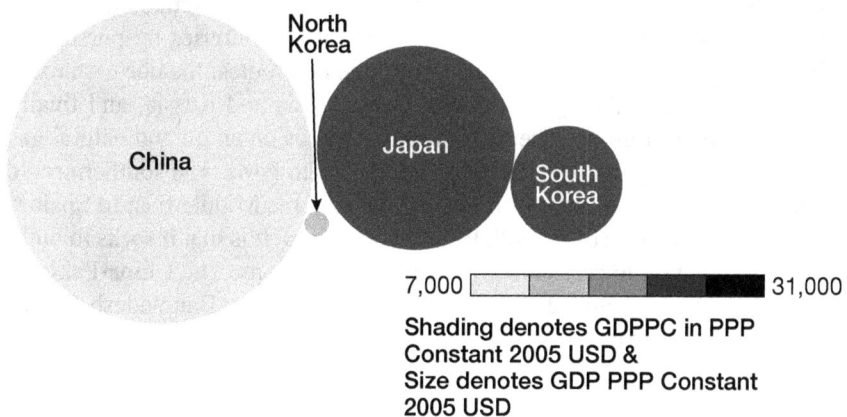

North
Korea

China

Japan

South
Korea

7,000 ▭ 31,000

Shading denotes GDPPC in PPP
Constant 2005 USD &
Size denotes GDP PPP Constant
2005 USD

East Asia–China Hierarchy

GLOBAL DYNAMICS

Global politics are sustained and modified by power distributions among great nations. Massive changes or earthquakes seldom occur in this distribution because change comes slowly. But when change arrives, the impact can be significant, even catastrophic for some nations. We call these *transitions*. A transition involves visible and invisible flows of power among contenders and the major variables of population, productivity, and political capacity. A transition may unfold peacefully or violently, as a factor of the relative power change between the incumbent leader and the challenger, as well as of the convergence or divergence in their respective orientations toward international norms. Tactically, a transition is also determined by the approach that the incumbent world leader and the rising superpower choose to take toward each other.

Many scholars, including the authors of this book, predicted that in the East Asia hierarchy, China would be a rising world leader based on its economic growth, technology, military strength, and political influence.[1] In this chapter, we examine the major Belt and Road (B&R) Initiative that could define the rise of China as a world leader. If it is successful, the economic and political influence of China will be increased substantially, confirming the leap from a regional to a global leader. If it fails, then China's ascent will slow down, potentially motivating more confrontational policies to avert a reversal.

CHINESE PROJECT DESCRIPTION, PURPOSE, AND JUSTIFICATION

In September 2013, during his visit to Kazakhstan, President Xi Jinping of China put forward the idea of building a "Silk Road Economic Belt."[2] According to China, the Silk Road Economic Belt aims to strengthen the economic cooperation and integration among Eurasian countries by pursuing a joint development strategy.[3] It consists of three key routes: the northern route starts from Beijing, then goes through Central Asia and Russia, and finally reaches Northern Europe. The second route focuses on an oil and natural gas pipeline, which departs from Beijing and transits to Paris. The southern route essentially is a road system from Beijing through the Middle East to Spain.[4]

An essential feature of the Silk Road Economic Belt is that it seeks to build four major economic corridors with different functions. The China-Pakistan economic corridor emphasizes oil transportation. The Bangladesh-China-India-Myanmar corridor focuses on enhancing China's trade with Association of Southeast Asian Nations (ASEAN).[5] The New Eurasian Land Bridge is the main route connecting China and Europe. The China-Mongolia-Russia corridor stresses national security and resource exploration.[6]

One month after his first announcement, President Xi advanced another proposal to build the "Twenty-First Century Maritime Silk Road," which will enhance maritime collaborative partnerships with Southeast Asian countries. It has two main dimensions. One route starts in Quanzhou (a coastal city in eastern China) and then transits the South China Sea, extending to Europe. The second route also departs from Quanzhou but stretches to the South Pacific Ocean. The partners of the Twenty-First Century Maritime Silk Road are not limited to ASEAN countries. This route is visualized as part of a comprehensive partnership and economic integration strategy aimed at ASEAN, South Asia, the Middle East, North Africa, and Europe.[7]

The combination of the Silk Road Economic Belt and the Twenty-First Century Maritime Silk Road is referred to the B&R Initiative. In effect it represents an aggressive new grand strategy for China and has the potential to be nothing short of an explosion onto the world stage—if fully implemented. Figure 3.1 shows the routes of the Silk Road Economic Belt and the Twenty-First Century Maritime Silk Road.[8]

The B&R Initiative follows the ancient Silk Road and Maritime Silk Road dating back to the Chinese Han Dynasty (206 BCE–220 CE). The stated goal of the B&R Initiative, according to Chinese authorities, rests on taking advantage of mutual interests across different countries. This principle is stated in the reassuring language of the document titled *Vision and Proposed Actions Outlined on Jointly Building Silk Road Economic Belt and 21st-Century Maritime Silk Road*: "The Initiative is harmonious and inclusive. It advocates tolerance among civilizations, respects the paths and modes of development chosen by different countries, and supports dialogues among different civilizations on the principles of seeking common ground while shelving differences and drawing on each other's strengths, so that all countries can coexist in peace for common prosperity."[9]

To achieve this goal, Xi Jinping summarized the mission of the B&R Initiative into five dimensions: policy coordination, facilities connectivity, unimpeded trade, financial integration, and people-to-people bonds.[10]

Flowery language aside, the B&R Initiative by any definition is global in scale and strategic in its application. It is a massive infrastructure project with implications for trade, resource extraction, economic development, and not the least, a launch pad for expanding Chinese influence globally. As such, the B&R Initiative is not just a precursor of a potential Chinese power transition with the United States but a specific step down that road.

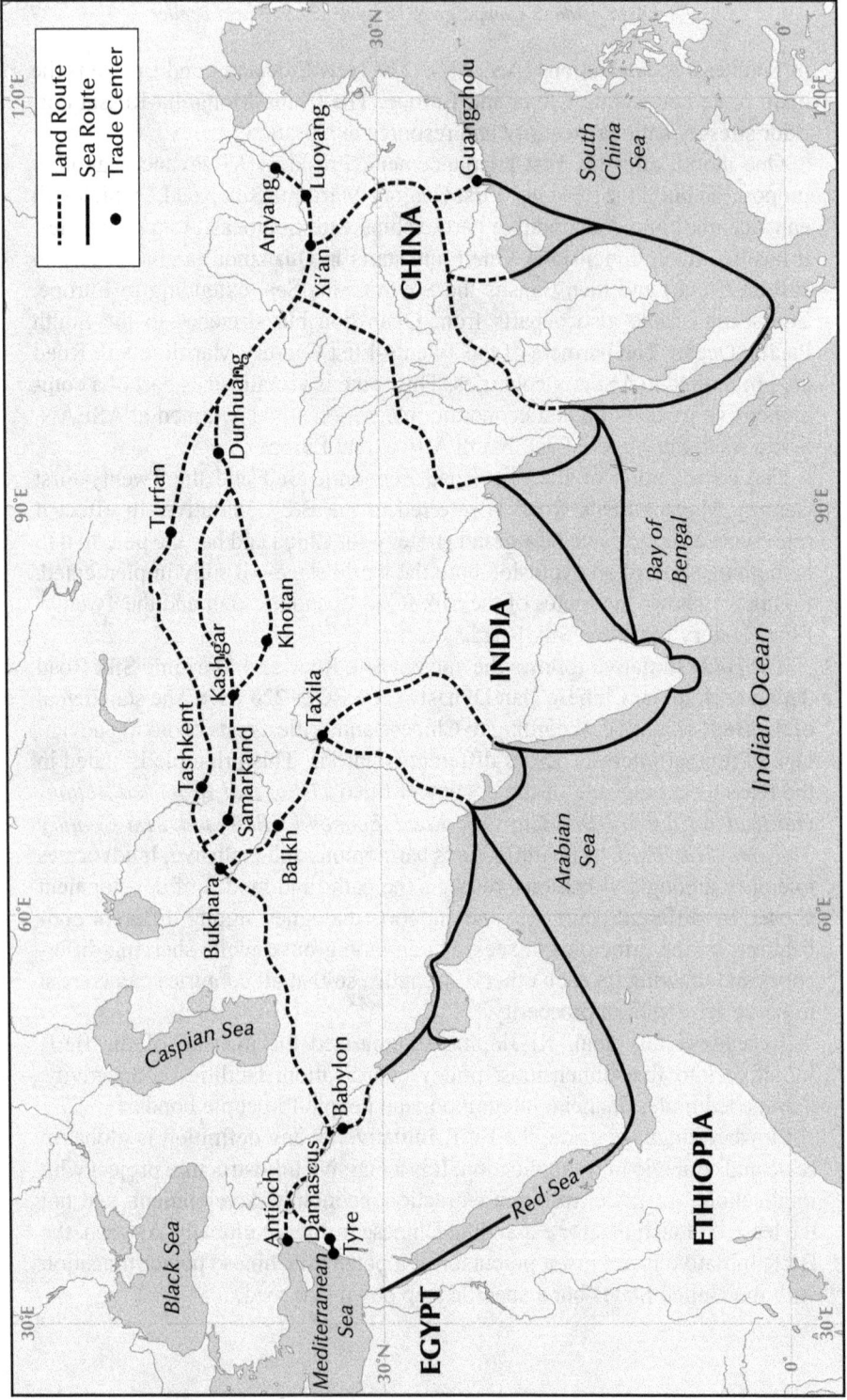

Figure 3.1. Major Routes of the Proposed Silk Road Economic Initiative

US INTERESTS IN THE B&R INITIATIVE

After the disintegration of Al Qaeda and the conclusion of the initial phase of the Arab Spring, the United States switched its attention back to Asia and put forward the "Pivot to Asia" strategy in 2011.[11] At the same time, tensions started to rise between China and some of its neighboring countries. Controversies included the Huangyan Island dispute between China and the Philippines, the Japanese government's nationalization of the Senkaku/Diaoyu Islands, and the escalating territorial dispute between China and Vietnam. Given complicated historical factors, China's neighboring countries have chosen to deploy a "double-track" diplomacy characterized as associating with China economically, while maintaining nominal political relationships with the United States.[12]

This double-track diplomacy has provided the United States with opportunities to address the anxieties that these countries have about China's rising power. The Trans-Pacific Partnership (TPP) Agreement, proposed during the Obama Administration, but canceled by President Donald Trump, illustrated the strategic objective of the United States in modulating China's rise.

The TPP would have created high-standard regulations in six major areas: environmental standards, labor standards, intellectual property standards, data flows, services, and state-owned businesses.[13] Despite cancellation, some US allies remained strong supporters of the TPP, including Japan and Singapore.[14] There is some evidence that Japan is still interested in enticing a future US administration into rejoining the TPP and reenergizing a Pivot to Asia strategy.[15] If the TPP could be resurrected by a new administration, this arrangement could become a potential strategic tool for the United States to preserve existing norms favored by the most developed societies.

CHINA'S INTERESTS IN THE B&R INITIATIVE

After more than thirty-five years of high growth, China's economy has entered a new phase called the "New Normal."[16] Overcapacity has become a serious factor, forcing Chinese companies to reallocate their resources overseas to seek opportunities.[17] Given this backdrop, the Chinese government put forward the B&R Initiative, based on both internal and external factors. It aimed to facilitate an upgrade of domestic economic structures as well to lock in regional support during a period of global ambitions.[18] By emphasizing "peaceful environment," China is attempting to increase its global political influence without alienating its neighbors. We delineate three key factors behind the Chinese government's decision to put forward the B&R Initiative.

The New Normal for China's economy began in 2012. According to the National Bureau of Statistics (NBS) of China, China's gross domestic product (GDP) growth rate decelerated from an average of 9.8 percent during 1979–2012 to 6.7 percent in 2016. Because of the diminishing return on investment and the fundamental change in trade structure, China can no longer rely heavily on using investment and export to drive economic growth as it did in the past thirty-five years.[19] As a result, the Chinese government defines this new developmental stage as New Normal, which accepts a slower economic growth rate but emphasizes the quality of economic growth.[20] A key feature of the New Normal economy is the overcapacity of many Chinese enterprises, especially heavy industries. Because the domestic market has gradually reached saturation, it becomes crucial for Chinese enterprises to actively seek opportunities overseas to absorb the overcapacity.

Given that most developing countries associated with the B&R Initiative are relatively weak in infrastructure, this offers substantial opportunities for business collaboration between Chinese enterprises and host countries. During the rapid industrialization of the past forty years, a large number of Chinese enterprises have accumulated abundant experience and expertise in building infrastructure facilities, such as high-speed rail, power stations, bridges, ports, freeways, and so forth. The rankings of Chinese enterprises in the list of Top 250 International Contractors has also been surging in recent years.[21] In 2016, China Communications Construction Group Ltd. ranked third on the list, Power Construction Corporation of China ranked eleventh, China State Construction Engineering Corporation Ltd. ranked fourteenth, and China Railway Group Ltd. and China National Machinery Industry Corporation ranked twentieth and twenty-third, respectively.[22] These companies' strong technology and professional expertise provide fundamental support for the implementation of China's B&R Initiative.

The B&R Initiative not only promotes economic integration but also sets the stage for a new national security framework. Within Chinese strategic planning circles and more broadly among the Chinese public, Western countries are viewed as having an interest in containing China's development.[23] Geographically, China's core industries are concentrated in coastal provinces, making them vulnerable to external attacks, according to Chinese analysts.[24] In addition, territorial tensions between China and several Southeast Asian countries raise the potential of security threats to shipping through the Malacca Straits.

From a Chinese perspective, the implementation of the B&R Initiative would help China reduce these regional political pressures and expand its strategic space westward.[25] Because China's western provinces still have large areas in which to develop manufacturing industries and infrastructure, the comprehensive economic cooperation and integration between those provinces and their inland neighboring countries would be part of a strategy to expand China's strategic space.[26]

In addition, the B&R Initiative reflects a change in the tenor of China's diplomacy. Since the Chinese government initiated the "reform and open-up" policy in the late 1970s, China's diplomacy can be divided into two stages. The first stage refers to the period from 1978 to 2012, which has been characterized as "keep a low profile and bide your time while also getting something accomplished."[27] Because the top priority during this period was economic growth, the Chinese government's diplomatic efforts were focused on building a stable environment. The late Chinese leader, Deng Xiaoping, put forward a general principle to resolve territorial disputes, which was to "set aside dispute and pursue joint development."[28] The fundamental reason for this "low-key" or "responsive" diplomatic stance was to avoid the escalation of disputes, which could have had a negative impact on economic development.[29]

The second stage started with the 18th National Congress of the Chinese Communist Party (CCP) in 2012, in which the new administration led by President Xi Jinping assumed leadership. Because at that point China had become the second-largest economy in the world in terms of GDP (first in purchasing power parity calculations) and the country is facing a more complicated international environment, the new administration has shifted to a more proactive foreign policy orientation.[30] Based on the current disclosed official documents, the B&R Initiative has become China's overriding strategy both domestically and internationally in the era of New Normal.[31] Given China's rapid economic development and rising influence in global affairs, some countries have urged China to shoulder more international responsibilities, instead of acting as a "free rider" of global economic liberalization.[32] In response to this argument, China has expressed its willingness to take more responsibilities and make greater contributions to the international community, but the government maintains that the scope of responsibility should be within China's current capacity.[33]

The B&R Initiative also serves the purpose of investing Chinese capital abroad. It has established three major financing platforms: the Asian Infrastructure and Investment Bank, the Silk Road Fund, and the BRICS New Development Bank.[34] China is the largest contributor to all of these financing platforms, providing indispensable capital support for infrastructure and various projects of the B&R Initiative. One by-product of these massive investments abroad is increased influence in the economic and political governance of the recipient countries.

China is calculating that the B&R Initiative will resolve some of the tensions with neighboring countries. According to Zheng Yongnian of the

National University of Singapore, China made a miscalculation in addressing the issue of the South China Sea without understanding neighboring countries' fear of facing a large power on their own.[35] Although China has put forth its "peaceful rising" slogan to mitigate the impact of the "China Threat Theory," this has not dampened the anxiety.[36] This suggests a move toward regional multilateralism.[37] The Chinese calculation is that shared economic interests will be more powerful than residual security fears. However, to date, the B&R Initiative has stirred up unexpected concerns in corridor countries.

OPPORTUNITIES OF THE B&R INITIATIVE

The B&R Initiative promises three positive results for China: (i) reducing disparity between the eastern and western provinces in China, (ii) advancing partnerships with foreign countries, and (iii) promoting a regional political framework that could lead to a de facto alliance system.

Because of the geographic limitations and unbalanced development policy since the early 1980s, the western provinces in China have fallen behind their eastern counterparts in terms of economic and social development. In addition, there are substantial distinctions in the level of openness between western and eastern provinces. According to the *Report of Regional Openness Index in China* published by the National Development and Reform Committee in 2012, the top three open provinces were Shanghai, Beijing, and Guangdong, whereas three western provinces (Guizhou, Qinghai, and Tibet) were ranked at the bottom of the table. The experience of China's economy has shown that openness contributes to higher economic growth. Therefore, it is crucial for western provinces to increase their trade, investment, and other outbound economic activities to facilitate growth.

The B&R Initiative offers unprecedented opportunities for the western provinces to use their unique advantages to drive economic growth. A long-lasting limitation for the western provinces is their weak infrastructure and supporting industries.[38] The efficiency of transportation cannot satisfy the needs of massive trade and investment. Because the connectivity of transportation infrastructure is one of the most significant components of the B&R Initiative, the western provinces will be able to seize the opportunity to implement various construction projects (e.g., road, railway, and air transportation) to lay a foundation for their economies to take off. Apart from the physical construction of infrastructure, the dialogue and negotiation mechanism included in the B&R Initiative will help western provinces reduce the transaction costs of international economic activities.[39] For example, several intergovernmental meetings have been dedicated to simplifying the customs procedures and improving the coordination of trade policies across countries.[40]

Compared to the Chinese government's previous plans to rebalance regional development (e.g., the West Development Strategy), a highlight of the B&R Initiative is to create an entity of shared interests by placing western provinces and neighboring countries into the same development framework.[41] Under this macro-level framework, economic integration would facilitate the efficient allocation of resources. In addition, the formation of the interest community would be helpful to reduce security risks (e.g., terrorist attacks) that have constituted a long-lasting threat to regional peace and development.

From an international perspective, along with China's new stage of economic development, the country's external environment has demonstrated three major characteristics. First, the economic relationship between China and the rest of the world has reached a new level, represented by closer economic cooperation in trade, investment, contracted projects, and exchange of human capital. Second, President Barack Obama's Pivot to Asia strategy brought about new challenges for China to deal with in its relationship with neighboring countries. Third, the antiglobalization policy and "America First" orientation under President Trump have changed the dynamics between the United States and Europe, which would indirectly leave more room to strengthen the partnership between China and Europe. Under these circumstances, the B&R Initiative has the potential to facilitate economic integration of the Asia-Pacific region and Eurasia. But potential is often difficult to translate into actual.

From a regional perspective, compared to the China-ASEAN Free Trade Zone, China has not established a mature platform for bilateral economic cooperation with South Asian countries. Because of complicated historical and geopolitical factors, South Asian countries have shown different attitudes about the B&R Initiative. India has concerns over the initiative based on the fear that it compresses its strategic space. Pakistan, once an enthusiastic supporter, now is unhappy with its financial terms.

Sri Lanka is the transportation hub located at the central sea route of the Indian Ocean, which is regarded as the "Crossroad of West and East." Because both China and Sri Lanka have competitive relationships with India, the two countries have common ground from a strategic perspective.[42] During Xi Jinping's state visit to Sri Lanka in 2014, the two countries signed a series of bilateral agreements covering the fields of economy, technology, and culture.[43] Sri Lanka was also the first country that officially announced its support for the B&R Initiative.[44] The two major projects that China has implemented in Sri Lanka are the construction of Hambantota Port and Colombo Port, both of which would improve the transportation condition of Sri Lanka and provide physical support for the advancement of the "Twenty-First Century Maritime Silk Road."[45]

As China's traditional close partner, Pakistan could play a key role within the framework of the B&R Initiative. Once completed, the China-Pakistan economic corridor would effectively connect South Asia, Central Asia, North Africa, and Gulf countries via economic and energy cooperation.[46] The operation of Gwadar Port would enhance China's energy security and strategic presence in the Indian Ocean.[47]

Recognizing the implications, neither the Sri Lankan nor Pakistani projects sit well with India, the largest and most important nation in South Asia. And even Pakistan is finding that cost sharing and financing details are not as attractive as once assumed.

The Central Asia route connects the Asia-Pacific region and Europe. The Central Asian countries have abundant resources of oil, natural gas, and minerals. However, because of geographic limitations, their level of economic development has fallen behind the Asia-Pacific countries. The B&R Initiative would provide opportunities to expand Central Asia's connections with other countries by building a series of transportation links.[48] For example, as the key components of the New Eurasian Land Bridge, the extension of Longxi-Lianyungang Railway and Lanzhou-Xinjiang Railway will function as main railway routes for the transportation of natural resources.[49] In addition, the China Railway Express will accelerate logistic transportation in Central Asia.[50] Considering the capital constraints of Central Asian countries, the Asian Infrastructure Investment Bank (AIIB) and Silk Road Fund promise to provide fiscal support for the construction of infrastructure projects.[51]

Another major international player in the B&R Initiative is Europe. In contrast to the China-US relationship, there are fewer policy disputes with the China-European Union (EU) dyad. In 2014, China and Europe published their positions in a document titled "Deepen the China-EU Comprehensive Strategic Partnership for Mutual Benefit and Win-Win Cooperation." This has functioned as the cornerstone for advancing the B&R Initiative in Europe. In addition, both parties have been actively seeking compatibilities between the B&R Initiative and various regional proposals, such as Jean-Claude Juncker's plan, which includes an investment of more than 300 billion euros in infrastructure. An effective connection between the B&R Initiative and Juncker's plan would promote connectivity in Eurasia and market expansion. Based on an estimation conducted by Bloomberg, the B&R Initiative would increase the trade volume between China and the other sixty-four member countries to US \$2.5 trillion per year by 2025 and create 3 billion middle-class individuals by 2050.[52] The spillover effect would benefit all of Europe.

Apart from economic cooperation, the B&R Initiative has provided new possibilities for building a comprehensive political partnership between China and Europe. Since the Trump administration has been implementing its "America-First" policy and demanding that its European allies shoulder more of the financial burden to maintain regional security, many European countries have expressed anxiety about the Atlantic Alliance. The meeting between President Trump and German Chancellor Angela Merkel accentuated these concerns as did other European and North Atlantic Treaty Organization (NATO) meetings.[53] Moreover, the US withdrawal from the Paris Accord has put Europe and China on the frontline of the fight against global warming.[54] In short, the drastic US policy shift has encouraged Europe's turn to China.

CHALLENGES FOR THE B&R INITIATIVE

Despite the promised benefits of the B&R Initiative, there are substantial challenges to overcome. Because the B&R Initiative could reshape the politico-economic structure of the Asia-Pacific region, it has brought about open and unstated anxiety within China and on the part of many of its neighboring countries. Here are the key arguments.

China

According to Chinese scholar Wang Yiwei, the United States may take several actions to impede the implementation of the initiative. First, the United States may use its special relationship with Saudi Arabia, located in the central route of the Silk Road Economic Belt, to create incidents that negatively affect the China project. Second, the territorial disputes between several Southeast Asian countries (e.g., the Philippines and Vietnam) and China have provided the United States with opportunities to enhance its military presence in the South China Sea and Indian Ocean. This could threaten China's implementation of the Twenty-First Century Maritime Silk Road. Third, because the United States has been encouraging the "color revolution" in Myanmar and Central Asia in recent years, it can use these countries to make Chinese inroads more difficult along these routes. Finally, given the potential competition between the AIIB and Asian Development Bank, the United States and Japan may take advantage of their traditional influence over the Asian Development Bank to increase difficulties for the AIIB.

In addition, the "New Silk Road" plan announced by the United States in 2011, but moribund at present, aims at the integration of Central Asia and Afghanistan. The strategic purpose of the New Silk Road is to establish a new regional geopolitical and economic structure dominated by the United States that will deter China, Russia, and Iran. Though the progress of the New Silk Road has decelerated since Secretary of State Hillary Clinton stepped down, it has encouraged China to strengthen its relationship with Central Asia.

India

Up to now, the Indian government has not officially indicated whether it supports or opposes the B&R Initiative. This suggests that India recognizes how the B&R Initiative might intrude on its own regional interests. According to Xie Gang, a China expert in India, there are three major reasons for India's ambiguous attitude concerning the initiative.[55] First, because the cost of investment for the B&R Initiative is estimated to reach US $8 trillion and a large proportion of the projects is associated with infrastructure, India has been concerned about its returns on the huge investment. Second, the Silk Road Economic Belt will go through several areas facing the threat of terrorist attack, such as the Kashmir region. This will increase the security risks for the implementation of the projects. Apart from economic and security concerns, the most important reason for India's negative attitude has to do with its geopolitical considerations. Under the framework of the B&R Initiative, China will strengthen its comprehensive partnership with Pakistan and Sri Lanka by building a China-Pakistan economic corridor.

The Twenty-First Century Maritime Silk Road will stretch out to the Indian Ocean, which has been traditionally controlled by India. Consequently, India has been worried about China's expansionist tendencies, which will cause its security environment to deteriorate.[56] India's absence in the B&R Initiative Forum held in Beijing in May 2015 further demonstrated its negative attitude toward the initiative. However, in summer 2017, both India and Pakistan joined the Shanghai Cooperation Organization led by China and Russia. India's position concerning China's B&R Initiative may be constrained by the framework of the organization that expects cooperation. That noted, India will place its own national security interests ahead of economic benefits from the B&R Initiative. Given India's economic size and influence in South Asia, it is close to being a veto player if it chooses to play that role.

Russia

Though having already become an official member of the B&R Initiative, Russia has been expressing some reservations about the initiative. As a large country with traditional influence in Central Asia and Eastern Europe, Russia has dedicated itself to establishing the Eurasian Economic Union to advance its economic interests in the region. However, three countries—Kazakhstan, Uzbekistan, and Kyrgyzstan—in the Eurasian Economic Union are also members of the B&R Initiative. Therefore, the Eurasian Economic Union could constitute competition with the B&R Initiative, thus increasing the uncertainties for the implementation of various projects in Central Asia and Eastern Europe. Consequently, it is crucial for China to find suitable channels to connect the B&R Initiative with the Eurasian Economic Union.

Structural Challenges

An essential feature of the B&R Initiative is operational decentralization. The Chinese government intends to establish regional platforms and let local enterprises play the major role in planning and carrying out various projects. Intergovernmental negotiation before the implementation process will lay the foundation. Decentralization has its merits, but it also creates the conditions for corruption.

Finally, from a political perspective, we surmise that the efficiency and effectiveness of the intergovernmental negotiation will be affected by the political distance between the two countries. Therefore, we will draw two figures (with respect to the Silk Road Economic Belt and the Twenty-First Century Maritime Silk Road) to demonstrate the index of political rights of the member countries of the initiative. The data for political rights were obtained from Freedom House. The range is from 1 to 7; the larger the value, the higher the level of autocracy.[57]

Figure 3.2 indicates that there exists a large variation in the level of democracy across countries on the route of the Silk Road Economic Belt. If we use China as the reference point, we see that it has the identical score for democracy as Turkmenistan and several neighboring countries in Central Asia. However, in regard to those countries in Eastern and Southern Europe, they have a substantially larger political distance from China. For example, the score for political rights in the Czech Republic, Lithuania, and Estonia is 1, which is on the opposite end of the spectrum from China. Because different levels of democracy could indicate different levels of flexibility in decision

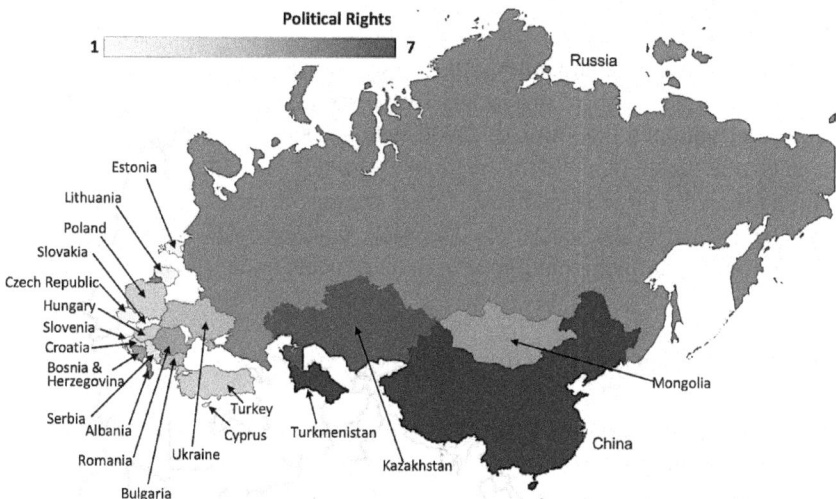

Figure 3.2. Political Rights of the Silk Road: Economic Member Countries

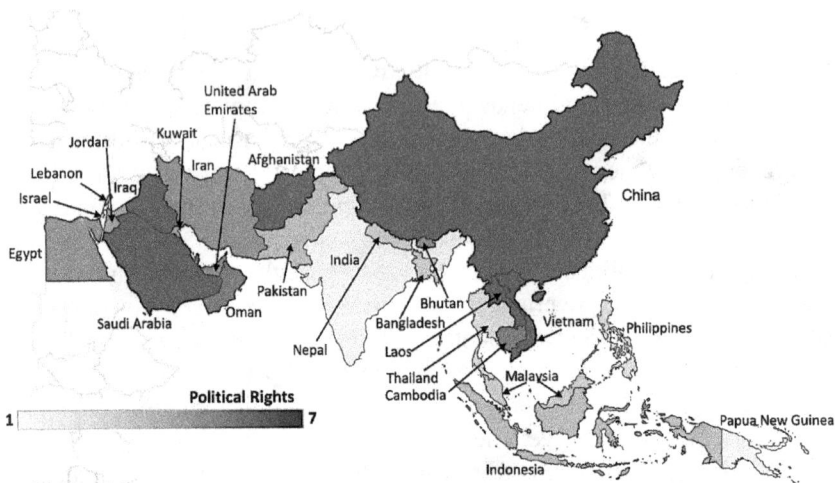

Figure 3.3.   Political Rights of the Silk Road: Maritime Member Countries

making, the large political distance between China and most member countries would add uncertainties for the governmental negotiation and smooth implementation of the projects.

Similar to the situation in figure 3.2, variations exist in the level of democracy among countries on the route of the Twenty-First Century Maritime Silk Road.[58] Two large economies, India and Indonesia, are the "most free" countries in the region, followed by several Southeast Asian countries (e.g., Malaysia, Singapore, the Philippines, Thailand, and Cambodia) with scores ranging from 4 to 5 as shown in figure 3.3.[59] Some neighboring countries (Vietnam and Laos) and Middle East countries (Iran) have the identical score for democracy as China. Combining those countries in figure 3.1, we calculated the average political distance between sixty-four member countries and China and obtained the value of 2.908 with the standard deviation of 2.149. Because the range of political freedom is from 1 to 7, the low mean value with a relatively large standard deviation suggests a lack of political foundations for economic and security cooperation, raising concerns about the effectiveness for the implementation of various projects under the B&R Initiative.

FUTURE COOPERATION AND CONFLICT

The successful completion of the B&R Initiative would connect China with India, Russia, Southeast Asia, the Middle East, Africa, and Europe and help to integrate these countries in a web of political, economic, and security cooperation. The question is whose interests will be served? Will the initiative be an operational arm of China, spreading Chinese influence across continents? Or will it usher in, as promised, a cooperative era of common benefits for all parties? We find it likely that both propositions will hold.

Given its comprehensive scope and strong support from the Chinese government, it is likely that the B&R Initiative will open new ground for Chinese enterprises in overseas markets and facilitate an economic but multidimensional cooperation between China and foreign countries. Given the complementary endowments and economic structures between China and other member countries, cooperation could help host countries improve their infrastructure and lay a foundation for a wave of economic growth. The initiative could help to facilitate global integration.

On the other hand, it is important to be aware of the challenges discussed in this chapter. Interference from Great Powers and political distance between member countries will compound uncertainties for the successful implementation of various projects under the framework of the B&R Initiative. In addition, the threat of terrorism and other types of extremism constitute potential destructive forces for the sustainability of the initiative. Lastly, if China attempts to exploit the initiative and use it for coercive purposes, it will raise local fears about China's ultimate intentions.

We note that there exists a trade-off between absolute gain and relative gain. Because the improvement of infrastructure will be conducive for the economy to take off, most developing countries will increase their absolute gain under the B&R Initiative. However, countries will compare their absolute gain with relative gain along with the implementation of the initiative. If countries (especially those in conflict with each other) find a large disparity between their absolute gain and relative gain, their support for the initiative could wane.

There is a potential trade-off between strategic and tactical opportunities. Grieco et al. discuss relative gains in international cooperation and conclude that absolute gains usually dominate in the short run, whereas the relative gains may dominate in the long run.[60] From this perspective, to strike a balance between absolute and relative gains while finding common interest will create boundaries leading to the success of the initiative. PTT also indicates that stability follows from the buildup of satisfaction with norms and institutions built by cooperative policies. The B&R Initiative promises such changes, but time will tell if the promise is delivered.

NOTES

1. Global Map shows region contours. The hierarchy map shows the relative size of the top contenders in this region. Data are World Bank, "World Development

Indicators," last modified March 27, 2016, http://documents.worldbank.org/curated/en/805371467990952829/World-development-indicators-2016.

2. Belt and Road Portal, "President Xi Jinping delivers important speech and proposes to build a Silk Road Economic Belt with Central Asia partners," last modified September 7, 2013, https://eng.yidaiyilu.gov.cn/qwyw/hyygd/1849.htm.

3. Ibid.

4. Ministry of Foreign Affairs and the Ministry of Commerce of the People's Republic of China, "Vision and Actions on Jointly Building Silk Road Economic Belt and 21st Century Maritime Silk Road," last modified March 28, 2015, http://en.ndrc.gov.cn/newsrelease/201503/t20150330_669367.html.

5. ASEAN is an acronym for the Association of Southeast Asian Nations, which includes Indonesia, Malaysia, the Philippines, Singapore, Thailand, Brunei, Cambodia, Laos, Myanmar, and Vietnam.

6. Yiwei Wang, *The Belt and Road Initiative: What Will China Offer the World in Its Rise?* (Beijing: New World Press, 2016).

7. For simplicity, we will use B&R Initiative to represent the "One Belt, One Road" Initiative for the rest of this chapter.

8. Figure 3.1 is adapted from Pakistan Defense, https://defence.pk/pdf/attachments/i3-silk_road_map_opt-jpeg.345307.

9. Ministry of Foreign Affairs and the Ministry of Commerce of the People's Republic of China, "Vision and Actions on Jointly Building."

10. Ibid.

11. Foreign Policy, "America's Pacific century," last modified on October 11, 2011, https://foreignpolicy.com/2011/10/11/americas-pacific-century/.

12. Yiwei Wang, 一带一路": 机遇与挑战 [*"One Belt, One Road" Initiative: Opportunities and Challenges*] (Beijing: Renmin Press, 2015).

13. New Zealand Foreign Affairs & Trade, "Text of the Trans-Pacific Partnership," last modified on January 26, 2016, https://www.mfat.govt.nz/en/about-us/who-we-are/treaties/trans-pacific-partnership-agreement-tpp/text-of-the-trans-pacific-partnership.

14. CNN, "Trump's TPP withdrawal: 5 things to know," last modified on January 23, 2017, http://edition.cnn.com/2017/01/23/politics/trump-tpp-things-to-know/index.html.

15. "Japanese efforts to entice US back to embattled TPP trade pact appear to have failed," Global Times, last modified on May 22, 2017, http://www.globaltimes.cn/content/1048155.shtml.

16. "Embracing China's New Normal: Why the economy is still on the track?" *Foreign Affairs*, last modified on May/June 2015, https://www.foreignaffairs.com/articles/china/2015-04-20/embracing-chinas-new-normal.

17. Ibid.

18. Wang, *"One Belt, One Road" Initiative.*

19. Jan Nederveen Pieterse and Jontae Kim, *Globalization and Development in East Asia* (New York: Routledge, 2012).

20. "Embracing China's New Normal: Why the economy is still on the track?"

21. "The 2016 top 250 international contractors 1-100," Engineering News-Record, last modified on August 2016, http://www.enr.com/toplists/2016-Top-250-International-Contractors1.

22. Ibid.

23. Y. Y. Xin and K. Li, 崛起大战略: "一带一路" 战略全剖析 [*Grand Strategy for China's Rising: A Thorough Study of the "One Belt, One Road" Initiative*] (Beijing: Taihai Press, 2016).

24. Ibid.

25. Ibid.

26. Ibid.

27. Maj Gen PJS Sandhu, *Rising China: Opportunity or Strategic Challenge?* (New Delhi: Vij Books India Pvt Ltd., 2010).

28. Ministry of Foreign Affairs of the People's Republic of China, "Set aside dispute and pursue joint development," https://www.fmprc.gov.cn/mfa_eng/ziliao_665539/3602_665543/3604_665547/t18023.shtml.

29. Xin and Li, *Grand Strategy for China's Rising*.

30. Angela Poh and Mingjiang Li, "A China in Transition: The Rhetoric and Substance of Chinese Foreign Policy under Xi Jinping," *Asian Security* 13, no. 2 (2017): 84–97.

31. Xin and Li, *Grand Strategy for China's Rising*.

32. Weizhun Mao, "Debating China's International Responsibility," *The Chinese Journal of International Politics* 10, no. 2 (2017): 173–210.

33. Ibid.

34. ZQ Zhu, "China's AIIB and OBOR: Ambitions and challenges," *The Diplomat*. Retrieved October 9, 2015, from http://thediplomat.com/2015/10/chinas-aiib-and-obor-ambitions-and-challenges/.

35. YN Zheng, 危机或重生? 全球化时代的中国命运 [*A Crisis or a Rebirth? China in the Age of Globalization*] (Zhejiang: Zhejiang Renmin Press, 2013).

36. Ibid.

37. Ibid.

38. Wang, *The Belt and the Road Initiative*.

39. Ibid.

40. Ibid.

41. Wang, *"One Belt, One Road" Initiative*.

42. Wang, *The Belt and the Road Initiative*.

43. Ministry of Foreign Affairs of China, "Xi Jinping meets with President Mahinda Rajapaska of Sri Lanka," last modified in 2014, http://www.fmprc.gov.cn/mfa_eng/zxxx_662805/t1159605.shtml.

44. Ibid.

45. Nash Jenkins, "China will build an extensive port city in Sri Lanka's capital," *Time*, last modified on March 11, 2016, http://time.com/4255129/chinese-port-colombo-sri-lanka/.

46. Wang, *"One Belt, One Road" Initiative*.

47. Ibid.

48. Ibid.

49. Ibid.

50. Ibid.

51. Ibid.

52. Kum Li, "Building a better world with B&R Initiative." CCTV, last modified on September 8, 2016, http://english.cctv.com/2016/09/08/ARTIzyLEMGjHs fqstY4MEUDa160908.shtml.

53. Randall Hansen, "Trump, Merkel, and the future of the transatlantic relationship," *The Globe and Mail*, last modified on June 2, 2017, https://www.theglobeand mail.com/news/world/trump-merkel-and-the-future-of-the-transatlantic-relationship/ article35188239/.

54. Michael D. Shear, "Trump will withdraw U.S. from Paris Climate Agreement," *New York Times*, last modified on June 1, 2017, https://www.nytimes.com/2017/06/01/ climate/trump-paris-climate-agreement.html.

55. Wang, *"One Belt, One Road" Initiative.*

56. Ibid.

57. Freedom House, "Methodology: Freedom in the World 2016," last modified in 2018, https://freedomhouse.org/report/freedom-world-2016/methodology; Wang, *"One Belt, One Road" Initiative.*

58. Figure 3.2 source: Freedom House, "Methodology: Freedom in the World 2016," last modified in 2018, https://freedomhouse.org/report/freedom-world-2016/ methodology.

59. Figure 3.3 source: Freedom House, "Methodology: Freedom in the World 2016," last modified in 2018, https://freedomhouse.org/report/freedom-world-2016/ methodology.

60. Joseph Grieco, Robert Powell, and Duncan Snidal, "The Relative-Gains Problem for International Cooperation," *American Political Science Review* 87, no. 3 (1993): 729–743.

Chapter Four

North America

The Peaceful Region

Patrick James and Athanasios Hristoulas

North America

North America Region

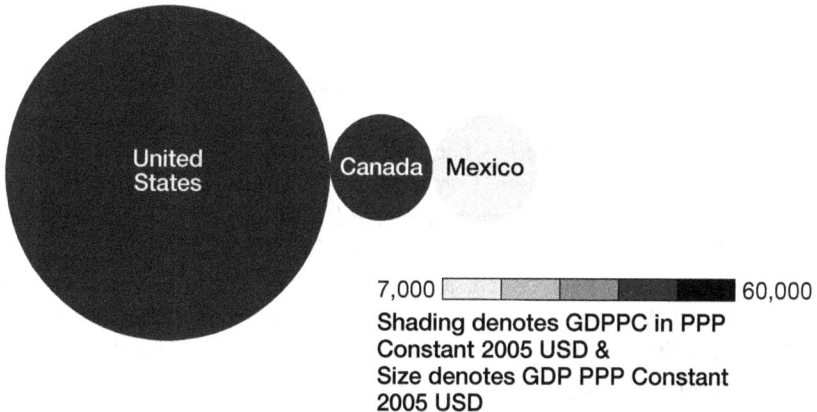

United
States

Canada   Mexico

7,000 ▭▭▭▭▭ 60,000
Shading denotes GDPPC in PPP
Constant 2005 USD &
Size denotes GDP PPP Constant
2005 USD

North America Hierarchy

THE PEACEFUL REGION

The North America hierarchy is a peaceful region in comparison to many other geographic regions covered in this volume.[1] From the twentieth century onward, there has been a scholarly consensus that there would be no shifts in power capabilities in North America in the foreseeable future and thus that no North American nation would overtake any other (a shift conducive to war). The United States, put simply, was and is the single preeminent state in this region. The absence of transitions and of any potential for conflict allows us to examine more closely other power transition phenomena that exist in peaceful regions.

Recognition of Washington, DC, as the preeminent capital on the continent was affirmed as early as 1903 when Great Britain declined to support Canada in its dispute with the United States over its boundary with Alaska. At that point, the last among the European colonial powers thus gave up any pretension to challenge the Monroe Doctrine in North America. US regional preeminence over the last century and into the new millennium stands in contrast to the history of other regions. As other chapters document, some regions that have experienced power transitions were involved in highly destructive wars between leading states. Although wars often rearrange international interactions, the dynamics of peaceful regions are equally interesting and important to understand.

North America as an international system is composed of three states: Canada, Mexico, and the United States. Although other states are adjacent to North America, such as those of Central America and the Caribbean, their inclusion in North America would not alter the analysis that follows.[2] French ownership of St. Pierre and Miquelon off the Canadian coast stands as a reminder of colonial times. Thus, the three-state system of North America creates three dyads (Canada–United States, Mexico–United States, Canada–Mexico) and one triad (Canada–United States–Mexico).

This chapter focuses on peaceful rather than confrontational or conflictual interaction. Power transition theory (PTT) anticipates both conditions. Historically speaking, there has been no power transition in North America to study for many generations. Furthermore, given the distribution of capabilities, *no power transition can be expected, if at all, for many generations to come*. This chapter is intended to convey, in effect, what happens in the presence of a firmly established, leading state. The time frame for analysis is from World War II onward. The evolution of the North American system will reveal political processes within dyads and the triad that resolve disputes by cooperation and bargaining but do not include efforts by either Mexico or Canada to supplant the United States.

This chapter unfolds in various sections, as will be explained. In section two, we will advance three propositions about what to expect regarding interactions in the absence of even a potential power transition. The third section focuses on the consolidation of US supremacy on the North American continent in the conduct and aftermath of World War II. To make subsequent events intelligible, we shall also devote some attention in this section to a brief overview of history of Mexico and Canada prior to that war. The fourth section focuses on politics and policies within the dyads and triad. Section five assesses the propositions based on interactions between and among the three principal states of North America. The sixth and final section sums up what has been learned and offers future insights.

PROPOSITIONS FOR PEACE

What sort of international politics should be expected when a power transition is virtually certain to be absent for generations into the future? Three deductions consistent with the theoretical foundations of power transition are offered here.

Strategic Cooperation Proposition: At a strategic level, states within a region with a dominant hierarchy will cooperate with the leader against external challengers.

The logic here is straightforward because all ongoing forces point in the same direction. Jacek Kugler has written about the risk associated with the decision to start a war.[3] For less-powerful states, the decision to support an external power against the established regional leader could involve extraordinary risk. The local dominant power might simply invade a less-powerful state to overthrow a regime that it would see as engaging in betrayal. In addition, it is more likely that less-powerful states within a given region will follow the lead of the local dominant power, rather than risk everything by casting their lots with any of its external rivals. Ongoing political and economic interactions can be expected to produce some degree of regional integration. This might fall short of a full-fledged regime for hemispheric cooperation, but it still would entail convergence in policy that makes strategic cooperation with the leader much more likely among lesser states than balancing against it via support for an external rival (for a slightly different path see chapter 11). The leader, in turn, is expected to cooperate with lesser states in its region as efforts are made to keep up with one or more rivals at the global level and to help socialize its neighbors into the peaceful alliance.[4]

Full cooperation, however, is not expected for a region with an ongoing and unchallenged leader. There is the tactical, as well as strategic, level to consider:

Tactical Competition Proposition: At a tactical level, states within the region will compete with the leader.

Competition is anticipated within limits even in the presence of an unchallenged leading state. Redistributive politics, as described by Lowi,[5] will exist precisely *because* of the amount of cooperation that occurs at the strategic level. In the realm of security, the question is: Who pays for it and how much? With regard to economic issues, queries are similar: What agreements will be made and how are benefits to be distributed? Disputes that naturally ensue in these redistributive contexts, in the presence of an unchallenged leader, will not rise to a strategic confrontational level.

Finally, we expect that the degree of integration in the region will rise and fall over time:

Oscillation Proposition: Contact will increase and decrease in cycles of varying length but seldom will it reach polar points of total separation or full integration.

This is a magnetic model of political processes. The leading state is the magnet in this metaphor. Lesser states will be pulled toward it, but then back away when they get too close in any given issue area. This is because lesser states seldom wish to be absorbed into one superstate. When movement away from the leader goes too far in a given issue area, and separation creates disadvantages because of the loss of cooperation, the process usually reverses itself. Very seldom, however, does oscillation ever result either in the absorption of a lesser state into the dominant power or in complete separation.

What are the criteria for falsifying these propositions? For the Strategic Cooperation Proposition, it is simple: a demonstrable challenge from one of the lesser states. The Tactical Competition Proposition would be refuted by the development of a pure hierarchy, in which the lesser states simply "took orders," as with a medieval tribute system. For the Oscillation Proposition, falsification would be straightforward as well. If the system settled on either integration into one country or full separation, that would mean an end to the process of moving closer or farther away.

Before moving forward with the story of bilateral and trilateral relations, a key assumption needs to be confirmed.[6]

The idea of exploring North America as a peaceful case of PTT depends on confirming (i) preeminent status of the United States and (ii) no challenger

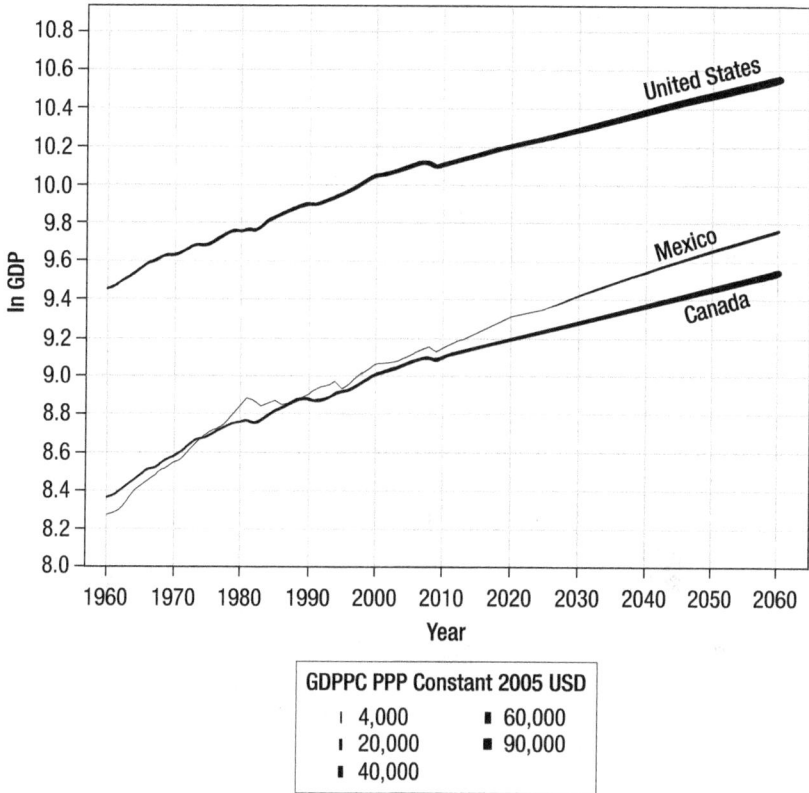

Figure 4.1. North America Power Trajectory

in sight. Figure 4.1 offers overwhelming confirmation on those points. The figure displays the United States, Canada, and Mexico in terms of relative national capability from 1960 to 2060. The United States leads by many orders of magnitude throughout this period. No change is in sight, with the United States maintaining control of about 15 percent of the world's economic capabilities. Given this enormous capability gap, Mexico and Canada show no sign of challenging the United States for regional leadership.

NORTH AMERICA: A HISTORICAL OVERVIEW

The United States and Canada

Relationships between the United States and Canada became peaceful following the British-American War of 1812–1815 (the War of 1812, as it is known in US historiography). Britain was involved with overriding matters in

Europe such as the Napoleonic Wars, so it allocated limited resources to the conflict with the United States. The war ended with the status quo antebellum on the Canadian front, with no boundary changes.[7] From that point on, an Era of Good Feeling emerged between Canada and the United States that continues to the present day.

Canadian Prime Minister William Lyon Mackenzie King and US President Franklin Delano Roosevelt signed the Ogdensburg Agreement on August 17, 1940, which institutionalized security cooperation in the event of an attack against the North American continent. This pact followed Canadian achievement of a foreign policy independent from that of Great Britain in 1931. The agreement signaled the onset of an era in which the principal security relationship for Canada would be with the United States rather than any state outside North America. With this development, each of the other two powers in North America now confirmed a primary connection in the realm of security with the United States.

Canada's participation in the coalition that won World War II is confirmed in numerous sources, written and otherwise. The exhibits at the Canadian War Museum make the case most clearly. Contributions are well known through stories passed on from one generation to the next; both successes and failures are long-remembered by Canadians and others. On the one hand, Canada led the failed raid on Dieppe, France, on August 19, 1942. It also actively participated in the Battle of the Atlantic and the Italian campaigns. Perhaps most important, Canadian forces took charge of securing one of the five beaches on the ultimately successful D-Day invasion of June 6, 1944. All of these events contributed to the Canadian sense of nationhood, notably as a state in and of itself that could act beyond the confines of the British Empire. Allied status in World War II also provided considerable positive momentum for the relationship with the United States.

The United States and Mexico

What about Mexico, the other US neighbor? For Mexico, of course, border disputes with the United States were more recent and far more conflictual than for Canada. Because of an early experience with conflict, Mexican foreign policy has historically emphasized independence and autonomy in foreign security policy. Of particular importance in that context is the specific impact of US-Mexican bilateral relations. Suspicion about US motives, which dates back to the war of 1846–1848, further solidified Mexico's commitment to autonomy, independence, and non-intervention during the Cold War.

As argued by one Mexican scholar, "the direct vicinity with such a colossus has cost Mexico the loss of more than half of its original territory, several military interventions, constant interference in internal political affairs and economic penetration at all levels. In few [other] countries, as is the case in Mexico, has the phenomenon of geographical situation operated as a major factor in foreign policy."[8] Awareness of such tensions went well beyond Mexico. For example, the ill-considered Zimmerman Telegram from Germany during World War I reinforced a fear that, under certain conditions, Mexico might side against the United States. This fear turned out to be groundless, at least in the context of that war, and no incident of its kind is known to have occurred since.

Not so well known, especially in the United States, are Mexico's contributions to the Allied effort in World War II. Mexico's main military contribution consisted of patrolling the Atlantic and the Pacific. Given the vulnerability of Allied shipping to German submarine attacks, Mexican efforts at sea had great value. This task became so important to Mexican decision makers that they separated the navy from the combined force structure. The Mexican government gave its navy the status of a ministry in its own right from that time onward. With the enhanced standing from that recognition, admirals obtained a direct line of communication to the president rather than having to go through the chief of staff.

Mexico's most important contribution to the war effort, in terms beyond its border for many years to come, was its agreement to the "Braceros" program with the United States. With the onset of that program, millions of Mexican migrants came to work on farms that had been left behind by US personnel sent off to fight in Europe and the Pacific. Thus, it would not be too much of an exaggeration to argue that Mexicans fed US soldiers and workers fighting the fascist regimes.

North America from the Cold War Onward

The nature of Mexican and Canadian collaboration with the United States changed somewhat with the onset of the Cold War. Canada continued to collaborate openly with the United States, but Mexico tried to distance itself to some extent from the United States and US policy during the Cold War. Mexico and Canada, prior to World War II, had very little connection with each other. The relationship had to build from near zero from 1945 onward. Bilateral relations for each dyad and the one triad in North America are revealing when studied in further detail.

Canada and the United States

With the emergence of the Cold War, security cooperation between Canada and the United States continued. For example, Canada became a member of the North Atlantic Treaty Organization (NATO) at its founding in 1949. The United States also established a permanent military presence in northern Canada to monitor Soviet activity. This began in earnest with the Distant Early Warning (DEW) Line in the 1950s and exists even now in the form of the Northern Warning System. The ongoing purpose is to detect intrusion into northern Canada by hostile forces, whether by Russia or some other actor.

The North American Aerospace Defense Command (NORAD) is the most important bilateral defense treaty between the United States and Canada. Created in 1957, NORAD's center is located in Colorado and jointly staffed by US and Canadian forces. The center provides early warning of missile and air attacks. NORAD defends North American air sovereignty and is responsible for providing air defense if an attack occurs.

The more than two thousand bilateral non-treaty-level military agreements have created a unique situation in the security relationship between Canada and the United States, viz., almost complete interoperability. It would not be an exaggeration to say that you could pluck a Canadian officer out of Kingston and put him or her in command of a New York-based National Guard platoon.[9]

Collaboration with the United States extended beyond security into many other areas (including law enforcement) and deepened across the board in the Cold War. In many ways, Canadian foreign policy came to mirror that of its southern neighbor. Canada became the "best friend" of the United States. Its connection with the United States became significant, for example, in matters of commerce as well as security. With the decline of Great Britain after World War II, Canadian businesses started looking south to take up the slack. This represented a notable departure from the past; Prime Minister Wilfrid Laurier had lost the federal election of 1911 for daring to suggest even limited free trade with the United States.

Difficult phases, to be sure, have arisen as a result of longstanding suspicions among Canadians that their country was compromising some of its foreign policy independence.[10] Yet there have been counterexamples, such as Canadian opposition to the Vietnam War in the 1960s and disagreement about recognition of the People's Republic of China (PRC), as well as connections with Cuba in the 1970s. Canada also had disagreements with the United States over missile testing in the 1980s. It is worth noting that the most intense period of tensions with the United States came during the years that Pierre Elliott Trudeau served as Canadian prime minister. However, a very close relationship between Ottawa and Washington resumed after the end of Trudeau's term in office; the security interests of both countries, for instance, continued to be intertwined.

Spillover from the military to the economic realm began with the Auto Pact in 1965 but did not advance much in the next two decades. On taking office as prime minister in September 1984, three months after Trudeau left office, Brian Mulroney stressed the advantages of further economic integration between the two countries. Canada signed a bilateral trade agreement with the United States in 1987, known as the Canada-United States Free Trade Agreement (FTA), which established for Ottawa the principles of free exchange in the North American context. The FTA set out what was important: an institutionalized mechanism to guarantee access to US markets. Even before the FTA, the bilateral trade relationship between Canada and the United States had been the largest in the world for a long time. Canadian decision makers at the time of the FTA wanted to make sure that the political climate in the United States would not subsequently affect trade relations between the two countries. Canadian decision makers, for example, did not want to have to worry about the political consequences of opposing the United States on foreign policy issues such as South Africa. Prime Minister Mulroney's government also had concerns about protectionist tendencies within the US Congress. From the Canadian perspective, a FTA between the two nations that established explicit rules would protect Canada's export market to the United States.

The terrorist attacks on September 11, 2001, shifted the focus from economic exchange back to security in a dramatic way. As a result of the events of that day, security would come to dominate the agenda of George W. Bush's administration and, as a by-product, the agendas of Mexico and Canada as well. This shift had different consequences and outcomes for Mexico and Canada.

From the beginning, several members of Congress identified Canada—wrongly, as it turned out—as the country from which terrorists linked to Al Qaeda entered US territory to commit the attacks. After these accusations and, combined with the fact that some evidence existed that terrorist groups had been operating in Canada with impunity, Ottawa focused its efforts on two related areas: First, the Canadian government demonstrated that terrorists had not in fact used its territory as a springboard for their actions. Second, Ottawa made it known that Canada would continue to be a reliable partner and ally of Washington.

Canadian Prime Minister Jean Chrétien—in office from 1993 to 2003—quickly implemented a strategy to confirm that his government would act decisively to fight terrorism. Canada and the United States signed a border agreement in October 2001. The agreement outlined four areas for cooperation: the secure flow of people, the secure flow of goods, secure infrastructure, and coordination and information-sharing.[11] Second, the Chrétien government put a counterterrorism plan into action, spearheaded by the Anti-Terrorism Act, enacted by parliament in December 2001.

With regard to foreign policy over and above the bilateral connection with the United States, the Canadian government declared its intention to fight terrorism within the context of multilateral institutions such as the United Nations (UN). When the UN Security Council authorized the war in Afghanistan, Canada assumed an active role in military operations in the course of early 2002.[12]

Indeed, the degree of interoperability between the United States and Canada, described previously, often conflicts with Ottawa's stated policy and tends to produce convergence in practice. For instance, the Canadian government heavily criticized the US-led war in Iraq up to and beyond its outbreak in 2003. Prime Minister Jean Chrétien stated bluntly that Canada would not be part of the coalition of the willing that the United States had assembled to prosecute the war against Saddam Hussein. Yet, because of multiple exchange programs in effect at the time the war started, a small number of Canadian units found themselves taking part in combat. This involvement also extended to maritime operations. Canadian military involvement in Iraq, a conflict that Ottawa viewed with disdain, reveals the overwhelming momentum that exists in the domain of security cooperation with the United States.

Further examples of security cooperation between Canada and the United States in the context of North America—as outlined in the 2001 Smart Border plan and Beyond the Borders in 2009—include the Border Enforcement Team Program (IBETS), Integrated National Security Enforcement Teams (INSETS) led by the Royal Canadian Mounted Police (RCMP), and the Shiprider program. Canada and the United States also implemented the Integrated IBETS along twenty-three points of the US-Canada border. This binational program permits five security agencies to exchange information and to work together on a daily basis with local, state, and provincial authorities. These agencies cooperate on such matters as national security, organized crime, and illegal acts committed along the border. Agencies involved in IBETS include the RCMP, the Canadian Border Service Agency (CBSA), US Customs and Border Protection (CBP), the US Bureau of Immigration and Customs Enforcement (ICE), and the US Coast Guard (USCG).

Integrated Cross Border Maritime Law Enforcement Operations, or Shiprider, function similarly to IBETS but at sea. The initiative is spearheaded by the RCMP and the USCG. Shiprider authorizes specially trained and designated Canadian and US law enforcement officers to jointly crew marine vessels to enforce the law on both sides of the international boundary line. Armed Canadian and US law enforcement officers are able to transit back and forth across the border to interdict cross-border criminality in shared waterways. Shiprider operations are conducted under the control of law enforcement officers of the "host" country, assisted by the law enforcement officers of the "visiting" country. In Canadian waters, for example, operations are subject to Canadian laws, policies, and procedures and all operations are under the direction and control of Canadian law enforcement officers.[13]

Mexico and the United States

The Cold War experience highlighted Mexico's perceived need to stay out of superpower politics. This disposition led to a somewhat unsuccessful effort to maintain the foreign policy orientation of *non-alignment*.[14] Mexico attempted to eschew superpower politics in general, and US influence in particular, by taking a more active and independent role in international relations. Of particular political importance were attempts to establish solidarity with Arab and other nations in the developing world by openly supporting many of their causes.

For Mexico, the first multilateral security organization in the hemisphere, the Inter-American Treaty of Reciprocal Assistance (ITRA), proved to be a non-starter. Originally the commitment was assumed by most Latin American governments to serve as a hemispheric collective security arrangement against external aggression, but the "alliance" quickly expanded its role to include counteracting threats believed to originate inside certain communist states.[15]

Indeed, the United States envisioned the ITRA as a "Monroe Doctrine of the inter-American community, whereby members of the pact could legitimately decide to intervene within the affairs of a member state. A prime justification for such action would be 'communist political aggression.'" Given this emerging reality, according to Torres, the Mexican delegation sent to Rio de Janeiro to negotiate the multilateral security treaty became interested first and foremost in minimizing its military commitments and the organizational capacity of the ITRA. The delegation hoped to limit the capacity of the United States to project influence and interfere in the domestic affairs of Latin American countries.[16]

Mexico wholeheartedly supported yet another regional institution—the Organization of American States (OAS)—in its early years. The Mexican government believed that the new institution might have a chance to balance the influence of the United States within the context of hemispheric-only issues. However, the same events that led Mexico to attempt to undermine the goals of the ITRA also suggested that the utility of the OAS, as an instrument of Mexican foreign policy, would remain minimal. As noted by Torres,[17] starting in 1954 with the US intervention in Guatemala, Mexico began to argue that the organization had been converted into an instrument of US meddling in countries where it perceived political reform to be a communist-inspired threat against US national security. Given this scenario, Mexico saw its purpose within the OAS as maintaining an essentially defensive posture against the potential for intervention.

Thus, to say the least, the history of bilateral security between Mexico and the United States during the Cold War can be characterized as conflicted. Little communication and information sharing existed between the two sides during the Cold War and beyond. US law enforcement officials found themselves in frustrating situations, unable to deal with the inefficiency and corruption that often characterized working with Mexican officials. Mexican authorities tended to be overly sensitive to US unilateralism and lacked the technical expertise to achieve deeper cooperative mechanisms. In the end, no "security confidence" developed between Mexican and US authorities. Binational cooperation typically focused on reducing irritants and misunderstandings rather than on coordinating operations.[18]

Given the high level of anti-American sentiment in Mexico during the Cold War, this distancing from the United States and its policies served Mexican leaders quite well. Anti-American rhetoric reached its apex during the early 1970s under the stewardship of President Luis Echeverría. A reorientation in Mexican foreign policy, which had Cuban echoes, took place during his term in office. Echeverría tried to establish Mexico as a defender of the Third World. The Mexican president maintained strong ties with the communist government in Cuba and with Salvador Allende's government in Chile. Echeverría also provided political asylum for many refugees from various South American countries who were fleeing right-wing military dictatorships supported by the United States. On the surface, Echeverría appeared to be quite anti-American.

Echeverría's presidency, in a twist of irony, ended up heralding the beginning of US-Mexican military and law enforcement cooperation in the fight against drugs. US officials trained Mexican army and law enforcement at locations in Mexico and the United States. In addition, the United States routinely flew reconnaissance missions into Mexican airspace. At the time, this activity remained hidden from public view for obvious domestic political reasons. Cooperation continues to this day and has progressively deepened.

The signing of the Mérida Initiative (MI) on June 30, 2008, which provided Mexico with approximately $1.5 billion worth of equipment and training to fight the drug cartels, stands as a point of culmination in the cooperation between the two governments in this issue area. With undeniable impact already, the package is a unique development for at least two reasons. First, the MI seeks to place the problems of organized crime, drug trafficking, and violence associated with both in a multinational context. In the past, each country blamed the other for not doing enough to stop the consumption, production, and trafficking of illegal drugs. The MI recognizes that, on the contrary, each country must share responsibility for dealing with the serious public security and health problems associated with illegal drugs. The MI also affirms that the best approach is intergovernmental cooperation.

Second, although there have been instances of cooperation in the past, the MI marks the first time that Mexico asked for US assistance to strengthen its institutional capacity to respond to organized crime. Cooperation between both countries had been previously limited largely to the transfer of equipment and training for specialized units of Mexico's police and military. The scope of the MI goes well beyond the previous level of cooperation, including training and administrative help for Mexico's civilian law enforcement agencies and justice sector. Mexican foreign policy in relation to the United States, therefore, appears to be in a transition phase. Decision makers in Mexico seem to have abandoned strict definitions of defense of sovereignty and nationalism in favor of "pragmatism" and recognize the limits of what foreign policy can achieve on a unilateral basis.[19] Evidence of this can be found in the renegotiations of the North American Free Trade Agreement (NAFTA) and the muted response of the Mexican government to the Trump administration's aggressive border policies.

Canada and Mexico

For the most part, the history of Canada and Mexico in relation to each other can be described as one of benign neglect. Among the three major dyads in North America, the Canada-Mexico dyad is the only one without previous warfare—obviously, a good thing. Canadian-Mexican bilateral relations have been hurt, however, by a persistent fear on the part of Canadian decision makers that inclusion of Mexico in any "North American" agenda is not in their country's best interests. This is not a new phenomenon in Canadian foreign policy: During the negotiations leading up to the signing of the now-defunct NAFTA, Canada repeatedly tried to torpedo Mexico.

After September 11, Canadian policy makers tried to distinguish their country from Mexico, arguing that the kinds of security threats present at the Canada-US border differed from those at the Mexico-US border and, therefore, should be treated differently. Although Canada emphasized bilateral Canada-US responses to the terrorist attacks of September 11, Mexico pursued a trilateral approach. Ironically, this consisted of Mexican policy makers trying to convince US policy makers to treat their country more like Canada. A further area of contention between Canadian and Mexican decision makers focused on the pace of change in response to September 11. While Canada preferred an incremental, piecemeal approach to dealing with security threats, Mexico wanted what its foreign minister at the time, Jorge Castañeda, called the "whole enchilada," or a comprehensive renegotiation of NAFTA to include areas such as security and migration.

Where the question of bilateralism versus trilateralism in the era after September 11 is concerned, Ottawa argued that the issues facing Canada and the United States were (and still are) the efficient flow of legitimate goods and travelers within the context of heightened US security concerns. Canadian decision makers depicted the Mexican-US border, by contrast, as much more dangerous than their own. A high level of trade created complexity, as in the US-Canada context, but from Ottawa's perspective, the similarity ended there. From the Canadian point of view, the existence of illegal migration, drug trafficking, and corruption made the Mexican border with the United States much more challenging to manage.

Negotiation of a trilateral security mechanism would require much more time and—from a Canadian perspective—introduction of a third actor would unnecessarily delay the entire process or possibly stall it completely. Moreover, "smart border" technology at the Canada-US border had been in place for a while, antedating the terrorist attacks by a number of years. The same situation did not hold along the Mexican-US border. By design, therefore, Canada chose to differentiate itself (in terms of both issues and solutions) from Mexico. Although this stance could be justified on technical grounds, it also underscored important symbolic and political factors. Canada, in effect, depicted Mexico not so much as a partner but as a complicating ingredient in the neighborhood.

TRILATERALISM: CANADA, MEXICO, AND THE UNITED STATES

What can be said of these states in terms of *trilateral* relations? Finding the optimal level of regional integration presents an ongoing challenge to the principal states of North America. Although Canada, Mexico, and the United States have shared a common geography and to a great extent a common history, before NAFTA the region had been extremely fragmented in both political and economic terms. There existed, in essence, two bilateral relationships—one between Canada and the United States and the other between Mexico and the United States.

For example, whereas Canada and the United States had developed a close economic relationship after the end of World War II, which developed into the Canada-United States FTA in 1987, Mexico at that time had barely started to recover from a severe economic crisis. The economic trough of 1982 had been brought on by decades of economic mismanagement. Only in the 1980s and early 1990s did Mexico begin to implement practices amenable to free trade and thereby enter into an exchange envisioned in North American terms.

Pragmatism ultimately prevailed in the early 1990s when Mexico, Canada, and the United States entered negotiations to sign NAFTA. When the Mexican government approached the United States in the early 1990s to begin negotiation on an FTA, it took decision makers in Washington somewhat by surprise. This initiative signaled an important shift in Mexican economic policy. Mexico, put succinctly, would now be open for business. The signing of NAFTA signaled three fundamental changes in Mexican foreign policy: a new openness toward the United States, a dominance of economic themes in foreign policy, and a strategic reorientation toward participation in multilateral institutions.[20]

For Canada, which had narrow objectives after the FTA fell into place, free trade in North America had limited appeal. Canadian thinking stood in sharp contrast to how Carlos Salinas, the Mexican president at the time, sold North American free trade at home and abroad. Salinas argued that free trade in North America would help, for example, eradicate poverty in Mexico. Free trade also would raise the standard of living of Mexicans. Finally, a free-trade deal would increase the size of the middle class. Canadian decision makers did not consider any of these factors to be important. In that respect, conflicting objectives on the part of Canadian and Mexican decision makers further complicated an already less-than-amicable relationship between Canada and Mexico in the trilateral context.

Canada had already signed an agreement with the United States in 1987, so its decision makers saw little value in a further agreement that would include Mexico. In 1994, NAFTA, therefore, appeared to the Canadian side as simply an unnecessary extension of the agreement from 1987. The fact that the 1994 agreement would include Mexico stood out as a complicating factor. Canadian decision makers saw Mexico as a competitor who might undercut Canada's trade with the United States. Mexico, for example, had much lower labor costs than Canada. Therefore, initially, Canadian decision makers actually tried to convince the United States that NAFTA would not be needed. Canadian leaders argued further that Mexico would be an unreliable trade partner because of its underdevelopment and rampant corruption. This effort proved unsuccessful and placed Mulroney's government in a difficult situation: either participate in the process to negotiate a trilateral trade agreement or stick to the bilateral FTA agreement signed in 1987.

Mulroney's government decided that the better option, under difficult circumstances, would be to participate in the creation of a trilateral trade regime rather than stay on the sidelines. After all, whether or not Canada participated, the US and Mexican governments had decided to go ahead with an agreement anyway. Mulroney's government decided that it did not want to be left out; Canada had no choice other than to participate. Further, by entering into the process, Ottawa's negotiators might be able to influence the design of the agreement in a fashion more favorable to Canada. Therefore, it would not be completely accurate to argue that Canada participated in the NAFTA process for purely defensive reasons.

Canada's reservations—which led to a number of hiccups in the nego-tiations—did not prevent a regional FTA from going into effect on January 1, 1994. The three countries agreed to implement NAFTA in stages covering a twenty-year period. What should be highlighted, from the standpoint of re-gional integration, is the motivation of each state. Canada participated ostensi-bly to protect its economic relationship with the United States, whereas Mexico saw free trade as a way to modernize. Leaders in Mexico City remained open to the idea that North American free trade at some point in the future could incor-porate other types of cooperation. Although the United States participated ac-tively in negotiations, setbacks generally resulted from disagreements between Mexico and Canada. At one point, for example, to the extreme displeasure of the Mexicans, the Canadian delegation left the negotiations. The Canadians returned only after the US representatives intervened.

When NAFTA went into effect, a grassroots insurgency movement in the south of Mexico took possession of towns and villages in the state of Chi-apas. After a number of armed confrontations with Mexican Armed Forces, the two sides declared a cease-fire. Demands from the group, called the Zapatista Army of National Liberation, focused on fears that the FTA would have negative effects on the peasant-based agricultural system that existed in southern Mexico.

The rebellion in Chiapas and subsequent related events made headline news in Mexico and abroad. The Mexican government felt a tremendous amount of pressure from its foreign allies and friends to negotiate a settlement of the dispute. The timing of the rebellion could not have been worse for the Mexican government. Throughout the early 1990s, the Mexican government had been trying to portray the country as being in the midst of political and economic modernization. Mexico, argued President Salinas, would soon join the ranks of advanced Western democracies on an equal footing. The rebel-lion demonstrated to both domestic and international observers that the path would be much more complicated than initially thought.

Mexico's newfound commercial allies, Canada and the United States, had some sympathy for the Mexican government. Ottawa and Washington acknowledged that Mexico, in the process of transformation, needed some help to achieve its goals. The United States and especially Canada offered the Mexican government assistance in various areas of governance. During the negotiations for NAFTA, Canada had adopted human security as a pillar of its foreign policy and Mexico offered an ideal opportunity to apply some aspects of the doctrine. Mexico needed help and Canada offered it, thus bringing the two countries into closer bilateral relations. The latter half of the 1990s could be characterized by ever-increasing bilateral and trilateral trade as well as political friendship, especially between Canada and Mexico.

The election of George W. Bush altered the political dynamics in the region. Bush, to begin with, stated publicly that the best friend of the United States was Mexico. This perturbed Canadian decision makers, who historically had viewed their own country as the best and closest ally to the United States. To make matters worse, Bush's first foreign visit as president of the United States was not to Canada, as a long-standing tradition stipulated, but rather to Mexico, to meet with that country's new president, Vicente Fox. Pictures of Bush and Fox enjoying the sun over lunch at the Mexican president's ranch did not alleviate Canadian concerns.

During that initial meeting, which took place on February 21, 2001, Bush and Fox discussed opening up NAFTA to include other areas of cooperation such as security and migration. Discussion included the possibility of a social cohesion program for Mexico paid for by the other NAFTA partners. To say the least, this constituted a tectonic shift in bilateral political and economic relations. To quote Bush: "Mexico is the first foreign country I have visited as President, and I intended it to be that way. Our nations are bound together by ties of history, family, values, commerce, and culture. Today, these ties give us an unprecedented opportunity. We have a chance to build a partnership that will improve the lives of citizens in both countries."[21]

With this new climate in US-Mexican relations, therefore, Mexico proposed a renegotiation of NAFTA in early 2001. Mexico City was looking for two things: (i) a migration agreement that would permit Mexicans to enter the United States in search of jobs and (ii) a program paid for by the United States and Canada designed to help modernize Mexico's economy. In return, Fox promised deeper security cooperation with the United States. Ultimately, Fox wanted something resembling the European Union (EU). As noted previously, the Mexican foreign secretary, Jorge Castañeda, referred to the plan as the "whole enchilada."[22]

Canadian decision makers, who had assumed that their relationship with the United States would remain more important than any other US relationships, ended up in a panic. Not only did it look like Canada would play second fiddle to Mexico, but renegotiation of NAFTA also came onto the table—something that Canadian decision makers vehemently opposed.

Unfortunately for Mexico, the plan ended up on the backburner a few months later when the terrorist attacks of September 11, 2001 occurred.

Because of this, subsequent negotiations focused on "securitizing" North America; Mexico appeared to have accepted wholeheartedly and even encouraged multilateral security mechanisms among the three NAFTA partners. Although terrorism remained the central security focus for Canada, Mexico, and the United States in the weeks and months following September 11, the prospect of NAFTA+ still seemed plausible. As with members of the EU and the common threat presented by the Soviet Union, terrorism would push the three North American countries closer together. However, the moment anti-terrorism became a less salient concern, at least within Canada and Mexico, the perceived need for a deeper North American bond began to wane.

Although terrorism remained on the radar screen, figuratively speaking, Canada's decision makers saw little utility in working with Mexico to manage this threat. Canada believed that the threat could be met in coordination with the United States in a bilateral and piecemeal fashion and not in the grandiose vision of a united North America as espoused by Mexican Foreign Minister Castañeda. Canada wanted a border agreement to assure the free flow of goods and services but only with the United States. Mexico's desires to trilateralize the process in 2001–2002 looked, to Ottawa, like a complicating factor. Canada itself tried to go trilateral with the Security and Prosperity Partnership (SPP) in 2005, but the process, as anticipated by Canadian decision makers, proved to be too complicated and cumbersome. Ottawa also had come to realize by 2006–2007 that the focus of the SPP—to manage the threat posed by terrorism—simply did not reflect the reality of the second half of the decade. For Canada, other threats had emerged in the context of North America that required the country to refocus its attention.

ASSESSING THE PROPOSITIONS

Three propositions have been put forward about peaceful processes in a region with no power transition looming. Each proposition will be considered in turn. Evidence from North America in the years since World War II supports the Strategic Cooperation Proposition. Canada signed the Ogdensburg Agreement and fought alongside the United States in World War II. Cooperation continued significantly after the war; NATO, NORAD, and the DEW Line are just the most visible manifestations of US-Canadian cooperation. Canadian forces also fought in the Afghan War as a US ally. Over time, the interoperability of US and Canadian forces became quite extraordinary. More than two thousand military agreements have been signed by these two states. Components of the Beyond the Borders initiative, notably IBETS and

Shiprider, project cooperation well into the future. Canada, in sum, supports rather than challenges the United States at a strategic level on the continent.

Evidence for Mexico is less clear but still points in the same direction. Mexico supported US efforts, especially at sea, in World War II. It also worked alongside the United States in the early years of the OAS. The Echeverría regime instituted major military and law enforcement cooperation with the United States in an effort to counteract the trade in illegal drugs. The MI stands out because of assistance to Mexico provided by the United States for purposes of security. Currently Mexico does not challenge US leadership at a strategic level but instead cooperates in security and trade with its northern neighbor in regard to China and Russia.

Developments in North America also favor the Tactical Competition Proposition. Mexico entered the Cold War with an interest in maintaining at least some distance from the United States, exemplified by at least a limited involvement in the nonaligned movement. Tensions developed over ITRA and then the OAS, which followed an initial period of cooperation. Conflict over matters related to law enforcement, as well as Mexican expressions of sympathy for Cuba and Chile, also occurred at various times. Thus, the bilateral relationship between Mexico and the United States features conflict at a tactical level over multiple issues, such as immigration and trade cooperation. Evidence from Canada also supports the tactical proposition. Canada sparred with the United States over opposition to the Vietnam War, recognition of the PRC and Cuba, and missile testing. The FTA represented cooperation on the one hand, but its details reflected at least some degree of conflict on the other hand; clearly, Canada had not simply signed an agreement dictated by the United States. In addition, Canada initially opposed the Mexican-inspired NAFTA, risking, perhaps, the ire of the United States. Finally, tensions developed with the security-fixated United States in the period after September 11, notably regarding opposition by Canada to the Iraq War. Under the Trump administration, Canada has been pressured to renegotiate trade agreements.

The Oscillation Proposition receives support from the history of North America during and after World War II. Mexico and Canada clearly jumped on the bandwagon with the United States during that war. Soon after, Mexico pulled away because of concerns about dominant tendencies on the part of the United States concerning Latin America. Canada, by contrast, got even closer to the United States through a series of security agreements with a tinge of the Cold War. Yet neither state came close to either a non-relationship with the United States or to being absorbed within its borders. A review of cooperation and conflict in relation to the preceding two propositions about the strategic and tactical levels confirms the existence of irregular cycles of attraction and repulsion for both Canada and Mexico vis-à-vis the United States.

The Oscillation Proposition incorporates the newest twist resulting from the advent of the Trump era. After castigating both Canada and Mexico and threatening to abolish NAFTA, President Donald Trump imposed adjustments to the arrangement. This subsequently led to passage of a similar agreement called the United States–Mexico–Canada Agreement. The previous proposal of an EU-type NAFTA has been postponed but may resurge in the future. On the security side, the US attempt to build a southern wall has created a firestorm of opposition.

US policy has damaged but not fundamentally altered cooperative relations in North America. The structural condition of overwhelming preponderance and relative satisfaction has restrained members of the triad from any real confrontation. Without major structural changes, we anticipate that this oscillation will continue.

FUTURE COOPERATION OR CONFRONTATION

North America holds the structural conditions for peace anticipated by PTT. The United States is in place, quite firmly, as the leading state in the region for generations to come. Canada and Mexico, as the other principal states in North America, cooperate with the United States at the strategic level in opposition to potential challengers from outside the region. Economic interaction is extensive but varies substantially over time. Ottawa and Mexico City argue with Washington over any number of issues in more tactical terms. An oscillating model seems to best describe the pattern of economic interactions in the region.

The United States is the magnet, with Mexico and Canada attracted to it up to a point but repelled when relations get too close. This follows logically from the desire of each lesser state to collaborate with the United States yet also protect its independence and sovereignty to the extent possible under conditions of extreme asymmetry. The result is a process of oscillation—pulling toward and drawing away, in alternation. As much larger challengers from Asia emerge from their slumbers, the regionally dominant United States will find that deeper collaboration with Canada and Mexico is central to its well-being if not survival.

Significant future policy options at the global level flow from this analysis. The dramatic rise on the part of China over recent decades will likely push the United States to alter its go-it-alone policies. If China matches or even surpasses the United States at the global level, the United States will first look to strengthen its base of support close to home and then seek to build up cooperation with other Western allies, which will be a worldwide effort to preserve stability against a rising dissatisfied challenger. Such cooperation, if successful early on, could move to economic integration in the face of a dynamic economic challenger.

The emergence of significant regional dissent is unlikely in the foreseeable future. No nation has a greater capacity than the United States to associate itself with Mexico or Canada, thus overcoming a likely counter by the United States. As indicated at the outset, North America is a relatively satisfied but highly asymmetric region, the security of which is assured by the preponderance of the United States. This makes North America a stable region by world standards. Consequently, the region has been spared the damaging side effects of conflictual power transitions that are commonplace elsewhere.

NOTES

1. Global Map shows region contours. The hierarchy map shows the relative size of the top contenders in this region. Data are World Bank, "World Development Indicators," last modified March 27, 2016, http://documents.worldbank.org/curated/en/805371467990952829/World-development-indicators-2016

2. Although at times Caribbean states (notably Cuba) have played significant roles with regard to international interactions with North America and other regional powers, that is not true on an ongoing basis. The states of Central America and the Caribbean are quite limited in capabilities and could not directly intrude into the stability of the North American region. The basic observation that North America is an exemplar of stable interactions driven by steep hierarchy supports the power transition theory argument that neither the necessary nor sufficient conditions for a severe war involving dominant and one *potential* challenger continue to be absent.

3. Jacek Kugler and Frank C. Zagare, *Exploring the Stability of Deterrence* (Boulder, CO: Lynne Rienner Publishers, 1987).

4. This line of reasoning is consistent with the argument put forward by Grieco in 1995, regarding German policy on the economic and monetary union (EMU). German willingness to make sacrifices to facilitate success of the EMU seemed to fly in the face of concerns about relative gains. However, Germany, as the leading power within Europe, experienced greater salience from relative gains and losses vis-a-vis *external* rivals, such as Japan. Thus, Germany propped up the EMU to compete more effectively with Great Powers beyond the region (Birol Yesilada, Jacek Kugler, Gaspare Genna, and Osman Tanrikulu, *Global Power Transition and the Future of the European Union* [London: Routledge, 2018]). Also note the role of "socialization" in modern power transition theory in Ronald L. Tammen, Jacek Kugler, and Douglas Lemke, "Foundations of Power Transition Theory," in *The Oxford Encyclopedia of Empirical International Relations Theory* Volume 2 (Oxford: Oxford University Press, 2017): 51–52.

5. Theodore J. Lowi, "Four Systems of Policy, Politics, and Choice," *Public Administration Review* 32, no. 4 (July–August 1972): 298–310.

6. Figure 4.1 source: World Bank, "World Development Indicators." Forecast based on growth rates adapted from PWC 20250, "The World in 2050," last modified August 29, 2017, https://www.pwc.com/gx/en/issues/economy/the-world-in-2050.html.

7. In 1812, US President James Madison declared war on Great Britain. On the border with Canada, US defeats at Detroit and Queenston Heights frustrated attempts to annex Canadian territory or capture Montreal. Americans were successful at Lake Erie and managed to defeat Native American Tecumseh's Confederacy, which was supported by the British. These successes secured vast new territories for the United States without territorial loss by Canada.

8. Mario Ojeda, *Alcances y límites de la política exterior de México* (Mexico City: El Colegio de México, 2018), 87–88, 1981.

9. Greg Anderson and Christopher Sands, eds., *Forgotten Partnership Redux: Canada-U.S. Relations in the 21st Century* (Amherst, NY: Cambria Press, 2011).

10. Stephen Clarkson, *Uncle Sam and Us: Globalization, Neoconservatism, and the Canadian State* (Toronto: University of Toronto Press, 2002).

11. US Department of State, "U.S.-Canada Smart Border/30 Point Action Plan Update," last updated December 2002, https://2001-2009.state.gov/p/wha/rls/fs/18128.htm.

12. Patrick James, *Canada and Conflict* (Oxford: Oxford University Press, 2012).

13. Public Safety Department of Canada, "Integrated Cross-Border Maritime Law Enforcement Operations (Shiprider)," last modified on December 1, 2015, http://www.publicsafety.gc.ca/cnt/brdr-strtgs/brdr-lw-nfrcmnt/ntgrtd-crss-brdr-mrtm-eng.aspx.

14. Peter H. Smith, *Talons of the Eagle: Dynamics of U.S.-Latin American Relations* (Oxford: Oxford University Press, 1996).

15. Ibid.

16. Blanca Torres, *De la Guerra al mundo bipolar: México y el mundo* (Mexico City: Senado de la República, 2000).

17. Ibid.

18. David Shirk and José María Ramos, "Binational Collaboration in Law Enforcement and Public Security Issues on the U.S.-Mexican Border," *Center for U.S.-Mexican Studies*, last modified May 2003, https://escholarship.org/uc/item/92f7c3cw.

19. Ana Covarrubias, "El problema de los derechos humanos y los cambios en política exterior," *Foro Internacional* 39, no. 4 (1999): 429–452.

20. Ibid.

21. The American Presidency Project, https://www.presidency.ucsb.edu/ (consulted).

22. "Mexico goes for the whole enchilada," *The Guardian*, last modified on September 5, 2011, https://www.theguardian.com/world/2001/sep/05/immigration.usa.

Chapter Five

Europe

The EU Yesterday, Today, and Tomorrow

Gaspare M. Genna, Birol Yesilada,
and Osman Goktug Tanrikulu

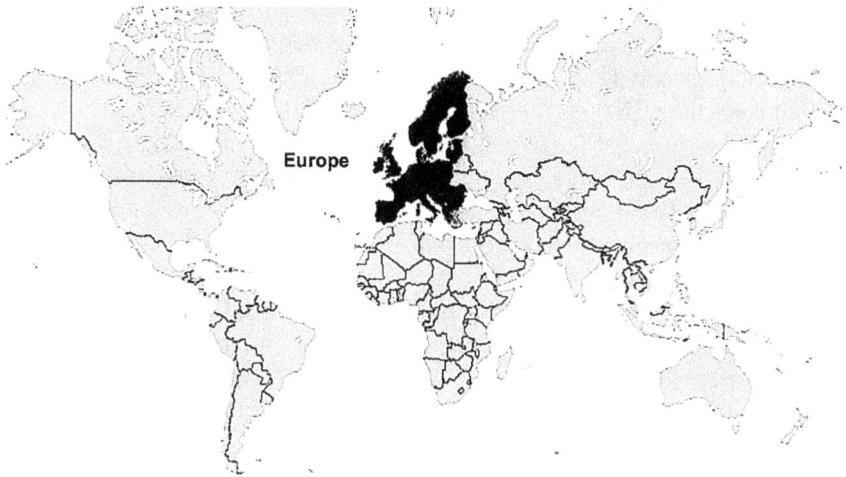

Europe

Europe Region

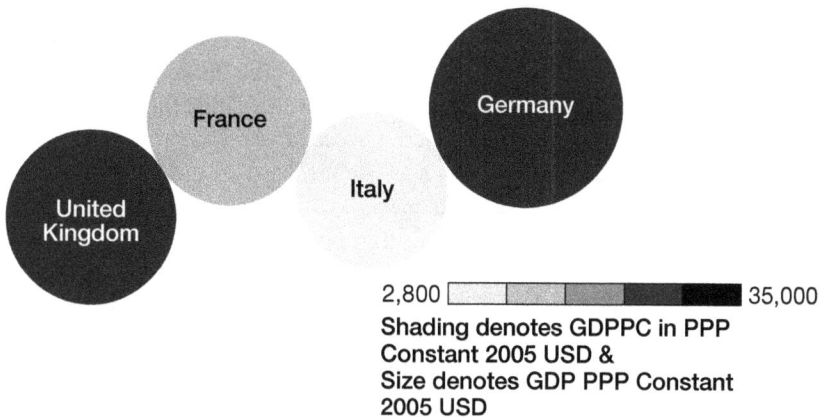

France

Germany

United
Kingdom

Italy

2,800 ▭▭▭▭▭ 35,000

Shading denotes GDPPC in PPP
Constant 2005 USD &
Size denotes GDP PPP Constant
2005 USD

Europe Hierarchy

IN THE BEGINNING

The European Union (EU) is the classic example of cross-national integration anticipated by power transition theory (PTT) when societies are satisfied and choose cooperation over confrontation.[1] Despite Britain's exit from the economic agreement with the EU, the United Kingdom remains a member of the North Atlantic Treaty Organization (NATO) and has long-term and solid security links to the continental powers. Historically, interactions in Europe were vastly different. Previous transitions led to massive conflicts that not only destroyed Europe but also had global repercussions. Moreover, Europe is the cradle of past Great Powers, many of which created colonial empires far larger than the mother country.

Power transitions in Europe led to massive confrontations between the most powerful global powers following the beginning of the Industrial Revolution around 1820. However, today, no single European nation can match the productivity of the global giants, the United States and China. In third and fourth place Japan and India may be mentioned. Japan's production dwarfs the output of Germany, and India early in its economic spurt has just overtaken Great Britain. Considering such facts, one can conclude that no single European nation can now play a role at the global level. However, if one takes into consideration the EU, the story is different. With or without Britain, today the EU has a gross domestic product (GDP) a bit larger than that of the United States and oversees a population larger than that of the entire North American region.

In the ruins of World War II, a European political elite from six countries designed a new direction for their societies. By rethinking the tenets of Westphalian sovereignty, they chose regional integration to bring peace and prosperity to the continent during a time of global confrontation marked by the Cold War. In the context of the democratization of Germany and Italy and encouragement of institutionalized cooperation, European membership expanded. After the collapse of the Soviet Union, most of the erstwhile Warsaw Pact states of Central and Southeastern Europe, and the Baltic countries of the former Union of Soviet Socialist Republics (USSR), joined the EU. Slovenia and Croatia, former Yugoslav republics, also became EU members.[2]

The arc of integration is based on specific ideas and some degree of idealism. These principles were adopted piecemeal in other regions around the world. However, unlike those regions, Europe has achieved a high level of integration, in fact the highest in the world. EU member states owe this, in part, to special regional and systemic developments that pushed policy makers to accept comprehensive unity.[3] For example, just as the rise of the Cold War served as a push for the original six to sign the early agreements that increased cooperation between West European members of NATO, the end of the Cold War served as a catalyst that pushed member states to sign the Maastricht Treaty.[4] Thus, ideas, in and of themselves, cannot help explain European integration. If ideas or "political will" were all that had been necessary, other similar levels of integration would appear in Africa and South America. To put it another way, architectural blueprints do not build houses. One would need a team of builders with ability, capacity, and shared views to erect houses.

This chapter explains Europe's high level of integration and prospects for its future by examining two important factors and their interaction: power asymmetry and satisfaction derived from preference convergence. First, the EU's evolution is briefly traced to see why these two factors were crucial in increasing the level of integration. Then three major challenges facing the EU are examined with the aim of understanding how they will affect future integration.

HOW THE EU GOT HERE

Europe, like all regions, is an ordered subhierarchy within the global hierarchy.[5] Figure 5.1 shows the spread of European membership from the original six members to twenty-eight members over time. That figure was recently reduced to twenty-seven.[6]

As already mentioned, the EU is an evolving community that started with six countries: France, Germany, Italy, Belgium, the Netherlands, and Luxembourg. It has grown rapidly and then expanded at a fast pace following the collapse of the USSR. Today Britain's "Brexit" marks the first time a nation is choosing to exit from the EU.[7] Britain is not excluded because the Brexit process is still evolving.

Members of the EU are relatively affluent and are forecast to continue to be the leaders in economic performance per capita.[8] After British departure, the EU will still have three of the four largest most productive economies in Europe. Without Britain, the EU will continue to approximate the output of the United States (see Chapter 4). Figure 5.2 details the total output of the four largest economies with Russia (not included) following in a distant fifth place.[9]

Like other regions, Europe is subject to power transitions as a result of uneven economic growth rates among the larger states. Figure 5.2 illustrates the growth of Europe's largest economies: France, Germany, Italy, and the United Kingdom.[10] At its beginning, the European integration experiment included only three of these four economies because of British self-exclusion. Germany and France were in the middle of transition and opted for a negotiated postwar settlement. Germany peacefully transitioned as the regional leader by

Figure 5.1.   Development of the European Community

first moving ahead of France and then Britain in the mid-1950s. During this time, member states established the European Coal and Steel Community and the customs union.

As Germany was visibly gaining economic power, the United Kingdom began its quest for membership. The British effort, however, was thwarted by France under Charles de Gaulle who questioned the British commitment to European integration and wished to retain for France a leadership role in the integration process. As figure 5.2 demonstrates, when a convergence of preferences did not emerge, the stronger economy of the United Kingdom could be used as leverage against French preferences. France rebuffed British entry twice during this time frame, first in 1963 and then again in 1967. During the 1960s and 1970s, the French economy was gaining strength against the British economy. Both governments shared an antifederalist view of integration.[11]

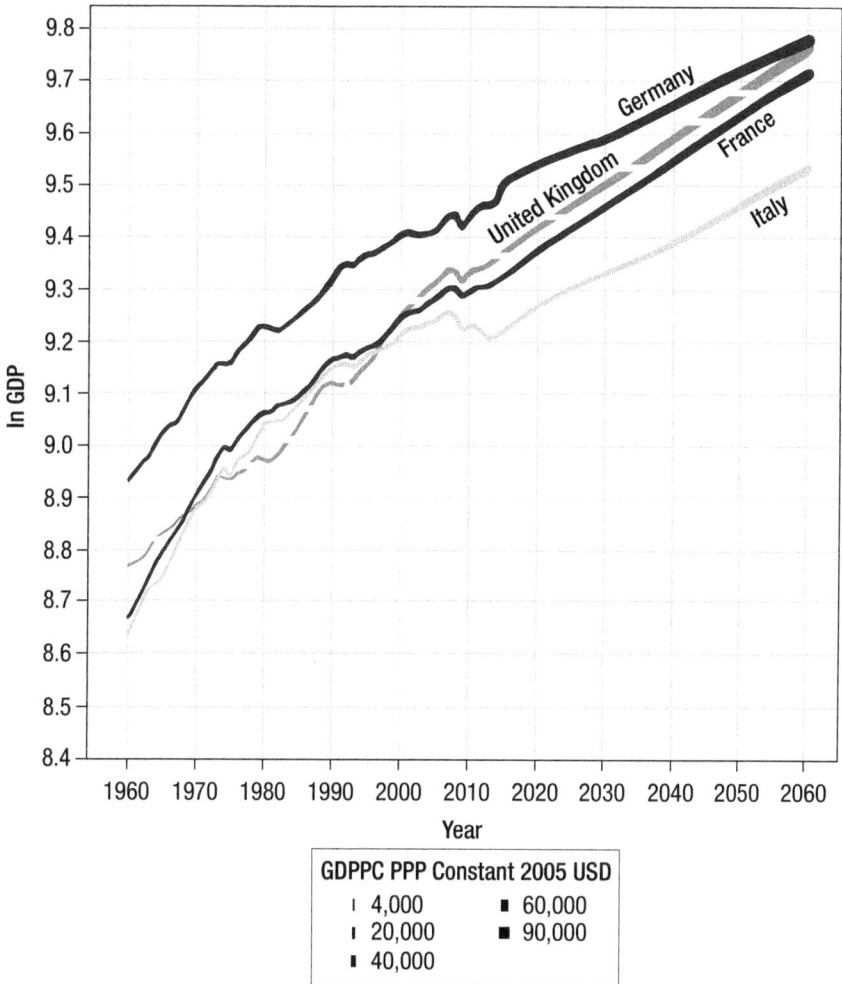

Figure 5.2. Gross Domestic Product of Four Largest Economies of the European Union

However, de Gaulle's stance on British membership was prompted by his opposition to the strong Anglo American alliance, which threatened de Gaulle's view of a "European Europe." As PTT posits, when states experience power parity and are not satisfied with prevailing conditions, the likelihood of integration decreases.[12] The membership issue was settled after France's economy crossed an important threshold, and Georges Pompidou replaced de Gaulle as president in 1969, thereby allowing the United Kingdom to enter.

The German role in the integration process involved its capacity to lead. Figure 5.3[13] illustrates the level of German power asymmetry vis-à-vis other

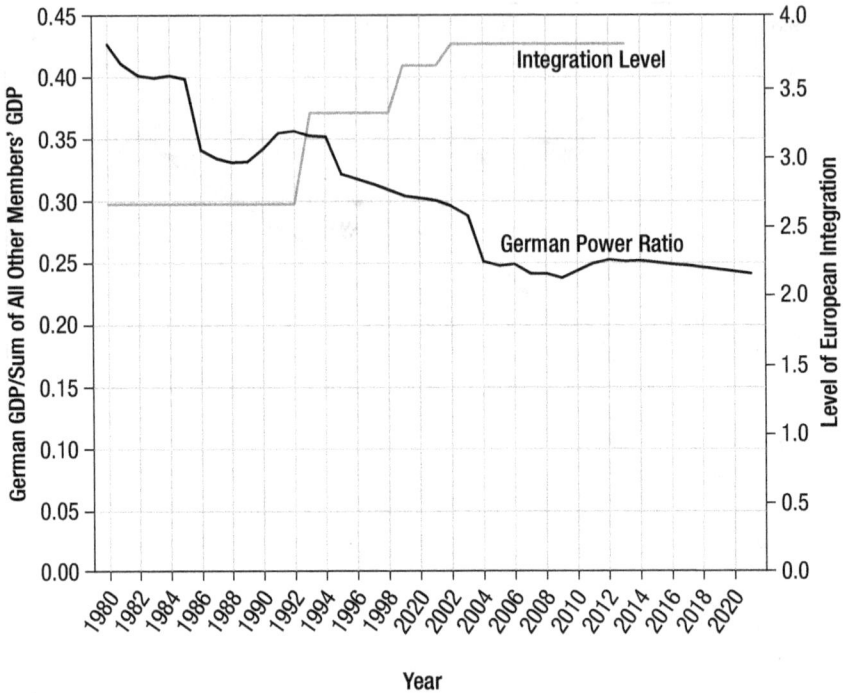

Figure 5.3. Germany's European Union Power Ratio and Level of European Union Integration

member states that allowed the creation of European institutions consistent with German preferences. The decline of its power ratio is not a result of its economic performance, as demonstrated in figure 5.2. The downward slope is due to the increasing number of states joining the EU, thereby increasing the denominator of the power ratio. As figure 5.3 also illustrates, as Germany's relative power ratio decreases, the level of institutionalized integration increases. It other words, German power at the early stages of integration created institutions that could reflect its preferences into the future.

Germany could not lead the process of integration on its own; it needed the willing support of other member states. It could use its economic leverage only when other states shared its values. In other words, there had to be a preference convergence with German positions. The strongest partner in this effort was France. The sturdy bond between these two former continental rivals formed the central pivot of progress toward integration. However, as figure 5.4[14] indicates, the preference of the United Kingdom for a less-integrated Europe often meant that it sought a special place. One clear example involved the efforts in drafting the Treaty on the European Union. The importance

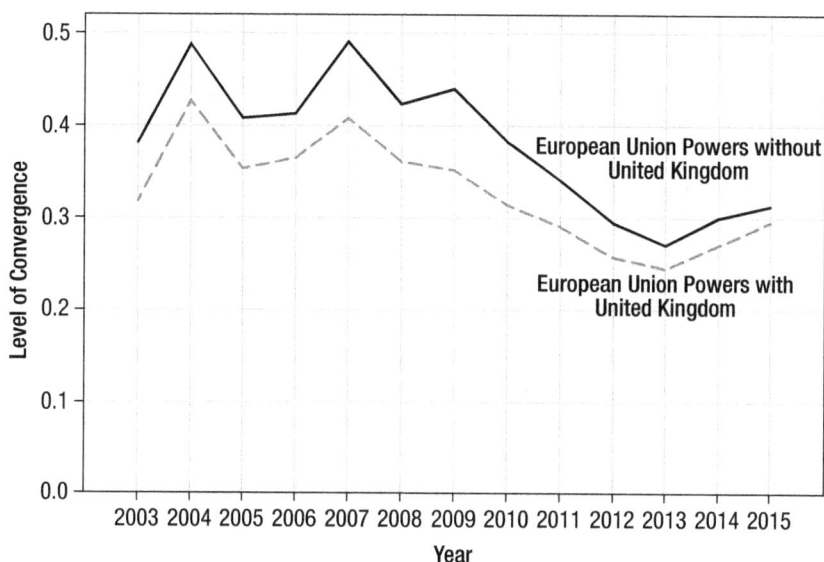

Figure 5.4. European Union Trust Convergence among European Union Powers

of this treaty cannot be understated because it was a major leap forward in integration. The treaty established the powers of all current institutions and the architecture of the single currency, namely the economic and monetary union (EMU). During the negotiations, a power preponderance of Germany over France is observed with preference convergence, but German preponderance over Britain occurs without preference convergence. The German and French governments went into partnership to sell the ideas behind the Treaty on European Union, including the EMU, to their respective constituencies.[15]

The French government's position (under François Mitterrand) for EMU was in line with that of the German government (under Helmut Kohl), although the French initially believed the franc would play a larger role. Both leaders envisioned a supranational EU with the establishment of the EMU as a major cornerstone.[16] Therefore, the proposal for an autonomous European System of Central Banks (ESCB) and European Central Bank was in line with their thinking. Also, although the British government (under Margaret Thatcher) was apprehensive about the reunification of Germany, the French government of François Mitterand calmed similar French fears by arguing that a united Germany in the EU would lock it into a cooperative mode.[17] Mitterrand needed to surrender his early idea of the franc's dual role in the EMU with the deutsche mark because of France's economic problems in the early 1990s. In fact, the French and German central banks that coordinated actions to prop up the franc scotched this notion.[18] As a result, the French viewed "importing" German stability as more beneficial than having the franc serve as a coanchor for the monetary system.

In addition, Kathleen McNamara[19] accurately describes the convergence of several members (e.g., France, Italy, Luxembourg) from previously Keynesian policy orientations to monetary orthodoxy. She states that it was the shift to monetary orthodoxy (a move according with Germany's preference) that led to the creation of the European single currency. However, this does not explain why Britain did not join because, under Thatcher, Britain also adopted a shift away from Keynesian policy and toward orthodoxy. In the dispute between Britain and France, the German position centered on the realization that the single currency also included the acceptance of changes in sovereignty, which allowed monetary policy to be decided at the European level, a shift toward supranationalism. Therefore, the sum of preferences includes convergence with both the type of policy (monetary orthodoxy) and the location of policy decisions in the ESCB. The British preferred the former. Despite the power asymmetry between Britain and Germany, the lack of preference convergence was not conducive for integration. The result was the formation of the single currency without British inclusion.

This pattern of preference convergence among the top EU powers, excluding Great Britain, continued into the twenty-first century. Figure 5.4 plots the convergence level of public trust in EU institutions among the four largest EU economies (France, Germany, Italy, and the United Kingdom). The public trust in EU institutions is used as a good proxy for preference convergence toward the EU because it indicates how well Europeans believe these institutions are working for them.

In general, trust in government institutions tends to track well with government policy outcomes. Therefore, if individuals trust EU institutions, they are also likely to be satisfied with EU policy outcomes. Also, given that all EU member states need to be fully functioning democracies,[20] voters will elect politicians who share their preferences concerning the EU. The grey line in figure 5.4 includes all four top powers, and the solid line excludes the United Kingdom. Preferences are more similar without the United Kingdom in the grouping during the entire period.

Figure 5.5[21] magnifies preference convergence by disaggregating the data into country pairs. The convergence between Germany-France and that between Germany-Italy track well with each other and are higher than the Germany-UK pair. British trust in EU institutions consistently came in dead last over the course of the UK's membership in the EU. Based on this observation, it is not surprising that the UK voted to leave the EU.

Currently, there are three major challenges facing the EU. Each will test the ability of the member states to maintain unity or deepen integration. Our

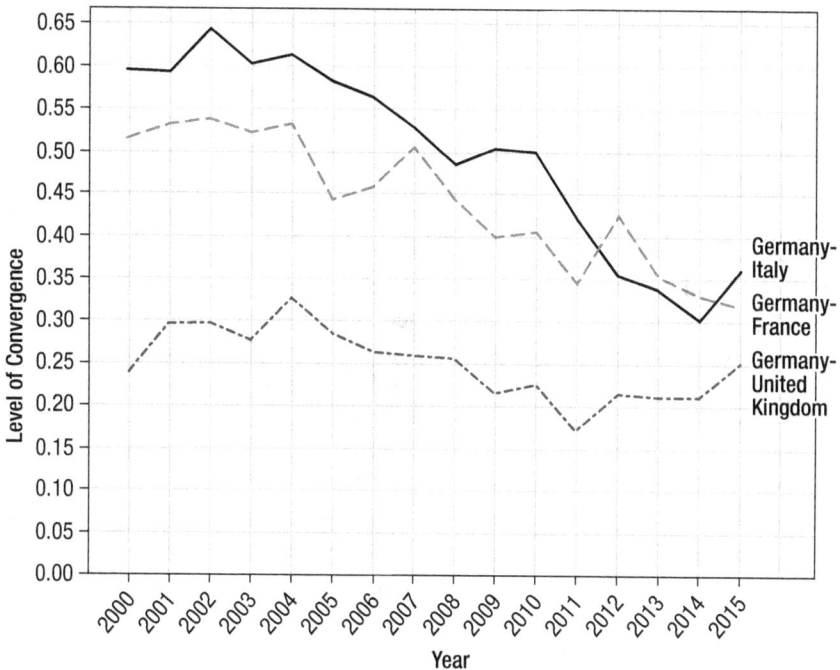

Figure 5.5. European Union Trust Convergence by Pairing European Union Powers

forecasts following power transition are based on the interaction of power asymmetry with preference convergence.

CHALLENGE 1: BREXIT

The Treaty on the European Union, as amended by the Treaty of Lisbon, outlines how a member state can cancel its EU membership (Article 50). On June 23, 2016, the British, by a referendum vote of 52 percent, asked their government to be the first member state in EU history to withdraw. The official process of Britain's exit from the EU, Brexit, would not begin with this vote because it was advisory. According to Article 50, the process begins when "A Member State which decides to withdraw shall notify the European Council of its intention" consistent with "its own constitutional requirements." The "constitutional requirements" would involve the UK Parliament passing an act asking the government to begin the withdrawal process. That has now happened. The terms of the withdrawal are in the European Council's hands and, with that, in the hands of the more powerful member states.

The British decision to leave is not surprising given the lack of preference convergence (see figures 5.4 and 5.5). The question is, what does this mean for the United Kingdom and the EU? There are many scenarios that can be played out. However, the power transition perspective points to the likelihood that the United Kingdom will remain engaged in Europe even without centralized EU decision making, while simultaneously following many of the major policies in place, including accepting EU citizens into the United Kingdom as workers. In addition, there is a good likelihood of a Scottish secession from the United Kingdom. As for the EU, the departure of the United Kingdom means a stronger preference convergence among the top EU powers with a possible Scottish entry adding to power asymmetry. These two factors point to a more integrated EU, one that is more federal than intergovernmental.

Beyond the negotiation process, Brexit will have an impact on UK-EU relations. The United Kingdom's withdrawal from EU membership is not the same as its complete separation from the EU. The projected profile of this relationship is one of degree that depends on the negotiating leverage of the United Kingdom vis-à-vis the EU. Given the asymmetric power relations, it is unlikely that the United Kingdom has much leverage. One indicator is that the UK's trade dependency on the EU since 2010 shows that the average trade total has continued to decline as a result of the protracted negotiations over Brexit.[22]

Given the strong preference convergence of the top three powers, their small economic stakes in British trade, and the strong need for Britain to maintain trade with the EU, it will be the EU (especially the top three powers) that will have leverage over the United Kingdom. When the EU makes regulatory policy in the future, it will mean that the United Kingdom will need to adopt the new policies; otherwise it will be faced with nontariff trade barriers. In other words, the United Kingdom will lose its voice in decision making because it will no longer have membership in the commission, council, or the European parliament, while needing to accept the decisions if it wishes to remain part of the free trade area, which it will need to maintain and grow its economy.

What does all this mean for the economic future for the United Kingdom? According to the *Financial Times*,[23] the long-term effect of Brexit on Britain's national income ranges from −7.8 percent[24] to −3.0 percent.[25] This will have a significant impact on Britain's power position in the European hierarchy. Domestically, Brexit is likely to cause serious domestic problems in unemployment, inflation, and potential stagnation.

On the other hand, Brexit will increase the EU's budget deficit. Prior to Brexit, Britain's contribution to the EU budget was set at 19.4 billion euros, which includes its rebate and customs duties. In return, Britain received 7 billion euros in agricultural and regional subsidies. The difference of 12.4 billion euros makes up roughly 5 percent of the EU's annual budget that needs to be picked up by other member states. This loss will be in part compensated as Britain has tentatively agreed to hand over about 60 billion euros to secure this divorce that will be paid out to Brussels for decades.[26] The result, again, points to little sympathy for Great Britain from the EU and a greater need to for British political and business leaders to preserve Britain's economic ties with Europe.

EU migration is a second and vexing problem. The influx of EU citizens into the United Kingdom was one of the major reasons given by the "leave" campaign. It is estimated that, in 2015, 3 million non-British EU citizens lived in the United Kingdom, representing approximately 5 percent of the population.[27] Most of them are there for work, representing approximately 7 percent of the total workforce. At the same time, the number of British citizens living in the rest of the EU in 2015 was approximately 1.2 million. Given these figures, there would be a strong joint inclination on the part of the EU to require that the United Kingdom maintain free mobility of labor. Should the United Kingdom require EU immigrants to follow the same migration criteria as non-EU immigrants, most would leave the United Kingdom and the number of new EU immigrants would drop significantly. The EU top powers, especially Germany, will likely require labor mobility to continue, and the United Kingdom will likely accept this, given its EU economic dependence.

The last outcome is that Brexit may prompt Scottish secession; 62 percent of Scots voted to remain in the EU. In fact, the majority of voters in every Scottish voting district voted to stay in the EU. This contrasts with England, where 52 percent voted to leave.[28] The results display a clear preference divergence between the two. Power dynamics suggests that Scotland will split from the United Kingdom. A referendum for Scottish independence is predicted shortly after Britain's full exit from the EU. This would allow Scotland to remain or rejoin the EU, whereas England, Wales, and Northern Ireland will leave. The loss of such a large portion of the United Kingdom will further diminish its power and influence in Europe.

Brexit also will finally have a significant impact on EU power ratios. The British departure will reaffirm Germany as the power broker within the EU once more. In recent years, Germany's GDP has been increasing above 20 percent of the other EU member states and will further increase with the potential departure of Britain.[29] In addition, as indicated by figures 5.4 and 5.5, preference convergence for a more united Europe would be higher. The interaction of the two indicates that Europe will potentially see an increase in the level of integration. Since with the financial crisis in 2008, the publics of the member states have less trust in the EU. However, the trend began reversing in 2013. In part, support is driven by further institutionalization. In an effort not to repeat the last recession, a banking union as well as political union (a federal EU) has been proposed and will now have a much higher likelihood of adoption. Given the desires of "more Europe" and without the influence of an antifederal United Kingdom, an accelerated evolution of political union is highly probable.

CHALLENGE 2: COMMON FOREIGN AND SECURITY POLICY

The Treaty on European Union (Maastricht Treaty) established an integration structure based on three pillars, one of which would be the realization of a Common Foreign and Security Policy (CFSP). The idea of such a uniform policy for all EU member states moved forward under the amended Treaty on European Union (Lisbon) when it created the office of the High Representative of the Union for Foreign Affairs and Security Policy, who heads the European Defense Agency as well as a diplomatic corps referred to as the European External Action Service. The EU is challenged by not having a clear, united CFSP. Currently, the High Representative and the President of the European Council can speak for the EU. This creates a condition where contradictory statements can be made. In addition, the CFSP is currently under the unanimity voting rule so that one member state can veto a policy position. One high-profile case that led to EU disunity was the US-led invasion of Iraq. Given no consensus, each member state went its own way.

Why have a CFSP? A simple answer would be to further European integration. However, to have a CFSP for its own sake is not enough. Like many other integration efforts, the rationale for the CFSP is tied to the single market. An integrated economy, like that of the EU, can be vulnerable to external shocks manifested unevenly in individual states. For example, monetary coordination was once needed so that if one currency's exchange rate dramatically changed vis-à-vis the US dollar or Japanese yen, it would not send an uncontrolled shock to the other currencies. Supporting EU integration, monetary coordination was eventually strengthened and replaced by a stronger control mechanism, the single currency, among a subset of member states.

Unilateral foreign and security policy actions can also send shocks to other member states. A single or small group of member states could decide on actions that could affect prices, currency values, foreign investment, or the ability to borrow from international markets. One extreme example would be the case of armed conflict. Should one or more member states be involved in a major war with a third party, it could impact economic relations among the remaining member states. Should one or more member states be physically invaded by a third party, this too could harm the other member states' economies. Russia's threats against the Baltic states, if carried out, would involve NATO.

If these extreme examples are not convincing, all that is needed is see the fallout of the current refugee crisis. The large populations attempting to escape North Africa, the Levant, and Afghanistan have pressured the resources of the member states that are geographically the closest to the source conflicts. The limited resources to secure the EU's external border and house and feed refugees puts pressures on members' budgets, which makes it more difficult to fulfill EU obligations. The movement of refugees further west and north causes many of the same problems for these other receiving countries. A few member states have dealt with the problem by resurrecting border controls not seen since the late 1980s. By limiting mobility, member states are dismantling one of the most important characteristics of a unified economy. Therefore, having a single voice to set policies is critical.

Also important is force projection to be a major player in noneconomic terms. If the EU wants to be influential abroad as a global power, it will need an integrated military force with heavy lift capability. The current emphasis on the EU's "soft power" is a limited tool in meeting serious foreign and security policy challenges. In December 1998, Britain and France signed the St. Malo Declaration calling for an autonomous European defense capability, which, at the time, was viewed as a necessary step toward establishing the EU's CFSP with a joint European army. However, the plan did not lead to a significant EU defense force and capability because most members' governments did not show sufficient interest and were planning to reduce defense spending. Yet, the St. Malo Declaration signaled the desire of the EU to establish its own integrated defense force that would act independently of the United States and NATO when needed.[30]

For an EU defense force to be effective, the participation of Germany is essential, yet German law prohibits deployment of German troops abroad without approval from Parliament. The major armed forces with overseas deployment capability, though significantly lower than those of the United States, remained the British and the French. The removal of the British armed forces through Brexit will have a serious impact on Europe's military capabilities and will make the EU even more dependent on NATO and the United States for its security. Data in table 5.1 and figure 5.6[31] demonstrate the military capabilities and defense spending of the United Kingdom relative to other countries. Assessment of preferences shows that the EU and Britain

Table 5.1. Comparative Military Power

	Overall Ranking	Active Personnel	Tanks	Aircraft	Nuclear Warheads	Aircraft Carriers	Submarines	Budget ($)
United States	1	1,430,000	8,325	13,683	7,506	10	72	612,500,000,000
Russia	2	766,000	15,000	3,082	8,484	1	63	76,600,000,000
China	3	2,285,000	9,150	2,788	250	1	69	126,000,000,000
India	4	1,325,000	3,569	1,785	80–100	2	17	46,000,000,000
United Kingdom	5	205,330	407	908	225	1	11	53,600,000,000
France	6	228,656	423	1,203	300	1	10	43,000,000,000
Germany	7	183,000	408	710	0	0	4	45,000,000,000
Turkey	8	410,500	3,657	989	0	0	14	18,185,000,000
South Korea	9	640,000	2,346	1,393	0	0	14	33,700,000,000
Japan	10	247,746	767	1,595	0	1	16	49,100,000,000
Israel	11	176,500	3,870	680	80–200	0	14	15,000,000,000
Italy	12	320,000	600	795	0	2	6	34,000,000,000
Egypt	13	468,500	4,767	1,100	0	0	4	4,400,000,000
Brazil	14	328,000	489	748	0	1	5	33,142,000,000
Pakistan	15	617,000	3,124	847	90–110	0	8	7,000,000,000
Canada	16	68,250	201	404	0	0	4	18,000,000,000
Taiwan	17	290,000	2,005	775	0	0	4	10,725,000,000

Poland	18	120,000	1,063	475	0	0	5	18,170,000
Indonesia	19	476,000	374	381	0	0	2	6,900,000,000
Australia	20	58,000	59	395	0	0	6	26,100,000,000
Ukraine	21	160,000	4,112	400	0	0	1	4,880,000,000
Iran	22	545,000	2,409	481	0	0	31	6,300,000,000
Vietnam	23	412,000	3,200	413	0	0	1	3,365,000,000
Thailand	24	306,000	740	543	0	1	0	5,390,000,000
Saudi Arabia	25	233,500	1,095	652	0	0	0	56,725,000,000
Syria	26	178,000	4,950	473	0	0	0	1,872,000,000
Switzerland	27	135,000	200	175	0	0	0	4,830,000,000
Spain	28	123,300	415	531	0	1	3	11,600,000,000
Sweden	29	14,000	280	216	0	0	5	6,215,000.000
Czech Republic	30	21,060	123	109	0	0	0	2,220,000,000
Algeria	31	512,000	1,050	404	0	0	6	10,570,000,000
Netherlands	32	47,660	0	160	0	0	4	9,840,000,000
Mexico	33	267,500	0	373	0	0	0	7,000,000,000
Belgium	34	33,000	52	166	0	0	0	5,085,000,000
North Korea	35	690,000	6,600	943	<10	0	78	7,500,000,000

Note: Gray cells indicate world leader.

Source: The Center for Arms Control and Non-Proliferation (Macias, Bender, & Gould, 2014).

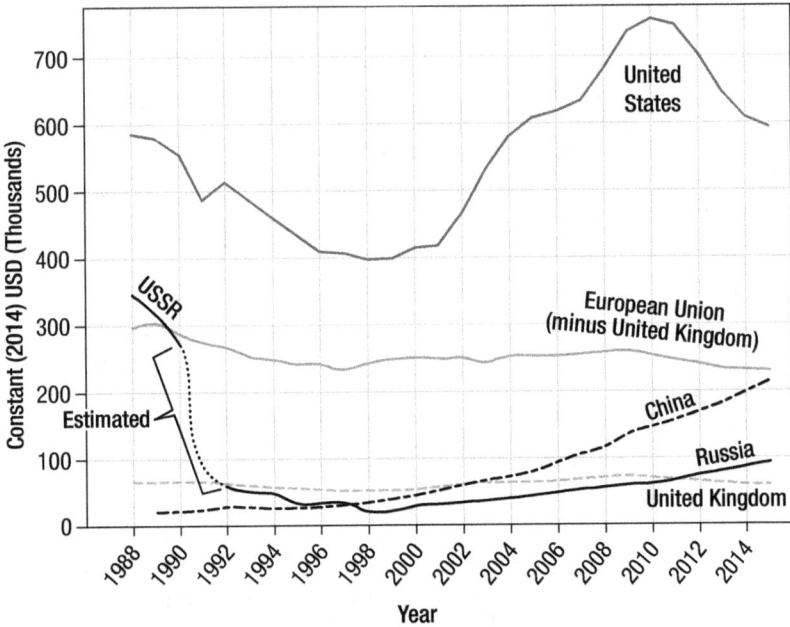

Figure 5.6. Military Expenditure by Country in Constant USD M (1988–2015)

both agree that NATO is essential for stability, and despite recent divergence in preferences, the United States concurs. However, the departure of Britain that shifts toward the United States and away from Europe suggests possible instability within NATO. Assuming that current trends persist, if not today then soon enough, implementing a fully functioning CFSP will require creating distinct EU capabilities separate from NATO. Therefore, one could argue that Brexit will ultimately contribute to closer defense cooperation among EU members if they are to establish their own integrated defense and intelligence capabilities while concurrently weakening the globally preponderant NATO alliance the West built after World War II.

CHALLENGE 3: NEIGHBORHOOD AND ENLARGEMENT PAINS

Does the EU have the capacity to reengage in meaningful enlargement policy that would bring the Western Balkan potential members? Can the EU revamp accession negotiations with Turkey? Might the EU restart negotiations with Ukraine?

Following the financial crisis of 2008, the subsequent problems associated with the lack of serious consensus on fiscal union and the continued budget deficits in many member states, one cannot help but wonder whether the EU has the necessary resources to pursue future enlargement. When he took office in 2014, Commission President Jean-Claude Juncker made it clear that "no further enlargement will take place over the next five years" and added, "ongoing negotiations will continue," but he added that "the EU and its citizens needed to take a break from enlargement so that we can consolidate what has been achieved and digest the addition of 13 new member states in just 10 years."[32] In light of Brexit, the enlargement challenge becomes even more critical from a financial, as well as political, perspective for candidates and potential candidate countries. For example, Turkey's never-ending accession negotiations will be different without pro-Turkish UK government lobbying for membership. Given Brexit, does Germany or France have the financial capacity, or the political will, to be the leader for mapping future enlargement? And if so, how will this be regarded in the rest of the now much enlarged EU?

First, prospects for further expansion are dim. When a regional leader's capacity to provide support for the EU is taxed to its limit, integration reaches a plateau and slows down.[33] With Brexit, the burden of regional leadership is likely to increase further for Germany. In addition, governments of several member states are adamantly opposed to Turkish or Ukrainian membership and support for the West Balkan countries is also questionable. Given Vladimir Putin's military intervention in Ukraine, unless current member states wish to risk a war with Russia, Ukraine's membership in the EU is unthinkable.

A second factor that can provide insight into how and why EU enlargement is likely to move forward is the values preferences of current and prospective member states. Based on information available from the World Values Survey project, one can calculate the relative convergence of social values using the Inglehart-Welzel indices and chart it on a time-series map.[34] In a previous study, Yeşilada found that convergence of social values is a strong predictor of how likely countries will move toward deepening integration.[35] Convergence of social values is an important component of Human Development (HD) Theory, which is also known as modernization theory.

The basic premise of HD theory is that socioeconomic development results in profound changes in basic human values that shape politics. But how is it that these values can lead to changes in a political system? Ronald Inglehart and Christian Welzel[36] provide some direction through their two compound variables that capture more than 78 percent of cross-national variance in social change across the world. To reflect value convergence, they capture individuals' relative religiosity and social values along two dimensions.

The first dimension is religious (traditional)-secular (autonomy) values, which reflect the contrast between societies over religion and religiosity. The more traditional societies place greater emphasis on religion, and more secular-rational ones do not. Inglehart and Welzel[37] also found that a wide range of values is associated with this dimension.

For example, societies near the traditional pole emphasize the importance of parent-child ties and deference to authority, along with absolute standards and traditional family values, and reject divorce, abortion, and euthanasia. They tend to have high levels of religious values and national pride coupled with a nationalistic outlook. Societies with secular-rational values have the opposite preferences in these areas. The second key dimension of cross-cultural variation is linked with the transition from industrial society to postindustrial societies, which polarizes materialist (survival values associated with industrialization phase of development) and postmaterialist (self-expression/post-industrial). The shift toward more postmaterialist values corresponds with transition to the postindustrial phase of economic development and an advanced welfare system, which provide many individuals with an overwhelming sense of existential security.[38]

Figure 5.7[39] shows the values map of Inglehart and Welzel for selected EU countries along with Turkey and Russia. The map plots results from the World Values Survey for the I-W indicators of materialist-postmaterialist and traditional-secular values over time. This map accurately reflects the relative value proximity among EU members and their neighbors. The arrows indicate the change in direction for each country, and each point represents average factor loadings along the two measures of I-W. The values map displays not only the type of values each country has, but also how much those values change over time and how close countries are to each other in terms of these values. The data on the map start from 1991 and the arrows are provided for 1996, 2000, 2005, and 2011 for each country, respectively.

Accumulated in the upper-right quadrant, the top European countries exhibit secular and postmaterialist values. Poland is on the traditional side of the coordinate system, but it is moving toward the values of the main group, Germany, France, Italy, the Netherlands, and Spain. Britain shifted away from the main group several years prior to Brexit. Turkey is not only far away from the main group but is also moving in the direction of the traditional end of the spectrum. In contrast to Turkey, Russia is on the secular side of the coordinate system; however, Russian values are distant from the top EU group, stressing materialistic concerns and being more concerned with survival rather than postmodern values.

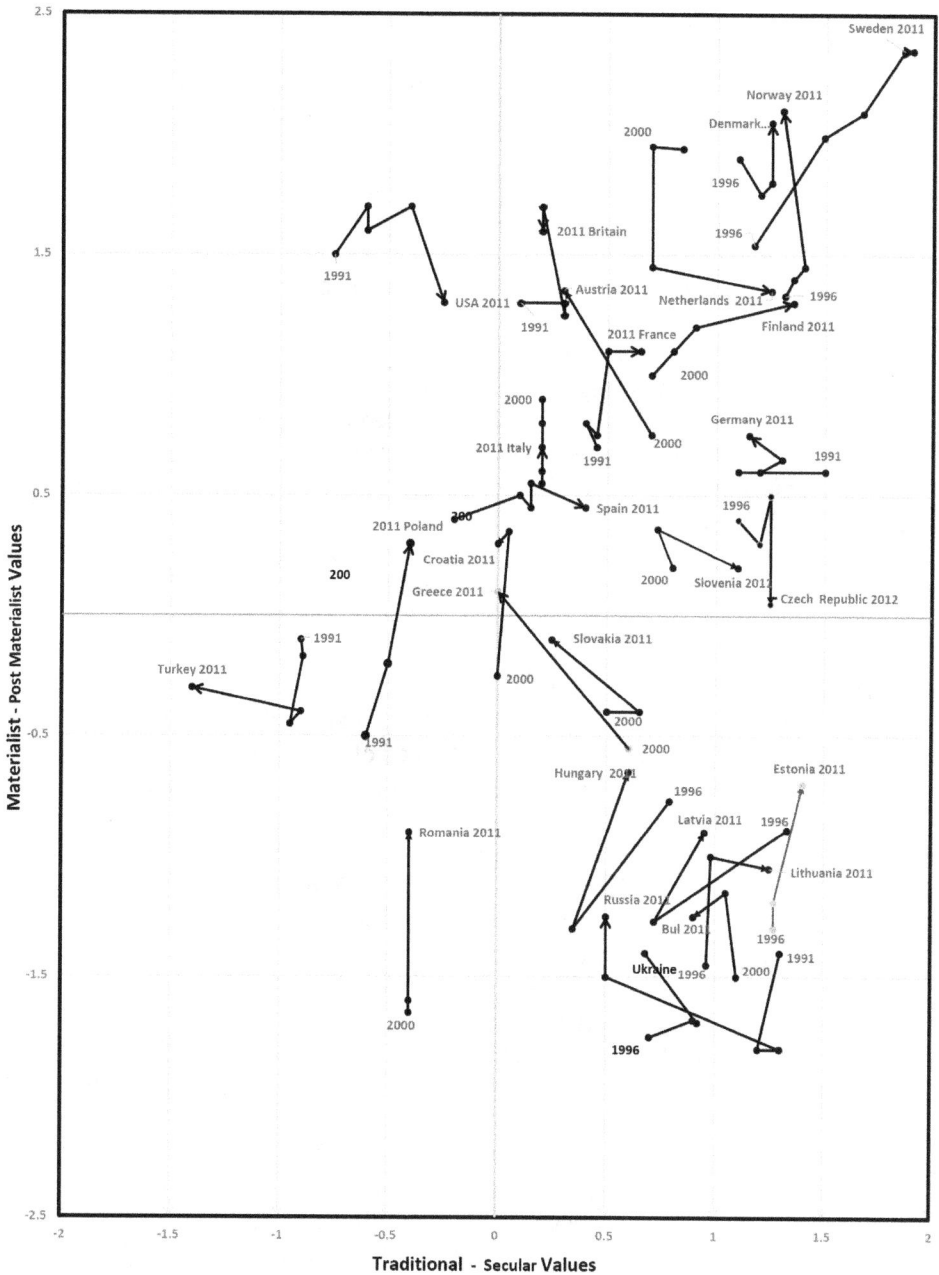

Figure 5.7. Values Map of European Union Countries, Russia, Ukraine, and Turkey (1991–2011)

Given such results, it is not surprising that EU-Turkish relations are at an all-time low, reinforced by President Recep Tayyip Erdoğan's power grab during the last several years and opposition to Turkey's membership by key EU countries. As if this was not sufficient, the failed coup in July 2016 and subsequent crackdown on all suspected opponents of Erdoğan in Turkey drove this relationship toward a potential train wreck. In response to the declaration of a state of emergency in Turkey, suspension of Human Rights Declaration by Erdoğan, arrests, and reported torture of thousands of individuals, the EU put the Turkish government on notice and suspended the European Community Action Scheme for the Mobility of University Students (ERASMUS) program in Turkey.[40]

The Austrian and Danish governments have called for suspension of Turkey's candidacy status, but the Commission called for restraint and sent clear warnings to the Turkish government to restore democracy and human rights. The reaction in Turkey to the EU's decisions has been hostile to both the EU and the United States. Pro-Erdoğan media quickly spread the rumor that the coup had been staged by the US and NATO allies to keep Turkey locked under their control. Public opinion's anti-Western orientation in Turkey is not surprising given how much social values in this country have shifted toward more conservative values during the last ten years.[41]

The pattern of values observed has implications for preferences because values drive preferences. If value preferences in Turkey and Germany eventually converge, that would increase the likelihood of Turkish membership. The current pattern, however, is one not of convergence but of divergence. Given this lack of cooperation, Turkish membership is unlikely. Current policy supports the perspective derived from PTT. EU cooperation with Turkey regarding the refugee crisis looked promising at first, but it started to unravel with the failed coup, which exposed the Turkish government's true values as it shifted away from democratic governance. The human rights violations in the weeks following the coup harmed relations in and prospects for salvaging cooperation on the refugee crisis.

Regarding Ukraine, key developments stand in the way of future enlargement and the improvement of neighborhood policy. Ukraine's geographic position close to, and historical ties with, Russia add complexity. Despite Russia's decline in power following the collapse of the USSR, Russia holds local power preponderance in Ukraine that could be reversed only if the EU and NATO were to get fully engaged. Given the divergence of values between Russia and the EU, and despite the power asymmetry, one predicts little cooperation regarding Ukraine. There are two issues in dispute between the EU and Russia where Ukraine is concerned. The first involves Russia's "permission" to allow Ukraine eventually to join the EU or at least have closer economic ties with the twenty-eight-nation community. The other is the disposition of the Ukraine's sovereignty vis-à-vis its eastern provinces and Crimea.

FUTURE CONFLICT AND COOPERATION

Within the European Regional Hierarchy, the likelihood of a severe conflict among EU members or with Britain is extremely low. Indeed, this region stands out as the most stable and cooperative, on par with North America. Several transitions took place between 1948 and today, and none were even noticed because of the high level of satisfaction among EU members. Such patterns fundamentally distinguish the present from the past, where confrontation dominated cooperation.

Integration is the hallmark of the EU and any consolidation of its structure requires a deepening of relations. Our analysis of Europe's integration centers on two important factors. The first is the need for a member state to play the role of regional leader. Germany has played this role in the development of the EU. The other elements are trust and preference convergence. Convergence reduces the number of disagreements and allows for a more uniform political structure to develop. Member states that trust EU structures are more pro-integration, and members of countries whose values converge seek to further institutional coordination.

The EU faces major challenges moving forward. Britain's exit from the EU means that the remaining member states, particularly the more powerful Germany and France, may push for deepening EU integration, reflecting their close level of preference convergence. Germany, which is strongly committed to the EU, will also be able to improve its ability to lead the integration process. Brexit will reduce the power of the EU marginally, but the likely consequences to the British economy will be far greater. The United Kingdom's attempt to dislodge itself totally from the EU will encourage Scotland to rethink its union with England and file for another independence referendum. Our analysis indicates that, although the EU will not immediately achieve a deepening of institutions, it will maintain and strengthen current ones.

On the security front, the EU may move to the development of the CFSP. Without British membership and as a consequence of US vacillation, a CFSP independent from NATO may emerge. Britain has often been the major player in the CFSP discussion because of its larger military capacity, but it has also been the member state that did not wish for the EU to be independent of NATO. So, without the United Kingdom, the EU can move forward more energetically with an independent CFSP but with diminished military capability. If member states collectively decide to beef up their military capabilities, then a robust CFSP remains possible. But because it is unlikely for Germany, France, or Italy to agree to this, it is more likely that the CFSP will weaken and the EU will increasingly depend on NATO.

The EU will face confrontational conditions regarding enlargement and its neighbor policy. The continuing divergence of values between Turkey and the EU member states dramatically reduces the likelihood of future Turkish membership. Turkey's large size exacerbates the situation since large size means more policy-making influence. The type of value divergence is critical because the trend in Turkey is to move away from values hospitable for democracy. The values divergence also harms EU-Turkish cooperation regarding the refugee crisis. The EU will continue to denounce Turkey's human rights violations, which will make Turkey less disposed to host refugees fleeing violence from its south and east.

The most significant external threat comes from Russia. A revival of the EU's attempts to accept Ukraine as a member will be nearly impossible, given Russia's opposition and ongoing territorial aggressiveness. Unless there is a democratic regime change in Russia, which is highly unlikely, EU relations with Russia will be driven by fundamental differences over Ukraine and Russian aggressiveness more generally, including political interference in European elections. Russia's localized military superiority, despite significant population and economic retrenchment, will cause Europeans to act cautiously when dealing with Russian provocations. This favors Russian aggressiveness.

NOTES

1. Global Map shows region contours. The hierarchy map shows the relative size of the top contenders in this region. Data are World Bank, "World Development Indicators," last modified March 27, 2016, http://documents.worldbank.org/curated/en/805371467990952829/World-development-indicators-2016.

2. Desmond Dinan, *Europe Recast: A History of European Union*, 2nd ed. (Basingstoke: Palgrave Macmillan, 2014).

3. Erick Eriksen and John Fossum, *Democracy in the European Union: Integration Through Deliberation?* (London: Routledge, 2003).

4. Wayne Sandholtz and John Zysman, "Recasting the European Bargain," *World Politics* 42, no. 1 (October 1989): 95–128.

5. Douglas Lemke, *Regions of War and Peace* (New York: Cambridge University Press, 2002).

6. Figure 5.1 source: "Members of the EU," last modified August 31, 2017, https://europa.eu/european-union/about-eu/countries_en.

7. Sara B. Hobolt, "The Brexit Vote: A Divided Nation, a Divided Continent," *Journal of European Public Policy* 23, no. 8 (2016): 1259–1277.

8. Jorge Nunez-Ferrer and David Rinaldi, "The Impact of Brexit on the EU Budget: A Non-Catastrophic Event (CEPS, September 7, 2016)," accessed July 20, 2019, https://www.ceps.eu/ceps-publications/impact-brexit-eu-budget-non-catastrophic-event/.

9. Figure 5.2 source: World Bank, "World Development Indicators," last modified March 27, 2016, http://documents.worldbank.org/curated/en/805371467990952829/World-development-indicators-2016.

10. Figure 5.2 source: Forecast based on growth rates adapted from PWC 20250, "The World in 2050," last modified August 29, 2017, https://www.pwc.com/gx/en/issues/economy/the-world-in-2050.html.

11. Desmond Dinan, "Governance and Institutions: A Transitional Year," *JCMS: Journal of Common Market Studies* 37, no. S1 (1999): 37–61.

12. Brian Efird and Gaspare M. Genna, "Structural Conditions and the Propensity for Regional Integration," *European Union Politics* 3, no. 3 (2002): 267–295.

13. Figure 5.3 source: World Bank, "World Development Indicators," last modified March 27, 2016, http://documents.worldbank.org/curated/en/805371467990952829/World-development-indicators-2016.

14. Figure 5.4 source: European Commission, "Eurobarometer 87.3: Standard Eurobarometer 87, May 2017," Ann Arbor, MI: GESIS [distributor], Inter-university Consortium for Political and Social Research [distributor], 2017-12-22, last modified August 31, 2019, https://doi.org/10.3886/ICPSR36876.v1.

15. Madeleine O. Hosli, "The Creation of the European Economic and Monetary Union (EMU): Intergovernmental Negotiations and Two-Level Games," *Journal of European Public Policy* 7, no. 5 (2000): 744–766.

16. David McKay, *Rush to Union: Understanding the European Federal Bargain* (Oxford: Clarendon Press, 1996).

17. Martin Holland, *European Integration: From Community to Union* (London: Pinter Publishers, 1994); Wayne Sandholtz, "Choosing Union: Monetary Politics and Maastricht," *International Organization* 47, no. 1 (1993): 1, https://doi.org/10.1017/S0020818300004690.

18. McKay, *Rush to Union.*

19. Kathleen R. McNamara, *The Currency of Ideas: Monetary Politics in the European Union* (Ithaca, NY: Cornell University Press, 1999).

20. Gaspare M. Genna and Taeko Hiroi, *Regional Integration and Democratic Conditionality: How Democracy Clauses Help Democratic Consolidation and Deepening* (London: Routledge, 2014).

21. Figure 5.5 source: European Commission, "Eurobarometer 87.3: Standard Eurobarometer 87, May 2017," Ann Arbor, MI: GESIS [distributor], Inter-university

Consortium for Political and Social Research [distributor], 2017-12-22, last modified August 31, 2019, https://doi.org/10.3886/ICPSR36876.v1.

22. Office for National Statistics, "UK Perspectives 2016: Trade with the EU and Beyond," last modified May 25, 2016, https://www.ons.gov.uk/businessin dustryandtrade/internationaltrade/articles/ukperspectives2016tradewiththeeuand beyond/2016-05-25.

23. Chris Giles, "Brexit in Seven Charts—the Economic Impact," *Financial Times*, last modified June 27, 2016, https://www.ft.com/content/0260242c-370b -11e6-9a05-82a9b15a8ee7.

24. London School of Economics, accessed February 27, 2019, http://www.lse .ac.uk/.

25. "Economic, Industry, and City-level Forecasts and Analysis," Oxford Economics, accessed February 27, 2019, https://www.oxfordeconomics.com/.

26. Margaret Malone, "European Union, 2017," *Administration* 66, no. 1 (2018): 69–81.

27. Full Fact, "EU immigration to the UK," last modified March 18, 2019, https:// fullfact.org/immigration/eu-migration-and-uk/.

28. Graeme Cowie, "Implications for Scotland of leaving the EU," House of Commons Library, last modified June 29, 2018, https://researchbriefings.parliament.uk/ ResearchBriefing/Summary/CDP-2018-0166.

29. World Bank, "GDP (current US$)," accessed October 5, 2016, https://data .worldbank.org/indicator/ny.gdp.mktp.cd.

30. Stockholm International Peace Research Institute, "SIPRI Military Expenditure Database," 2016.

31. Figure 5.6 source: Stockholm International Peace Research Institute, "SIPRI Military Expenditure Database," 2016.

32. Friends of Europe, "Europe's World," accessed February 27, 2019, https:// www.friendsofeurope.org/.

33. Gaspare M. Genna, Birol Yesilada, and Peter Noordijk, "Political Performance, Leadership, and Regional Integration in Europe," in Jacek Kugler and Ronald L. Tammen, eds., *The Performance of Nations* (Lanham. MD: Rowman & Littlefield, 2012), 97–118.

34. Ronald Inglehart and Christian Welzel, *Modernization, Cultural Change, and Democracy: The Human Development Sequence* (Cambridge: Cambridge University Press, 2005).

35. Birol Ali Yesilada, Osman Goktug Tanrikulu, Jacek Kugler, and Allison Hamlin, "Power Transition and the Future of European Union Integration," paper presented at the International Studies Association Annual Conference, Atlanta, GA, last modified March 15, 2016, http://works.bepress.com/birol_yesilada/31/.

36. Inglehart and Welzel, *Modernization, Cultural Change, and Democracy.*

37. Ibid.

38. Daniel Bell, *The Coming of Post-Industrial Society: A Venture in Social Forecasting* (New York: Basic Books, 1976).

39. Figure 5.7 source: Calculated from survey data at World Values Survey: R. Inglehart, C. Haerpfer, A. Moreno, C. Welzel, K. Kizilova, J. Diez-Medrano,

M. Lagos, P. Norris, E. Ponarin, B. Puranen, et al., eds., 2014. *World Values Survey: All Rounds—Country-Pooled Datafile 1981–2014.* Madrid: JD Systems Institute, last modified August 31, 2019, http://www.worldvaluessurvey.org/WVSDocumen tationWVL.jsp.

40. The ERASMUS program is a student and faculty exchange mechanism among EU member and associate states.

41. Birol A. Yeşilada, "The Future of Erdoğan and the AKP," *Turkish Studies* 17, no. 1 (2016): 19–30. https://doi.org/10.1080/14683849.2015.1136089.

Chapter Six

Europe

A Nationalist Dream and the Effects of Zero Migration on Political Power

Tadeusz Kugler

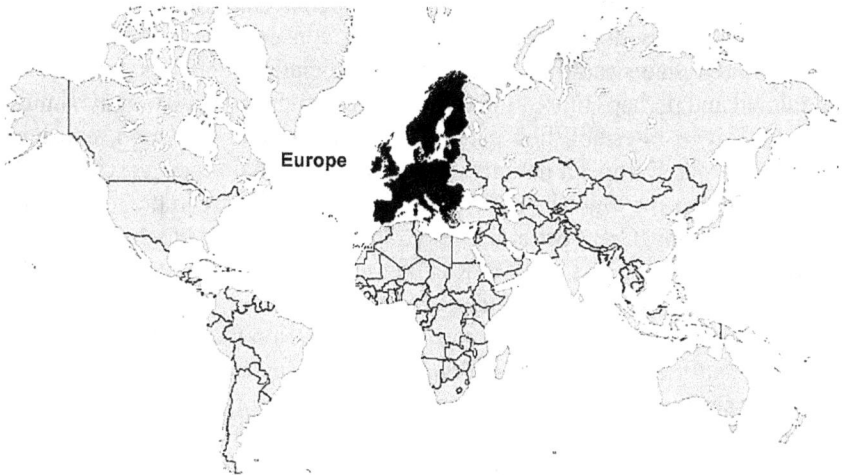

Europe Region

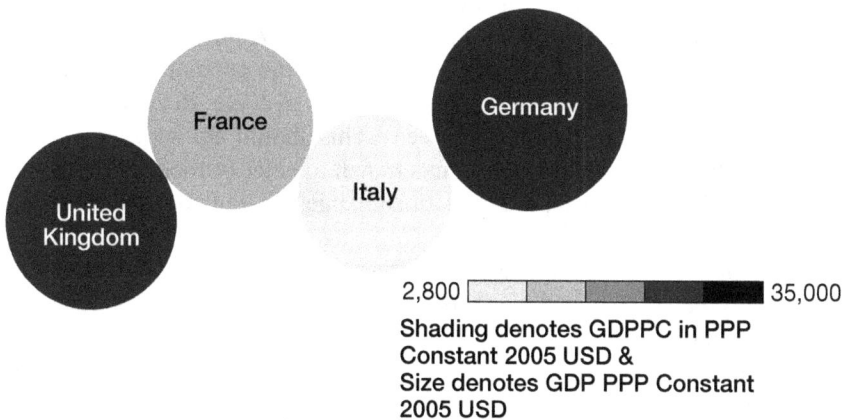

2,800 ▭▭▭▭▭ 35,000
Shading denotes GDPPC in PPP
Constant 2005 USD &
Size denotes GDP PPP Constant
2005 USD

Europe Hierarchy

EUROPE'S DEMOGRAPHIC DILEMMA

The European hierarchy has been host to the most devastating wars in recent memory.[1] Before the two great wars, members of the European region
expanded rapidly, driven in part by technological advantages acquired early
in the Industrial Revolution. Using this advantage, Spain, Portugal, England,
France, the Netherlands, and even Belgium expanded into the Americas, Africa, Asia, and Oceania.

The colonial phase was driven in part by prospects of riches but also by fast
population growth. As the Spanish, English, Dutch, French, and eventually
Portuguese empires crumbled, affluence, political modernization, and a stable
population drove democratization. A central question is why these European
societies turned inward. From a hierarchical perspective, the declining relative power of individual European states was a consequence of the emergence
of the United States and the Union of Soviet Socialist Republics (USSR). An
additional and perhaps more fundamental answer lies in population dynamics.

Following well-established patterns of demographic transition, educated
and prosperous European nations were unable to sustain their previous size.
Integration was the logical solution. This came in response to the relative decline of Germany, Great Britain, France, and Italy compared to developments
in the United States and the USSR. The same pattern is reoccurring now as
China and India go through the fast-growth phase.

Power transition theory (PTT) considers population the indispensable base
of power but focuses on gross national product to assess the dynamic nature
of power accumulation. This chapter emphasizes the often overlooked population variable. Europe is the perfect place to consider the effect of stable and
declining populations on the future capacity of a region to maintain its status
in the international system.

Europe is not the only region affected by low fertility. In the near future,
Russia, Japan, and China will face the implications of shrinking populations. Note, however, that the differences are large. Among members of the
European Union (EU), on average 16 percent of the population is younger
than age fourteen, and in the African Sahel on average 46 percent of the
population is younger than age fourteen.[2] This should not surprise anyone
given the short distance Sahel migrants transit to enter Europe. This chapter
seeks to explore the impact of population changes on transitions both within
and across regions.

Population is a key component of international and regional power. Population size creates the boundaries and framework for determining the long-run
economic and security success of a country.[3] Countries with a relatively small
population, in comparison with other global entities, can compensate for
that relative deficiency with high productivity. In Europe, large-scale public
education programs, the successful assertion of women's rights and partici-

pation in the workforce, and investments in infrastructure and technological innovation have all combined to create an extraordinary increase in worker productivity. But what will happen when larger population countries, as predicted, also increase their worker productivity? The competitive playing field shifts to the large *and now* productive set of relatively underdeveloped Great Powers. This is the power of population.

Within the EU, difference in national power is no longer a question of government efficiency, which has roughly plateaued, but of population. Differences in immigration policy, birth rates, and social ability to assimilate members of the foreign-born population will all be the key components of future power dynamics within the region. These regional population dynamics will have a significant impact at the global level. Should the United Kingdom wish to challenge Germany as the regional preeminent power within Europe, then current political rhetoric to radically restrict immigration flows undercuts its likelihood of doing so.

Restrictive immigration policies radically limit domestic population growth rates and disrupt the internal opportunities of nations to dramatically decrease the expectations of future total gross domestic product (GDP) and, subsequently, power.[4] The recent Brexit vote and the rise of nationalistic European political parties, such as Britain's United Kingdom Independence Party (UKIP) or France's National Rally (prior to June 2018, the National Front), build on a foundation of anti-immigration beliefs.[5] If adopted, they have the potential to undermine the EU's commitment to the free flow of populations, which produced the largest global economy in the world.

This is an ironic twist. Nationalist proponents argue for an expansion of national power without understanding that their anti-immigration policies severely handicap their stated objective of increasing relative power. Eventually, the European immigration crisis will be settled. The eventual immigration decisions for migrants, outside the EU, will pose no direct threat of armed conflict inside the EU. On the horizon, however, very real population-power conflicts loom. An external confrontation between the United States-European Union and Russia supported by China lurks behind the scenes.[6] Slowing external immigration and splitting the EU weakens the Western coalition substantially.

INTERACTIONS BETWEEN RESTRICTED IMMIGRATION AND DECLINING GREAT POWERS

Europe has developed political parties that have gained popularity by supporting a nativist belief that immigration should be either restricted or even ended. In common public policy discourse both options are promoted.[7] Yet, even without restrictions, the population of Europe as a whole is declining.

The two countries with the largest foreign-born populations, France and the United Kingdom, have maintained relatively stable populations because they have been major recipients of non-EU migrant populations. Immigrants arriving principally from former colonies, such as Algeria for France and the Caribbean for Britain, have prevented a decline in the populations of both nations.

Starting in 2016, the largest recipient of immigration has been Germany because of the refugee crisis, and this process has reversed imminent population decline.[8] Prior to the refugee crisis, the EU consistently enacted pro-immigration policies within its jurisdiction. For example, Britain accepted a large influx of Polish migrants following the collapse of the USSR. France's position as a full member of both the EU and Schengen Area helped to support the free flow of populations from its colonies and former Soviet republics.

Opposition to further immigration has emerged, and a common restrictive immigration policy consistent with British proposals is developing and is likely to prevail.[9] The implications of a more robust anti-immigration posture affecting non-EU nations may be compensated by enhancing internal EU migration. Britain, after Brexit, will not have the ability to compensate for low fertility unless it reinvigorates a pro-immigration posture aimed at its previous colonies. Such decisions suggest the possibility of lower growth for the EU and possibly a much sharper decline for the United Kingdom.

Anti-immigration policies restrict economic growth. The history of the United States shows that immigration is a tool for growth. The United States has benefited enormously from large migration flows. When the United States temporarily enacted radical immigration restrictions at one point, growth fell. The series of Alien Exclusion Acts between the 1880s and 1924 decreased the total inflows of immigration by nearly 90 percent. These acts were eventually reversed, but in the meantime they had reduced potential output substantially. Interestingly, the flow of immigrants into the United States in 1929 was roughly on the same scale as those currently in the United Kingdom. Immigration can be heavy even when restricted. The outcomes of those anti-migration policies in the United States were not consistent with the goals originally postulated to increase US national power. These hard lessons were not learned in the United States or in Britain.

The vote by the majority of citizens of England and Wales to leave the EU is one of the most dramatic reversals of a strong European trend toward integration.[10] In population-policy terms, Brexit is a prime example of the move from rhetoric to policy action. The marketing behind the "Leave" campaign focused on immigration, emphasizing the more than 300,000 immigrants who come to the United Kingdom every year. The EU became a cause célèbre among many British. Immigration to Britain became the great unifier of political action in favor of restrictions.[11] What was lost in the popular discussion is that the population flow was legal and mainly the result of UK domestic politics. The EU direct actions were secondary.

The British choice to leave reflects a shift in domestic preferences. The growth of anti-immigration policies will likely continue, although at a slower pace, and more restrictive policies will move to the books. Although analysts have been focused on the anti-immigration rhetoric, what is far more important and less appreciated is that Britain is willingly giving up the potential for increasing national power and economic growth. The new nationalistic parties throughout Europe, affected by the Brexit trend, are blindly supporting policies contrary to the long-term best interests of their own countries. Similar trends are emerging in the United States. The long-term implications for the relative capabilities of the Western coalition that has dominated world politics since 1945 are profound—a disaggregation of the United Kingdom from the EU reduces the community marginally. Britain, on the other hand, falls out of the set of potential challengers and becomes a minor Great Power. A potentially isolated United States will remain a Great Power but will lose its dominant posture without direct support from the EU. Underlying all these divisions are dramatically different population shifts.

Restrictions on immigration are not confined to large European nations. Early moves to adopt immigration restrictions started with small far-right parties in the smaller members of the EU, such as Jobbik in Hungary, True Finns in Finland (now called the Finns Party), the Danish People's Party in Denmark, and the Golden Dawn in Greece that then impacted the now-defunct British National Party in the United Kingdom and the new Alternative für Deutschland (AfD) in Germany. The increased popularity of these smaller parties (and their larger counterparts, such as France's National Front, which was recast in June 2018 as the National Rally, and the UKIP) put pressure on mainstream center-right parties to accept many of their policy positions, if only as a method to rally center-right and right-wing voters. Although not monolithic, mainstream political parties, such as the Conservative Party in the United Kingdom and the new Les Republicans (a rejuvenated center-right party) in France, have adopted some of these new restrictive policies.

Captured by their rhetoric, what these parties have failed to realize is that population is the critical element of national power. No other single aspect of national capabilities is as important to national power as population. Any rapid or large-scale change to UK immigration flows following Brexit, for example, will alter not simply the potential economic success of the country but also its role as a power broker in Europe. Current assessments show that Britain could be the largest and, hence, most powerful, nation within Europe in time, if it remained a member of the EU. Given current conditions and trends, the United Kingdom could be anticipated to overtake Germany in economic power around 2040. But this transition is unlikely without continued immigration growth. Limiting population growth limits the potential of the nation's total economic and political power.

What are the consequences of one or more major European countries reducing immigration to zero or heavily curtailing the influx of new residents? How would the policy of an anti-immigration umbrella reorganize and rework the basic political fundamentals of the continent and alter the expected power trajectories of Europe?

POPULATION DYNAMICS

The demographic structural influences on political power and economic growth pose an interlocked complex challenge. First, as economic growth increases, mortality rates fall quickly, followed by a decline in birth rates. In most developing societies this creates a short-term phenomenon called a "youth bulge."[12] This expansion is further associated with a baby boom that often follows major wars. The declines in fertility then create a new phenomenon known as the "demographic transition," or simply the movement from a young growing population, in a developing country, to an old declining one.[13] After the population stabilizes, a new stage of long-term population decline characterizes nations.

Attempts to restart domestic fertility rates after exiting the transition have so far failed internationally. The richest countries are now becoming increasingly dependent on immigration as a means to restore or even shore up a declining labor force. The United Kingdom has been one of the most successful at this policy and consistently has had some of the highest levels of immigration seen within Europe in general as well as in the world at large.

Population growth originates from three factors. The first is the fertility of the population, the second is total mortality, and the third is more complex, based on the demographic structures of the population.[14] It is the imbalance between young and old populations that produces a growth momentum: in other words simply growth in the population created by the proportion of the population in cohorts with expected child production. Because cohorts are fixed beyond birth, the principal way to alter population size in the developed world is immigration. Migration is most heavily influenced by policy. Mortality is affected by the creation and maintenance of a universal healthcare system, and major sanitation works in the early twentieth century decreased mortality steadily and continuously. Continued increasing access to more advanced medical care, and other aspects of health and safety, increase life expectancy in a population, adding to the population size.

Fertility, the expected number of children born to the average women in the society, is more nuanced. Improvements in women's rights and access to contraception are two important policy actions that contribute to declining fertility rates. Momentum, indirectly affected via policy choices, is the outcome of those two effects. Declines in mortality, especially infant mortality, create larger-than-expected cohorts and subsequently a higher-than-traditional youth population. So, even with future declines in fertility, growth continues. Immigration influences population growth because on average it is a younger cohort with higher fertility rates. It is the fourth and final factor that is the most malleable and continuous in modern politics: the decision to allow the foreign-born to reside permanently within a country.

DEMOGRAPHIC FLUCTUATIONS

Using the United Kingdom as an example of a developed major European power, figure 6.1 illustrates the expected sources of UK growth, in millions of people, from 2010 to 2050. It assumes a constant domestic policy within the United Kingdom in terms of both access to health care and the quota for immigration. The first is particularly important because it shows expected declines in mortality with life expectancies continuing to increase. Notice first that growth via fertility is in sharp decline. As mentioned previously, a characteristic of the developed world is declining fertility. Least-developed societies generate eight to nine children per woman, and developed societies

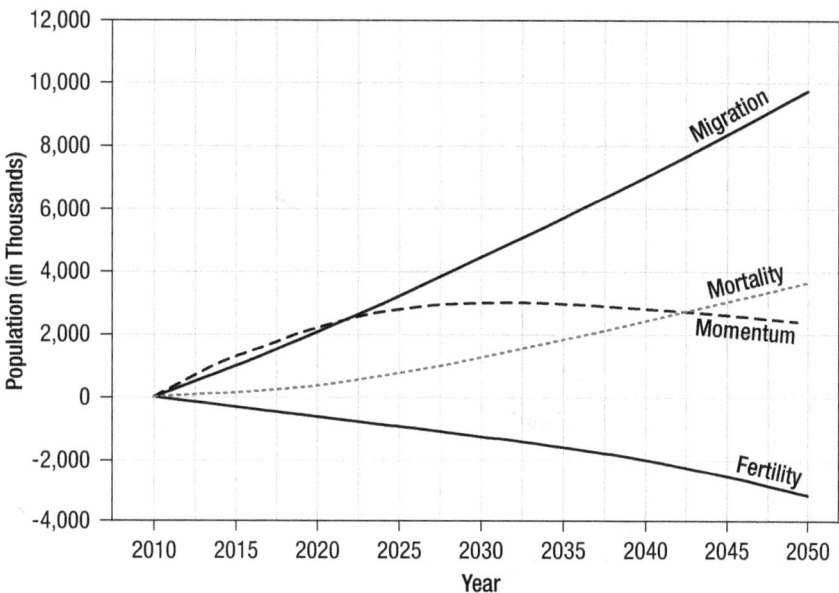

Figure 6.1. Sources of British Population Growth

fall to, at, or even below, two children per woman. A rate of two births per female allows for the population to replace itself via domestic population growth without the need for immigration to replace lost labor.

Subsequently, both momentum and continued declines in mortality increase a population, with the largest proportion of growth being expected to be created via a consistent immigration policy. Note that figure 6.1 does not show the total expected population growth, only the sources of it. Simple evaluations can be made by noticing that, with zero immigration, growth does continue (assuming no extreme out-migration) in small amounts well into the middle of the century.[15] This growth is small enough to be near stagnation, and that change from growth to stagnation, and subsequent decline, will have remarkable domestic and international political effects.

The difference in capabilities between the most radical policy choice of zero migration and the continuation of current immigration policy is illustrated in figure 6.2.[16]

The effects of change in immigration policy take decades to become noticeable. This lag is a key reason for declines in population being ignored in most political debates. Yet a United Kingdom with more than 10 million additional population, versus one without, would be likely to be the second- or third-most powerful country in the region. The difference is almost an entire metropolitan London (or two Scotlands) with all the additional benefits toward a greater tax base, larger GDP, and increased innovation. However, this effect will be seen only by 2050, well beyond the time horizons of a political

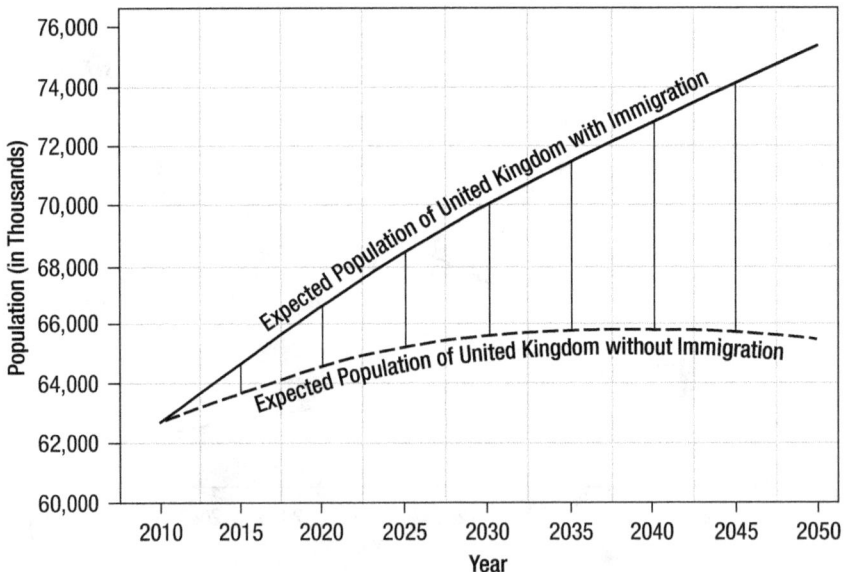

Figure 6.2. The Outcome of Nationalism within the United Kingdom

actor. The political focus is on short-term political gains versus long-term losses, leading to an obvious choice for all but the most farsighted leader and informed electorate.

EUROPEAN FLOWS OF POPULATION AND POWER

The twenty-eight nations of the EU are primarily dependent on immigration to sustain their current populations. The few seeing actual growth are those with a greater degree of liberal policies on inflows of population. Investigating the four largest members in figure 6.3, both the Germans and the Italians are projecting expected population declines. Only France and the United Kingdom see some reasonably small gains by 2050. Immigration is more than simply legal allowance but primarily societal acceptance. The ability to build a new life as part of a new community is the most important reason why people migrate, and this graphic attests to the greater degree of perceived difficulty in that achievement.

A further complexity is that three of these countries are in a true united labor market with total allowance for population movement, residence, and work. Yet, even with these legal allowances (at least for a certain proportion of EU countries), the United Kingdom stands as the country with the highest growth

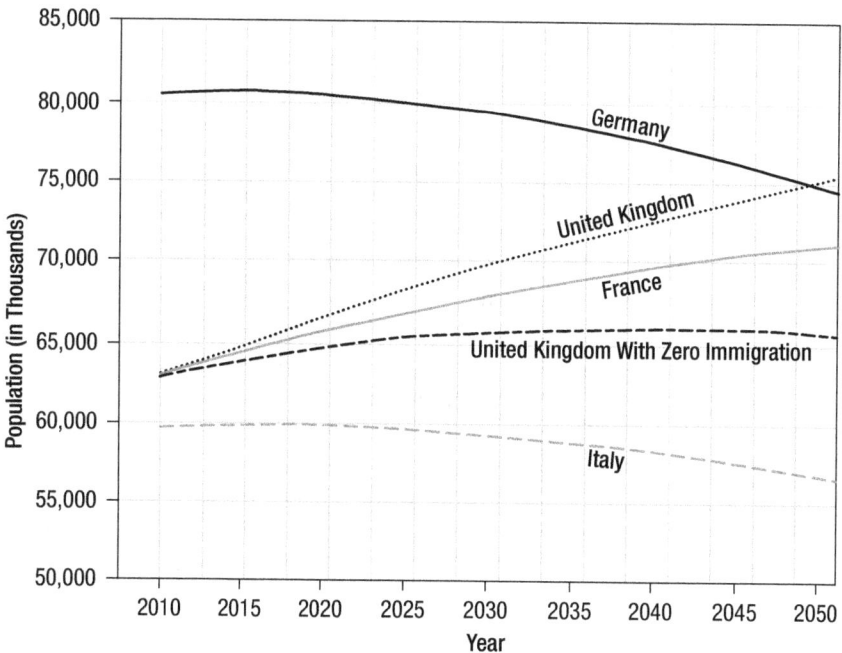

Figure 6.3. Europe and the Future

rates because of its acceptance of the largest total and proportional (for major countries) number of immigrants to Europe, making the recent Brexit vote even more surprising. Figure 6.3 focuses on population because this is the core element that determines, over time, the rise and fall of GDP. The reason is a combination of both simplicity and understanding, that at the stage of development seen within the EU, the small differences in labor efficiency or governmental capacity are well within the limits of error of long-range forecasting. More problematically, declining population as a result of increased mortality, falling fertility, and limited migration results in aging societies. Italy and Germany lead in these categories. The portion of the population moving to retirement and, hence, dependency is rising fast as a proportion of the whole. Even with additional labor force flows, the countries themselves are, in effect, less able to grow economically, meaning that simply using population underestimates the economic situation within declining countries by 2025.

The current expected forecast is for Germany to experience increasing population decline after 2025, dropping by the mid-2070s. Italy shows a similar but, sharper, trajectory. The United Kingdom and France increase linearly, moving toward total stagnation in their respective populations by 2050, with growing numbers of people in their seventies. The most dramatic consequence is a potential to create a population transitional event between the United Kingdom and Germany after 2040.

The most important aspect of figure 6.3 is the consequence of zero immigration. As the United Kingdom implements Brexit and were it to follow anti-immigration policies afterward, its relative power decline will be sharp.[17] The anticipated 10 million population decrease by 2050 would undermine whatever chance the United Kingdom has of becoming the largest entity in Europe. Within the EU, only France will have the required population growth and scale to compete with the Germans. The EU will be led by this bilateral structure, replacing the triumvirate that has been leading the union thus far.

Figure 6.4 illustrates a stark scenario resulting from potential migration constraints driven by nationalism.[18] By 2050, major European nations with zero migration would be far less strong than they would be if they could maintain current levels of immigration. Note the remarkable potential decline in both Germany and the United Kingdom, each of which is facing a loss estimated at 10 million people. France and Italy would lose 5 million each.

These numbers suggest a contraction of populations and severe aging distortions induced by the reduced fertility and the expansion of aging cohorts. Such older, less-mobile societies would face the much larger but declining population of China, a massive and still-expanding India, and a now large and exploding Africa.

There is a stark contradiction between future national potential driven by larger populations and the nationalist desire for ethnic or cultural homogeneity.

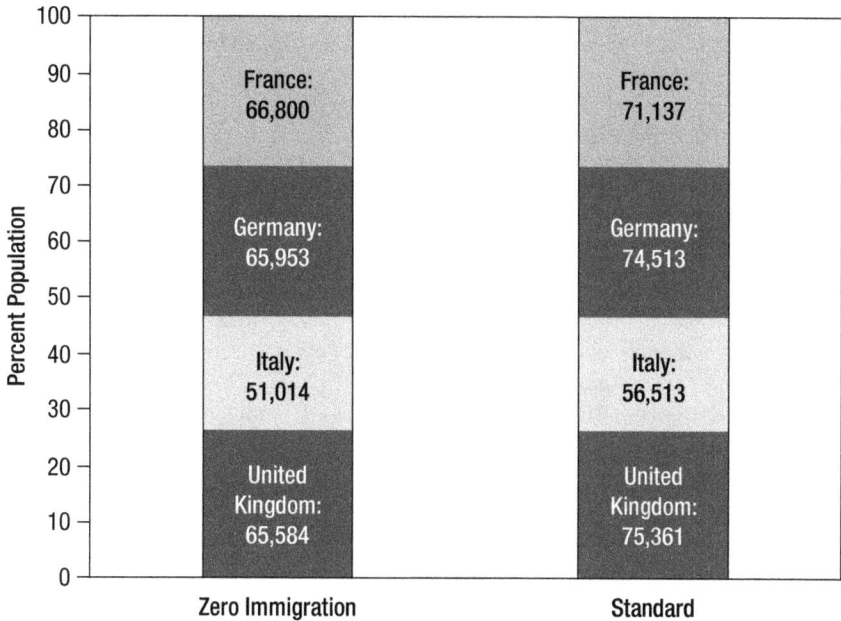

Figure 6.4. Percent Population in Select European Nations Comparing Zero Immigration with Current Standard Policy (Totals in Thousands)

FUTURE CONFLICT AND COOPERATION

From a population perspective, the likelihood of a new conflict within Western Europe is minimal. The reported potential for international conflict that looms as the EU faces a disgruntled Russia alone is also minimal. The potential for conflict, assuming Russia and a rising China join forces, would induce profound structural global changes. Europe plus the United States, given their advantage in productivity, could easily hold back any threat from the East.

In a more distant future, the potential for conflict may be centered increasingly between nations with expanding, youthful populations and developed nations with contracting and aging populations.

NOTES

1. Global Map shows region contours. The hierarchy map shows the relative size of the top contenders in this region. Data are World Bank, "World Development Indicators," last modified March 27, 2016, http://documents.worldbank.org/curated/en/805371467990952829/World-development-indicators-2016.

2. For this particular calculation, the subregion of sub-Saharan Africa contains Mali, Burkina Faso, Niger, and Chad. For this book, all the nations south of the Maghreb are included.

3. Tadeusz Kugler, *Political Consequences of Population Dynamics* (Athens: University of Georgia Press, 2020)

4. Philip Rees, Pia Wohland, and Paul Norman, "The Demographic Drivers of Future Ethnic Group Populations for UK Local Areas 2001–2051," *Geographical Journal* 179, no. 1 (March 2013): 44–60.

5. Matthew Goodwin and Caitlin Milazzo, "Taking Back Control? Investigating the Role of Immigration in the 2016 Vote for Brexit," *The British Journal of Politics and International Relations* 19, no. 3 (August 2017): 450–464.

6. Douglas Lemke and Ronald L. Tammen, "Power Transition Theory and the Rise of China," *International Interactions* 29, no. 4 (2003): 269–271.

7. Eric Kaufmann, "Introduction: The Politics of Immigration: UKIP and Beyond," *Political Quarterly* 85, no. 3 (July–September 2014): 247–250.

8. European Commission, "Together against Trafficking in Human Beings," accessed February 27, 2019, https://ec.europa.eu/anti-trafficking/node/4598_en.

9. Birol Yeşilada, Jacek Kugler, Gaspare Genna, and Osman Tanrikulu, *Global Power Transition and the Future of the European Union* (London: Routledge, 2017).

10. Sara B. Hobolt, "The Brexit Vote: A Divided Nation, a Divided Continent," *Journal of European Public Policy* 23, no. 9 (2016): 1259–1277.

11. Goodwin and Milazzo, "Taking Back Control."

12. Henrik Urdal, "A Clash of Generations? Youth Bulges and Political Violence," *International Studies Quarterly* 50, no. 3 (September 2006): 607–629.

13. Dudley Kirk, "Demographic Transition Theory," *Population Studies* 50, no. 3 (1996): 361–387; Tim Dyson, *Population and Development: The Demographic Transition* (New York: Zed, 2010).

14. Nico van Nimwegen and Rob van der Erf, "Europe at the Crossroads: Demographic Challenges and International Migration," *Journal of Ethnic and Migration Studies* 36, no. 9 (2010): 1359–1379.

15. Figure 6.1 source: United Nations, Department of Economic and Social Affairs, Population Division, *Demographic Components of Future Population Growth: 2015 Revision* (New York: United Nations, 2015).

16. Kirill Andreev, Vladimíra Kantorová, and John Bongaarts, "Demographic Components of Future Population Growth," *United Nations, Department of Economic and Social Affairs: Population Division*, Technical Paper No. 2013/3 (New York: United Nations, 2013), accessed July 21, 2019, https://www.un.org/en/development/desa/population/publications/pdf/technical/TP2013-3.pdf; figure 6.2 source: United Nations, Department of Economic and Social Affairs, Population Division, *Demographic Components of Future Population Growth.*

17. Figure 6.3 source: United Nations, Department of Economic and Social Affairs, Population Division, *Demographic Components of Future Population Growth.*

18. Figure 6.4 source: United Nations, Department of Economic and Social Affairs, Population Division, *Demographic Components of Future Population Growth.*

Chapter Seven

Eurasia

Russia Plus

Kristina Khederlarian,
Allison Hamlin, and Jacek Kugler

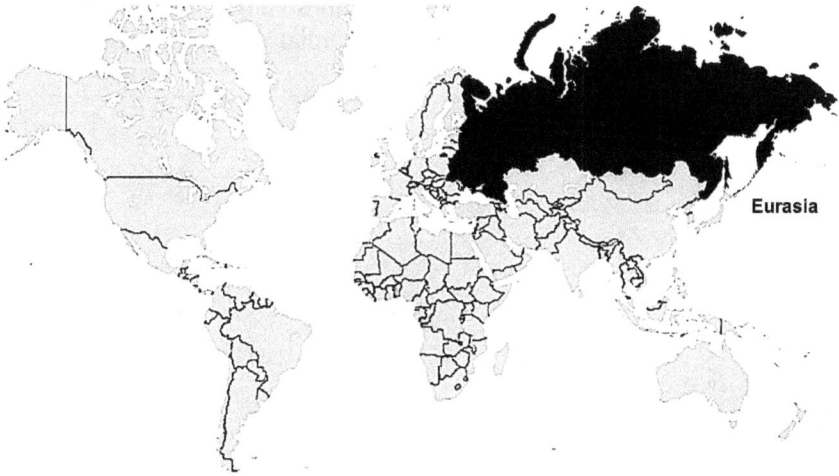

Eurasia

Eurasia Region

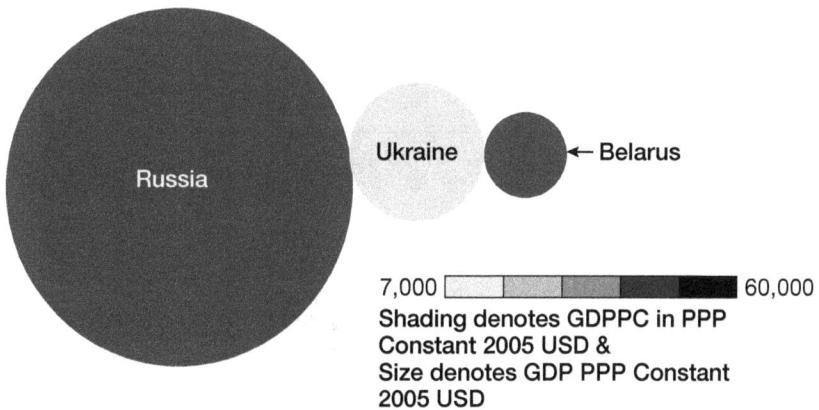

Russia

Ukraine

← Belarus

7,000 ▭▭▭▭▭▭ 60,000
Shading denotes GDPPC in PPP
Constant 2005 USD &
Size denotes GDP PPP Constant
2005 USD

Eurasia Hierarchy

SETTING THE STAGE

As a result of the collapse of the Union of Soviet Socialist Republics (USSR), the larger Eurasian hierarchy splintered into many distinct pieces.[1] A portion morphed into states of Central Asia, another became a portion of Eurasia, and the former members joined Europe, becoming full members of the European Union (EU) and North Atlantic Treaty Organization (NATO). Today this region is best described as Russia and its near-abroad neighbors Ukraine and Belarus. But the halo effect of the old USSR remains. Russia still considers nations in the Central Asia region and the Baltic states as lost territory with Russian-speaking populations and, thus, as targets for reacquisition.

Figure 7.1 represents Eurasia as a region heavily dominated by Russia.[2] However, unlike North America, where relations among the United States, Canada, and to a lesser degree Mexico are cordial and largely cooperative,

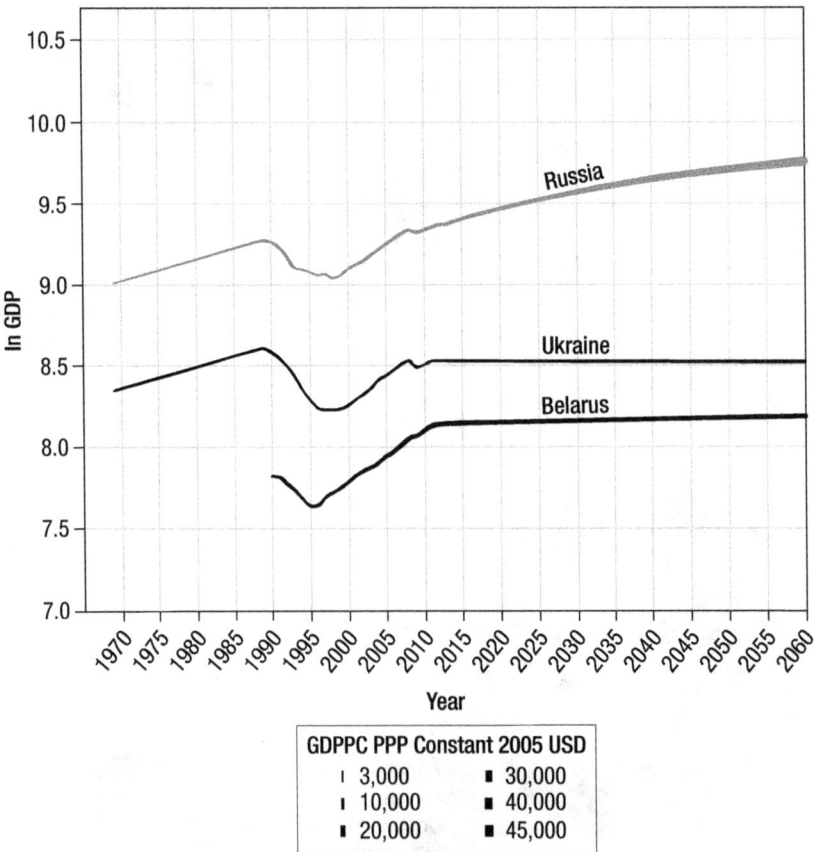

GDPPC PPP Constant 2005 USD	
ı 3,000	∎ 30,000
ı 10,000	∎ 40,000
∎ 20,000	∎ 45,000

Figure 7.1. Eurasia Power Projections, 1970–2060

Russia's relations with its former republics are conflictual. This is particularly true in the case of Ukraine. Although Russia and Belarus have reached a modus vivendi based on overwhelming Russian power, Russia continues to press forward in other areas with a plan to restore, wherever possible, lost Russian dominance. This is clearly seen in Ukraine and Moldova.

REGIONAL DECLINE

Before the split of 1991, the USSR had been suffering economic decline. The deceleration of economic growth began in 1973 and the most of fifteen states that emerged after the collapse carried this slow economic growth pattern into their postsplit economies.[3] The centralized strategies of the USSR had kept these republics removed from the rest of the international system, and the slowdown of the economy was not easily identified; nor was it easy to address. This slowdown of the Soviet Union has been mostly credited to a decrease in microeconomic efficiency, an increase in military spending, and the inefficient exploitation of natural resources.[4]

Although the Russian Federation could boast of being the largest of the fifteen states, it also inherited a similarly slow growth rate. Prior to the collapse of the USSR, the Russian Federation had accounted for more than 60 percent of the gross domestic product (GDP) and 50 percent of the population of the Soviet Union. The Russians constituted the majority of the Soviet military forces as well. The Russian Federation took devastating blows in GDP between 1991 and 1998, as it transitioned into a crony market economy. GDP in the Russian Federation dropped by 42 percent between 1990 and 1998, while fixed investment fell by 17.5 percent during the same years.[5]

Similar economic blows hit the rest of the region, with Belarus and Ukraine taking substantial drops in their respective GDPs as well. In 1987–1988, only a very low proportion of the region's population lived in poverty, but once the USSR dissolved, this spiked. In 1987–1988, 2 percent of the population in the Russian Federation and Ukraine lived below the poverty line, and the comparable figure for Belarus was 1 percent. In the period 1993–1995, the Russian Federation saw 50 percent of its population living in poverty; in Ukraine the figure was a shocking 63 percent. Belarus was slightly better off than its neighbors, with 22 percent living in poverty but still strikingly worse off than what it had been in the days of the USSR.[6]

This poor economic performance was paired with a declining population in Russia. The population disaster has largely been traced to the high male mortality rate seen in the adult population, as well as the deterioration of the healthcare system.[7] Fertility rates in Russia were low already, which accounts for much of the long-term population decline as well. This affected the entire region of Eurasia.

As a result of these factors, the Russian Federation barely compares with the United States and China today. According to the World Bank, Russia's GDP, purchasing power parity (PPP; current international) in 2018 was $3.9 trillion compared to $20.5 trillion in the United States and $25.4 trillion in China.[8] The new Russia is but a pale shadow of its former self.

EURASIAN HIERARCHY

This chapter evaluates the long-term evolution of power dynamics in the Eurasian region. It also analyzes the global implications of Russia's pivot toward China and away from both the EU and the United States. Russia today is no longer a superpower, but it continues to play a role in the world arena largely due to its over-commitment to military power and its global nuclear capabilities.

Given the massive preponderance of Russia over Belarus, Moldova, and Ukraine, power transition theory (PTT) anticipates instability in this region, driven by Russia's dissatisfaction. Simply put, Russia dominates this regional hierarchy. Fundamental shifts that stabilize relations can take place only as a result of internal changes within Russia.

Russia is dwarfed to the west by the EU and to the east by China. Internal politics in Russia are complicated because the collapse of the USSR created a number of new republics in Central Asia. In the Baltic states, Ukraine and Belarus, Russian expatriates continue to live in independent states under very new and diverse governments. The Baltic states joined North Atlantic Treaty Organization (NATO), thus blocking attempts to reabsorb them into Russia. Only the two contiguous states of Belarus and Moldova, which were the food baskets of the USSR, remain unattached on the western border. The states in the Central Asia region continue to have ties with Russia, but the prolonged conflict in Chechnya, combined with the Russian intervention in Syria, has soured relations with the Muslim minorities in this region. Considering Russia's current confrontational posture along its borders plus outside interests vying for influence in the region, Eurasian stability is at risk.

The Russian confrontational posture was not inevitable. Following the fall and the formal dissolution of the USSR on December 26, 1991, most international observers anticipated a period of peaceful reconciliation and the emergence of new opportunities for cooperation between East and West. The long Cold War was over. As Russia tilted toward neutrality, many observers anticipated, or hoped for, greater association with the West.

Specific actions seemed to follow this optimistic path. In 1998, recognizing the prominent role that Russia could play among the top industrialized societies, the United States and the EU invited Russia to join the Group of Seven (G7).[9] In 2012, relations with the West further improved when, after almost twenty years of tortuous negotiations, the World Trade Organization (WTO) officially welcomed the Russian Federation to join its ranks. This inclusion finally granted Russia the right to have a say in global trade forums. Moreover, as the Baltic states joined the EU and NATO, Russia was added to the G7 *and* became an associate observer in NATO.

Global actors including the EU, the United States, and even China anticipated that admitting Russia into the WTO would raise the country's international prestige, while enhancing its economic and political interactions. With such benefits, Russia could be persuaded to adhere more closely to established norms of the international system. At the 1995 Oslo summit meeting, Russian President Boris Yeltsin and US President Bill Clinton agreed to expand Russia's observer status in NATO and even anticipated plans for its full membership. Just before the Georgia and Ukraine crises, Russia-West relations were slowly improving. Concurrently, China was building economic ties with the West and repairing the damage that the suppression of dissent in Tiananmen Square had done to East-West relations. Global interactions were shifting in a manner that no longer resembled that of Cold War behavior.

These expectations of cooperation were shattered by Russia's annexation of Crimea in 2014. The crisis in Ukraine marks a significant signpost in world politics. Russia's annexation of Crimea reversed the previous trend that saw Russia gravitating toward the Western alliance and the EU. It shattered the processes of both reconciliation and accommodation. The Ukraine crisis generated not only a regional conflict but also the beginnings of a possible global realignment.

The United States and the EU levied sanctions on Russia but failed to implement promises agreed on at the 1994 Budapest Memorandum of Security Assurances. In this agreement, the United States, Russia, and the United Kingdom provided security assurances for Ukraine in the event of the threat or use of force against its territory or sovereignty. All three countries promised to respect Ukraine's sovereignty and existing borders. Satisfied by this Budapest Memorandum on Security Assurances, Ukraine finally agreed to join the Non-Proliferation Treaty and allow all of its nuclear weapons to be transferred to Russia by the end of 1994 for decommission.[10] Despite the bright outlook for future cooperation, these commitments dissolved when Russia invaded Crimea and part of Ukraine. To the surprise of many, China responded by tacitly accepting the Russian aggression.

This was in fact quite counter to long-held Chinese declarations supporting national sovereignty.

Absorbing sanctions from the West, Russia now bids to take its business East. For the first time in history, an emerging economic coalition creates a link between Russia, with its very large and advanced militarily capabilities, and China, a rising developing economy whose market power and overall productivity will eventually surpass that of the United States. This paints a new picture for Eurasia, on a canvas where Western influences fade and the prospect of a new Sino-Russian global alliance structure rises to the surface.

The fact is that Russia is no longer a superpower, *but* it dominates Eurasia. Facing a population decline, an economy characterized by slow growth and starving for Western technological transfers and investments, Russia now intends to sustain its economy on large military transfers and petroleum oil and natural gas contracts with China. Encouraged by its successful aggression in Crimea and the tepid response from the United States, Russia now feels comfortable siding with Bashar al-Assad in Syria and Nicolás Maduro in Venezuela. These Russian incursions well beyond their borders must be seen as spasms of past greatness and not as embryos of the creation of a new Russian empire.

Turning our attention to global stability, the Crimean crisis is central in evaluating the power dynamics of the region. Stability in the core of Europe is a global concern. The Middle East and North Africa, including Iraq, Iran, Kuwait, Tunisia, Yemen, Egypt, and Syria, account for only about 10 percent of the world's population and GDP, and yet conflicts in the Middle East seem to consume a large amount of the world's attention. By contrast, Eurasia contains a substantially larger population and more than half of the total global output. Therefore, instability in Eurasia poses a much greater threat than conflict in the Middle East.

Looking at the relevance of this region, we see that many global wars, starting with the French Napoleonic Wars that ended in 1815 and continuing with World Wars I and II,[11] were fought, in part, over control of Russian Eurasia. This did not happen by accident. Eurasia is the birthplace of large and powerful nations, which often develop high levels of dissatisfaction with their neighbors. Many of these nations have long understood that control of Eurasia is essential for global dominance.[12] Thus, the relatively small number of casualties in Ukraine compared to the losses incurred in the severe violence common to the Middle East is quite misleading. The Crimea–East Ukraine crisis involves core Eurasian territory, which raises the stakes among all the global players.

The Ukraine crisis not only poses a threat to regional stability but, if not addressed, also has the potential to gradually infect the entire international system. It could be an important signal that the solidarity of NATO is no longer a given, and it could also be an early warning sign that China intends to take sides on important Eurasian issues, and not just those associated with trade. This could be a precursor to China seeing itself as a Eurasian power rather than as an Asian power. Taking a look at power dynamics down the road, this could also trigger increasing tensions within the next generation of regional and global challenges of the EU, China, India, and the United States, with Russia acting as the spark that ignites conflict.

Cooperation at the global level has declined with the erosion of satisfaction among the main contenders. The Crimea crisis shattered any chance in the foreseeable future of Russia joining the EU or NATO. The possibility of a preponderant satisfied Western alliance, which could secure a dominant position for the West beyond 2050, has now evaporated.[13]

Instead, an increasingly dissatisfied Russia has joined a more assertive China. This new informal coalition confronts the West in Ukraine and in the South China Sea. As relations between East and West sour, interactions between China and Russia are on the rise. This has been seen throughout the 2014–2019 time period, where Sino-Soviet relations have steadily improved with economic agreements that secured oil exports from Russia to China, joint military exercises in the Mediterranean, close coordination on issues in contested regions close to Korea, and specifically in actions involving the South China Sea. Economic investments by China in Russia are on the rise, and the substantive military sales and technological transfers from Russia to China indicate a new level of satisfaction between these two societies.

RUSSIA'S NEW FOREIGN POLICY

Since the dissolution of the USSR, there have been conflicting schools of thought in the Russian foreign policy establishment. Torn between policies that favor more friendly relations with the West and those that advocate for a Russia-first strategy, the country has seen a shift in policy as of late. The hopeful days of cooperation are over. Under the leadership of Vladimir Putin and Dmitry Medvedev, the country has turned away from Atlanticist policies that preferred closer ties with the United States and other Western nations. In recent years, Russia has turned back to a more nationalistic strategy. It has become known for its cross-regional confrontations, which can be seen in its attitudes regarding the EU community (see chapter 5, figure 5.1). Despite the robust attempts of Russia to regain the dominance it once had, attempts at confrontation with the EU, or the United States for that matter, would fail to yield favorable outcomes for Russia. Russia simply does not have the power it once had.

Seeking to avoid dependence on Europe, Russia's TurkStream pipeline transports gas through Bulgaria then on to Serbia, Hungary, and Austria. This allows Russia to completely bypass Ukraine, although still allowing the Russians to strengthen their relationship with Turkey and their presence in the Balkans. But more important than Russia's pipeline to Europe is its natural gas pipeline to China. According to the International Energy Agency (IEA), China is expected to be the world's top importer of natural gas by 2019.[14] This will undoubtedly be aided by its strategic partnership with and pipeline to Russia.

FUTURE CONFLICT AND COOPERATION

The Eurasian regional hierarchy is heavily dominated by Russia. Unlike North America, where relations among the United States, Canada, and to a lesser degree Mexico are cordial, relations between Ukraine and Russia are confrontational and conflictual. Given the massive difference in capabilities, this relationship cannot be altered without a serious restructuring. The Ukrainian bid to join the EU and even NATO was an attempt for such a structural realignment. Given the reaction of the West to the Soviet invasion in Crimea, it is clear that this option is foreclosed unless there is a fundamental change within Russia, or if the West were ready to face a direct confrontation with Russia. Neither of these options is particularly likely.

The implications for regional stability emerging from dynamics within Eurasia could result in a protracted conflict but also present an opportunity for extended stability. Preserving the current status quo will lead to intermittent flare ups, with the potential to escalate to a severe conflict. To avoid this condition, a permanent resolution of the Crimea dispute and settlement of conflictual action along the eastern border of Ukraine is a precondition for stability. A move toward the West by Ukraine could generate change within Eurasia and could result in reconciliation with the EU. A very distant possibility is that Russia, which is now close to China, could become an interlocutor between East and West. The prerequisite for such an unlikely outcome is a return to stability.

Globally, our assessment of the powers at play indicates that a united West can lead globally for the next two decades. During this period, Western leaders could attempt to incorporate Russia, China, and India into an alliance favoring maintaining the status quo. However, the foreign policy required to achieve such shifts is more complex and difficult to implement than the confrontational path seeking to realize short-term goals. This strategy requires patient *strategic thinking*; something that is extraordinarily difficult for leaders impatient to realize immediate goals and satisfy their constituents' demands, but it will be absolutely essential if global peace is to be maintained. Russia adds very little to the overall power of China. By 2030, China and Russia will be far less powerful than the combination of the United States and the EU.[15] The West will continue its dominance over the East, provided that the West remains united. Global policy makers should reconcile primary disputes now to ensure a peaceful future.

NOTES

1. Global Map shows region contours. The hierarchy map shows the relative size of the top contenders in this region. Data are World Bank, "World Development Indicators," last modified March 27, 2016, http://documents.worldbank.org/curated/en/805371467990952829/World-development-indicators-2016

2. Figure 7.1 source: World Bank, "World Development Indicators," last modified March 27, 2016, http://documents.worldbank.org/curated/en/805371467990952829/World-development-indicators-2016. Forecast based on growth rates adapted from PWC 20250, "The World in 2050," last modified August 29, 2017, https://www.pwc.com/gx/en/issues/economy/the-world-in-2050.html.

3. Angus Maddison, *The World Economy, Vol. 1, A Millennial Perspective* and *Vol. 2, Historical Statistics* (Paris: OECD Publishing, 2006).

4. Ibid.

5. Ibid.

6. Branko Milanovic, *Income, Inequality and Poverty during the Transition from Planned to Market Economy* (Washington, DC: World Bank, 1998), accessed July 21, 2019, http://documents.worldbank.org/curated/en/229251468767984676/pdf/multi-page.pdf.

7. Barbara Anderson, "Russia Faces Depopulation? Dynamics of Population Decline," *Population and Environment* 23, no. 5 (May 2002): 437–464.

8. World Bank Website, "GDP, PPP (current international)," (2019), accessed on April 8, 2019, https://data.worldbank.org/indicator/NY.GDP.MKTP.PP.CD?locations=RU-US-CN.

9. The G7 members are Canada, France, Germany, Italy, Japan, the United Kingdom, and the United States. These advanced economies produce more than 50 percent of global output.

10. John J. Mearsheimer, "Why the Ukraine Crisis is the West's Fault," *Foreign Affairs* (September/October 1994), accessed on July 21, 2019, https://www.foreignaffairs.com/articles/russia-fsu/2014-08-18/why-ukraine-crisis-west-s-fault. Anticipating a confrontational environment, Mearsheimer argued that "foregoing the deterrent of nuclear weapons would not be prudent. Clearly nations that seek peace take risks equal or even larger than those that seek to gain through war." For the sequence of

agreements, see "Ukraine, Nuclear Weapons, and Security Assurances at a Glance," *Arms Control Association* (July 25, 2017), accessed on July 21, 2019, https://www .armscontrol.org/factsheets/Ukraine-Nuclear-Weapons.

11. Historians remind us that, prior to the rise of the nation-state associated with the Treaty of Westphalia signed in 1648, the Mongol invasions of the thirteenth century were also fought to control Eurasia.

12. Although no one since the Mongols in 1241 have approached dominance over this whole region, a successful challenger would achieve the level of "hegemonic dominance" suggested by John Mearsheimer, *The Tragedy of Great Power Politics* (New York: Norton, 2001) as the overriding goal of Great Powers. Robert Keohane, *After Hegemony Cooperation and Discord in the World Political Economy* (Princeton: Princeton University Press, 1984) attributed hegemony to the United States but empirically the United States only preserved overwhelming preponderance from the end of World War II to mid-1950s. A. F. K. Organski and Jacek Kugler, *The War Ledger* (Chicago: The University of Chicago Press, 1980).

13. Yelena Tuzova and Jacek Kugler, "Global Financial and Structural Implications of the Ukraine Crisis," *Journal of Business and Economics* 9 (2018): 666–678.

14. "International Energy Agency," accessed April 07, 2019, https://www.iea.org/.

15. It is clear that the per capita productivity of Russia and China is far lower than that of the dominant Western allies, suggesting that the technological advantage will remain with the West at least until mid-century.

Chapter Eight

Middle East

Levant

Marina Arbetman Rabinowitz and Zeyad Kelani

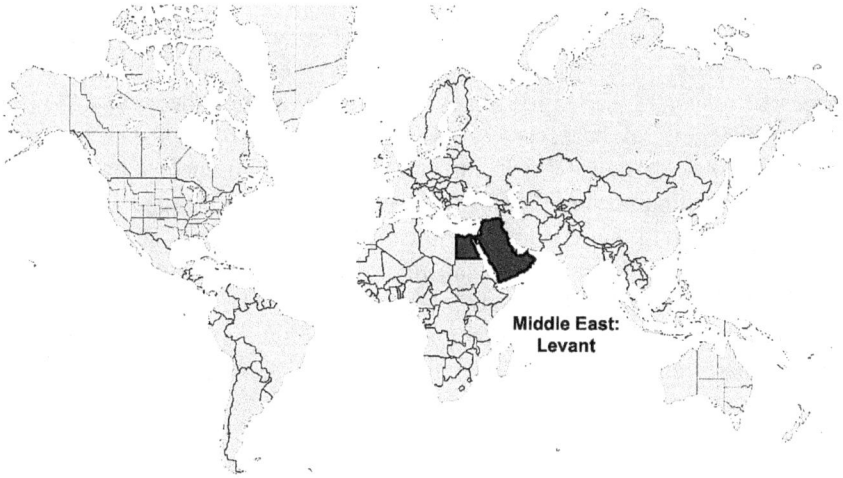

Middle East: Levant Region

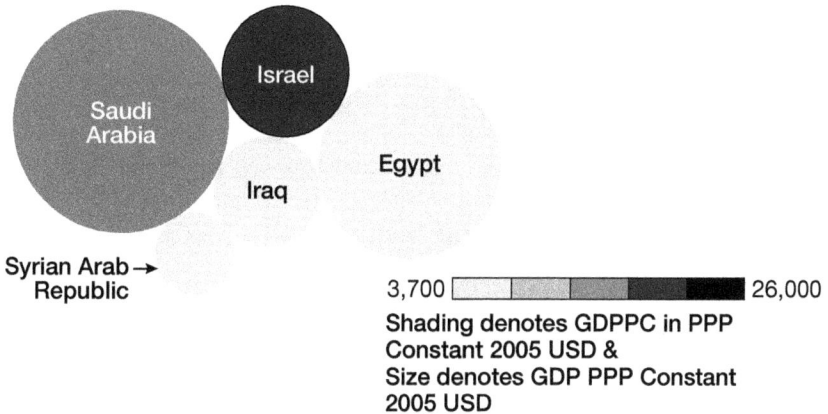

3,700 ▭▭▭▭▭ 26,000

Shading denotes GDPPC in PPP
Constant 2005 USD &
Size denotes GDP PPP Constant
2005 USD

Middle East: Levant Hierarchy

In the Middle East, the Levant is a part of the world always in the news, always noisy, and with the kind of noise that portends conflict.[1] The historic search for a magic potion for peace in the area has centered on the resolution of the Israeli-Palestinian conflict. At the global level, US and European administrations have tried, and failed, in their diplomatic efforts to bridge the communication gap and advance negotiations for peace in this region.

The protracted Israeli-Palestinian conflict has been a permanent feature of this region since 1948, when Israel fought back Arab attempts to destroy that nation. This conflict is characterized by low but constant levels of violence, frequently exaggerated in a news cycle that emphasizes the conflict end of the spectrum. In the more than seventy years since Israel became a nation, there have been on average between one thousand and twelve hundred conflict-related deaths per year.

Today, however, conflict in the Levant has exploded to involve Iraq, Iran, Yemen, Turkey, Saudi Arabia, and Syria, not to mention the continued presence of Russia and the United States. As power transition theory (PTT) posits, regional stability is secured by a dominant power *satisfied* with regional norms and rules. The Levant is characterized by the absence of both. Israel has been and still may be a significant power in the region, but the presence of Turkey and Iran in the adjoining region, along with actions by global powers such as the United States and Russia, affects all outcomes in this very divided region. Though still powerful and once dominant, Israel certainly has never been satisfied with regional norms and rules. Analysis of the interactions among these countries will not only shed light on transitions but also identify potential regional dominant powers that will set the rules of interaction and can create the conditions for cooperation or conflict.

POWER TRANSITIONS IN THE LEVANT

A look at the distribution of power in the region (see figure 8.1) provides an overview of past events and a glimpse of the future.[2] The ranking of powers has not dramatically changed since the 1950s, although Iran has lost steam in its trajectory. The projections show a smooth path. Following World War II there were several dyadic power transitions between Israel and Egypt that generated conflict based on dissatisfaction between the contenders until a settlement between Egypt and Israel took place. Then, the intensity of this turbulent period subsided.

Conflict shifted to civil wars within Lebanon, and, more recently, Syria and Yemen. Today the powerful regional players—Iran, Turkey, and Saudi Arabia—are fueling conflicts in Syria, Yemen, and beyond. The underlying

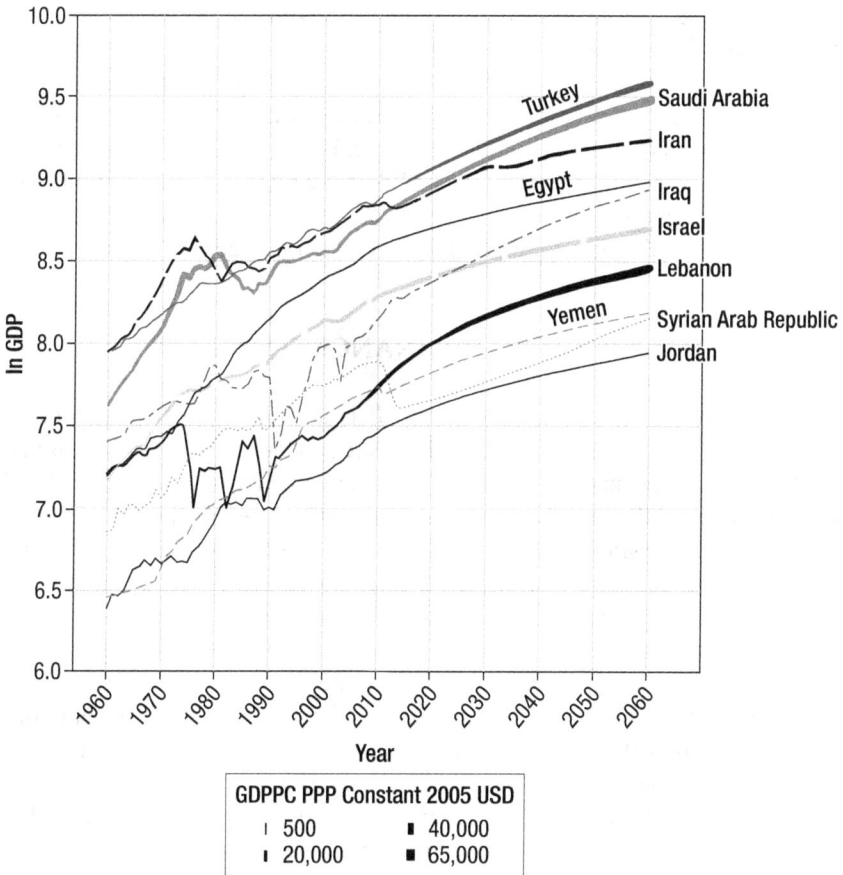

Figure 8.1. Power Transitions in Middle East: Levant plus Turkey and Iran (1960–2060)

structural reason is that Iran and Saudi Arabia are going through a period of power transition, with Turkey and Iran waiting in the wings (see chapter 9). Our forecasts show that Saudi Arabia is now the third-most powerful nation in the Levant hierarchy. Saudi Arabia is smaller than Iran and Turkey, which are included in the Middle East Northern Tier region. This external competition between Middle East hierarchies may realign alliances within the Levant hierarchy.[3]

Israel dominated the western region through 1980. After that, Israel unexpectedly did not keep up in terms of political performance, specifically the ability to extract resources from its population or relative political extraction (RPE).[4] Although Israel declined in RPE, Egypt and Saudi Arabia increased their governmental efficiency. Israel still dominates the immediate region—Lebanon, Syria, Jordan—but it no longer dominates Saudi Arabia or Egypt.

This means that, as long as the peace agreement with Egypt holds, so will the peace, a fact fully understood in Tel Aviv.

Interregional competition within the Middle East hierarchies directly affects interactions within the Levant and Northern Tier hierarchies. Saudi Arabia, threatened by Iran, is shifting toward Israel. If this evolution continues, a dominant coalition in the larger Middle East will emerge should Egypt also join in. Regardless of potential alliances, within the Levant hierarchy the Saudis are becoming the dominant leader, replacing Israel.

POWER AND GOVERNANCE EFFICIENCY

Power is not a unidimensional concept. It is a more sophisticated concept than its commonly used proxy, gross domestic product (GDP). As the original work on political capacity has shown and many other works have tested and applied successfully, the adjustment of economic prowess by how capable the government is at using its resources produces a much more accurate measure of power.[5] The measure of RPE is designed so that this metric can be used for comparative purposes. The average political capacity of a country is set at one.[6] Countries that have the capacity above one perform better than the norm, and countries with a capacity below one are the underperformers. Of course, the sample chosen will influence the relative values, so in general, this indicator is calculated based on all countries in the world, adjusted by their levels of development and other specific characteristics.

The range between the countries with low and high political capacity has narrowed in the last twenty years. Until the 1990s, Israel and Egypt had one and a half times to twice the political capacity of the average country in the region.[7] On the weaker side, Saudi Arabia had very low capacity in the same periods. Most countries converged toward the average in the late 1990s and oscillated around this level in the years prior to the financial crisis in 2008. The only exception was Jordan, which was above average.

Egypt, Israel, and Jordan had very high political capacity given their level of economic development. The gap between capable and less-capable governments ranged from 2.0 to 0.2, indicating very large disparities. From 1990 to 2005, the gap diminished with Lebanon being one of the countries that increased its capacity and Saudi Arabia showing a less-volatile positive path. Syria started a predictable steep decline, which reached the point where state governance was non-existent. In the postwar period, we expect this to rebound. Surprisingly, Israel also showed a decline in political capacity.

But even more striking is the generalized weakening of governance in the region, and all the countries seem to be following this downward trend with some countries at a faster pace than others. Egypt's level of political capacity has been below average for twenty years, but the trend started to reverse in 2011. Israel had a very capable government since its inception but has had a downward trend and has been below average for the last ten years. Saudi Arabia clearly demonstrated an upward trend but has also been losing relative political power in the last ten years. This means that more problems are foreseen for this subregion if internal instability continues. In this case, a replication of 1973 would yield a volatile situation with the outcome contingent on US and now, perhaps, Russian actions.

THE SUBREGION TODAY: KEY COUNTRIES OF THE LEVANT

Saudi Arabia

Saudi Arabia is the major player in the region, not only because of its position as the birthplace of Islam but also its strong ties to the West through oil. It is the regional dominant power but reluctant to foster regional strategic policies. This aversion stems from the country's isolationism and its strong hold on the traditional interpretation of Islam (Wahhabism). Its regional involvement is directed toward preserving some peace to protect its business interests. Being the reluctant dominant power leaves Saudi Arabia open to external influence and scrutiny and forces it to impose its values in other countries.

Saudi Arabia wants to preserve its social and religious norms while continuing business as usual with the West. Its enmity with Iran also has historical and religious roots.[8] Saudi Arabia is concerned with the expansion of Iran and the historical hostility between Sunni and Shiites. Iran is fostering internal strife among the Shiites in the eastern provinces of Saudi Arabia and, on the other side of the country, is focusing on sabotaging Saudi oil production. This hostile relationship has stimulated Saudi involvement in Syria and Yemen, and quietly in other places, with the goal of containing or rolling back the influence of Iran.

For example, Saudi Arabia is backing the Yemeni government against the Houthis, and Iran is supporting the militias backed by the Zaidi Shia minority. In 2011, Yemeni President Ali Abdullah Saleh, accused of being authoritarian among other things, handed over power to his deputy, Abdrabbuh Mansour Hadi, whose conciliatory tone was taken as a sign of weakness and precipitated a civil war.[9] Internally, the Houthis have a strained alliance with ex-president Saleh, with the common goal of overthrowing President Hadi, who left Yemen in 2015 fearing for his life. In 2018, Saudi Arabia took over the port city of Hodeidah on the Red Sea, with support from the United Arab Emirates (UAE), with the objective of stopping Jihadist militants from Al Qaeda and allied Iranian rebels from interrupting trade through the Red Sea.

The Houthis' resistance is seemingly fading but the contest continues; however, the withdrawal of the UAE generates a new protracted regional conflict.

The most interesting change for Saudi Arabia is the start of business and political relations with Israel. The motivation comes from outside and inside the region. In the quest to control Iran in Yemen and Syria, Saudi Arabia has joined forces with Israel in both conflicts, and Israel is conducting a significant military role, mainly out of sight. If this newfound collaboration holds, it may be possible that Saudi Arabia can help to bring some resolution to the Israeli-Palestinian conflict.

Egypt

With interests and a role in North Africa as well as in the Middle East, Egypt strives to maintain a presence in both North Africa and the Middle East more broadly. But its main goal seems to be to monetize its role with the European Union (EU) rather than exercising its brokering capabilities.[10] According to Jonathan Marcus, citing Davis Kirkpatrick in a 2018 British Broadcasting Company (BBC) article,[11] the relations between Egypt and Israel are going beyond the formalities. Reportedly, because Egypt is worried about extremist activity in the Sinai Peninsula, Israel is attacking these groups with unmarked drones. This covert antiterrorism alliance between Egypt and Israel could create conditions for cooperation on other fronts. Egypt's president, Abdel Fattah el-Sisi, who won a disputed reelection with 97 percent of the vote in April 2018, supports "normalization" of relationships with Israel, partly to secure US aid and good diplomatic relations but also to preserve security cooperation against terrorist organizations, including Hezbollah and Hamas.[12]

From an economic point of view, Israel's ten-year deal worth $15 billion to export natural gas to Egypt from the Tamar and Leviathan operations through the East Mediterranean pipeline highlights the importance of the relationship. Egypt needs energy to continue its path of economic growth, which was set back when regulated low prices made investment in natural gas development unviable before el-Sisi. In 2015, the Zohr gas field was discovered and the availability of natural gas can now propel Egypt on a long-term path to self-sufficiency.[13] The lack of operational export pipeline routes, as well as the need to develop transport technology, limits Egyptian energy capabilities and flexibility. But a joint venture involving Egypt, Israel, and Saudi Arabia would benefit each party and serve to foster peace in the region.

Israel

Israel's once-dominant position in the Levant and the larger Middle East has faded. Although it retains a powerful military and the support of the United

States, population growth and economic development on its periphery have generated viable challengers. In addition, opposition groups such as Hamas and Hezbollah are joining forces to oppose Israel.[14]

Because of Israel's *relative* decline in power, it has opened public and private cooperative corridors with moderate Sunni governments. There are practical reasons for the moderate Sunnis in the region to be receptive to these initiatives. Iran, a powerful nation in the region, is increasing its conventional military strength and could at a future date expand its nuclear capabilities. This creates more than unease in the Sunni world. And this potential threat to Israel has not gone unrecognized in Tel Aviv.

The Israel-Iran cross-regional interaction is antagonistic, fueled by Iran's strategic missile programs and its intervention in Syria. Given Israel's powerful military, the moderate Arab bloc (Saudi Arabia, Jordan, and Egypt) undoubtedly understands Israeli interests and benefits from cooperation with Israeli military and intelligence.

Syria

Syria is the playground for many countries in the larger Middle East. In 2011, Syrian pro-democracy demonstrations met with a harsh government crackdown. By 2015, the confrontation between the Sunni Muslim majority and President Bashar al-Assad's Shiite Alawite sect had intensified. This division opened the door for Islamist state Jihadist groups and Al Qaeda to get involved and for Iran to assist the Shiite Muslim militia financially, including via the Lebanese branch of the Hezbollah movement. Iraq, Afghanistan, and Yemen have assisted the Syrian Army.

In 2015, President Assad asked Russia for assistance.[15] The global coalition of the United States, United Kingdom, and France supported the Syrian Democratic Forces (SDF), an alliance of Kurdish and Arab militias. Turkey supported the rebels, but with the real objective of containing the Kurdish militia. Saudi Arabia, keen to contain Iran's influence, has supported the anti-Assad coalition. And the Israelis, concerned about shipments of Iranian weapons to Hezbollah in Syria used to attack them, are joining forces with Saudi Arabia.

Syrian anti-Assad Islamist rebels have declined substantially despite support from the United States, Saudi Arabia, and Israel. Assad is in control because more assistance has been provided by the other side—Iran, Russia, and Shiite allies including Hezbollah. Active hostilities are drawing to a close. The Syrians, with Russian and Iranian support, are succeeding on the battlefield. As the United States exits Syria and the Middle East more broadly, countries in the region will be calculating how to attract new external support, including from willing partners Russia and Iran.

THE UNITED STATES, RUSSIA, AND CHINA

The United States used to be the link to Israel and the mediator in the region, but US foreign policy has adopted more transactional strategies and has lost credibility as a power broker. The United States offers mainly indirect military support through rebels in Syria and military aid to Israel. In effect, the United States is withdrawing, piecemeal, not only from the Middle East but also from the world scene at large.

Russia intervened in Syria in 2015 at Assad's request. Russia is following a policy similar to the one that it implemented in Afghanistan for decades, choosing to challenge the West in foreign lands. The Russian investment in Afghanistan turned out to be disastrous, but the country's heavy investment in Syria seems to be paying off thus far. The costs of intervention in Syria are high. Figure 8.2 shows relative power and indicates how intervention relies not on power but on salience.[16]

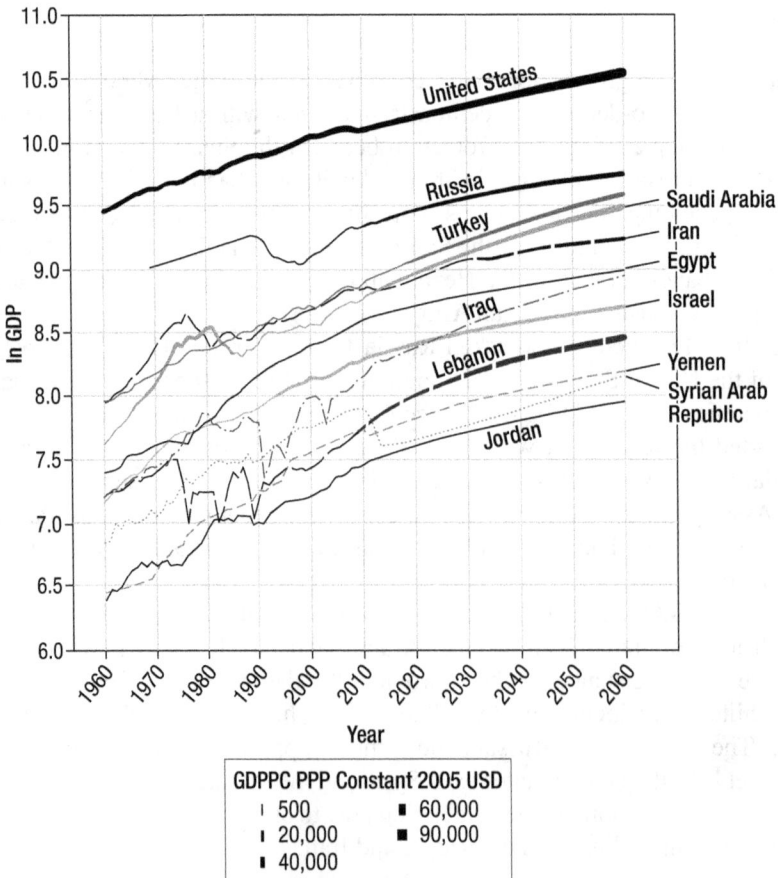

Figure 8.2.   Levant plus Turkey, Iran, Russia, and USA

Russia has strategic reach in the Levant. It demonstrates more interest, historically and currently, in intervention than the United States does. A coalition of Saudi Arabia, Egypt, and Israel could provide a regional roadblock to Russian ambitions. That is why current cooperation operations are so tantalizing.

Another potential Levant factor is China, which already has large investments in Egypt as well as a defense contract with Israel. However, its financial interests have thus far not involved influence operations. Traditionally, China has claimed to separate business and politics. But in recent years, it has demonstrated that it can and will use economic leverage to support Chinese interests (see chapter 2).

FUTURE OF CONFLICT OR COOPERATION

A new hierarchy is in the making in the Levant. Fundamental structural shifts are driven by the growth of Saudi Arabia and concerns with possible actions of Iran and Turkey along with vulnerability to external influences from the United States and Russia. Syria is the classic case study.[17] The Levant region is undergoing a massive transition and today lacks a dominant, satisfied leader. Israel, the modern society that dominated this region in the past, has declined and has been overtaken by Saudi Arabia and Egypt. This transition has been obscured because Israel has nuclear capabilities that no other state in this region possesses. The emerging dominant power based on wealth is Saudi Arabia, but it lacks the population size to confront Iraq or Turkey.

There is one option that would secure peace in the Levant and the Northern Tier of the Middle East. If Saudi Arabia with its vast resources, Egypt with its large population, and Israel with its advanced technological know-how were to create a de facto alliance, this grouping would dominate the Middle East. The old dynamics in the Middle East would change. Neither Turkey nor Iran could act with impunity in the region. If a stabilizing coalition does not form, however, there will be an increasing risk of conflict.

Economic factors cannot be overlooked. Oil is the main commodity that the Middle East exports to the rest of the world. Without this asset, controlled largely by Saudi Arabia and the small Gulf states, the Levant would not be a critical element in the global interactive environment. Economic alignments surrounding commodities do not always follow political alliances.[18] Our observation is that politics will dominate economic interests.

The future story is that Saudi Arabia will dominate the Levant portion of the Middle East, while Turkey-Iran will compete over the domination of the Northern Tier. These competitions will frame region-wide politics. The hope for regional peace, so long unfulfilled, will depend on new and unexpected alliances. As utopian as it may sound, a coalition of powers, led by Saudi Arabia, Egypt, and Israel could, one day, resolve at least one long-standing issue, the thorny Palestinian question. Region-wide, the lack of a dominant leader in the Middle East suggests that there will continue to be conflict, in the absence of hard-to-achieve unanimity among the Big 5—Turkey, Iran, Saudi Arabia, Egypt, and Israel. In the past, Israel dominated all Middle East competitors, particularly when economic growth and effective political performance were taken into consideration.[19] That now has changed, and there is a leadership vacuum waiting to be filled.

APPENDIX
GDP PPP CONSTANT 2005 USD EXTRAPOLATION METHOD

Constructing the Extrapolated GDPPP and Population Dataset (1960–2060) dataset:

- GDP Figure is multiplication of GDP per Capita (RPC 2018 Components) × Population
- GDPPC_PPP Constant 2005 from RPC components file, Source: World Development Indicators by World Bank
- For population estimates, we use Probabilistic Population Projections based on the World Population Prospects till year 2100: The 2015 Revision
- For GDP PPP Constant 2005 growth rate estimates we use PWC GDP 2050 growth rate estimates.

NOTES

1. Global Map shows region contours. The hierarchy map shows the relative size of the top contenders in this region. Data are World Bank, "World Development Indicators," last modified March 27, 2016, http://documents.worldbank.org/curated/en/805371467990952829/World-development-indicators-2016.

2. The term *Levant* is defined in multiple ways. In some use it refers to Israel and its near neighbors. Other writers include a broader grouping of countries to include Saudi Arabia and Turkey. And frequently, *Levant* is a synonym for the Middle East in general or at least the western portion thereof. For our purposes here, the Levant refers to Israel, Egypt, Saudi Arabia, Syria, Lebanon, Jordan, Iraq, Yemen, Kuwait, Bahrain, Qatar, and the United Arab Emirates (UAE). We address Turkey and Iran as part of the Northern Tier, separately in chapter 9.

3. Figure 8.1 source: World Bank, "World Development Indicators," last modified March 27, 2016, http://documents.worldbank.org/curated/en/805371467990952829/World-development-indicators-2016. Forecast based on growth rates adapted from PWC 20250, "The World in 2050," last modified August 29, 2017, https://www.pwc.com/gx/en/issues/economy/the-world-in-2050.html.

4. TransResearch Consortium, "Relative Political Capacity Dataset," 2013, http://transresearchconsortium.com/.

5. A. F. K. Organski and Jacek Kugler, *The War Ledger* (Chicago: University of Chicago Press, 1980): 64–101. See also Jacek Kugler and Ronald L. Tammen, *The Performance of Nations* (Lanham, MD: Rowman & Littlefield, 2012).

6. TransResearch Consortium, "Relative Political Capacity Dataset."

7. Ibid.

8. Athina Tzemprin, Jugoslav Jozić, and Henry Lambaré, "The Middle East Cold War: Iran-Saudi Arabia and the Way Ahead," *Politička Misao* 52, nos. 4–5 (2015): 187–202.

9. "One Vote, One Man," *The Economist* 402, no. 8773 (February 25, 2012): 59.

10. Similarly, Brazil as the reluctant dominant power in Latin America is more interested in engaging Europe and United States than in the region.

11. Jonathan Marcus, "Israel's 'Air Strikes' in Sinai Show Its Growing Arab Ties," *BBC News*, February 5, 2018, https://www.bbc.com/news/world-middle-east -42950490.

12. Linah Alsaafin, "Abdel Fattah El-Sisi Narrowly Misses 100 Percent of Vote in Egypt," *Al Jazeera*, April 2, 2018, https://www.aljazeera.com/news/2018/04/abdel -fattah-el-sisi-narrowly-misses-100-percent-vote-egypt-180402112319879.html.

13. "Fluiten Sealing Systems for Gas Processing Plant," *World Pumps* no. 4 (April 2017).

14. Michael C. Horowitz and Philip B. K. Potter, "Allying to Kill: Terrorist Intergroup Cooperation and the Consequences for Lethality," *Journal of Conflict Resolution* 58, no. 2 (March 2014): 199–225.

15. Bashar Al-Assad, "Syria's President Speaks: A Conversation with Bashar Al-Assad," *Foreign Affairs* (March/April 2015), https://www.foreignaffairs.com/ interviews/2015-01-25/syrias-president-speaks.

16. Figure 8.2 source: The World Bank, "World Development Indicators," last modified March 27, 2016, http://documents.worldbank.org/curated/en/8053714 67990952829/World-development-indicators-2016.

17. Note that Turkey, Saudi Arabia, and Iran were deeply involved in the Syrian conflict before it became an international battleground for both the United States and Russia. Turkey and Saudi Arabia then played a less-visible role.

18. Oil production is a clear example. In June 2018, all twenty-four countries in the Organization of the Petroleum Exporting Countries (OPEC)+ group began negotiating an increase in production. The present global production is 32 million barrels/day and inventories seem to be back to typical levels after a period of excess surplus (World Oil Market Prospects for the Second Half of 2018). Russia wants to foster domestic investment and increase output by 1.5 million barrels/day. Iran opposes the increase in production, and Saudi Arabia and most other countries are willing to compromise, allowing an increase in production to between 300,000 and 600,000 barrels/day.

19. Organski and Kugler, *The War Ledger*, 90.

Chapter Nine

Middle East

Northern Tier

Ali Fisunoglu

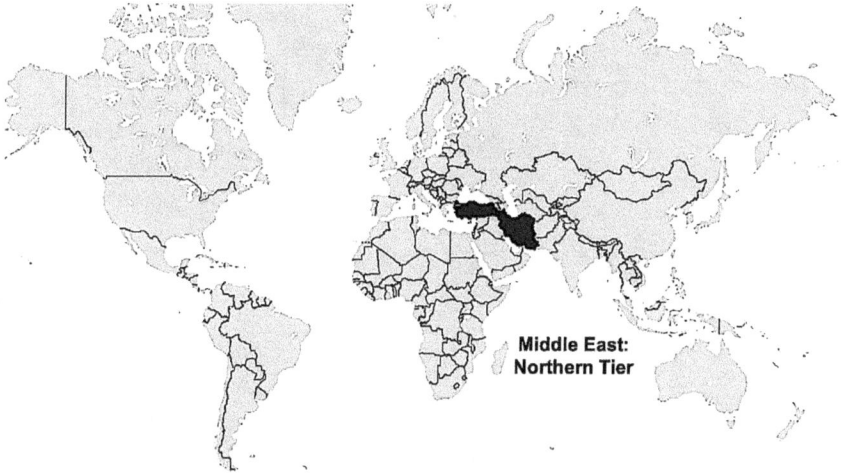

Middle East: Northern Tier Region

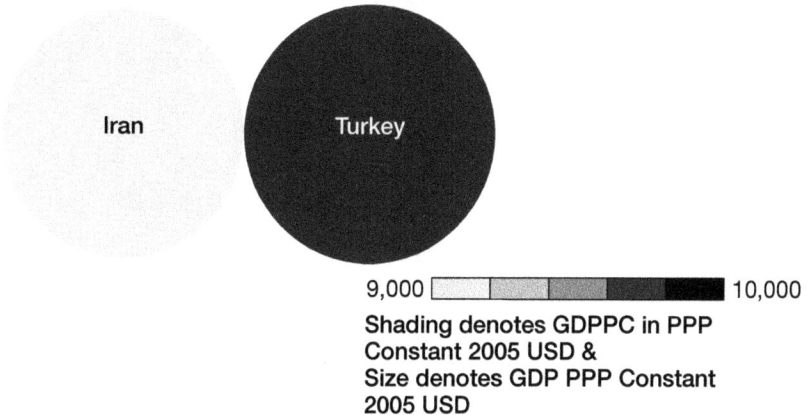

9,000 ▢▢▢▢▢ 10,000

Shading denotes GDPPC in PPP
Constant 2005 USD &
Size denotes GDP PPP Constant
2005 USD

Middle East: Northern Tier Hierarchy

In the Middle East, the Northern Tier hierarchy has long languished in the shadow of conflict.[1] Ominously, there is little evidence that this is changing. Israel, the economically most advanced society in this region, is no longer dominant, but after reaching an accommodation with Egypt, it remains capable of defending its existence because its neighbors are less-powerful Syria, Jordan, and Lebanon. This leaves Turkey and Iran as the main competitors in the Northern Tier region, with Saudi Arabia advising from the wings.

Consider the evidence in figure 9.1: Iraq—once a potential major competitor in the Middle East—acknowledged the superiority of Iran by settling the Iran-Iraq War of 1980–1988.[2] Further declines in Iraq's capabilities following the Gulf War in 1990–1991 served as a prelude to US intervention in 2003. Iraq, still dealing with the consequences of these events, can no longer

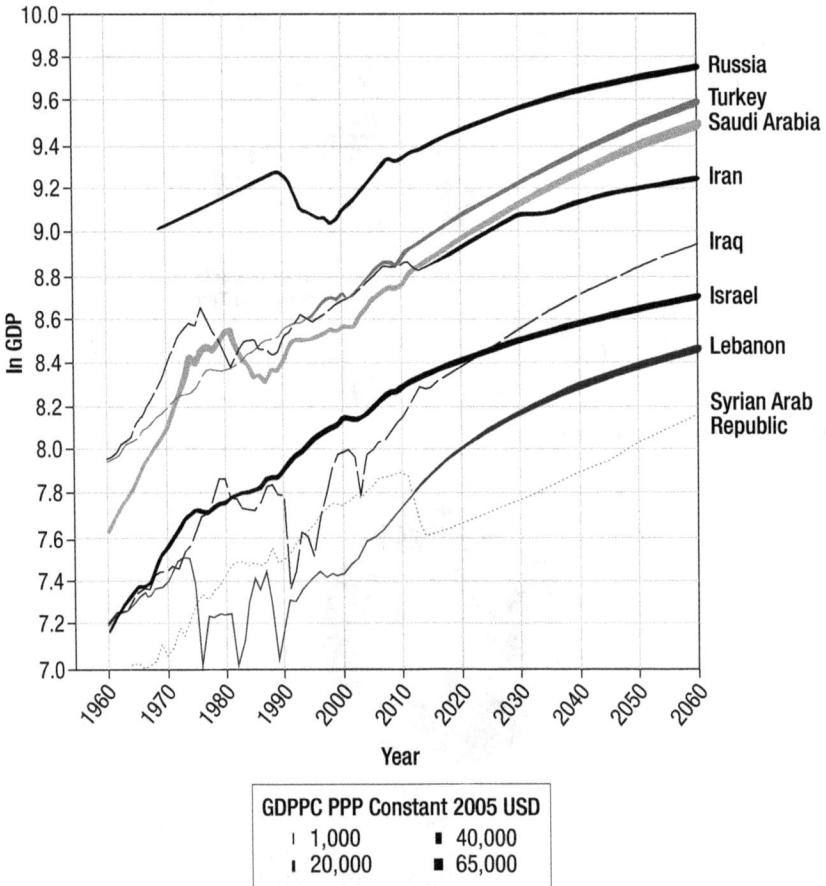

GDPPC PPP Constant 2005 USD	
ı 1,000	∎ 40,000
ı 20,000	∎ 65,000

Figure 9.1. Power Projections in the Middle East Northern Tier

compete with Iran because much of Sunni Iraq remains under the influence of local groups. A strong Kurdish minority seeks separation. Internal dissent now offers more significant challenges for Iraq than the external expansion on which Saddam Hussein was focused.

Saudi Arabia, also a relatively large state in the Middle East, lacks the population base to confront the two main giants. Saudi Arabia appears powerful on paper because its oil exports give its rulers considerable influence beyond the borders of their country. However, despite the fact that Saudi Arabia is considered a great power within the Middle East, it is not a potential challenger in the hierarchy of the Middle East.

Israel has been a central leader in the Middle East for the last sixty years. Despite its advanced economic status, Israel can no longer deploy sufficient boots on the ground to control even small neighbors like Lebanon or Syria. Israel's advanced military tactics and credible nuclear threat can hold at bay any current competitor, but its offensive actions are now limited and its relative decline in capabilities will continue.

Israel and Saudi Arabia, through alliances and financial connections to the United States and Europe, will continue to exert influence over regional affairs. But unless this coalition extends to include Egypt, which can provide the needed population, they will not be the central protagonists determining regional norms; nor will they be the key protagonists of the future. This position will rest with Turkey and Iran.

The United States is among the global giants that can still influence outcomes in the Middle East. The United States has been overcommitted to this area since September 11, 2001. Retrenchment is likely because its interest is waning after two Gulf wars. Moreover, the United States has continued to incur human and material costs as a result of the conflicts in Afghanistan, Syria, and Iraq. China has not made its position clear, but it seems unlikely that it will remain silent for long. Russia, despite its fall from Great Power status, has re-emerged as a major actor. But Russia's current relatively high level of interest and involvement are unlikely to be sustained. Russia is a limited power and is rapidly declining in relative terms. Moreover, it is increasingly overshadowed by China. In the Middle East, in any case, the emerging competition is between Iran and Turkey. That is the focus of this chapter.

ANALYSIS OF PENDING CONFLICTS

Since before World War II, the Middle East region has been characterized by confrontation and conflict. A considerable amount of friction was generated by the emergence of Israel as a new nation. The Arab-Israeli conflict has masked the quiet regional changes shifting dominance away from Israel and Iraq. Now attention centers on the Iran-Turkey regional hierarchy. These two countries present a classic case of what generated conflict when two nations are equal or near-equal in power and when either one or both are dissatisfied with their roles in the region.

The long and severe war between Iran and Iraq from 1980 to 1988 was caused in part by power parity and global interventions.[3] Following the short-term Iraqi occupation of Kuwait in 1990, Iraq was engulfed in two wars that directly involved the United States. The outcome of these asymmetric conflicts was devastating for Iraq. Likewise, the outcome of the Syrian civil war was altered by Russian intervention. These actions contributed to the rise of violent Jihadist militant groups tacitly supported by Iran.

As seen in figure 9.1, despite some economic difficulties, Turkey is the most powerful country in the region. It currently holds almost 50 percent of the total power of the region. Iran follows Turkey with approximately 35 percent, Iraq with about 10 percent, and Syria with less than 5 percent.

In addition to the actual power it holds, Turkey has also sustained higher growth rates in the last three decades than other countries in the hierarchy. Yet this trend does not guarantee that Turkey will keep its dominant position in the region, as Iran is a close second. Moreover, as the civil war in Syria shows, relations in the region are contingent on the actions of Great Powers. Whether it was the end of the Cold War or the decline of competitors that resulted in a dramatic leap for Turkey is less important than the ground truth that favors Turkey, as documented by the Turkish invasion of 2019.

Turkey's power alone is almost equal to the sum of Iran, Iraq, and Syria. This suggests that the Iran-Iraq-Syria-Turkey regional hierarchy is currently a transitional hierarchy,[4] which is intriguing because it confirms the prevalent views that Turkey and Iran are competing for regional dominance. In the recent past, Turkey was dominant. In fact, it exceeded the threshold of 20 percent considered to determine a dominated hierarchy. For a short period in the 1970s, Turkey's relative power was in decline due to Iran's high growth rates. Between 1972 and 1978, Iran briefly became the most powerful country in the region. However, Iran's high growth rate and, thus, the country's dominance in the region came to an end with the Iranian Revolution in 1979. After 1980, Turkey increased its level of dominance in the region partly due to international events (e.g., the Iran-Iraq War, sanctions against Iran, and the end of the Cold War with particular effects on Syria) and partly due to internal events (e.g., economic restructuring).[5]

In the early post–World War II period, Turkey did not act alone. As a founding member of North Atlantic Treaty Organization (NATO), it held a preponderant position in the Middle East, and its candidacy for entry into the European Union (EU) promised continued economic dominance and massive collective superiority over any potential contender in the region. But now EU candidacy is dormant, and Turkey has been embracing more traditional Islamic values, moving away from the secular values shared by leading EU nations.[6] Turkey is gradually shifting away from the Western alliance. Initiatives and coordination with Russia—temporarily affected by the war in Syria—are reducing previous tensions with that country. But at the same time, China is showing more interest in Iran.[7] This suggests that Turkey and Iran may clash in the future over leadership roles in the Middle East.

With the reimposition of sanctions on Iran, and ongoing domestic problems in Iraq, Syria, and Turkey, along with the instabilities in the global economy, there is ample opportunity for regional disputes pitting Turkey against Iran. Both sides enjoy support from opposing global powers, whose involvement may influence the outcome of their rivalry.

POTENTIAL SCENARIOS FOR THE FUTURE

Because of the frequent destabilizing events in the region, producing forecasts for the Middle East is particularly challenging. To mitigate uncertainty regarding the future, this chapter will review ten sets of distinct forecasts generated by International Futures[8] between 2009 and 2017, and extract low-, medium- (normal), and high-growth scenarios for each country.[9]

Using power transition logic, this chapter explores the future of the Iran-Turkey, Iraq-Turkey, and Syria-Turkey dyads. Of particular interest are differences in the interactions between power forecasts and the level of satisfaction. Figure 9.1 indicates the capability projections for the countries in this region. Turkey will remain the most powerful and dominant country in the region through 2030; it is expected to hold approximately half of the power in the region until then, followed closely by Iran, which will keep its relative power in the region at 35 percent. Iraq is expected to show a slight increase from 12 percent to 15 percent, and Syria is estimated to decline to around 2 percent.

No power transition is expected in the region for the next fifteen years under such growth projections. Still, there is a potential convergence between Iran and Turkey toward the latter half of the next decade in some scenarios.[10]

In particular, if Iran were to demonstrate three percentage points higher than average real growth rates than Turkey until 2030, these countries would come to a dangerous parity. This scenario is possible when Iran's performance is high and Turkey's performance is relatively low.

Considering current events in the region, Turkey is on the path for a lower equilibrium, whereas Iran is improving its potential, at least in the short run. Turkey's economic growth has been slowing since 2007. Between 2002 and 2006, Turkey's growth averaged an impressive 6 percent. However, this declined to a little above 3 percent between 2007 and 2015,[11] and it continues to remain around this level in the medium run.[12]

Increasing authoritarianism in Turkey, waning relations with the EU and its Western allies, increased domestic instability with frequent terrorist actions committed by the Islamic State of Iraq and Syria (ISIS) and Kurdistan Workers Party (Partiya Karkeren Kurdistan [PKK]), coupled with a failed coup attempt, the refugee crisis, and economic issues with trading partners are only some of the factors that pull Turkish growth down. The inflation and unemployment rates have also shown steep increases after 2015. Turkey also needs to carry out considerable political and economic reforms if it wants to achieve higher growth rates. Iran's growth is uncertain. Iran's relations with the United States suffered a blow since the Trump administration was sworn in. The United States withdrew from the Iran nuclear deal in May 2018 and reenacted sanctions in November 2018.[13] China, France, Germany, Russia, and the United Kingdom are trying to restore the nuclear deal. The Group of Seven (G7) meeting in 2019 provided no major developments.[14]

Orderliness, defined as the ratio of the dominant state's power to the total power of contenders in the region, is projected to decrease over the next twenty years. Iran and Iraq's gains play a major role in this decrease. Turkey will remain the most powerful state, but the region will become closer to being a disordered hierarchy. The decline in the orderliness of the hierarchy will be exacerbated if Iran's growth increases in line with the aforementioned discussion reflected in figure 9.2.[15]

Decreasing orderliness in the hierarchy means that Turkey would need to consider whether all sides are satisfied with the status quo. It might face greater difficulties in maintaining its preeminent role. Moreover, Turkey will have less time to deal with other global issues. For example, the decrease in the orderliness in this hierarchy might have implications for the attention that Turkey can give to other actors and topics, such as mediating in other regions. The next section turns to a discussion of Turkey-Iran relations followed by summaries of relations with other Middle East states.

Orderliness, 1950–2030

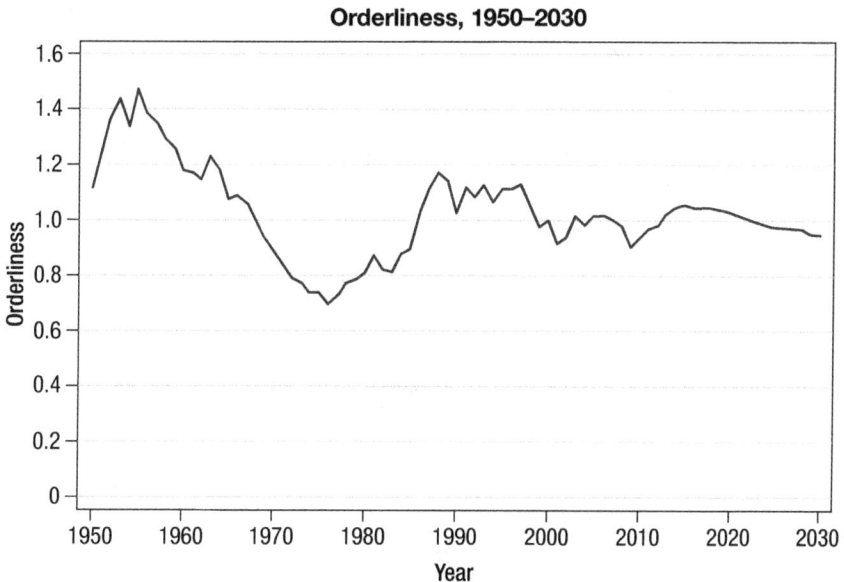

Figure 9.2. Orderliness of the Hierarchy, 1950–2030

RELATIONS OF TURKEY WITH IRAN

As shown in the previous figures, Iran is the second-most powerful country in the region. The projections suggest that Iran's power has been approaching that of Turkey, but there still is a sizable gap. The conflict-cooperation spectrum of Turkey and Iran is broad. Turkey and Iran are at odds but cooperate in many areas. One of the areas of cooperation is gas transport, which has been improving in recent years. After Russia, Iran has the second-largest natural gas resources in the world. Turkey has been buying large quantities of natural gas from Iran despite protests by the United States and remains interested in continuing to be a major player as an energy transit country between Iran and other parts of the world. The Turkish government has made it clear that it does not want its economic ties to Iran to vanish, but differences over actions in Syria have strained relations.

Another area of cooperation between Iran and Turkey is the fight against terrorism. Both Iran and Turkey provided assistance in the fight against ISIS in Syria. They also cooperate in their stance regarding Kurdish groups in the region. Turkey and Iran host the largest and second-largest Kurdish populations in the region, respectively,[16] and they both strongly oppose Kurdish separatism. Turkey views the Kurdish issue as a vital national security threat. For instance, on May 11, 2009, when Iranian soldiers were engaged in combat with terrorists, five mortar shells fell on Turkish soil,[17] but a diplomatic crisis did not materialize. The clear stance against the Kurdish aspirations to self-rule was demonstrated again during the Iraqi Kurdistan independence referendum in September 2017. Both Iran and Turkey opposed the referendum. To coordinate the efforts to prevent Kurdish secession, Turkish President Recep Tayyip Erdoğan visited Iran on October 4, 2017. Several days before Erdoğan's visit, the military chief of general staff of Turkey, Hulusi Akar, visited Tehran, the first-ever visit for a top Turkish military official since the 1979 Iran Revolution.[18]

The confrontational stance of previous decades has not diminished. In July 1999, Iran claimed that the Turkish Air Force had bombed targets around Piranshahr, an Iranian city about forty miles south of the border between the two countries. The Turkish side responded that its air force had bombed only PKK training camps in southeast Turkey and that there was no violation of Iranian air space. The Iranian side insisted that Turkey had bombed targets in Iran and added that there were no PKK camps in the region. Iran asserted that "Turkey deliberately attacked its border forces."[19]

Another event that raised tensions between the two countries took place when Iran disturbed Azerbaijan's oil explorations in the Caspian Sea and violated Azerbaijan air space. In response, Turkey's Chief of General Staff Hüseyin Kıvrıkoğlu visited Baku, bringing a squadron of F-16s and the Turkish Air Force aerobatic team, which performed an air show over Baku.[20] The 2020 confrontation over the future of Idlib that involves Turkey, Iran, and Russia further adds to a potential confrontation in this region.

This was a clear message to Iran that Turkey was the dominant country in the region and would not tolerate actions challenging its allies. Nonetheless, the stability of the borders and the lack of territorial pretensions at each other's expense is a considerable help. Moreover, the Justice and Development Party (JDP) leadership in Turkey appears to have built a good rapport with Iranian counterparts, and such crises are not seen as often.

At the same time, Turkey maintains an increasingly tenuous relationship with the United States, Israel, and the West.[21] This dual stance forces Turkey to juggle between its mixed good-bad neighbor policies vis-à-vis Iran and its relations with the West, specifically the United States. There is considerable fear in US circles that Iran is trying to destabilize Iraq's recovery. The United States, Turkey, and Iran supported different factions in Syria, which was interpreted as a contest for influence. It is also unclear whether the JDP rapport with Iranian representatives will continue once changes in governments take place. In the 1990s, the Iranian regime was seen as trying to destabilize the secular order in Turkey. The very different regimes in the two countries limit the extent of possible cooperation. In the past, the sides were engaged in increasing their zones of influence, especially in Central Asia.

Iran's nuclear program is the most serious threat to the stability of the region and to Iran-Turkey relations. Turkey has indicated that it wants the Middle East to be free of nuclear weapons, including those now held by Israel. Iranian acquisition of such weapons would alter the regional order and probably force Turkey to consider a nuclear option. The president of Turkey has underscored that Turkey wanted only to see Iran limit its nuclear program to peaceful uses. Supporting a pro-Iran stance in 2010, Prime Minister Erdoğan made it clear that he did not believe that Iran had a nuclear weapons program. To this end, Turkey, along with Brazil, went out of its way to facilitate an agreement being reached on Iran's nuclear program in 2010 that would be satisfactory to Iran, the United States, and other permanent members of the United Nations Security Council (UNSC). When this proposal was rejected, Brazil and Turkey were the only two countries voting against the UNSC resolution imposing further sanctions on Iran. This suggests that the possibility of Iran having a nuclear weapons program has not provoked any particular concern in Ankara. Turkey might be the most powerful actor within the hierarchy, but it often coordinates with Iran to maintain stability.

The Syrian war is a major challenge for the Iran-Turkey relationship. The long Syrian war was fought substantially by outsiders as much as by Syrians. Iran and Turkey both endeavored to increase their influence directly and indirectly by empowering proxies in the war zones. The Russian intervention dramatically increased their influence in the region and opened the door to Turkish aggressiveness.

Figure 9.3 displays the likelihood of cooperation and conflict between Iran and Turkey.[22] The baseline scenario, where both countries show normal growth patterns, paints a potentially peaceful future for the dyad. The power gap between these countries will remain significantly wide given anticipated levels of dissatisfaction. Turkey is expected to remain the dominant actor in the region and sustain relatively stable relations with Iraq. Enhanced cooperation is not foreseen, but conflict is not expected to emerge even when these regional contenders reach the limit of dissatisfaction with the status quo.

The peaceful interaction presented in figure 9.3 would be altered if Turkey does not dominate power relations. A significant potential for conflict emerges if Iran achieves high growth rates. Figure 9.4 shows a scenario where Turkey has normal growth rates and Iran has high growth rates. This would increase opportunity for conflict.[23] A second opportunity for conflict appears when Iran's power approaches parity and then overtakes Turkey. Cooperation is still possible if these two countries are satisfied with either

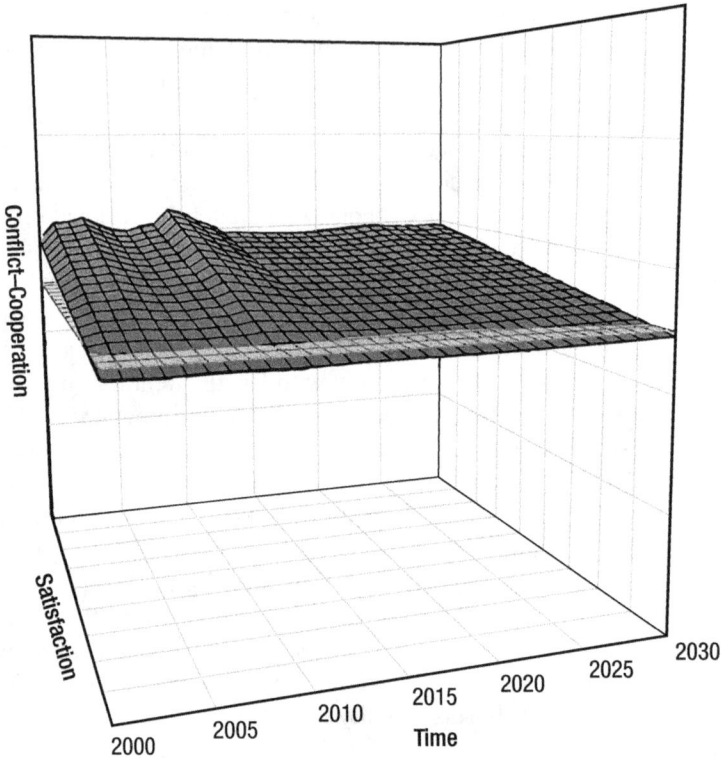

Figure 9.3. Forecasting Conflict and Cooperation, Iran-Turkey, 2000–2030 (Normal-Normal)

option, but the likelihood of conflict is notably higher when the countries are dissatisfied. Turkish leaders are seemingly aware that dissatisfaction can create severe problems, though the United States remains skeptical about such cooperative ventures.

The role of external powers is a common feature in the Middle East, and it profoundly affects the regional order.[24] Events in Israel, Syria, Iraq, and Saudi Arabia have been directly affected by US and Russian interventions. This analysis indicates that the primary recipient of external aid, Israel, will no longer dictate policy in the Middle East. The United States continues to have influence in the Middle East in certain situations, but this influence is waning because of the Trump administration's incoherent withdrawal strategy.

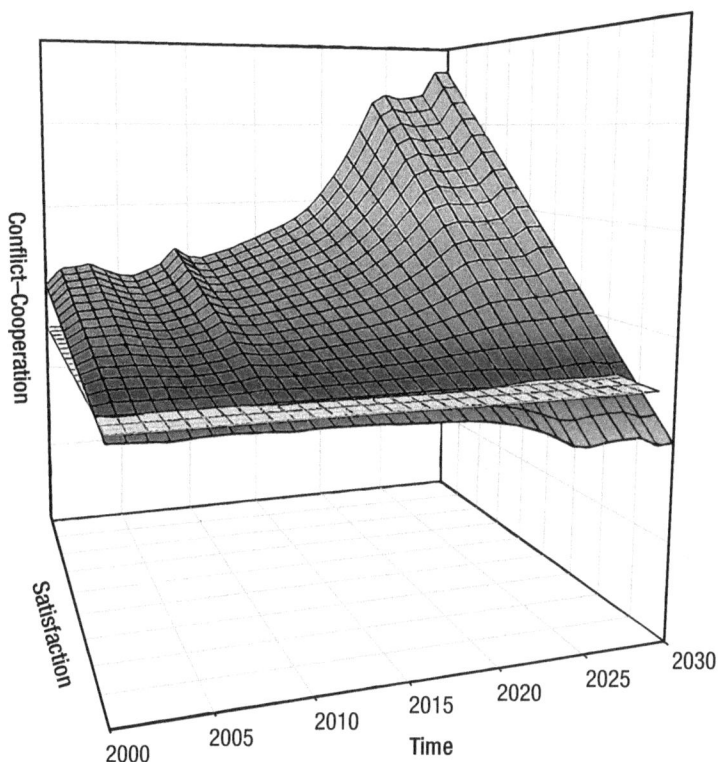

Figure 9.4. Forecasting Conflict and Cooperation, Iran-Turkey, 2000–2030 (High-Normal)

The one unifying element is Iran's interest in military nuclear capability, which does not appear to be in the interests of any country outside Iran. Israel has made it clear that a nuclear Iran is unacceptable. In the early 1980s, an Iraqi nuclear site was attacked by Iranian air strikes and then by Israeli air raids. A repetition of such behavior is unlikely but not outside the realm of possibility.

Regime change in Iran or Turkey could alter the regional status quo regardless of whether it occurs as a result of external pressure or domestic upheavals. However, regime changes are not necessarily a guarantee for enhanced cooperation. Overall, the problematic relations of these countries are an important matter affecting the region.

FUTURE CONFLICT AND COOPERATION

Iraq is no longer a powerful country in the Middle East hierarchy. Syria and other smaller nations do not have good prospects for making a leap to challenge the two dominant nations in the region, Iran and Turkey.

Assessments are distorted in part because Iraq's power is difficult to forecast, with its rich oil reserves combined with internal political uncertainties. If Iraq continues to muddle through economic and political difficulties, Turkey will remain the dominant nation in the region and will be able to preserve stability.

In sum, Iraq and Syria will remain medium powers in the region. The role of Israel will decline. Given recent history, it is unlikely that Iran will surpass Turkey and become the dominant country of this region before 2030.

The Great Powers may withdraw from involvement in the region given the costs of conflict or may become more involved as China and the United States compete for dominance in global politics. China's role, perhaps foreshadowed by its tacit consent to the Russian annexation of Crimea, may give us a clue as to what a new geopolitical world will look like in the Middle East.

Within this regional hierarchy, shifts in EU-Turkish relations could produce the most significant changes for the region. It is unlikely, given Brexit, that the EU and Turkey will reestablish negotiations on EU membership. If this occurs, it would lead to a Turkish-led stability in the region.

A key element here is the regional status quo, wherein Turkish foreign policy choices are particularly relevant. Turkey is likely to remain dominant, but it might be reaching the zenith of its superiority. Turkey's earlier foreign policy sought to have "zero problems" with its neighbors. That policy failed. Turkey is now transitioning to a governance system that allows for higher policy volatility, and it is responding to significant conflictual developments in the region.

This regional hierarchy has the potential to become even more unstable and disorderly in the future. The security of the region requires that Iran and Turkey work together. If they are assisted quietly by Saudi Arabia, Israel, and Egypt, the prospect for Middle East peace may unexpectedly improve. To make progress toward peace, these nations need to find common ground, as unlikely as this coalition seems on paper. But there are hints that some version of this unanticipated coalition may be possible. In the absence of such new developments, the Middle East will remain the site of episodic conflict.

NOTES

1. Global Map shows region contours. The hierarchy map shows the relative size of the top contenders in this region. Data are World Bank, "World Development Indicators," last modified March 27, 2016, http://documents.worldbank.org/curated/en/805371467990952829/World-development-indicators-2016.

2. Figure 9.1 source: World Bank, "World Development Indicators," last modified March 27, 2016, http://documents.worldbank.org/curated/en/805371467990952829/World-development-indicators-2016. Forecast based on growth rates adapted from PWC 20250, "The World in 2050," last modified August 29, 2017, https://www.pwc.com/gx/en/issues/economy/the-world-in-2050.html.

3. The Iran-Iraq War provides an interesting avenue to test power transition theory. In 1979, Iran was the more powerful country, but its power was decreasing while Iraqi power was increasing. Thus, there was a movement toward parity. Moreover, Iraq's relative political capacity was more than twice as high as Iran's (approximately 0.9 vs. 0.4 on average during war years). Jacek Kugler and Ronald L. Tammen, eds., *The Performance of Nations* (Lanham, MD: Rowman & Littlefield, 2012). Furthermore, one should factor in Iraqi overestimation of its abilities, the extent of the third-party support to Iraq, and the Iranian domestic upheaval.

4. Brian Efird, Jacek Kugler, and Gaspare Genna, "From War to Integration: Generalizing Power Transition Theory," *International Interactions* 29 (October 2003): 293–313, classified regional hierarchies as dominated hierarchies, transitional hierarchies, and disordered hierarchies. According to its definition, a *dominated hierarchy* exists if the relative power of the dominant country is at least 1.2 times as great as the total power of all contenders combined. If it is between 0.8 and 1.2 times, the hierarchy is a transitional hierarchy. Finally, if it is less than 0.8 times, it is a disordered hierarchy. Because the most powerful country in this hierarchy is Turkey, the ratio of Turkey's power to the sum of Iran, Iraq, and Syria's powers is used to find the orderliness of the hierarchy for this study.

5. The analysis of the military expenditures in this region showed that Turkey has spent the most in the post–Cold War era, while the differences between other nations are smaller. It should be noted that, for the whole period, specific events, such as Syria's conflict with Israel, Turkey's conflict with Cyprus, the Iran-Iraq War, and later Iraq's conflicts caused the values to display a high variance. Focusing only on the last decade, note that Iraq's values for 2002–2005 are missing and its pre-2002 and post-2005 values did not show a significant change, except for 2012–2015, where the country's military spending increased from around 3 percent of the gross domestic product (GDP) to up to 5 percent in 2015 because of the Iraq government's struggle with ISIS (World Bank, accessed on July 23, 2019, https://data.worldbank.org/). Whereas Turkey and Syria's expenditures are relatively stable, Iran has increased its military expenditures since 2004, which may signal increased dissatisfaction. Still, Iran's nominal expenditures are significantly below those of Turkey. Iran spent $10.2 billion in 2015 whereas Turkey spent $15.3 billion. Iran's military expenditures constituted 2.5 percent of its GDP in 2015, whereas Turkey's expenditures constituted

2.1 percent of its GDP in 2015 ("SIPRI Military Expenditure Database," SIPRI, last modified 2018, https://www.sipri.org/databases/milex).

6. Birol A. Yeşilada, Brian Efird, and Peter Noordijk, "Competition among Giants: A Look at How Future Enlargement of the European Union Could Affect Global Power Transition," *International Studies Review* 8, no. 4 (December 2006): 607–622.

7. Zhao Hong, "China's Dilemma on Iran: Between Energy Security and a Responsible Rising Power," *Journal of Contemporary China* 23, no. 87 (2014): 408–424.

8. Several other long-term GDP estimates were examined, including forecasts from Office of the Director of National Intelligence, "National Intelligence Council-Global Trends," last modified 2012, https://www.dni.gov/index.php?option=com_content&view=article&id=398&Itemid=776; USDA, "United States Department of Agriculture Economic Research Service," last modified 2015, https://www.ers.usda.gov/; Centre for Economics and Business Research, "Leading Economic Forecasts and Analysis," last modified 2017, https://cebr.com/, to check the accuracy of the International Monetary Fund's forecasts. The comparisons revealed that the "normal" forecasts for Turkey and Iran appeared to be consistent. However, most of the aforementioned sources provide inconsistent forecasts for Iraq and Syria. Thus, it is not possible to confidently confirm the accuracy of the forecasts for these two countries. In this chapter, the main interest is in the power measures.

9. The average compound annual growth rates between 2014 and 2030 for low, medium, and high scenarios, respectively, for Iran are 2.05 percent, 3.75 percent, 6.2 percent; for Iraq the rates are 2.6 percent, 5.2 percent, 7.8 percent; for Syria, 0.7 percent, 2.5 percent, 3.7 percent; and for Turkey, 3.3 percent, 3.9 percent, 4.5 percent.

10. There is a small probability of a transition between Iran and Iraq if Iraq's real growth rates will be on average 7 points higher than those of Iran. This high an interval between the growth rates of Iran and Iraq did not arise in any forecasts that were reviewed. Thus, this possibility is omitted.

11. Daron Acemoglu and Murat Ucer, "The Ups and Downs of Turkish Growth, 2002–2015: Political Dynamics, the European Union and the Institutional Slide," *The National Bureau of Economic Research* NBER Working Paper no. 21608 (October 2015).

12. OECD, "Developments in Individual OECD and Selected Non-Member Economies: Turkey," *OECD Economic Outlook* (2017), no. 1: 250–252.

13. The Guardian, "EU Powers Resist Calls for Iran Sanctions After Breach of Nuclear Deal," last modified July 1, 2019, https://www.theguardian.com/world/2019/jul/01/eu-powers-resist-calls-for-iran-sanctions-after-breach-of-nuclear-deal.

14. British Broadcasting Company, "G7 Summit: Trump would meet Iran's Rouhani if circumstances were right," last modified August 26, 2019, https://www.bbc.com/news/world-us-canada-49475744.

15. Figure 9.2 source: World Bank, "World Development Indicators," last modified March 27, 2016," http://documents.worldbank.org/curated/en/805371467990952829/World-development-indicators-2016. Forecast based on growth rates adapted from PWC 20250, "The World in 2050," last modified August 29, 2017, https://www.pwc.com/gx/en/issues/economy/the-world-in-2050.html.

16. Institut Kurde de Paris, "The Kurdish Population," accessed January 12, 2017, http://www.institutkurde.org/en/info/the-kurdish-population-1232551004.

17. Reuters, "Suspected Iranian shells hit Turkish soil-officials," last modified May 11, 2009, http://www.reuters.com/article/middleeastCrisis/idUSLB734832.

18. Hurriyet, "Üçlü tatbikat iddiası," last modified October 3, 2017, http://www.hurriyet.com.tr/uclu-tatbikat-iddiasi-40597780.

19. Robert Olson, "Turkey–Iran Relations, 1997 to 2000: The Kurdish and the Islamist Questions," *Third World Quarterly* 21, no. 5 (2000): 871–890.

20. Robert Olson, "Turkey-Iran Relations, 2000–2001: The Caspian, Azerbaijan, and the Kurds," *Middle East Policy Council* 9, no. 2 (Summer 2002): 111–129.

21. Olson, "Turkey–Iran Relations, 1997 to 2000."

22. Figure 9.3 source: Author's calculations using the International Futures modeling system, which relies on World Bank, "World Development Indicators," last modified March 27, 2016, http://documents.worldbank.org/curated/en/80537146 7990952829/World-development-indicators-2016.

23. Figure 9.4 source: Author's calculations using the International Futures modeling system, which relies on World Bank, "World Development Indicators," last modified March 27, 2016, http://documents.worldbank.org/curated/en/805371467990952829/World-development-indicators-2016.

24. Douglas Lemke, *Regions of War and Peace* (Cambridge: Cambridge University Press, 2002).

Chapter Ten

North Africa

Beyond the Arab Spring

Amir Bagherpour and Ashraf Singer

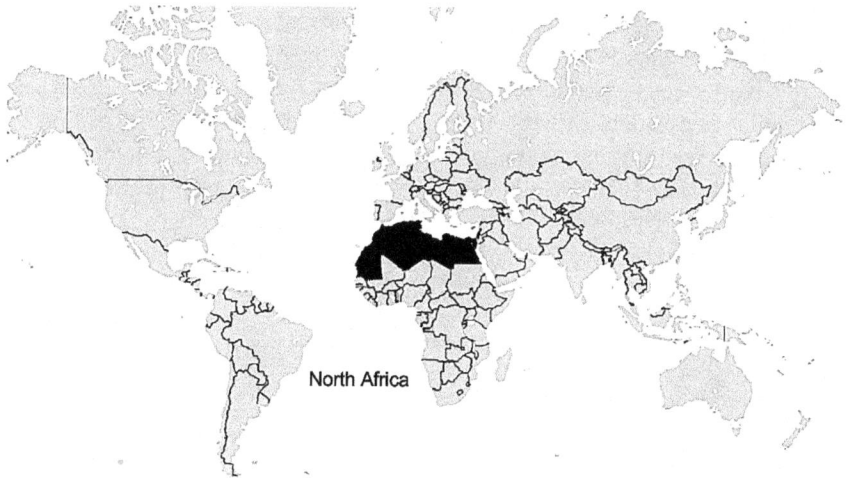

North Africa Region

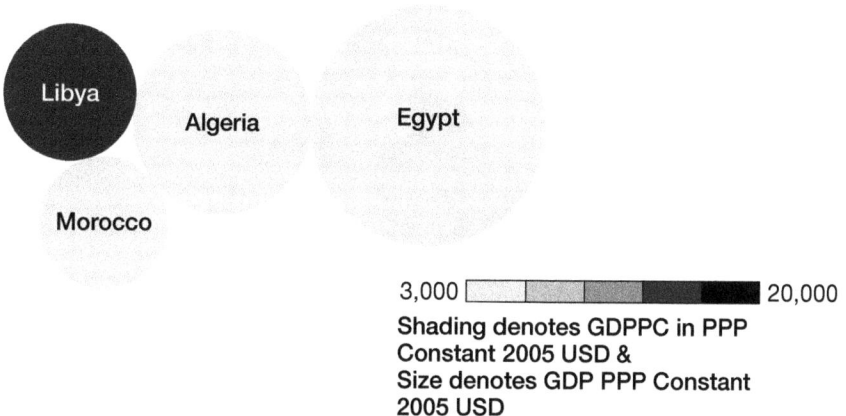

3,000 | 20,000

Shading denotes GDPPC in PPP
Constant 2005 USD &
Size denotes GDP PPP Constant
2005 USD

North Africa Hierarchy

TRANSITIONS IN NORTH AFRICA

This chapter assesses power dynamics in North African hierarchy.[1] The first objective analyzes the impact of changing standings in the regional hierarchical structures and levels of dissatisfaction to assess whether major conflicts or peace between states would be more likely. The second objective is to view the region through the lens of a stakeholder analysis. Previous work has demonstrated that by comparing the strength of a deeply dissatisfied opposition to the strength of the government one can anticipate the severity of conflicts.[2] That principle is applied to the North Africa region.

In North Africa, structural changes at the intrastate level forecast relative stability in the region. Figure 10.1 shows the reason for this assessment.[3] Egypt is the dominant country in the region and the only one likely to increase its relative power capabilities. The main reason for this expected growth is continuing population growth. Algeria, the second-most powerful nation in this region, is declining in relative terms despite significant hydrocarbon reserves. Libya and Tunisia are also expected to decline in the foreseeable future. The common thread is the weak political performance of governments. In addition, continuous competition will persist over how these countries should

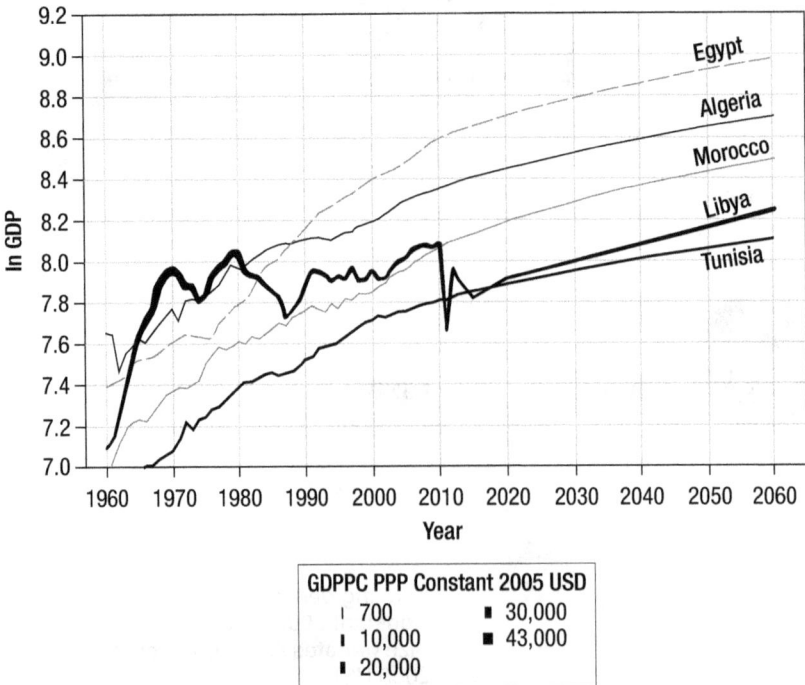

Figure 10.1.   **Relative Capabilities of North African Nations**

be governed and who should govern them. Morocco is the exception to this observation but faces potential instability on its southern border.

Regional relationships, either cooperative or competitive, are limited among North African states. The two largest nations, Egypt and Algeria, are separated by geographic distance across inhospitable desert terrain. Thus, opportunities for cooperation or conflict are curtailed because both lack power-projection capabilities outside their borders. Moreover, North African nations often are still focused economically and politically on relationships with European nations. Egypt is also heavily invested in extra-regional interactions with Israel and more recently with Sudan while engaging economically with Saudi Arabia. Algeria still focuses on France for much of its political and economic interests. Given these characteristics, very little regional coordination has taken place. Despite past historical attempts, most notably Gamal Abdel Nasser's framework for Pan-Arabism, integration is not a priority for these countries. This disinterest in regional integration may be contrasted with the potential strategic, economic, and political benefits of association with Europe.

This nonregional focus on the part of North African nations may be traced, in part, to the colonial legacy. Ironically, as a by-product, the postcolonial period evolved to the point that countries in this region have a stronger commitment to ex-colonial powers than to each other. Compared to other regional hierarchies treated in this volume, North Africa is more dependent on nations outside its own hierarchy and is less integrated economically within the region than North American and even Latin American nations, which also had colonial histories.

Because the largest two potentially dominant nations in this region, Egypt and Algeria, are poorly integrated and lack the capacity to interact directly, internal disputes within these states are more relevant than disagreements between neighbors. North Africa serves as a prime example of a region where interstate disputes are relatively insignificant compared to domestic problems.

After a period of relative stability, North Africa became the epicenter of the Arab Spring. In 2011, it experienced three major political upheavals in the span of a few months. These domestic convulsions led to the fall of Zine El Aedine Ben Ali in Tunisia, Hosni Mubarak in Egypt, and Muammar al-Qaddafi in Libya. Algeria avoided a change in government but is currently undergoing similar convulsions. Morocco is the exception to this pattern of internal turmoil but even that state faces potential instability on its southern border.

The domestic changes in government originating in North Africa inspired instability in the Arab world. Domestic changes encouraged Sunnis in Syria to rebel against their government. This created a violent dispute that drew in foreign militants and opportunistic governments that eventually devastated this society. A thwarted challenge to the government in Bahrain and turmoil in Saudi Arabia eventually contributed to produce the bitter civil war in Yemen.

As governments in these states weakened, emerging opposition groups found a power vacuum in which to operate and the unstable conditions they prefer. [4]

MEASURING INTERNAL DYNAMICS

To assess a state's internal dynamics,[5] the strength of each standing government is compared to the strength of the local rebel forces. In this chapter, subject matter experts (SMEs) assess the relative strength and policy of the government and opposition.[6]

Because insurgencies or rebellions rarely are recognized as legitimate parties at the onset of any civil war, the practicality of gaining empirical data on the size and strength of such an opposition is difficult. Simulations offer a novel alternative to capture power dynamics through expert surveys. In a simulation context, experts are asked to assess the relative power capabilities of opposition groups in comparison to standing governments and then report the position that each group adopts along with the importance they attach to such differences. Experts on each nation are asked to estimate the relative influence of powerful stakeholders, the position they adopt in support of or opposition to the government, and the importance each stakeholder attaches to its preferred outcome. This process provides a rough map of the effective influence of competing parties and allows an assessment of the power dynamics that lead to the rise or fall of governments. These data allow multiple dynamic assessments to be generated.[7]

The first assessment represents current conditions that can be empirically verified by contrasting the median outcome with existing reality. The second assessment reflects forecasts based on agent-based interactions where one assumes that each contender seeks to maximize net gains.[8] These assessments estimate the relative stability and instability of governments as they face an emerging or declining opposition. The results reported were obtained in 2017–2018, providing an overall assessment of the likely futures of the governments in the aftermath of the Arab Spring uprisings. In each case, our pre-event simulations accurately forecast the outcomes of conflict.

The first simulation is with Egypt, the dominant nation in the North Africa region. All simulation data were collected by the authors.

EGYPT

As the largest state in North Africa, Egypt continues to struggle with internal dissent. With a population of nearly 100 million, Egypt is by far the largest

Arab state. It is experiencing two ongoing insurgencies: one led by pro-Muslim Brotherhood groups across the country and another led by Islamic State of Iraq and Syria (ISIS)-inspired Islamists in the Sinai. Following the overthrow of President Mubarak and the subsequent coup overthrowing President Mohamed Morsi, who was supported by the Muslim Brotherhood, Egypt transitioned to a quasi-military-run government with the election of President Abdel Fattah el-Sisi.

Egypt has played a significant role in its geopolitical environment in the Arab world. It can do so based on its size, population, and economic and military strength. Originally, Egypt gained increasing importance during the Cold War. But the changes that have taken place in the Middle East since the 1990s have contributed to the erosion of Egypt's extra-regional position. Smaller but wealthier countries such as Saudi Arabia and the United Arab Emirates (UAE) are playing an increasingly more important role. Sudan, Egypt's neighbor to the south, fractured into two states despite Egypt's support for North Sudan and the preservation of union.

Since the reassertion of military power by General Abdel Fattah el-Sisi, economic reforms have been modest. Egypt continues to struggle under depressed economic conditions but a wary public seemingly prefers stability to the risks of another political upheaval.

To analyze systematically the evolution of power within all the states in North Africa and determine the relationship between such dynamics and civil war, this chapter uses the distribution of influence within the country using a simple scale, as shown in figure 10.2. At the left extreme are located domestic and foreign stakeholders that actively oppose the government and seek to replace the existing leadership. Next to these are actors that oppose the government passively but are unwilling to take direct action. On the extreme right of this scale are domestic or foreign actors that actively support the existing leadership. Passive supporters of the government are located to the left of the active groups. Domestic and foreign actors that are neutral fall in the middle of this distribution. The capabilities of stakeholders willing to support or oppose the government are indicated by the height of each grouping. This height is calculated by a simple multiplication of the size of each stakeholder multiplied by the importance that stakeholder attaches to the outcome.[9]

Figure 10.2 summarizes the general support for and opposition to the Sisi government in 2018. This representation should hold until major changes in the size or identity of the key players take place.

When the majority of the groups falls on the support side, confrontation is unlikely. When most of the groups are found in the opposition and particularly the active opposition, the government has a tenuous hold on power. When the relative size of the opposition and that of the government is at parity, consistent

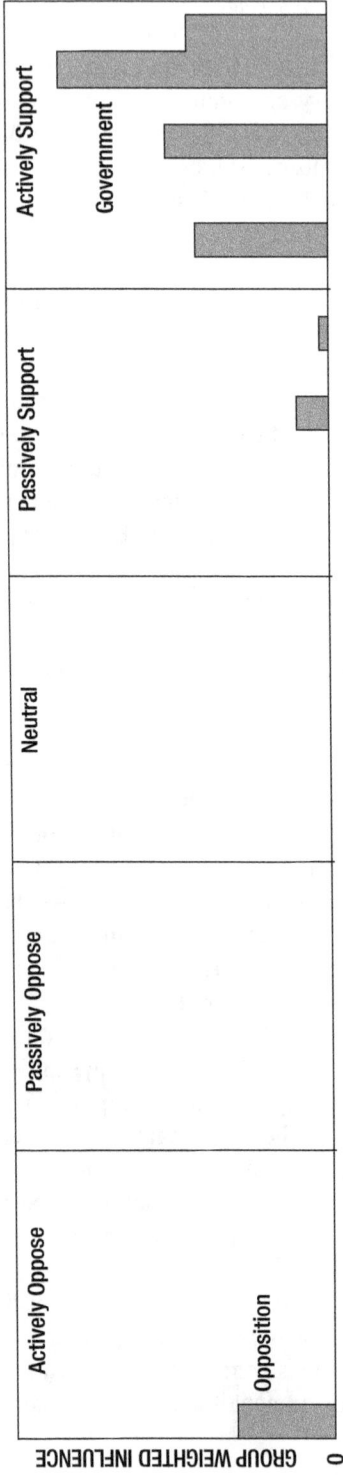

Figure 10.2.   Support for Government in Egypt, 2018

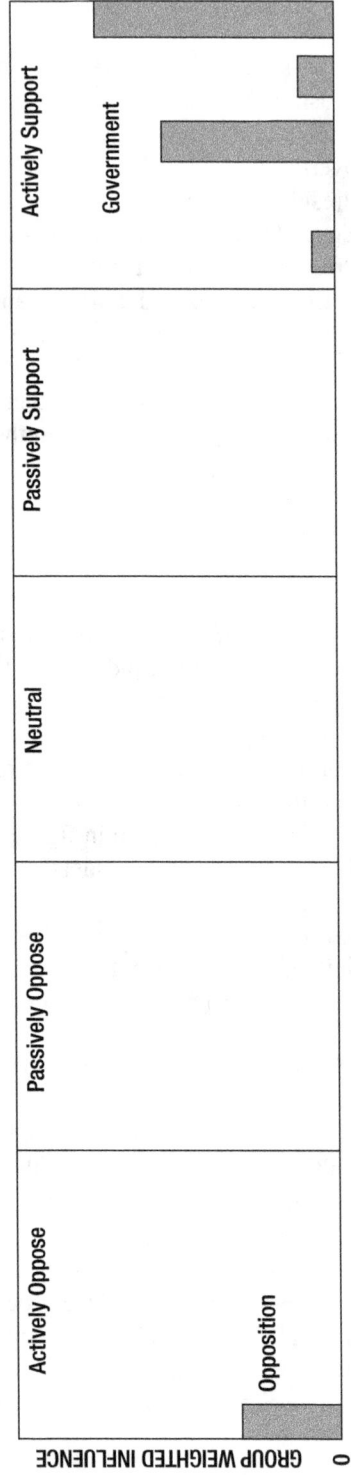

Figure 10.3.   Projected Support for Government in Egypt, 2018

with power transition postulates, civil war is likely. The intensity of the conflict is predicted by the distance between the contending parties.[10]

A forecast helps to understand the situation in Egypt. If conditions remain unchanged, the forecast indicates the anticipated outcome when all the contenders seek to maximize their net gains. But there can be unanticipated change such as foreign or domestic intervention, a leader assassination, or direct support for one side or the other by an outside power, as was the case in 2015, with Russia's intervention in Syria.

With regard to Egypt, the government of General Sisi has consolidated power while the opposition remains unchanged. Given the difference in capabilities, the government can no longer be challenged directly by the opposition led by the Muslim Brotherhood, and there is no room for accommodation. The distance between these contenders is extreme. The iron-fisted Sisi government will continue to confront the weaker but determined opposition. Conflict will persist.

There is strong support for the government from most of Egyptian society. Passive Sisi supporters are expected to become active supporters of the government. Support for the opposition, composed of the Muslim Brotherhood and Jihadist groups including Al Qaeda, ISIS, and Ansar Bayt al Maqdis, remains in place. But Egyptians seemingly prefer stability as a priority over the chaos they experienced in the eight years following the removal of Mubarak.

The persistence of a strong opposition suggests that insurgencies have been reduced in strength but remain active. Ongoing security threats are expected to continue. Currently, figure 10.3 suggests that opposition success remains highly unlikely because the contending factions are not united and individual groups have no chance to overthrow the Egyptian government. Thus, unless a major shift in relative influence takes place, comparable to the original Arab Spring, opposition groups will persist only as a destabilizing force that threatens public safety but not as an existential threat to the Sisi government.

In sum, Egypt is sharply divided between supporters and opponents of the government. Yet the government is preponderant and can impose stability. This creates an environment where terror tactics will likely continue, followed by responses from the government. However, given polarized sides, insurgencies are unlikely to be fully defeated in any near-term time horizon.[11]

ALGERIA

Algeria is the second-largest nation in North Africa. Its population in 2018 reached 42 million. With a gross domestic product (GDP) per capita almost twice that of Egypt and a stable base in hydrocarbons that Europeans seek, Algeria once was seen as a potential competitor to Egypt for regional dominance.

However, the lack of consistent growth led to a relative decline on Algeria's part and parity between these two Arab nations is no longer likely.

Internally, Algeria has had a troubled history with democracy. In the 1990s, the army annulled parliamentary elections won by the Islamists. This action prompted a violent eleven-year civil war, which claimed more than 100,000 lives. With the support of the military, President Abdelaziz Bouteflika ruled Algeria from April 1999 to April 2019. During the 2010 Arab Spring, Algeria avoided the popular uprising events experienced by neighboring nations.

Currently, Algeria faces potential instability. After guiding the country through a moderately stable postwar period, in March 2019 a seriously ill Bouteflika, at eighty-two years of age, failed in an attempt to run for reelection. This sparked mass demonstrations and his resignation. Currently there is an acting president as Algeria sorts out their succession crisis. Algeria's potential growth is unlikely to be realized in the absence of significant political and economic reforms.

Algerian data on stakeholders were collected in 2018 to determine the stability of the government in power. Results are presented in figure 10.4 with forecasts in figure 10.5.[12]

Algeria is the one state that remained undisturbed during the Arab Spring. This picture of a stable environment proved deceptive. The evolution of 2019 events (see figures 10.4 and 10.5) indicate that Bouteflika managed to survive because of his ability to maintain support from the military and domestic coalitions in addition to regional and international support from external players such as France.

The Algerian regime crafted after the Arab Spring made the military an essential part of its winning coalition. Analysis indicated that this stability would remain as long as President Bouteflika remained in power. Figure 10.5 correctly indicated that Algeria was stable. President Bouteflika fully consolidated his power and little or no change in the governing structure of Algeria took place. The government coalition was highly committed to stability of the regime. A weakness detected at the time of our analysis was that, without Bouteflika's presence, group solidity would dissipate. In 2019, Bouteflika attempted to remain in power despite ill health. This posture generated an unexpectedly strong opposition to his rule, reinvigorating aspirations similar to those observed during the Arab Spring.

Testing these effects in 2019 *prior* to the president's resignation demonstrated that the military would gain control over the government. Dissent is widespread but not integrated or strong enough to withstand determined action by the military establishment as shown in figure 10.6.

Our forecast shows that there will be a change of government in Algeria from Bouteflika to a military-supported candidate with little substantive alteration of

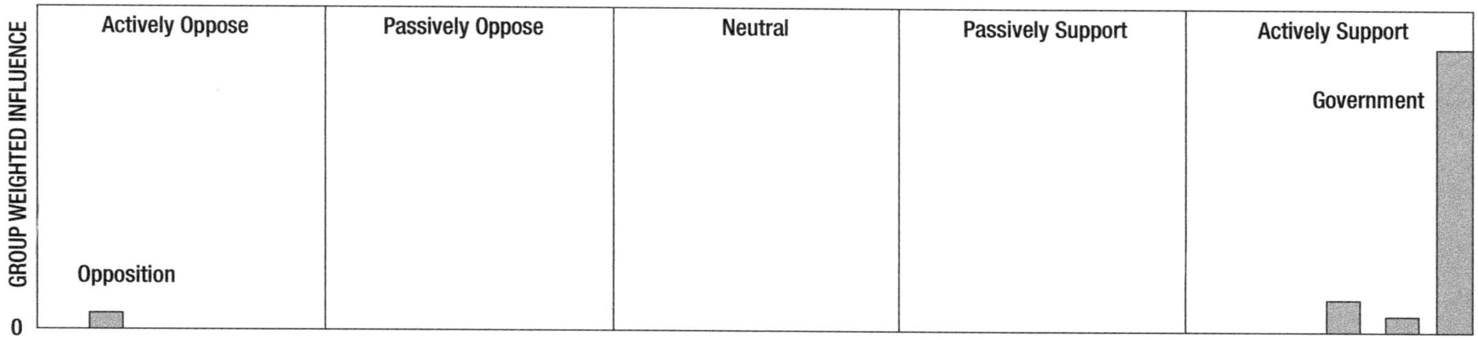
GROUP WEIGHTED INFLUENCE
0
Actively Oppose
Passively Oppose
Neutral
Passively Support
Actively Support
Opposition
Government
Figure 10.4. Support for Government in Algeria, 2018

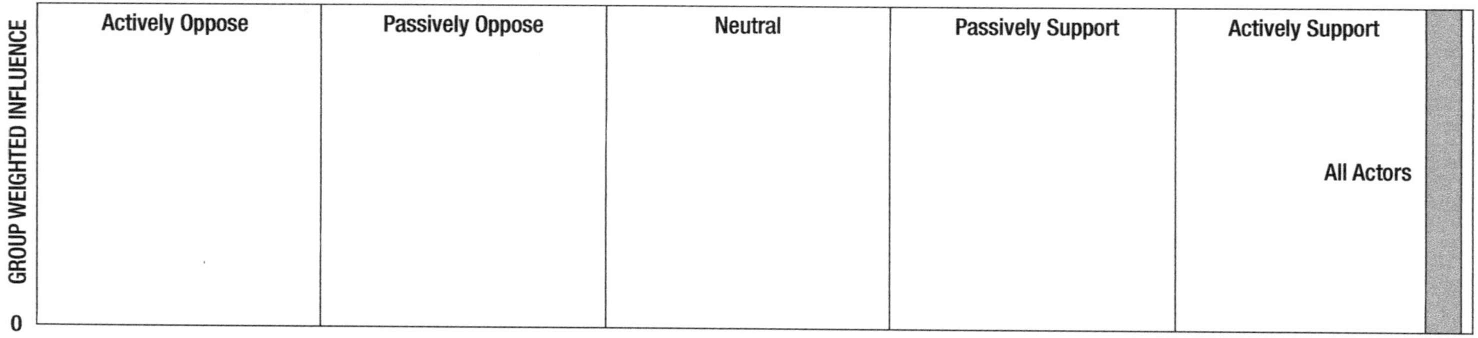
GROUP WEIGHTED INFLUENCE
0
Actively Oppose
Passively Oppose
Neutral
Passively Support
Actively Support
All Actors
Figure 10.5. Projected Support for Government in Algeria, 2018

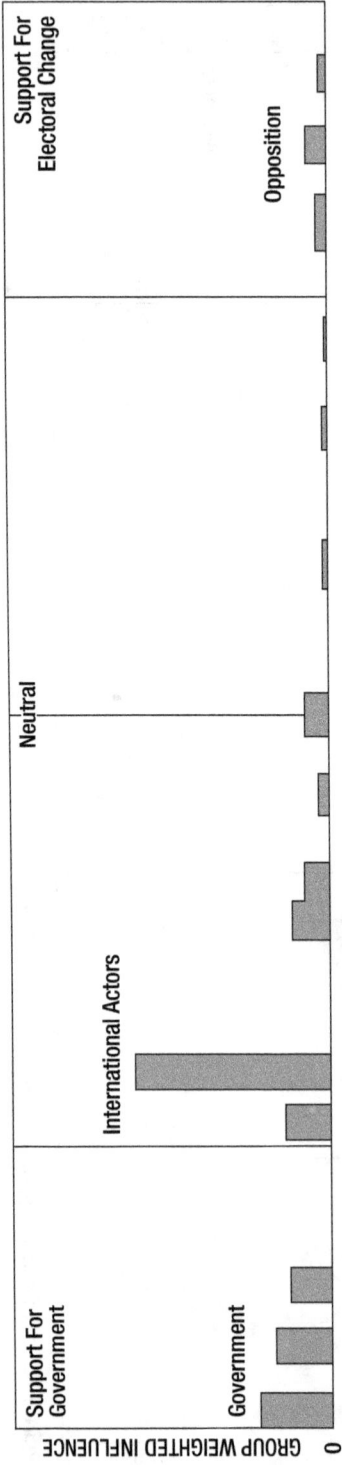

Figure 10.6. Support for Government in Algeria, 2019

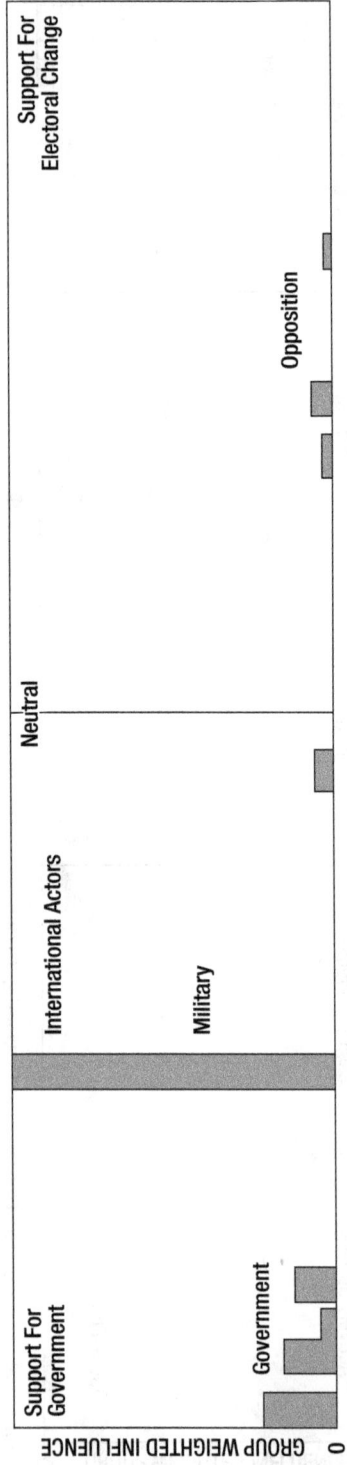

Figure 10.7. Projected Support for Government in Algeria, 2019

policy. The military will be the decisive voice in determining the successor, and there is little appetite for radical change in this powerful institution.

Results in figure 10.7 indicate that the military likely will take over the government and react to the protests in Algeria by creating a stable coalition in the aftermath. The army remains the preponderant force in Algeria. The military is expected to consolidate power and the opposition to slowly but surely dissipate. The demonstrations in March and April 2019 are not a sign that the military government is on the verge of falling from power as has happened in other Arab countries. The Algerian army can consolidate power and rely on allies abroad, especially France and Russia, which is seeking new opportunities in North Africa. That noted, Algeria will likely remain stable under a leadership directly influenced by the military.

LIBYA

Despite its international visibility and large oil deposits, Libya is a relatively small member of the North African region, with a population of less than 7 million. The regime of Qaddafi (1969–2010) was overthrown as a direct consequence of the Arab Spring. The Qaddafi regime intentionally avoided building centralized bureaucratic institutions and throughout its existence faced challenges from Western powers and occasional uprisings in remote areas within Libya.

Using the same simulation scale as presented in the analysis of Egypt and Algeria, the assessment of Libya is quite different. Figure 10.8 shows that contending groups are at parity in terms of influence, and no coalition manages to emerge as a preponderant entity.[13]

The forecast in figure 10.9 shows that groups diverge rather than converge over time. Four distinct factions now emerge that are similar in size.

The distribution of influence indicates that, consistent with classic conditions set by power transition, the conflicts in Libya will likely continue to escalate. The Government of National Accord (GNA), officially recognized by the United Nations and North Atlantic Treaty Organization (NATO) allies, continues to face significant resistance from militias and Islamist groups in Benghazi and Sirte. The Tripoli-based GNA has failed to consolidate its authority over allied factions consisting of Zintan militias and the Libyan National Army (LNA) led by Libyan general Khalifa Hafter. This loose coalition of forces will passively support the GNA but, if the opportunity exists, may even seek to seize control of the government. Their interests do not lie in sharing power but in seizing power.

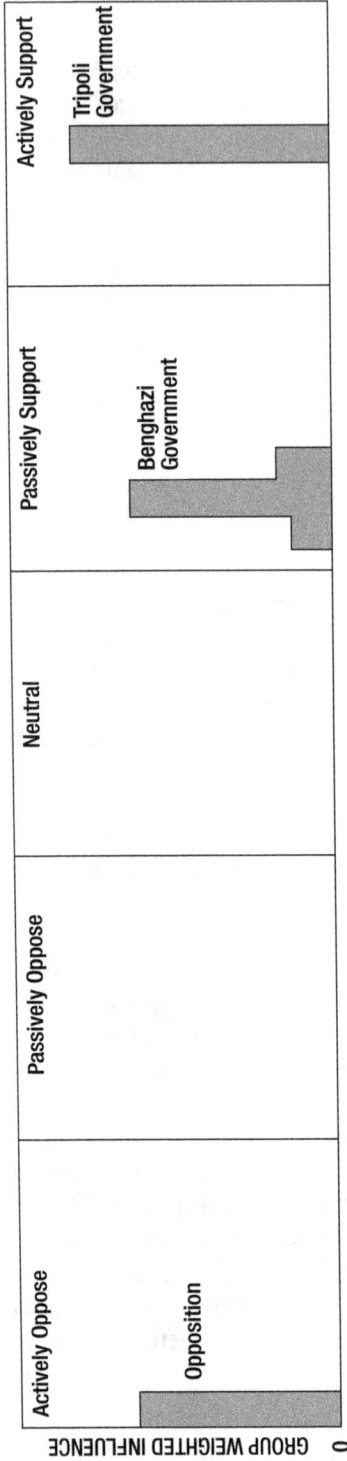

Figure 10.8. Support for Government in Libya, 2018

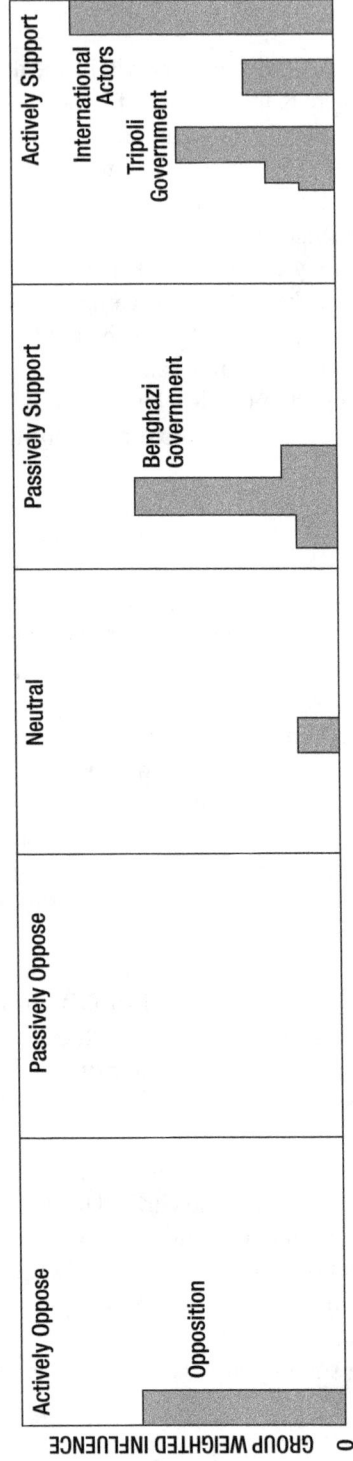

Figure 10.9. Projected Support for Government in Libya, 2018

Projections indicate that Libya's leadership will remain fragmented between the Islamist-led faction in Benghazi and Sirte and less-extreme but poorly consolidated forces in Tripoli and Misrata. Current actors and groups include militias in Tripoli, the Special Deterrence Force, and Misrata militias, each of which will seek to exploit their own interests despite the interests of virtually all other factions. Islamists in Benghazi and Sirte will continue to resist the GNA, while Zintan-based and Haftar-led forces will fail to support the officially recognized government except as is advantageous to their interests.[14] Given the relative military parity among these groups, it is likely that conflict will be consistent and indecisive.

Because of the relative parity and distance between opposing factions, conflict will continue in Libya because of gridlock. In the absence of a preponderant coalition, Libya is expected to remain in limbo between crisis and war for the foreseeable future. The emergence of a preponderant grouping, by cooperation or imposition, is required to reassert stability.

TUNISIA

Tunisia is a relatively small society in North Africa with 11 million people. Following the overthrow of dictator Zine El Abidine Ben Ali in early 2011, Tunisia has proven to be a relatively rare success story in North Africa and the Middle East after the Arab Spring. Tunisia's newly elected government is the only party democracy that continues to avoid the major conflicts plaguing its neighbors. Tunisia's transitional government has made commendable progress in drafting the Transitional Justice Act in a comprehensive and rational manner. Of the twelve members of the independent commission charged with drafting the law, only two are members of the Ministry of Justice, and the other ten are from various civil society organizations. The mission of these members is to measure public opinion by talking to people around the country and getting to know what the victims of Ben Ali's dictatorship want and what their expectations of the transitional justice process are. However, stability is not certain. Tunisia is religiously, linguistically, and ethnically homogenous. Its population is 98 percent Sunni, and citizens have strong ties to the Tunisian diaspora in countries such as France, Italy, and Libya.

Tunisia's case has distinguished itself in two areas: the proper management of the transition process and a rational and methodological approach. The late Tunisian President Habib Bourguiba ruled between 1957 and 1987, building a network of modern, centralized institutions. Tunisia lacks a precise segregation of ethnic, tribal, or religious sectarianism that is so divisive in other countries. The Renaissance Party's view of Egypt differs greatly from the Muslim Brotherhood's view of that country. Brotherhood leaders suffered decades of systematic repression and marginalization within Egypt. It can be said that their political agenda was largely formed in the jails of the regime. On the other hand, the leaders of the Renaissance Party spent the years of Ben Ali's rule in exile. The Renaissance Party leader Rashid Ghannouchi was in London from 1991 to 2011. Several senior party figures were also exiled there. This period of time had a clear impact on the modernization of the political ideology of the Renaissance Party and prompted it to adopt a more inclusive and peaceful model of reconciliation. The Tunisian army is professional and committed to non-interference in politics and respect for republican rule. The army, however, played a decisive role in the overthrow of Ben Ali and the subsequent transitional period. It was effective in this role partly because of its relative abstention from Tunisian politics.

Tunisia faces a risky polarization in the widening gap between secular liberals and hardline Islamists. Tunisia's secularism is energetic and unmatched in the Arab world. Under Bourguiba and Ben Ali, Tunisia was the only Arab country to ban headscarves in state institutions. However, Tunisia's Jihadists demand a purely religious state and have expressed their willingness to attack cultural activities they consider non-Islamic. Thus, Tunisia may be contrasted with Egypt, where consensus was reached regarding Islam as the religion of the state. In Tunisia, the vast distance between these two cultural extremes makes it difficult for the two groups to agree on a common vision of the state.

Tunisians built not only a new set of state institutions but also a culture of accountability and the rule of law. This is how Tunisia will be able to engage the participation of pre-revolutionary figures in political life, including Sibsi and Kamal Marjane; in their lifetime, Tunisia will change for the better. Tunisia has built a stable, comprehensive, and rule-based state that allows for broad reconciliation and real development in Tunisian society.

Using the same scale as presented in the analysis of the previous three North African states, the assessment of Tunisia shows that the government has successfully co-opted opposing coalitions to support its policies. Figure 10.10 shows that influential factions have moved to support or passively support the government and no major outliers remain. Such shifts augur well for a stable government not directly threatened by internal dissent.[15]

Despite concerns about the flow of foreign fighters and recruitment by ISIS, our simulations suggest that Tunisia is relatively stable as seen in figure 10.11. Opposition to the current government in Tunisia is expected to decrease slightly as major groups increasingly support the government. The indifferent or small opponents are not extreme, but their support for the government will likely not increase. At the time of our simulation there was

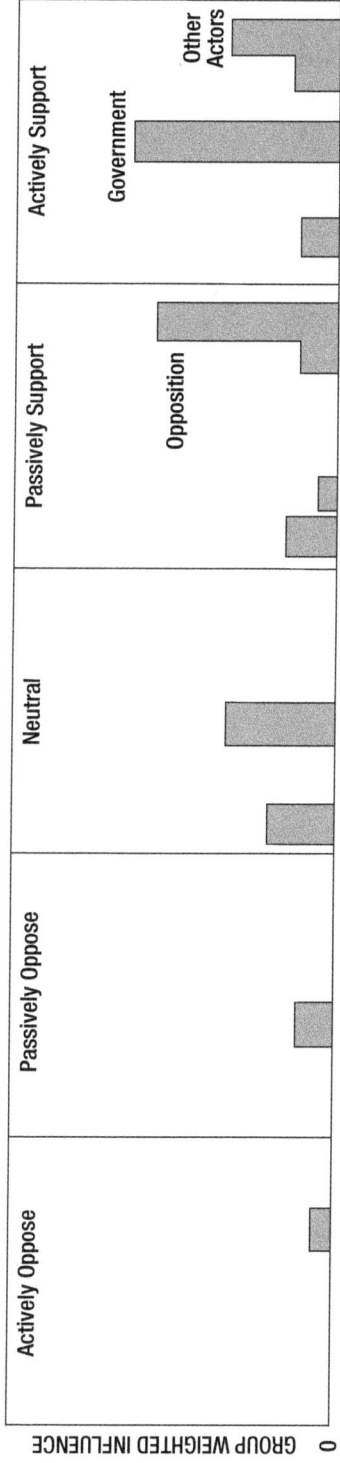

GROUP WEIGHTED INFLUENCE   0

Figure 10.10.   Support for Government in Tunisia, 2018

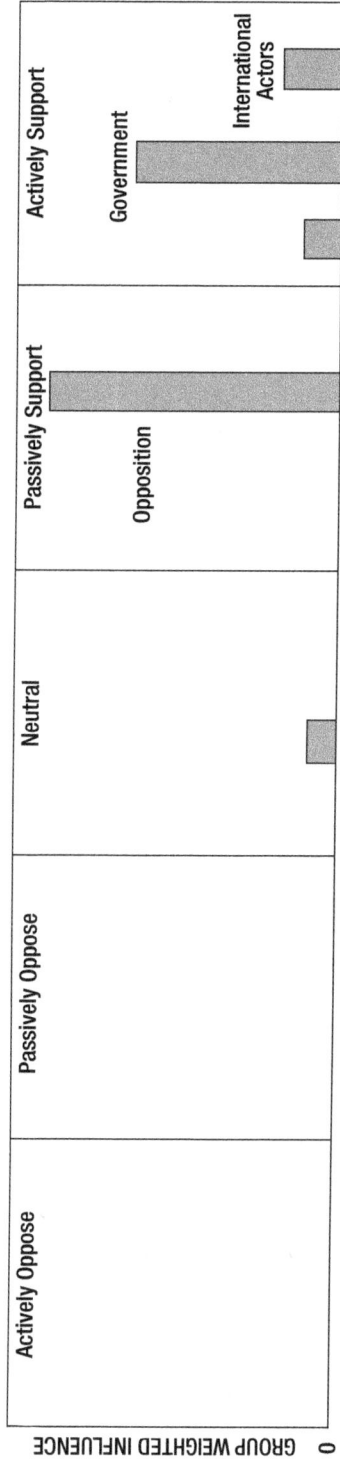

GROUP WEIGHTED INFLUENCE   0

Figure 10.11.   Projected Support for Government in Tunisia, 2018

little to no active opposition. All groups passively opposed to the government reduce their opposition, but active support does not increase substantially.[16]

A concern not captured in this scale comes from external excursions. Over the past few years, Tunisia's government and media have promoted anti-Assad postures. Because of low income and commitment to Sunni leadership, Tunisia was the largest supplier of ISIS fighters both in absolute terms (with at least 6,500 fighters) and in per capita terms (with 571.4 foreign fighters per every million Tunisian citizens). Now that the crisis in Syria is winding down, many of these radicalized fighters will return to Tunisia, posing a potential problem for the relatively calm and democratic state. The threat of instability prompted by ISIS and new extreme Islamist groups may emerge with little warning.

Despite such concerns, the picture emerging from Tunisia is one of stability, as the government is slightly preponderant over the opposition that—unlike in other neighboring states—is satisfied and rather supportive of government policies.

MOROCCO

Morocco is a relatively large member of the North African region with a population of about 35 million people in 2018. It is the most stable country in North Africa. Morocco's income at about US $3000 per capita falls between that of Egypt and Algeria. Although it has had a history of internal conflict, it has not experienced any of the instability observed in the 2010 Arab Spring and subsequent years as seen in figure 10.12.

Analysis based on the same structures used for previous nations indicates that stable conditions will persist as shown in figure 10.13.[17] The government is preponderant in this region and only a very small ISIS group—capable of terrorist acts—opposes the government. Opposition parties are supportive of the government.

This forecast suggests that there will be little or no opposition to the government in Morocco. Although Morocco has grassroots Islamists and an ISIS presence, the threat is extremely low and is declining. Morocco is very stable.[18]

One source of conflict, not considered here, is Morocco's occupation of the Western Sahara. The Western Sahara, an ex-colony of Spain originally partitioned between Morocco and Mauritania, has been occupied by Morocco's army since 1987. Western Sahara is on the list of United Nations Non-Self-Governing Territories and a source of tensions between Algeria and Morocco. The African Union has given the Sahrawi Arab Democratic Republic full recognition and accepted it as a member state, which has led Morocco to

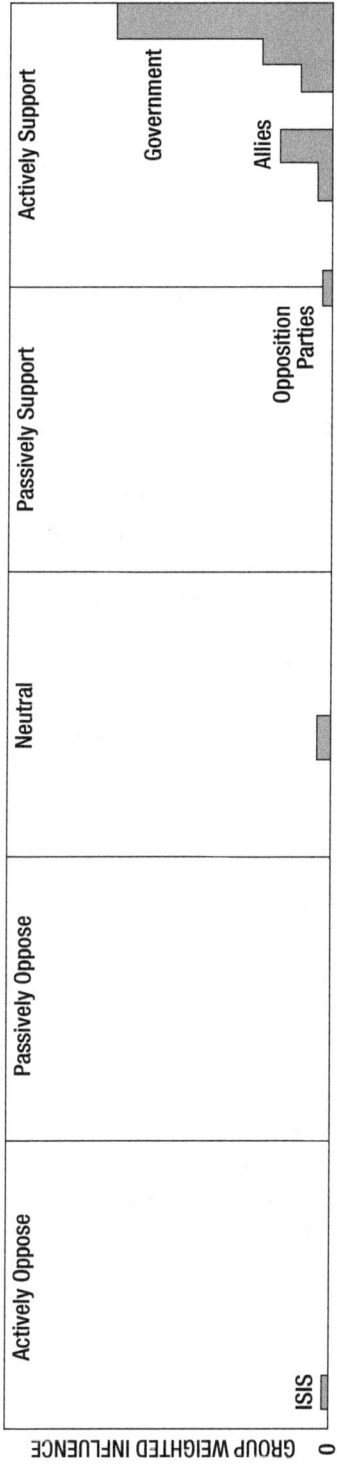

Figure 10.12. Support for Government in Morocco, 2018

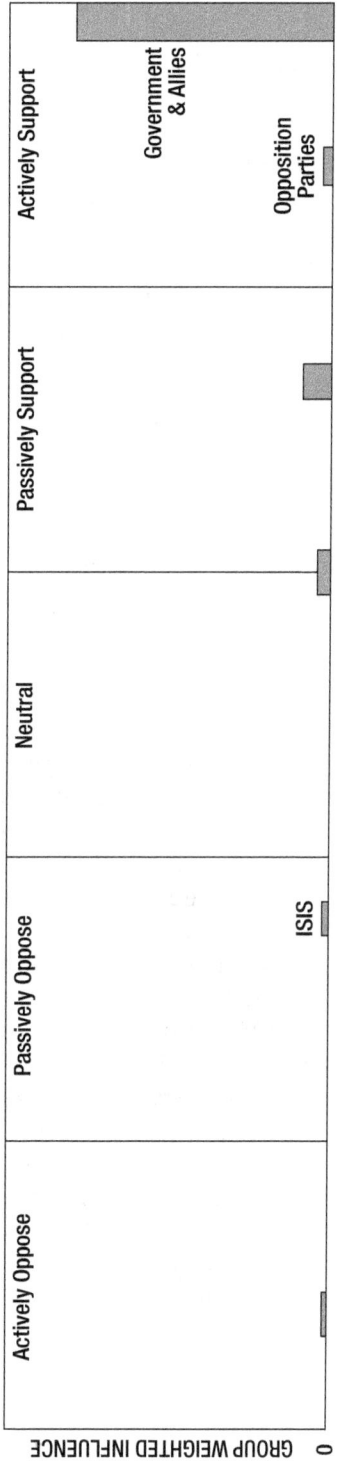

Figure 10.13. Projected Support for Government in Morocco, 2018

leave the union. The Polisario Front is seeking independence and has threatened to return to armed hostilities unless a settlement is achieved. Talks were renewed in late 2018 after the United States pushed to make the continued presence of United Nations (UN) peacekeeping forces in the region contingent on progress toward settling the dispute. Although not likely, this dispute could escalate into a regional confrontation between Algeria and Morocco.

Within Morocco, the power structures investigated are once more consistent with the power transition perspective. Satisfied groups supportive of a dominating government maintain stability in the country.

FUTURE CONFLICT AND COOPERATION

The North African region tends to look north rather than west or east. Its conflicts are internal rather than external. It has a preponderant power, Egypt, that does not act like one. Pan-Arab cooperation has not emerged, largely because these societies are weak and prone to internal dissent. Egypt, the likely leader of any integration movement, has been focused on the Middle East region and Israel and, to a lesser degree, on Sudan's partition in the sub-Saharan region. Neighbors within North Africa have been overlooked. Libya's weak attempt to unify the Arab world and much of Africa under Qaddafi did not get anywhere. Perhaps confrontations with the United States and Europe vitiated all such efforts. Most important, North Africa still looks to Europe far more than to neighbors for trade, technology, and investments. Given these circumstances, the dangers of interstate war in North Africa are low but so are those for integration despite a common culture and religion.

Analysis indicates that the most serious threats to this region have been and continue to be civil wars. Analysis of the period after the Arab Spring shows that Morocco and, to a large degree, Tunisia have retained stable governments. The previously stable Algeria is facing limited domestic dissent coupled with leadership change. Egypt has reestablished, after a short democratic experiment, a military-supported autocracy while opposition is brewing in the Sinai. Libya is undergoing a protracted civil war with no end in sight.

North Africa remains fragmented and isolated. Nations there sometimes are pushed and pulled by the winds of change, but often they return to the comfort of stability. Many of the North African internal conflicts can be understood according to the same rules that govern intrastate conflict. Power parity of opposing competitive groups stimulates long and bitter conflict. Governments and coalitions with substantial advantages in power resources maintain the peace.

NOTES

1. Global Map shows region contours. The hierarchy map shows the relative size of the top contenders in this region. Data are World Bank, "World Development Indicators," last modified March 27, 2016, http://documents.worldbank.org/curated/en/805371467990952829/World-development-indicators-2016.

2. Michelle Benson, Dimitry Panasevich, Andy Hira, and Jacek Kugler, "Violence and Political Capacity," in *Political Capacity & Economic Behavior,* eds. Marina Arbetman and Jacek Kugler (Boulder: Westview Press, 1997); Michelle Benson and Jacek Kugler, "Power Parity, Democracy and the Severity of Internal Violence," *Journal of Conflict Resolution* 42, no. 2 (1998).

3. Figure 10.1 source: World Bank, "World Development Indicators," last modified March 27, 2016, http://documents.worldbank.org/curated/en/805371467990952829/World-development-indicators-2016. Forecast based on growth rates adapted from PWC 20250, "The World in 2050," last modified August 29, 2017, https://www.pwc.com/gx/en/issues/economy/the-world-in-2050.html.

4. Jacek Kugler, Amir Bagherpour, Mark Abdollahian, and Ashraf Singer, "Pathways to Stability for Transition Governments in the Middle East and North Africa," *Asian Politics and Policy* 7, no. 1 (2015): 5–38.

5. Time measure of power chosen in this book is gross domestic product (GDP) that reflects the size of populations and the productivity of such populations. Alternatively, the Correlates of War project proposed a CINC measure that gives equal weight to two indicators each of industrial, population, and military capabilities, adds these, and divides them by the number of indicators.

6. Successful efforts to measure the strength of the opposition used internal assessments of North Vietnam capabilities during that war. Alternate substitutive measures in determining the strength of an opposition's material resources proposed by Marina Arbetman Rabinowitz examine the size of the black market related to a rebel group's necessary need for capital and tangible resources. Marina Arbetman and Jacek Kugler, *Political Capacity and Economic Behavior* (Boulder: Westview Press, 1997). Yet these do not directly capture the size, composition, or military and political capabilities of the opposing forces.

7. Arshin Adib-Moghaddam, *On the Arab Revolts and the Iranian Revolution: Power and Resistance Today* (London: Bloomsbury, 2013).

8. For a detailed description of the method used please see Mark Abdollahian, Jaehoon Lee, Zining Yang, and Khaled Eid, "The Future of Korea's Trade and Business Portfolio in North Africa: A Deep Horizon Political Economy Scan of Algeria, Morocco and Tunisia," *Korea Institute for International Economic Policy* 16, no. 11 (2016). Senturion Inc. graciously authorized the use of forecasts in this analysis.

9. The disposition of support by domestic and foreign actors reflects the assessments of subject matter experts regarding the position that actors with varying level of influence adopt at a given point in time. The projected outcome reflects the anticipated shifts of these actors using Senturion, an agent-based model designed to determine the most likely positions that competitors will adopt in the future. Senturion

Inc. provided some of the data and allowed the use of their model for these forecasts and assessments.

10. Final results from Leila Fadel confirm Islamists winners in Egypt's elections.

11. Tests for exogenous and endogenous error were conducted along with statistical robustness test on all inputs. The outcome was robust. The median outcome is active support for Sisi in forty of forty simulations that alter positions randomly.

12. Robustness using simulated forty alternative futures at ±25-point variance show results are strong. The median indicates active support for the Bouteflika government in all 40/40 alternative futures.

13. Robustness using simulated forty alternative futures at ±25-point variance shows results are robust. The median indicates mixed active support for the government in all 40/40 alternative futures.

14. Robustness test on all inputs using simulated forty random alternative futures with ±25-point variance shows the median that remains at active support for the government of national accord (GNA) government (37/40 alternative futures 92.5 percent). Libyan National Army forces that are passively in support of the GNA will not shift for or against the government.

15. Robustness using simulated forty alternative futures at ±25-point variance shows that results are robust. The median indicates support for the government in all 40/40 alternative futures.

16. Robustness test using forty alternative futures simulations with ±25-point variance under normal distribution shows highly robust active and passive support for the government.

17. Figure 10.13 source: World Bank, "World Development Indicators," last modified March 27, 2016, http://documents.worldbank.org/curated/en/80537146799095 2829/World-development-indicators-2016.

18. Robustness test with simulated forty alternative futures at ±25-point variance under normal distribution shows the results presented are highly robust. Active support for the current government in all 40/40 alternative futures emerges.

Chapter Eleven

Sub-Saharan Africa

Civil Strife

Nicholas M. Coulombe and Kristin Johnson

Sub-Saharan Africa

Sub-Saharan Africa Region

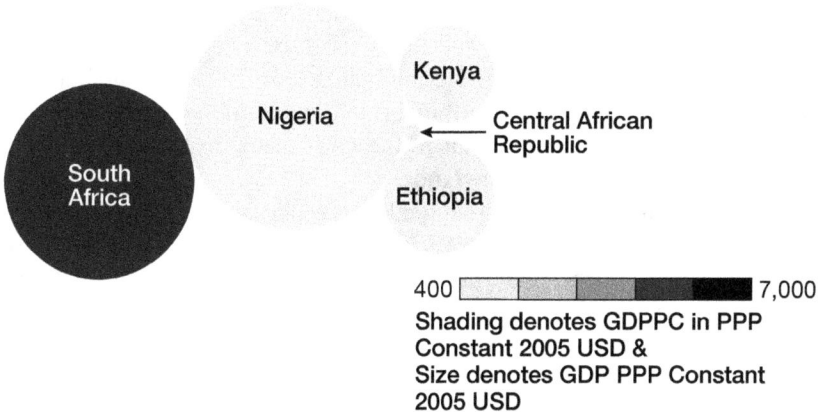

Kenya

Nigeria

Central African Republic

South Africa

Ethiopia

400 ▭▬▬▬ 7,000
Shading denotes GDPPC in PPP Constant 2005 USD & Size denotes GDP PPP Constant 2005 USD

Sub-Saharan Africa Hierarchy

LOCALIZED CONFLICT

Sub-Saharan Africa is a rising continent. Both its division into relatively small states with relatively small populations and generally low levels of economic development limit the power reach of the existing states.[1] In the global context, Egypt and Nigeria, the largest in the continent by population, each account for less than 1 percent of global economic output.[2] Despite rapid population growth (Nigeria will match the US population by 2050), no African state is expected to break into the top thirty global powers by 2030.

In 2016, the combined output of the most powerful nation-states—Egypt, Nigeria, and South Africa plus Algeria—just exceeds the output of Brazil or Indonesia but falls far behind the output of Germany or Japan and is dwarfed by the United States, the European Union (EU), and China. The potential global influence of African states is unlikely to change in the foreseeable future unless further integration takes place.

At the top of the sub-Saharan regional hierarchy, no power transitions are likely. Despite an apparent power parity across the two regions within Africa, the geographical distance between the leading states—Egypt and Nigeria—is such that confrontations are unlikely to occur because these nations have limited ability to reach each other. For this reason, despite the relative dissatisfaction of African states with the international norms applied to the regions, severe international wars have been rare.[3] Each of these two large nations dominates a region. The presence of such isolated regions prevents cross-national conflict.

Africa—like Spanish South America but unlike North America—consolidated along local, rather than global, lines. Lemke's categorization adapted for the creation of our hierarchies reflects such divisions.[4] The North Africa hierarchy incorporates Egypt as the dominant state together with Algeria, Tunisia, Libya, and Morocco (see chapter 10). The sub-Saharan region covered here is an amalgamation of several smaller hierarchies. In the Horn of Africa, Ethiopia dominates following the partition of Sudan. Nigeria is preponderant in the Gulf of Guinea. South Africa is preponderant in the Central Lowlands.

Although some violent cross-national interventions have taken place, the most severe have been the civil wars in Sudan, Eritrea, and Somalia that resulted in major restructuring of the states in this area. The conflicts in Sudan led to the partition of the largest African state and the emergence of South Sudan as a new state. The Boko Haram crisis has rekindled the Biafra conflict and disclosed deep fissures in Nigeria. Such political fissures reflect the reality that many African states are still in the nation-building stage.

THE PERSISTENCE OF INTERNAL
INSTABILITY AND CONFLICT

Sub-Saharan Africa, filled with weak states with limited territorial control, is an anomaly in the international system. Conflict there is characterized by its intrastate nature rather than warfare or conflict between countries. Competing groups within states, characterized by Lemke as "autonomous political entities (APEs)"[5] remain the most important drivers of major conflict within the region. The most severe conflicts in the region began as intrastate conflicts, notably the Biafra war in Nigeria, the second Congolese War, and the two Sudanese civil wars between the north and south of the now-divided Sudan and South Sudan. Parity between groups and the salience of divisions remain critical determinants of conflict within states. Future major conflicts within the region are also likely to be internal, in some cases expected to comprise groups spanning national boundaries, and in many cases, conducted not between a rebel force and the government but between competing internal autonomous political entities. This is a region that forces scholars to look inward for answers. Subnational political actors in this region are the more appropriate unit of analysis.[6]

The historical pattern of conflict in sub-Saharan Africa is responsible, in part, for this dynamic. Even prior to colonial intrusion and the scramble for Africa, low population density and relatively poor soil quality facilitated population movements and limited permanent settlement. Nunn notes that the African slave trade functionally decimated the coastal regions of well-established nations, leaving few political structures tied to fixed geographic boundaries.[7] Conflicts were evident in both the pre- and postcolonial period; however, these conflicts were largely based on population differences in contrast to territorial control.[8]

The artificial political boundaries imposed during the colonial era largely endure on the continent today, yet populations and conflict often transcend geopolitical boundaries, and in the process, contribute to a phenomenon commonly referred to as *conflict contagion*.[9] In contrast to the international system, where disputes over territory provide the impetus for conflict, territorial conflict in sub-Saharan Africa is often confined to resource-rich regions of a country or a valuable natural asset such as a river.

Little incentive existed in colonial and postcolonial Africa to establish institutions such as tax structures, bureaucracies, and standing militaries in part because territorial protection did not function as a foundation for conflict in most African populations.[10] In the absence of interstate conflict, established institutions lacked accessibility and relevance to populations throughout politically defined territories. Colonial enterprises, often based on monocropping or concentrated mineral extraction, resulted in the creation of dual economies. Single-crop production governed the cash economy and subsistence agriculture comprised much of the remainder of economic activity. Infrastructure investments such as railroads concentrated trade and settlement along transit lines for the extraction of goods, rarely extending beyond a range necessary to transport raw materials.

This stands in contrast to other regions where state building and state capacity flowed from warfare—a mechanism for establishing revenue streams based on the transfer of individual resources in the form of taxes to the government.[11] But in Africa there were few established institutions that "reached" the population. Thus, commodity-dependent revenue streams contributed to the creation of rentier states or neo-patrimonial regimes that excluded much of the population.[12] These trends were exacerbated by high levels of foreign aid and development assistance, further decreasing incentives to expand tax structures and limiting incentives for governments to facilitate redistribution.[13]

The consequence of this unusual "state-building pattern" is a society where multiple and conflicting centers of social organization emerged.[14] This is reflected in vertical formal institutional structures and horizontal informal social structures operating independently. This geometry requires a focus on small organized political actors as the unit of analysis rather than on the state. Rather than signaling vulnerability to equally weak neighbors, the consequence of these developments is the facilitation of competing political actors within subnational geographic units. Traditional analyses identify these conditions as rendering a country ripe for the predation of resources and territory by neighboring governments. Instead, the geographic and political boundaries within the region have remained relatively unchanged, whereas internal conflicts drive seizures of land, predation, and the resulting political and territorial changes.

Throughout the region, territorial control by nonstate actors and even within governments has increasingly been driven by resource endowment. The vast wealth associated with oil and gas or mineral deposits can change the capabilities of governments, opposition groups, and nonstate actors, creating a volatile environment characterized by the potential for dynamic growth or decline. Where resource control is vulnerable to seizure, national governments are vulnerable. Disruption in resource rents for oil-dependent states can result in a rapid decline for governments and rapidly evolving parity with opposition factions.

Nigeria is the preponderant nation in the sub-Saharan regional hierarchy. It is an oil-dependent state with surprising endurance, despite numerous conflicts. Concurrently, the Central African Republic (CAR) and South Sudan

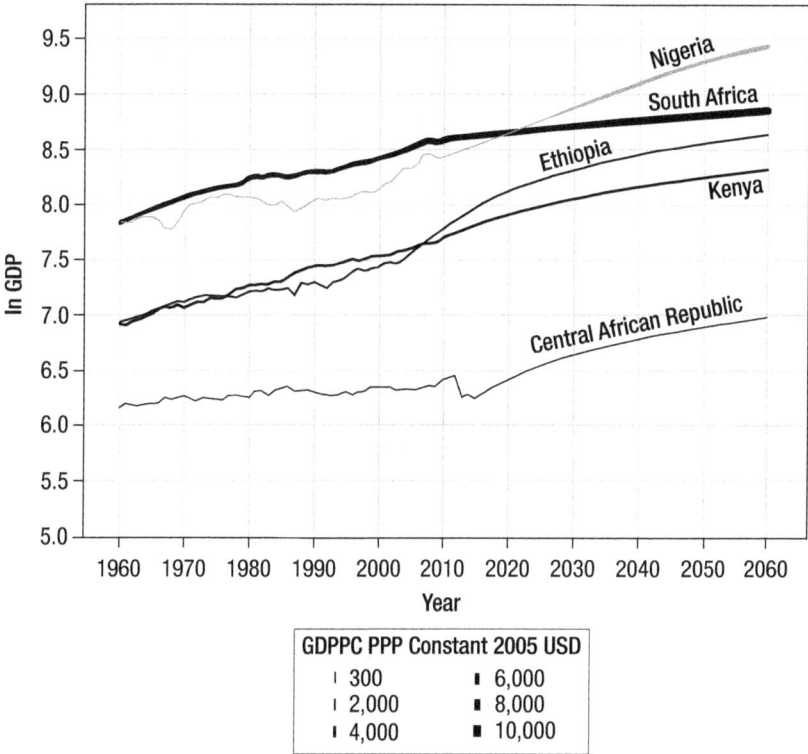

Figure 11.1. Power Projections of Selected Sub-Saharan African States

demonstrate how resource access drives capabilities and domestic instability. Finally, potential for conflict is assessed between the two regional powers of Kenya and Ethiopia, given the fast rise of Ethiopia (figure 11.1).[15]

NIGERIA

Nigeria is the preeminent (most dominant) country in sub-Saharan West Africa. It is characterized by a significantly larger population, economy, and resource endowment in the form of oil and gas revenues than any other country in the region. Nigeria is a founding member of the African Union, is committed to regional stability, and has sent security forces to unstable neighbors such as Liberia and Somalia. It supplies the largest regional contingent of military forces and support to United Nations (UN) peacekeeping missions. Consequently, large-scale instability in Nigeria would threaten prospects for stability in the entire region.

For the past two decades, Nigeria has been identified as a country on the verge of collapse. Citing a reliance on natural resources, legitimacy crisis, and religious, ethnic, and linguistic divisions, Collier and Hoeffler identified Nigeria in 1999 as the state most likely to experience significant civil war or collapse.[16] Over the past five years, the alarm has been raised annually surrounding prospects for the collapse of the Nigerian state. For example, a 2013 report for the Strategic Studies Institute and the US Army War College argues that Nigeria's continued dominant role and national unity is in jeopardy because of corruption, piracy, organized crime, and regional terrorist and insurgent challenges.[17] These refrains are echoed throughout the popular press and continue today.

Although these challenges are real, Nigeria does not risk impending collapse. No single or combined opposition groups possess sufficient power to challenge the state. Political decentralization of the state structures has contributed to the fragmentation of violent political movements, resulting in numerous small-scale opposition movements that are unlikely to coordinate efforts given massive discrepancies in grievances.

The most visible challenge can be found in Boko Haram, ranked as the world's deadliest terror group by the Global Terrorism Index in 2017 (GTI 2017). With reports of more than twenty thousand killed and well more than 2 million displaced between 2009 and 2015, the impact on northern Nigeria has been substantial. By 2014, Boko Haram had succeeded in capturing territory within the northern states of Borno, Asamawa, and Yobe.[18] A delayed and inadequate response by Nigeria's military raised concern about the capability of Nigeria's federal government to maintain security and political order.

By the end of 2015, however, Boko Haram no longer held territory, and a multinational effort had been mobilized to combat the insurgency. Improvements to Nigeria's military including increased funding, staffing, and commitment to professionalization need to continue under President Muhammadu Buhari. With limited military efficacy, Boko Haram lacks the capability to mount a real challenge to the Nigerian federal government. In addition, the group prompted cooperative multilateral efforts, including a multinational force involving Cameroon, Chad, Benin, and Niger to secure Nigeria's borders with its neighbors.

Nigeria's military is challenged on multiple fronts, including regional actors that do not operate across national borders. A relatively recent group, the Niger Delta Avengers (NDA), established in 2016, is arguing for secession of the Niger Delta region and greater self-determination. This is potentially a substantial challenge for the Nigerian government because the conflict has resulted in significant reduction in oil output, from 2.2 million barrels per day to 1.6 million barrels per day.[19] With a federal government that is dependent on oil revenues, this represents a clear and present danger. Yet precedents are in place for resolution of this conflict. First, the Nigerian military has carried out significantly more effective suppression of the NDA than it had done in the case of Boko Haram. Second, previous military activities organized around these claims (e.g., the Movement for the Emancipation of the Niger Delta) have negotiated successful solutions with the Nigerian government and are urging the NDA to do the same.[20]

Part of the success of Nigeria's strategy in managing these conflicts has been one of decentralization. The 1994 constitutional establishment of thirty-five additional states, and the 1997 arrangement for oil-producing states to retain 13 percent of resource rents generated within state borders prior to redistribution create both political and economic incentives for local elites to remain committed to the current borders.[21] This has served the federal government in additional ways as well. State governments and elites are reduced to small powers that cannot challenge the authority or control of even a weak and illegitimate central government. Some states, including northern states, remain reliant on federal subsidies, whereas the oil-producing regions enjoy control over a larger set of revenues of resource rents. This model, in part, replicates the rentier-state model operated by the federal government at the state and local level, reducing challenges by state and local governments.

Prior work identifying this pattern of reproducing regimes patterns subnationally has been demonstrated in countries ranging from Mexico's subnational authoritarianism[22] to India's inequality[23] to Argentina's rentier states.[24] It is unsurprising that an implicit strategy of Nigeria's constitution has been to empower local elites through resource endowment and control in two ways. First, the constitution assigns uneven redistribution of oil rents. State governments with oil production are able to retain some revenues, rendering control of appointments to state office as an opportunity for neo-patrimonial distribution and functional resource control. Non-oil-producing states are supported by subsidies, once again realized through oil rents and redistributed.

In each case, oil revenues or subsidies comprise the majority of state-level revenues, resulting in the concentration of resources available for distribution in the hands of local elites. In the short and even medium term, these local elites have massive disincentives to challenge federal authority because they benefit from the status quo. Only long-term declines in oil revenue or in oil prices are likely to result in a substantial challenge mounted against the federal government.

Other fault lines consistently identified as salient include adoption of Sharia law by northern Nigerian states (in contravention of rules set down by the federal secular state), indigenous-settler conflicts, and ethnic mobilizations in the south provoked by resource allocations. Although the ethnic challenges have been discussed, the allowance for Sharia law has actually resulted in an increase in political legitimacy at the state and local level. Other conflicts remain localized, including settler-indigenous conflicts in central Nigeria.

In sum, Nigeria is an important dominant state. It is simultaneously fragile and cohesive, in some ways strong yet weak. It is a study in contrasts yet undeniably the most powerful and influential nation in its region. Despite a dominant economy, the military remains a work in progress and the country is experiencing instability from several sources. The key is that none of these is sufficient to challenge the national government because their relative capabilities fall significantly below that of even a weak and ill-equipped military. Decentralization, in the case of Nigeria, has resulted counterintuitively in the fracturing of opposition and the limitation of a major challenge to the central government. Empowerment of state and local elites for resource distribution has shifted questions of illegitimacy and distrust from the central to the local governments and also has highlighted local authorities as the center of protest.

In the current period, Nigeria can be characterized as a relatively weak state, with a low level of legitimacy, whose sovereign authority will nonetheless not be challenged in the near term. One of the few likely sources of systemic instability that may render Nigeria vulnerable in the long term is enduring low global oil prices. Even piracy and vandalism are unlikely to disrupt Nigerian production in a way similar to what happened in South Sudan. Nigeria has responded to the highest levels of vandalism resulting in the loss of 355.69 thousand metric tons of petroleum by increasing offshore production.[25]

Nigeria's role as the dominant state will endure. The distribution of power between major regional actors has and will continue to be relatively static. Nigeria enjoys a significantly larger population, economy, and resource endowment in the form of oil and gas revenues than its neighbors and any other country in the region. The current effort to quash Boko Haram has resulted in Nigeria's coordination with neighbors Chad, Cameroon, Benin, and Niger. Despite internal instability with constant low-level political violence, Nigeria has served as a stabilizing political and security force in the region.

SOUTH AFRICA

South Africa is the preponderant state in the central lowlands of the sub-Saharan region, although it is still suffering from widespread corruption and poverty more than twenty years after apartheid. Known for its diverse population, South Africa suffers from vast inequality that was established during its colonial days of Dutch and British rule. Since Nelson Mandela won the long-awaited victory over the National Party in 1994, the African National Congress (ANC) has been the dominant political power in the country. The elections of 1994 signaled a "democratic breakthrough" for South Africa and started a movement to change the political landscape and power in the country.[26] During apartheid, South Africa suffered the ramifications of discriminatory practices. Nigeria positioned itself as a strong opponent of the National Party's discriminatory policies by placing sanctions on South Africa. Since Mandela changed the course of the nation, South Africa has been vying for regional leadership in Africa.

South Africa remains the dominant power in this subregional hierarchy.[27] Much has been done to respond to the political struggles of a formerly segregated population and repair the damage of South Africa's painful history. However, South Africa today is not the same as it was during the Mandela era. Strides have been made to tear down the walls of racial segregation, but corruption and white exodus have slowed the economy, suggesting that South Africa still has a long road of recovery ahead.

On the positive side, South Africa has made significant strides in dismantling political norms around the dehumanization of black residents and introducing democracy. However, economic growth has been slow in recent years. The economy in South Africa grew by only 1.3 percent in 2017, and the World Bank projects growth in 2018 at 1 percent, with a slight increase back to 1.3 percent in 2019.[28] In 2018, South Africa saw an increase in poverty to 19 percent, and in the second quarter, the overall unemployment rate rose to 27.2 percent among the general population and 50 percent among the youth.[29] There seems to be little room for poverty to be alleviated, as the population in South Africa continues to grow, while there has been little growth in per capita gross domestic product (GDP) since 2014.

Paired with slow growth rates, South Africa has experienced significant levels of governmental corruption across all three major political parties in the country. After dealing with allegations of corruption, fraud, money laundering, and racketeering around an arms deal, ANC president Jacob Zuma stepped down on February 14, 2018.[30] Onlookers had high hopes that Cyril Ramaphosa would pull South Africa out of its dark era of poverty and corruption after apartheid, but the country has yet to see much change.

In 2018, the Great Bank Heist report was released, detailing the robbery of the VBS Mutual Bank, in which close to R2 billion was stolen.[31] More than fifty government officials are thought to have been involved in this scandal, signaling to the region that corruption in South Africa is rampant. Tensions in South Africa run high, as the government struggles to navigate scandals while addressing the remnants of apartheid inequality.

With the introduction of the land expropriation amendment to South Africa's constitution, ANC and Economic Freedom Fighters (EFF) supporters are hopeful that this change in governmental power will allow authorities to redistribute property in such a way as to heal the wounds of racial segregation and inequality of South Africa's past. This amendment passed in parliament with 209 national assembly members in favor, 91 against. The processing of this amendment has left Democratic Alliance (DA) supporters angry and threatening legal action against the government. But is this enough to pull South Africa out of its failing economy? Probably not.

Apart from the government corruption in South Africa, there are also major concerns about health and the overall quality of life that come with widespread poverty. Much like other countries in this region, South Africa has experienced the effects of the human immunodeficiency virus/acquired immunodeficiency syndrome (HIV/AIDS) epidemic. Life expectancy in South Africa took a shocking blow in 2005, when it dropped to fifty-two years. The country has been slowing recovering, and by 2016, life expectancy had increased to sixty-two years, similar to what it had been when Mandela took office in 1994.[32]

Despite desires to climb the regional hierarchy, South Africa will need to undergo significant changes to its internal political and socioeconomic climate to exercise real influence. A start was made by Mandela in the 1990s, but widespread corruption and poverty have left South Africa in a fairly stagnant economic condition, and slow growth has hindered or even reversed pro-growth initiatives.

From a transition perspective, no external challenger has emerged in the sub-Saharan region. Nigeria, the only potential challenger, exerts some influence only from a distance and is embroiled in domestic disputes. Internally, domestic instability is unlikely, despite a weak government, because organized opposition to the existing regime is feeble. The system-wide presence of corruption and weak national growth make it unlikely that government efficiency will increase. Given its current population distribution, South Africa has the potential to grow at development rates found in high-growth countries such as China or India. But it is currently squandering that opportunity.

THE CENTRAL AFRICAN REPUBLIC

In a departure from perspectives on internal conflict that emphasize wars between a single rebel group and the government,[33] conflicts in this region assume a variety of forms. This includes nonstate groups targeting each other and the creation of an opposition coalition composed of a constituency of rebel organizations.[34] The weak state capacity and limited reach of national governments compounds this problem and may explain in part the persistence of weak national governments in the presence of enduring internal conflicts. As Lemke[35] notes, the appropriate level of analysis for conflicts in the African context is often at the group level. Using this approach, problems that contribute to conflict are identified including relative distribution of power, grievances, dissatisfaction, and exclusion.

Conflict in the CAR reflects this framework. The current bout of civil unrest began in 2012 as a conflict between the Seleka rebel coalition and the government, following the failure of previous peace agreements. The Seleka coalition is composed of four independently organized opposition groups that coordinated to seize the capital city of Bangui in March 2013. The collective effort of these opposition groups was necessary to effect the temporary seizure of political power because independently none had sufficient strength to challenge the national government. This coalition has contributed to the extension of the conflict and the significant human suffering associated with it. The United Nations (UN) estimates that 2.2 million people were in need of humanitarian aid in the CAR in 2014.[36] Despite a January 2015 cease-fire after African Union and UN peacekeeping deployments, low-level conflict persists in the CAR.

One aspect of this conflict that illuminates a major trend in the region is the changing nature of territorial disputes. Historically, territorial control has not been a driving factor in conflict motivation in sub-Saharan Africa. But now, political actors prize territories rich in natural resources, whether as a source of funding for armed forces deployed in conflict, or in providing a critical determinant in the current and future capabilities of an opposition group. In the CAR, seizure of the diamond trade and gold-mining efforts in the eastern CAR by the Seleka coalition constituted an integral source of financing for their opposition effort. On the one hand, a combination of new tax structures created by Seleka on diamond mining, and a sharp increase in Seleka-controlled gold mining since 2012, allowed for the financing of several thousand mercenaries from Sudan and other conflict zones. The CAR has been able to recruit fighters with the believable promise of financial compensation. This led to their successful march on Bangui in December 2012.[37]

Utilization by the opposition coalition of the diamond trade to finance struggles recast the conflict as an identity-based frame founded on religion. Muslim opposition forces coercively extracted revenue from predominantly Muslim diamond traders, resulting in the identification of the conflict as religious rather than resource-based, despite the reality being one of in-group predation. This resulting conflict diffusion has resulted in spontaneous targeting of Muslims by Christian vigilante forces that have now been accused of intentional ethnic cleansing. Anti-Balaka Christian militias have now also targeted control of the diamond-rich western regions of the country as essential for security. Rather than a confined conflict between competing groups for political control, the conflict now focuses on civilians, forcing displacement and a widespread utilization of identity-based violence between Christians and Muslims throughout the country.

Two additional conflicts have influenced violence and stability in the CAR. A Chadian group, the Popular Front for Recovery (PFR), has been active in the northern regions of the CAR since 2008 and offered allegiance and support to the Seleka rebel coalition in part because of their mutually beneficial relationship in the gold and diamond trade. The Lord's Resistance Army, a particularly brutal terrorist organization, has also been active in the CAR (in addition to prior activity in Uganda and current activity in South Sudan, also in the eastern region of the Democratic Republic of Congo, and the CAR). As recently as this year, kidnappings in the CAR were attributed to the Lord's Resistance Army.

This example highlights the most frequent pattern of conflict that can be found in the region. Opposition efforts are often fragmented and individual groups may be insufficient to effectively challenge a government. In an environment where these efforts can coalesce along a common line of division, the seizure of plunderable resources can facilitate rapid increases in capabilities and create opportunities for real challenges to existing national governments. Regional and international actors are the sole stabilizing factors for many of these faltering central governments. For example, in the CAR, a transition government, constitutional revision, and prospects for peace came about only as a result of the continued engagement of the African Union (AU) and UN intervention.

SOUTH SUDAN

The 2011 referendum on the independence of South Sudan offered the promise of stability and cessation of conflict for the region. Following five decades of intermittent civil war with catastrophic humanitarian consequences, prospects for self-determination and improved human and economic development appeared to be improving. The 2011 referendum endowed the new government of South Sudan with significant oil-producing fields and the prospects of capitalizing wealth into real human development, infrastructure, and economic gains for a population that is among the poorest in the world.

The potential shape of divisions between Sudan and South Sudan was anticipated by Arbetman-Rabinowitz and Johnson in 2008. Since independence on July 8, 2011, South Sudan has been in conflict over divisions of the South Kordofan oil-producing region with Sudan. Currently under the control of Sudan, the region remains contested. However, even more salient divisions exist within the country.

Since independence, South Sudan experienced persistent internal conflict and ethnic mobilization. In 2016, the country ranked second on the Fragile States Index, preceded only by Somalia. The driving division in the country exists between two leaders, each with origins in the Sudan People's Liberation Army (SPLA). This split, between ethnically Dinka President Kir and ethnically Nuer Vice President Machar, has resulted in divisions within the military and mobilization along ethnic lines. Grievances include perceived exclusion of the smaller Nuer population from distributional benefits despite residence in the oil-rich upper Nile region.

Resources and reliance on resource rents have produced relative parity between Kir's and Machar's contingents. Traditionally, South Sudan has received more than 98 percent of its revenues from oil production. A dispute with Sudan over transit prices halted production in 2012. Subsequently, 2013 and 2014 witnessed a resumption in production, albeit limited as the country generated only a third of the output attained in 2012.[38] The 2013 civil conflict resulted in temporary closure of oil fields in Unity State (sometimes known as the Western Upper Nile) and limited production in its oil fields. The civil conflict, which lasted more than two years, resulted in such significant damage to oil infrastructure that a return to higher output levels was not possible until July 2016.

The case of South Sudan shows the impact that resource rents can have on both state capacity and the reach of constituent factions. Resource rents and distribution networks in this case represent both the impetus and the motivation for conflict and contribute to extended parity between groups.[39] Both Kir's and Machar's militia and military resources are ethnically organized with neo-patrimonial distribution networks. Consequently, support for each actor is conflated with resource control and economic well-being.[40]

Transit disputes with Sudan over the cost of oil transfer gutted the Kir government's revenues in 2012, creating vulnerability to challenge by Machar's previously weaker faction. It should be noted that South Sudan is dependent on pipeline transit through Sudan, despite current efforts to increase access to Kenyan ports. By 2013, Kir's government was sufficiently weakened by the revenue deficit that Machar's opposition militia (Sudan People's Liberation Army-Militia [SPLA-M]) had reached resource parity and was able to mount a credible challenge. The period of parity was extended by low levels of oil production and resource seizure on both sides. SPLA-M opposition forces were defeated only with external support from the Ugandan military.

The case of South Sudan demonstrates the significant consequences that resource reliance can have on relative capabilities. Contraction of the majority of revenues due to a dispute over transit costs with Sudan resulted in a rapid decline on the part of the Kir government. Low global oil prices only accelerated the decline, resulting in the creation of near parity between the SPLA and the SPLA-M.

Evenly matched and with significant resource endowments at stake, each side was able to garner support by promising future access and revenue to supporters. The 2013 conflict is identified as significantly enriching both Kir and Machar at the same time the country's coffers were being emptied. In September 2016, seven out of nine provincial (state) regions in South Sudan were experiencing conflict.[41] The weak and fractured military of South Sudan remains vulnerable, although a peace agreement was signed in 2018. Continued regional and external support are critical in precluding a resumption of hostilities.

These cases illuminate two key issues: Regional powers are critical factors in influencing and limiting the spread of instability, and resource rents can catapult or compromise capability. Dominant countries in the region, such as Nigeria, provide a critical role in regional stability and cooperation by providing financing and military support for AU interventions. However, even these dominant countries face internal challenges. The subsequent section discusses expectations for Nigeria to continue to manage its internal challenges and why it will remain the dominant country in the region.

KENYA AND ETHIOPIA

Cooperation or collision associated with a shift in the power hierarchy is present between these two countries. Kenya and Ethiopia eclipse other East African countries in both economic output and state capabilities. Since 2012, the two countries have been close to parity, with a rapidly growing Ethiopia on track to overtake Kenya economically sometime within the next five years. Traditionally, Kenya has enjoyed a prominent role as a political leader in the region, following a close alliance to Western democracies after its independence from Britain in 1963. These close ties to the West made Nairobi the headquarters for the UN in Africa in 1996. With a large English-speaking population and ties to the West, the banking and financial services sector has traditionally made Nairobi the financial hub of Eastern and Central Africa.

By contrast, Ethiopia struggled throughout the second half of the twentieth century, facing challenges of political cohesion, economic capacity, and overall state strength. The mid-1990s saw the beginnings of Ethiopia's transformation from a country ravaged by two decades of civil war, Soviet-sponsored dictatorship, secessionist movements, and famine to a politically stable country with substantial economic gains. From 2001 to 2013, Ethiopia averaged economic growth of more than 7 percent per year, becoming the only African country to keep up with booming Asian economies.[42] Population growth also exploded from 1990 to 2015, doubling in size from approximately 50 million to 100 million people.[43] A stable political order, combined with a rapidly growing population and strong economic growth and a slow opening of the country, has made Ethiopia a quickly rising regional power.

International and continental powers have recognized the changing role of Ethiopia since the start of the twenty-first century and accordingly have facilitated a steady expansion of Ethiopian influence in regional, continental, and world politics. External Chinese funding of the completion of headquarters of the AU in 2012 in Addis Ababa solidified the city as the political capital of the African continent. Since then, the Ethiopian capital has hosted the majority of all major AU activities, including yearly summits of all African leaders and multilateral peace talks in efforts to end such conflicts as the Sudanese crisis in Darfur.

Regionally, Egypt has recognized Ethiopia's ascendancy in the context of the 2015 Nile Deal by ceding the economic use of the Nile River to Ethiopia's elites, nurturing ambitions to expand the country's generation of power.[44] Ethiopia recently bid for a nonpermanent seat on the UN Security Council, resulting in an uncontested and successful outcome. Such institutional ascendancy contributes to building an overall feeling of institutional satisfaction and increased status.

Despite international and intergovernmental facilitation, several areas of contention remain between Kenya and Ethiopia, risking the outbreak of conflict. Both countries, and not just Ethiopia, are interested in and require hydroelectric power to further increase their economic development. Chinese economic intervention has put the two countries at odds with one another: Kenya requires additional hydroelectric power to pursue manufacturing agreements with China, but the Chinese are investing heavily in Ethiopian hydroelectric power generation.

Ethiopia aspires to become the powerhouse of East Africa in the near future, exporting electricity to Sudan, Somalia, Kenya, and perhaps Egypt. By exploiting hydroelectric power generation on the Omo River, Kenyan wind electricity production may be adversely affected. There are similar environmental overlaps that would create conflict between the two countries as they each attempt to expand their energy-production requirements.

More importantly, civilian border conflicts have also been rising over the past several years as a result of drought and ethnic divisions. Although conflicts over energy policy can be negotiated between states, community conflicts in border zones where neither government has a strong presence are not as manageable. In 2015, Kenya and Ethiopia attempted to begin a process to resolve the latent border conflicts between the pastoral communities in Marsabit County in Northern Kenya and the Borana zone in Southern Ethiopia.[45]

The program seeks to create a cross-border zone of economic development, and interethnic conflict management, that can ultimately stabilize what could otherwise be considered a flash point for the region. Currently the government is dealing with the remnants of the militarized Oromo Liberation Front, a group that promotes self-determination and has promised to give up the arms struggle in 2019. Despite this promise, there have been frequent cross-border incursions by local forces on both sides. Currently, both Marsabit and Borana are under-administered regions of each respective country, and governmental reach in executing policies, whether political or economic, is quite low. As in other cases, external support from the UN can contain conflicts, but whether they are resolved will depend on increased governmental involvement in the region by both the Kenyan and Ethiopian governments.

Ultimately, despite disagreements on a number of issues, ranging from border disputes to hydroelectric power cutting off water resources to pastoral Kenyan herders on the northern border, Ethiopia should remain satisfied because of the favorable treatment it has recently received in the UN and the AU. It is clear that both national governments and the international community are committed to a cooperative and mutually beneficial transition between Ethiopia and Kenya.

The major prospects for disruption of strengthening ties and cooperation are found in subnational conflicts created by nonstate actors in the region. Despite evidence of cooperation for future ties, one needs look no further than South Sudan to identify and understand the long-term influence of enduring conflict that can be facilitated by internal divisions and subnational actors.

FUTURE CONFLICT AND COOPERATION

The sub-Saharan regional hierarchy is dominated by Nigeria and, to a lesser degree, South Africa. However, the relative incapacity of the two leading countries, dictated by low levels of development, restricts their ability to secure stability in the region. Kenya and Ethiopia are sufficiently isolated by distance from Nigeria or South Africa. Both are undergoing a subregional transition and may choose conflict or cooperation in the near future. The large regional powers have limited influence on such outcomes.

External global factors play a substantial role in this region. Even though Africa is not on the top of the US agenda or that of China, or even the EU, these nations have interests in Africa. Analysis of structural changes in this region must be understood from a future perspective. China is already creating support structures in Africa, and this will require some response from Europe and the United States.

Unlike other regions considered, international organizations, and nongovernmental organizations play an important role in determining the economic future of nations within the sub-Saharan regional hierarchy. The actions or inactions of such institutions directly affect growth. In 2015, the World Bank launched an initiative referred to as the "Billion Dollar Map."[46] The objective of this endeavor is to create a public resource financed by public and private interests to identify geospatially undiscovered mineral resources throughout the African continent. Savings attributed to the effort include providing African governments with complete information to avoid underselling rights to resource development by clarifying the extent and scope of anticipated resource endowments and by facilitating wealth transfers for development.[47] One of the most frequent prescriptions for economic development and prosperity for the region concentrates on the location and exploitation of mineral and oil resources.

Resource endowments induce volatility and vulnerability throughout the region. Power can be enhanced by the seizure of assets, which in turn may strengthen the capacity to challenge a government. Declines in resource revenues for dependent states can result in rapid decline and vulnerability to challenge. Nigeria is relatively stable because resource rents are used to ensure short-term stability at the expense of long-term economic and human development. As in other parts of the region, African nations systematically discount efficient resource management, investment in new technologies, stabilization funds for the future, and investments in human development. In a region where subnational politics are likely to remain drivers of conflict, such investments should be undertaken to ensure domestic stability.

Despite disappointing economic growth and persistent inequality within South Africa, the ruling party in South Africa retains support from the majority of the population. But persistent corruption has given rise to domestic dissatisfaction with the government in general. International conflict is unlikely in the absence of a competitor with the capacity to challenge or be challenged. The preconditions for a civil confrontation of any severity are also absent at this time. Despite the lack of preconditions for conflict, cooperation is unlikely to emerge because low growth continues to be seen here, despite enormous potential for much faster expansion. The window of opportunity created by a very large active population is being squandered by a government with very low political capacity. Reversing this trend is possible but unlikely if the current path is maintained. Prospects for a restructuring of the current economic and political structures do not appear to be good.

The sub-Saharan regional hierarchy is far more constrained that most of the others assessed in this volume. The current distribution of capabilities suggests that, under Nigeria's leadership, a cooperative African community can emerge. Confrontation at the margin between Kenya and Ethiopia could be managed by supporting a convergence of norms and values.

Economic interventions by China forecast a wider role for this state in this continent. Due to weak and corrupt national and local governments in the area, it will be relatively easy for China to penetrate, influence, and perhaps control resource-rich regions in Africa. Inevitably this will draw in other global competitors, including the EU, the United States, and India. Thus, a region, which today is inward looking and decentralized, likely will find itself pulled into global politics.

The Africa of 2030 will be substantially different from the Africa of today. A burgeoning, increasingly productive population will position Africa on the cusp of a dramatic economic takeoff. But for now, the status quo in Africa will continue: internal conflict, relative underdevelopment, civil wars, corruption, and fractionalization.

NOTES

1. Global Map shows region contours. The hierarchy map shows the relative size of the top contenders in this region. Data are World Bank, "World Development Indicators," last modified March 27, 2016, http://documents.worldbank.org/curated/en/805371467990952829/World-development-indicators-2016.

2. International Monetary Fund, "World Economic Outlook Database October 2016," accessed February 28, 2019, https://www.imf.org/external/pubs/ft/weo/2016/02/weodata/index.aspx.

3. Douglas Lemke, *Regions of War and Peace* (Cambridge: Cambridge University Press, 2002).

4. Ibid.

5. Douglas Lemke, "Intra-National IR in Africa," *Review of International Studies* 37, no. 1 (2011): 49–70.

6. Douglas Lemke, "African Lessons for International Relations Research," *World Politics* 56, no. 1 (2003): 114–138.

7. Paola Giuliano and Nathan Nunn, "The Transmission of Democracy: From the Village to the Nation-State," *The National Bureau of Economic Research* Working Paper no. 18722 (January 2013), last accessed on July 14, 2019, https://www.nber.org/papers/w18722.

8. Jeffrey Herbst, *States and Power in Africa: Comparative Lessons in Authority and Control* (Princeton: Princeton University Press, 2014).

9. Alex Braithwaite, "Resisting Infection: How State Capacity Conditions Conflict Contagion," *Journal of Peace Research* 47, no. 3 (2010): 311–319.

10. Herbst, *States and Power in Africa.*

11. Charles Tilly, *From Mobilization to Revolution* (Boston: Addison-Wesley, 1978); A. F. K. Organski and Jacek Kugler, *The War Ledger* (Chicago: University of

Chicago Press, 1980); R. H. Bates, *When Things Fell Apart* (Cambridge: Cambridge University Press, 2015).

12. Herbst, *States and Power in Africa.*

13. Ibid.

14. Pierre Englebert, "Pre-colonial Institutions, Post-colonial States, and Economic Development in Tropical Africa," *Political Research Quarterly*, 53, no. 1 (2000): 7–36.

15. Figure 11.1 source: Global Map shows region contours. The hierarchy map shows the relative size of the top contenders in this region. Data are World Bank, "World Development Indicators," last modified March 27, 2016, http://documents.worldbank.org/curated/en/805371467990952829/World-development-indicators-2016.

16. Paul Collier and Anke Hoeffler, "Greed and Grievance in Civil War," *Oxford Economic Papers* 56 (2004): 563–595.

17. Gerald McLoughlin and Clarence J. Bouchat, *Nigerian Unity: In the Balance* (Carlisle: US Army War College Carlisle Barracks PA Strategic Studies Institute, 2013).

18. David Smith and Gillian Parker, "Nigeria Falls into 'a State of War' as Islamist Insurgency Rages," *The Guardian*, March 8, 2014, https://www.theguardian.com/world/2014/mar/08/nigeria-state-war-islamist-insurgency.

19. OPEC: Saudi Arabia, "Annual Report," accessed Feb. 28, 2019, https://www.opec.org/opec_web/en/publications/337.htm.

20. Stephanie Hanson, "*MEND: The Niger Delta's Umbrella Militant Group*," The Council on Foreign Relations, last modified March 21, 2007, http://www.cfr.org/nigeria/mend-niger-deltas-umbrella-militant-group/p12920#.

21. McLoughlin and Bouchat, *Nigerian Unity.*

22. Agustina Giraudy, "The Politics of Subnational Undemocratic Regime Reproduction in Argentina and Mexico," *Journal of Politics in Latin America* 2, no. 2 (2010): 53–84.

23. Atul Kohli, "Centralization and Powerlessness: India's Democracy in a Comparative Perspective," in Zoya Hasan, ed., *Politics and the State in India* (New Delhi: Sage India, July 2000): 228.

24. Carlos Gervasoni, "A Rentier Theory of Subnational Regimes: Fiscal Federalism, Democracy, and Authoritarianism in the Argentine Provinces," *World Politics* 62, no. 2 (2010): 302–340.

25. Nigerian National Petroleum Corporation, "2014 Annual Report," https://www.nnpcgroup.com/NNPCDocuments/Annual%20Statistics%20Bulletin%E2%80%8B/2014%20ASB%202nd%20Edition.pdf; Nathan Nunn, "The Long-term Effects of Africa's Slave Trades," *The Quarterly Journal of Economics* 123, no. 1 (2008): 139–176.

26. Tom Lodge, *Politics in South Africa: From Mandela to Mbeki* (Cape Town: David Philip, 2006).

27. Uwem Jonah Akpan, "Nigeria and the Elimination of Apartheid in South Africa: An Assessment of Regional Diplomatic Initiatives," *Elixir Social Studies* 127 (2019): 2656–2663.

28. World Bank, "The World Bank in South Africa—Overview" (October 31, 2018), accessed March 11, 2019, http://www.worldbank.org/en/country/southafrica/overview.

29. Ibid.

30. "Why Jacob Zuma Resigned," *The Economist*, February 19, 2018, https://www.economist.com/the-economist-explains/2018/02/19/why-jacob-zuma-resigned.

31. Terry Montau, *The Great Bank Heist*. Report, Investigator's Report to the Prudential Authority. Vol. 1 (2018), https://www.resbank.co.za/Publications/Detail-Item-View/Pages/Publications.aspx?sarbweb=3b6aa07d-92ab-441f-b7bf-bb7dfb1bedb4&sarblist=21b5222e-7125-4e55-bb65-56fd3333371e&sarbitem=8830.

32. World Bank, "Life Expectancy at Birth, Total (Years)," (2019), accessed March 11, 2019, https://data.worldbank.org/indicator/SP.DYN.LE00.IN?locations=ZA.

33. Michelle Benson and Jacek Kugler, "Power Parity, Democracy, and the Severity of Internal Violence," *Journal of Conflict Resolution* 42, no. 2 (1998): 196–209.

34. Ida Rudolfsen, *State Capacity, Inequality and Inter-group Violence in Sub-Saharan Africa* (MA thesis, University of Oslo, 2013).

35. Lemke, "Intra-National IR in Africa."

36. Babacar Gaye, "Central African Republic: Security Council Briefed on Roll-out of UN Peacekeeping Mission," *UN News*, July 16, 2014, http://www.un.org/apps/news/story.asp?NewsID=48286#.V_AWrSR8moH.

37. Alexandre Jaillon, Filip Hilgert, Lotte Hoex, Steven Spittaels, and Yannick Weynes, "Mapping Conflict Motives: The Central African Republic," *International Peace Information Service* (21 November 2014), accessed on July 14, 2019, http://ipisresearch.be/publication/mapping-conflict-motives-central-african-republic-2/.

38. Robert Mason, review of *A Poisonous Thorn in our Hearts: Sudan and South Sudan's Bitter and Incomplete Divorce*, by James Copnall, *African Affairs* 114, no. 456 (July 2015): 486–487.

39. Alex de Waal, "When Kleptocracy Becomes Insolvent: Brute Causes of the Civil War in South Sudan," *African Affairs* 113, no. 452 (July 2014): 347–369.

40. Ibid.

41. Michelle Benson, "Let's Talk about Tax: Constitutional Confusion around Revenue Roles Is a Recipe for Conflict in South Sudan," *Africa in Fact* 32 (2015): 39–42.

42. Harry Verhoeven, "Africa's Next Hegemon," *Foreign Affairs*, April 12, 2015, https://www.foreignaffairs.com/articles/ethiopia/2015-04-12/africas-next-hegemon.

43. World Bank, "Population, Total," last accessed on July 14, 2019, http://data.worldbank.org/indicator/SP.POP.TOTL?locations=ET&view=chart.

44. *Al Jazeera*, "Egypt, Ethiopia, Sudan Sign New Deal on Nile Dam," December 30, 2015, https://www.aljazeera.com/news/2015/12/egypt-ethiopia-sudan-sign-deal-nile-dam-151230105650388.html.

45. Gaye, "Central African Republic: Security Council Briefed on Roll-out."

46. David C. Ovadia, "Improving Access to Africa's Geological Information through the 'Billion Dollar Map' Project," *SpringerLink: Mineral Economics* 28, no. 3 (November 2015): 117–121.

47. S. Vijay Iyer, "Billion Dollar Map to Help Africa Turn Mining into Prosperity," World Bank Blog, last accessed July 14, 2019, http://blogs.worldbank.org/energy/billion-dollar-map-help-africa-turn-mining-prosperity.

Chapter Twelve

South America

Uncertain Voyage

Marina Arbetman Rabinowitz
and Ayesha Umar Wahedi

South America

South America Region

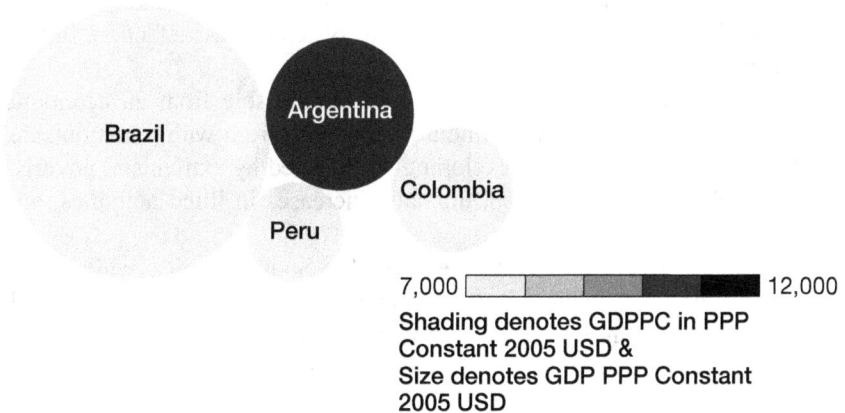

Brazil

Argentina

Colombia

Peru

7,000 ▢▨▨▨■ 12,000

Shading denotes GDPPC in PPP
Constant 2005 USD &
Size denotes GDP PPP Constant
2005 USD

South America Hierarchy

CURRENT STATUS AND DIRECTION

Less than half a century ago, South America was on the verge of a long-term catastrophe: the debt crisis. Though the worst was averted, an expected economic renaissance remains elusive as growth has been anemic. Economically and politically, South America remains the forgotten continent.

This should not be the case. The distribution of power in South America has been relatively stable over the past fifty years. Nations there have not been inclined to challenge the status quo, and there is a clear regionally dominant nation to provide leadership.[1] The absence of structural conditions for conflict has been supported by a strong and widespread nuclear weapons treaty, with the addition of numerous cooperation agreements.

This should have resulted in increased production, efficiency, trade flows, and other positive outcomes derived from economies of scale and interconnectivity. Furthermore, and defying expectations, democratic governance in the past twenty years has not improved the living conditions of the majority of the population. Instead the modus operandi has been one of regional and international apathy and domestic stop-and-go political and economic crises.

The South American regional outlook prior to 2016 was grim and then a modest recovery began in 2017 and leveled off in 2018 and 2019. It is expected to remain nearly flat, yet positive into the future. Venezuela and, to a lesser degree, Argentina are in the midst of severe recessions.[2] Regionally, Brazil, the reluctant dominant power, is not showing leadership partly because domestically its economic fundamentals are unsound and the level of poverty and maldistribution of income are staggeringly high.

Unless South America changes direction, the trends show negative weak economic performance on the part of all countries in the region. Without dynamic regional leaders this can easily lead to domestic instability. South American countries constantly change their positions in international agreements and treaties following domestic shifts in the political landscapes. Weak and short-lived regional cooperation leads to systemic dissatisfaction, further increasing the probabilities of conflict.

The fractured domestic scene seems insurmountable from an economic and a political point of view. Without intervention from within and outside, South America will mirror a developing world ruled by extremism, poverty- and instability-driven migration, dramatic increases in illicit activities, and internal conflict.

The United States has shown little interest in South America, while China is showing growing interest is economic and financial interactions. South America's links to the global economy are weak. The level of regional cooperation is extensive on paper but unconvincing in practice and marred by intra-organizational political disputes reflecting the individual countries' domestic left-right pendulum. The early promise of integration associated with Mercosur has not materialized.

To change directions, the domestic economic engine should be repaired with the assistance of tangible regional cooperation. It is essential that Brazil, the only country with the capacity to change negative patterns, redirect its world view and assume a vibrant regional leadership posture.

CHALLENGES TO THE REGIONAL HIERARCHY

The South American Regional Hierarchy incorporates major variations in output per capita income. The Southern Cone countries of Argentina, Chile, and Uruguay approach the level of advanced developed countries. Bolivia, Ecuador, French Guiana, Suriname, and Guyana, on the other hand, fall squarely in the least-developed set.

The United States has had a strong influence in South America. It has usually, though not always, promoted democracy in the face of military dictatorships, distributed aid to foster economic development (although at the expense of an increasing foreign debt), advanced free trade in the face of import substitution policies, and maintained a strong diplomatic presence. These are proper and useful objectives of a preeminent power—a role that the United States has played by extension. But that strong interest is no longer present.

The empirical evidence of the last twenty years shows that the United States has increasingly diverted its attention to other geographic areas. Despite this shift of focus, the level of international conflict in the region has not been affected. But the winds are changing; South America is becoming the priority of other major powers. China, Russia, and India to some degree are increasing their presence in South America, as seen by the increasing flow of investments and trade. South American nations now have choices for trading partners and the absence of US leadership suggests that they may well turn their attention to Asia.

Today, the European Union (EU) and the United States have retrenched and focused on their own domestic problems. Challenged by China as supported by Russia, they may not have the array of options to take the lead in all areas of the planet. Concurrently, a divergence in distribution of income and resources fueled by migration flows, technological and educational disparities, and the absence of workers' voices at negotiating tables has created a gap between the fast-growing Asian and the much slower South American societies. The main culprit, according to Robert Reich, is not wealth but a "grossly misshapen" wage structure clearly observed in the financial sector and in corporations.[3] South America has been hit hard by this model of maldistribution and derailed global growth, as well as by the steady decline of commodity prices.

China's interest in South America may or may not be benevolent. The immediate focus of the Chinese is on financial and economic matters. But political issues soon become associated with financial matters, and economic assets often require military power projection for protection. Thus, benign trade agreements are just the first stage of a cascading range of entanglements. Dependence on China is risky for South America. A large expansion may challenge the United States as well as draw other Great Powers into this region.

South American countries have been unable to establish and deepen economic ties to the rest of the world because their trade policies have oscillated between open markets and protectionist policies. The policy swings have also resulted in missed opportunities, wasted domestic resources, and underinvestment in infrastructure, especially in the transport sector, which is critical to the globalization process already heavily dependent on transport to organize supply chains.[4] This policy pendulum reflects the domestic political landscape of each country and has deprived South American countries of steady long-term international commercial relationships as well as the possibility to engage in internal long-term planning. Neither set of policies has worked. The main lesson is that the oscillations themselves have negative consequences; policy predictability and stability are more important than left or right, liberal or conservative orientation of policies.

At the global level, countries are faced with their own domestic issues and the presence of a dominant power whose interest in global issues is waning. Brexit is showing the tip of the iceberg. The strong ties within the EU are strained and global cooperation is in retreat. The consequences for the South American region are discouraging; as the global economy contracts, it leaves South America vulnerable to external shocks and further contraction from weakened global demand. In turn, the international system might refuel and accelerate the negative trends in South America by taking away the support system that was once offered.

There is no doubt that the behaviors of states outside the region have affected South America negatively. A future in which the United States neglects its role as the preeminent international leader and countries outside the region exclude it from global interaction may encourage South America to decouple from the international system. The economic standstill that the region has suffered over the last five decades is developing into large economic losses with countries declining at different rates. Although the region has remained relatively stable despite periods of negative growth and stagnation, continued economic decline has serious implications for instability in the region. If South America does not start gaining economic ground, ensuing domestic upheaval may turn these nations into net exporters of conflict amid despair and dissatisfaction with the system.

CONFRONTATION IN SOUTH AMERICA

The traditional colonization or institutional explanations of South America's decline are pessimistic and incomplete. The argument that structural beginnings have set the pace for a continuous bleak future overlooks the fact that in the seventeenth century, South America seemed to be full of possibilities, but long-term cycles of prosperity were followed by stagnation and a disengagement from the international system. South America kept abreast of the growing pace of advanced nations from 1870 to 1929 but stagnated after the mid-nineteenth century, at a time when gross domestic product (GDP) per capita in the United States grew between four- and sixfold.[5]

When analyzed relative to developed nations, the contraction of the GDP per capita in South America is appalling, especially since the 1930s. South America has not experienced sustained economic growth since that time. It has endured multiple stop-and-go episodes with a brief period of growth during the 1980s and another in the 1990s but then followed by a period of stagnation. Even the decade-long glimmer of hope resulting from the global commodity boom of 2003–2013 was short-lived, and as the commodity prices declined, the region returned to a familiar standstill that has become a defining feature of its economic landscape.[6] To understand this decline, explanations beyond the colonial and institutional narrative have to be brought into the analysis.[7]

The power distribution in South America has been dominated by Brazil as shown in figure 12.1. The country's economic clout is undeniable. Brazil's economy is four times as large as that of Argentina, which has the next-largest economy in the Southern Hemisphere. In 1996, Brazil's economy was 33 percent larger than the rest of South America combined. In 2019, Brazil still had a very large economy but by a smaller margin; now it is 30 percent larger than the rest of the southern continent together.[8] No other South American nation—with the possible exception of much-smaller Chile—has gained much against Brazil. Preponderance in the region suggests continued stability as the status quo is reluctantly maintained.

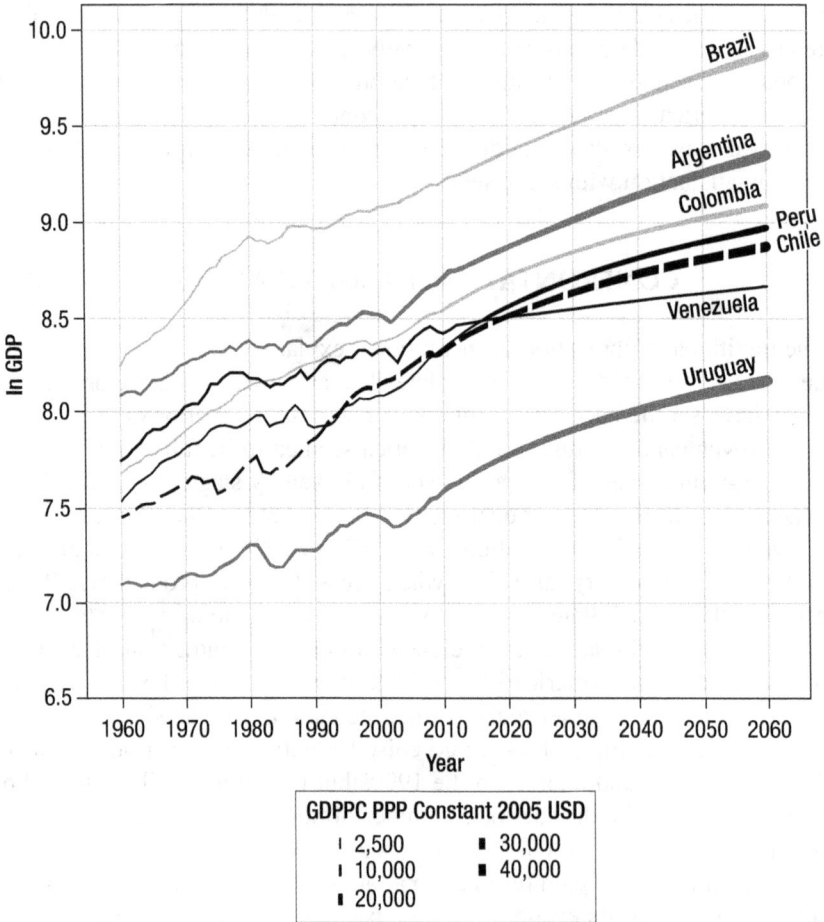

Figure 12.1.   Power Projections in Latin America (1960–2060)

COOPERATION IN SOUTH AMERICA

Brazil's disinterest in the region has resulted in failed attempts to lead. At the heart of regional disinterest has been an absence of a preponderant nation acting as an organizing force. Instead, Brazil, the largest economy in the region, has disengaged as a result of domestic challenges that get reflected in the wider region.

Support for cooperation emerges because South America has not gone through major international security challenges in the last decades, but neither has it developed a strong sense of cooperation that would foster the economic growth of the bloc of countries. There has been a proliferation of institutional agreements, but the most successful has been the Treaty of Tlatelolco, or Treaty for the Prohibition of Nuclear Weapons in Latin America and the Caribbean, which was signed half a century ago. That is not to say that there has been a total absence of international conflict; since the end of the Cold War there have been eleven territorial disputes, mainly over unresolved border issues.

The Treaty of Tlatelolco has defied the odds and has strengthened through the fifty years since it opened for signature in 1967. By now, thirty-three states have signed the treaty, which is "of permanent nature and shall remain in force indefinitely."[9] Treaty obligations prohibit testing, use, manufacture, production, acquisition, receipt, storage, installation, or possession of nuclear weapons. Verification by the International Atomic Energy Agency (IAEA) and the Agency for the Prohibition of Nuclear Prohibition of Nuclear Weapons in Latin America and the Caribbean (OPANAL) has been successful; in 2016 OPANAL completed its comprehensive safeguards and established that the Treaty of Tlatelolco sets a good example for other countries. The issue of nuclear war has become a non-issue in South America—an incredible achievement. South America has succeeded at denuclearization.

Before the Treaty of Tlatelolco was signed, the Latin America Free Trade Association (LAFTA) had come into effect. It includes twelve member-nation states, including Cuba. The goal was to create a free-trade zone, and several institutions have been created to support it.[10] It is important to note that LAFTA refers only to goods and not to services and does not include coordination of policies; therefore, little political or economic integration was ever anticipated and the expectation that richer nations within Latin America were going to support poorer nations has not come to fruition.

Union of South American Nations (USAN or UNASUR) likewise includes twelve countries. It was signed in 2008 and ratified in 2010 with the intention to model a community after the EU, including currency, parliament, and passports.[11] Another goal was to reduce the tensions between countries. It has been used to mediate peaceful outcomes in Bolivia, Paraguay, Venezuela, and Colombia. In addition, some opportunities for dialogue have succeeded in issues related to drug trafficking. Community of Latin American and Caribbean States (CELAC) was signed in 2011; it includes thirty-three countries and has the goal of promoting dialogue and political accords.[12]

Mercosur (the Southern Common Market), originating in 1988 but signed into effect in March 1991, includes Argentina, Bolivia, Brazil, Uruguay, Venezuela, and Paraguay. Although it showed initial promise, the devaluation of Brazil's currency in 1999 served as a blow to the agreement, one from which it has not fully recovered. The year 2012 showed some internal squabbles for Mercosur when Venezuela became a full member; the suspension of Paraguay over the impeachment of President Fernando Lugo resulted in the further politicization of the agreement. Reinforcing unification, Bolivia became a full member in 2015.

The purpose of Mercosur was to encourage free trade and the fluid movement of goods, people, and currency. It has expanded into a full trading bloc with the introduction of "loopholes and temporary exemptions" that have made it ineffective.[13] Yet, South American countries trade less with each other than with Asian countries, according to the International Monetary Fund (IMF).[14] The fact that Mercosur continues to be in trouble can be seen in the decline in intratrade. Most of the intraregional trade continues to be between Brazil and Argentina, but they, too, rank very low on trade openness compared to the rest of the world.

South America in general is not integrated into the global economy, which is becoming increasingly dependent on global supply chains for the production of intermediary or value-added goods. Although the benefits of increased trade especially within the region in enhancing supply chain networks are clear, countries in the region continue to underinvest in transportation and the infrastructure critical to enhancing global trade ties and diversifying exports beyond commodity trade. According to the World Trade Organization (WTO), regional value chains can serve further as a "natural bridge between domestic and global value chains," with political and economic advantages both domestically and at the regional level. Supply chain networks are still underdeveloped in South America, even though the benefits associated with participating in global value chains are undeniable.

South America's large collection of treaties and intergovernmental regional organizations has not contributed to deepening integration and economic growth. Brazil, the reluctant and powerful dominant power, has not taken the lead because for decades Brazilian elites have been more interested in establishing a more prominent role among developed countries than in looking into their own backyard. Furthermore, Brazil's trade with countries beyond the region has primarily focused on resources rather than manufactured or value-added goods. The dependence on commodity exports hit the Brazilian economy hard when the commodity boom came to an end. Brazil, Argentina, and South America in general have much to gain from strengthening intraregional trade and fostering supply chain networks that can make the region an important player in the global economy and change the bleak economic outlook to a more promising one.

REGIONAL LEADERSHIP

Brazil has been a reluctant dominant leader with fickle allies. South American countries continue to concentrate on their domestic issues, and those priorities overshadow regional cooperation. To make matters worse, the internal left to right, populist to autocratic, democratic political pendulum has made representation in international forums volatile amid constant changes and lack of policy affinity. A well-established network of regional organizations allows for dialogue and interactions among political figures and their staffers. This contact has the ability to foster trust and improvement in regional governance as well as other more tangible outcomes, like increased trade and capital flows within the region. These are all likely to promote peace and prosperity.

The future success of regional cooperation must include Brazil taking the regional lead. Brazil is recovering from a downturn, fueling domestic instability. This instability might prove to be sufficient to hinder cooperation across countries. Integration relies on a leader that gains the support and trust of allies to maintain order and strengthens compliance to international agreements. Bilateral and multilateral organizations, as well as alliances and security agreements that mirror national preferences and control distribution of preferences, are pivotal to maintaining the status quo.

South America has myriad regional agreements, many without the institutional capacity to implement decisions, and often the member countries' positions change as the domestic political environments shift. A dominant nation that can ensure an environment of satisfaction and trust will assist in conflict avoidance. The regional distribution of power is moving toward a danger zone where contracting economies will be achieving parity on their way down. Brazil as the leader needs to take a preeminent role in the regional challenges beyond international conflict, from economic growth, poverty, inequality, and international agreements to drugs, arms trafficking, internal violence, and crime. Brazil has started to spearhead some regional efforts such as the South American Defense Council and UNASUR.

Recall that, according to the IMF, South American countries trade far less with each other than with their Asian counterparts, and countries within the region continue to rank very low on trade openness.[15] Efforts to boost intraregional trade and integrate into global value chains have thus far proven unsuccessful. However, Pacific alliances are showing some promise. The Pacific Alliance (PA), composed of Chile, Colombia, Mexico, and Peru, has aimed to create an area of "deep integration" and has made modest progress as member countries have abolished 92 percent of their tariffs on trade.[16]

Mercosur, on the other hand, has not lived up to its promise, and the inclusion of Venezuela has challenged its effectiveness and weakened its momentum. Venezuela has introduced global competition by taking policy positions in concert with Russia and China. This affects the unity of the Organization of American States (OAS) and Mercosur. Central to the success of any future attempts at integration would be Brazil's progress in securing itself domestically and finding that its path to prosperity runs through closer ties in the region.

Many country representatives have cited the EU as a model for South America, despite its latest difficulties, but it has always involved more rhetoric than action. However, the Brexit experience suggests that the efficacy of such an alliance will depend on a carefully managed integration unique to the dynamics in the region. Besides, South American governments are far from the right candidates to abide by a supranational body. The future of their cooperation will be dictated by domestic economic necessity, humility when policy affinity needs to be bridged, and a dominant power that can be trusted to plan beyond its immediate internal needs. The current path that the region is following is one of lack of cooperation and economic isolation where the domestic problems continue to increase.

So far, South America has enjoyed relative cooperation under a clearly indifferent leader, Brazil. Even under conditions of parity among the other countries in the hierarchy, major international conflict did not follow suit. Border disputes have coincided with conditions of parity in 2000, 2005, and 2009 between Colombia and Venezuela, but the border disputes did not escalate and the last border skirmish was in 1995 between Peru and Ecuador.

The conditions for peace have prevailed in the region: an unchanged distribution of power with a clear regional dominant power and no threat of nuclear war. On the other hand, the system equilibrium is strongly based on indifference and distrust among the South American countries; the region as a whole is characterized by trade agreements that have not increased the minimal intraregional trade that exists, a disengaged leader, fractured domestic political scenes, economies that have been contracting for years, and international representation that changes direction. The early warnings of an oncoming crisis will stem from the distribution of power in the region and the engine that drives domestic economic growth.

THE FUTURE: CONFLICT OR COOPERATION?

Although peace has prevailed in the region, in general, the South American regional hierarchy is not free from conflict. As inequality worsens domestically, country after country may experience rising instability. Antigovernment sentiment will increase if governments continue to fail to deliver; spillovers from ensuing political chaos can change the outlook of conflict for the region. Consistent with power transition, the South American region has not gone through major regional conflict since the emergence of Brazil as a dominant power, and this structure will be preserved.

Dissatisfaction with the system and its lack of leadership as well as increasing domestic poverty, crime, and inequality can increase the likelihood of domestic unrest, which may spill over to regional instability.

Traditionally, preponderance is achieved by persuading allies to rally around the values reflected in the status quo where norms are shaped by the dominant power in that hierarchy. So why has Brazil been, until recently, such a hesitant leader? An external focus on global markets is a partial reason. A downturn in the world economy may reverse Brazil's unwillingness to trade with the rest of South America.

The lack of cooperation in the region is exacerbated by the increasing disengagement from the global system, as seen in the absence of strong supply chain networks and the slowdown of financial and trade flows. But global actors are not looking at the moment for new opportunities to expand, let alone to make risky investments when the domestic markets are on the brink of collapsing with every change of government. As the countries in the region contract further at different rates, converging toward the poverty trap, the presence of a strong leader in the region could foster stability. The success of the nuclear treaty demonstrates that when incentives are aligned, there is an organizing force for further integration. With these elements, regional cooperation can be successful. The regional outlook for South America will depend on whether the nations are successful in safeguarding themselves from a contracting global economy, which will be influenced by only a modest recovery in the United States and a possibility of further slowdown in the Chinese economy.

Brazil and the United States are the twin pillars of hope for South America. The central issue is: will they step forward or will inaction precipitate this relatively stable region into sustained domestic confrontations and eventually conflict?

NOTES

1. Global Map shows region contours. The hierarchy map shows the relative size of the top contenders in this region. Data are World Bank, "World Development Indicators," last modified March 27, 2016, http://documents.worldbank.org/curated/en/805371467990952829/World-development-indicators-2016.

2. OECD Development Centre, "Latin American Outlook 2019," last modified March 20, 2019, http://www.oecd.org/dev/latin-american-economic-outlook-2019-development-in-transition-launch-media-advisory.htm.

3. Robert Reich, "Why wages are going nowhere," *Salon*, August 5, 2018, https://www.salon.com/2018/08/05/why-wages-are-going-nowhere_partner/.

4. United Nations, "Economic Bulletin for Latin America," February 1962, https://repositorio.cepal.org/bitstream/handle/11362/10080/S6200129_en.pdf?sequence=1.

5. John H. Coatsworth, "Structures, Endowments, and Institutions in the Economic History of Latin America," *Latin American Research Review* 40, no. 3 (2005): 126–144.

6. World Bank, "World Development Indicators."

7. Ibid; Figure 12.1 source: Forecast based on growth rates adapted from PWC 20250, "The World in 2050," last modified August 29, 2017, https://www.pwc.com/gx/en/issues/economy/the-world-in-2050.html.

8. World Bank, "World Development Indicators."

9. "Treaty for the Prohibition of Nuclear Weapons in Latin America and the Caribbean (LANWFZ) (Tlatelolco Treaty)," Nuclear Threat Initiative–Ten Years of Building a Safer World, last modified April 29, 2019, https://www.nti.org/learn/trea ties-and-regimes/treaty-prohibition-nuclear-weapons-latin-america-and-caribbean -lanwfz-tlatelolco-treaty/.

10. Ibid.

11. Paul Kellogg, "Regional Integration in Latin America: Dawn of an Alternative to Neoliberalism?" *New Political Science* 29, no. 2 (June 2007): 187–209.

12. Andrés Malamud and Gian Luca Gardini, "Has Regionalism Peaked? The Latin American Quagmire and Its Lessons," *The International Spectator: Italian Journal of International Affairs* 47, no. 1 (March 2012): 116–133.

13. Shannon K. O'Neil, "Argentina and Brazil Grow Together," *Foreign Affairs*, July 13, 2016, https://www.foreignaffairs.com/articles/south-america/2016-07-13/argentina-and-brazil-grow-together.

14. International Monetary Fund, "Direction of Trade Statistics (DOTS)," last modified March 1, 2017, https://data.imf.org/?sk=9D6028D4-F14A-464C-A2F2 -59B2CD424B85.

15. Ibid.

16. *The Economist*, "No Brussels Here," July 7, 2016, http://www.economist.com/news/americas/21701788-how-latin-america-may-prosper-different-kind-integration -no-brussels-here.

Chapter Thirteen

Northeast Asia

Challenge of Nuclear Deterrence

Kyungkook Kang

Northeast Asia Region

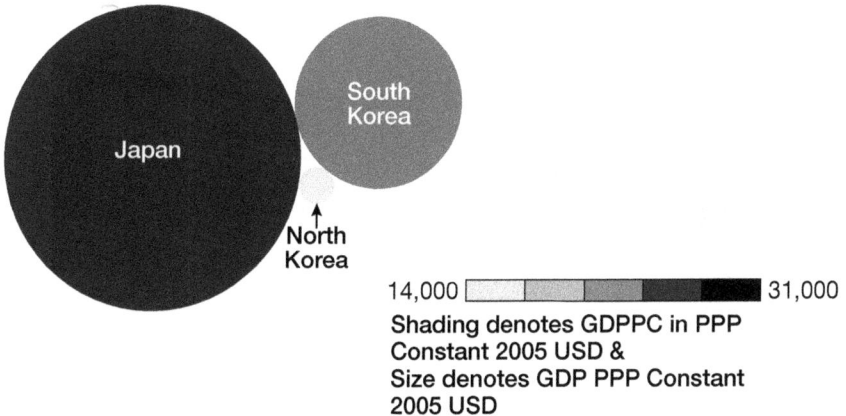

14,000   31,000

Shading denotes GDPPC in PPP
Constant 2005 USD &
Size denotes GDP PPP Constant
2005 USD

Northeast Asia Hierarchy

CLASH OF INTERESTS

The Northeast Asia Regional hierarchy is compact.[1] It is composed of Japan, South Korea, Taiwan, and North Korea.[2] Japan, economically the largest country by far, and South Korea are located at the edge of the US sphere of influence, with interested players China and Russia competing for influence. Japan is about five times as large as South Korea, but both states are among the best educated and most successful nations in the post–World War II era. Japan and South Korea face similar challenges. As figure 13.1 indicates, the main long-term economic challenges come from rapidly aging populations, inflexible labor markets, and heavy reliance on exports, which comprise half of each state's gross domestic product (GDP).[3]

Taiwan has a special, disputed political status. This developed country is now the only Asian state not recognized by a majority of nations. China reluctantly accepts the "one country, two systems" principle developed after US President Richard Nixon's visit in 1972 that reincorporated China into the international system and was designed to ameliorate China's increasingly controversial cross-strait relations with Taiwan. In Taiwan, advocates of unification and

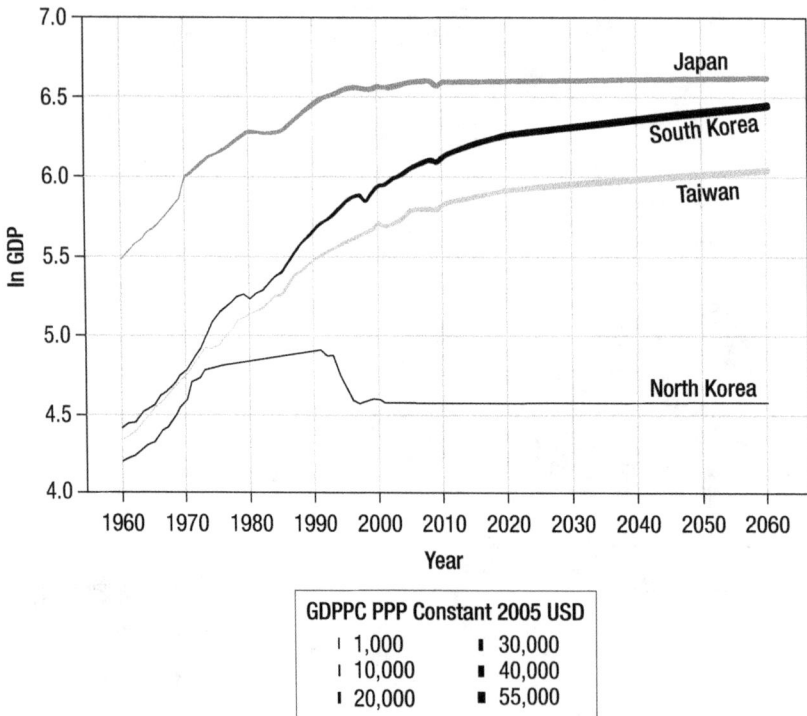

Figure 13.1. Power Projections of Northeast Asian States

supporters of independence vie for control, while China presses for integration. This dispute may lead to a severe confrontation between China and the United States as a power shift takes place in the coming decades.

North Korea is the least-developed society in this fast-growing economic region. However, it is the only one with an independent nuclear capability, which it has threatened to use in defense of its regime. Economically, South Korea dwarfs North Korea, and this massive superiority extends across conventional military capabilities.

One cannot analyze this region without directly assessing the impact of global Chinese and US interests on any future outcome on the Korean peninsula. Although there are indications of limited regional cooperation between Japan and South Korea—despite the still-open wounds left by events that transpired in World War II—the main security focus of Japan, South Korea, and Taiwan is related to US actions. Taiwan is, of course, the most exposed and would likely be absorbed by China, much like Macau, were it not for the US presence. The United States provides the security umbrella that, thus far, ensures stability in this region. An alliance change would shift potential outcomes quite dramatically. A US retreat from Asia would lead to a settlement of all disputes by a preponderant China.

This condition is well reflected in North Korea, which owes its very existence to China's willingness to send troops across the Yalu River in October 1950. This action thwarted the US-South Korean advance that would otherwise have reunified the peninsula. North Korea has relied heavily on Chinese support to ensure its security and recently added an independent nuclear capability to mitigate chances that South Korea would seek to revise the border in its favor and to improve its global image and coercive leverage with the United States.

Because of the massive asymmetry between China and Russia and members of the Northeast Asia region, this area is well suited to explore the role of nuclear weapons in this region and also to consider why North Korea has openly threatened its neighbors, despite being the smallest, most-impoverished, and seemingly dissatisfied nation in the region.[4]

On the basis of previous chapters, one might expect that Japan would dominate this region and that our attention would center on the evolution of cooperation in this very heavily dominated region. However, such a case would require assuming that the United States, China, and Russia do not and would not interfere directly in regional politics. They do. Thus, extending the region to include China, the United States, and to a lesser degree Russia provides a picture of total global dominance. This chapter focuses on the role of nuclear weapons precisely because any serious confrontation in this region is likely to involve directly two or three major nuclear nations.

Power transition has a different view of stability from that assumed by the doctrine of mutually assured destruction (MAD), and the Northeast Asia region provides an excellent case to define the differences. Albert Einstein argued in May 1946 that "the unleashed power of the atom has changed everything save our modes of thinking, and thus we drift toward unparalleled catastrophe. We shall require a substantially new manner of thinking if mankind is to survive." Nuclear deterrence among the Great Powers is already well documented. Stability is maintained only when a preponderant regional or global power is satisfied with existing norms. Otherwise, outcomes are far less certain.

REGIONAL DETERRENCE

The threat of a global nuclear war continues to be a central policy priority among nuclear-capable nations. At present, there are approximately 15,350 nuclear warheads globally.[5] Not only are the prospects for US-Russian arms control bleak after the recent crisis in Ukraine (which began in 2014), but other nuclear-club powers, including China, Pakistan, North Korea, and India, are increasing their warhead inventories. Furthermore, new challenges have emerged at the regional level in the past two decades.

The increasing technological sophistication of North Korea's nuclear missile program, already capable of reaching US territory, is now a matter of direct deterrence rather than extended deterrence from the perspective of Washington, which has fought only "away games." The modernization of Chinese nuclear weapons and the deployment of US defensive systems are playing crucial roles in power competition in East Asia, compounded by China and Russia boosting their bilateral nuclear cooperation. Nuclear and ICBM development missile tests by North Korea ironically strengthen South Korea's and even Japan's limited domestic support for developing their own nuclear deterrents.

Such competitions between nuclear-armed rivals occur in the name of deterrence.[6] The strong need to respond to such evolving challenges in Northeast Asia, which is visible from the statement made by the current prime minister of Japan. Discussing the purpose of Japan's new security-related legislation at a plenary session of the Lower House on July 16, 2015, Prime Minister Shinzo Abe delivered a forceful call: "By letting the world know that the Japan-US alliance will come into force should Japan come under threat, we improve our ability to pre-empt conflicts—that is, we strengthen our deterrent capabilities. This makes it all the more unlikely that Japan will come under attack."[7]

Of course, the simple and obvious way to avoid war is to eliminate these weapons through disarmament coupled with a robust international verification regime.[8] On May 27, 2016, at the Hiroshima Peace Memorial Park, US President Barack Obama presented his vision for strengthening the global effort to limit the spread of nuclear weapons. His historic visit as the first sitting US president to Hiroshima notwithstanding, his vision of a world without nuclear weapons met with an immediate opposition within Northeast Asia. Specifically, about three months later, North Korea claimed a successful test of a nuclear warhead that could be mounted on a ballistic missile. Despite waves of international sanctions, Pyongyang's nuclear program has been accelerated recently.

Although a vast number of academics and practitioners have endorsed Obama's principled stance in the name of "Global Zero," a major impediment to any disarmament proposal is directly linked not to its desirability, but to its enforceability. Over time, the potential for nuclear war has not been reduced; rather, it may have increased continually because a major obstacle to any disarmament proposal has been directly linked to the irreversible acquisition of technology. Consequently, ensuring stability through nuclear deterrence warrants a reexamination of previous approaches. Indeed, as Betts correctly points out, "deterrence isn't what it used to be," but a clear path toward stability has not yet been identified.[9]

New security threats in Northeast Asia require a thorough understanding of the theoretical structure regarding the dynamics of deterrence. The emergence of new technologies that may counter the comparative advantages of US military forces is expected to play a greater role in overall US strategic policy. The implications are apparent in the ongoing debate over the US forward deployment of tactical nuclear weapons and land-based missile defense system in Northeast Asia. Alternate perspectives suggest very different policy choices.

This chapter responds to the need to reassess the relevance of deterrence as both theory and practice in light of foreign policy issues facing Northeast Asia. Political leaders have a need to evaluate, assess rapidly, and reason about deterrence stability when they encounter new political crises. A reevaluation of deterrence theory is now mandatory because many of the factors believed to uphold strategic stability during the Cold War have faded or are absent in Northeast Asia. To that end, it is important to develop a well-established systematic outline that can aid practitioners and scholars to anticipate, trace, and alter the development of any potential severe crisis in the future. After reviewing the existing insights to show that alternate theoretical perspectives suggest very different policy choices, this chapter assesses a variety of pressing deterrence issues in Northeast Asia.

THE LURE OF THE COMFORTABLE ADVICE:
CLASSICAL DETERRENCE IN NORTHEAST ASIA

Shortly after the atomic bombings of Hiroshima and Nagasaki, Bernard
Brodie and other leading scholars urged policy makers to turn their attention from "win-war strategies" to "deterrence strategy."[10] To this day,
classical deterrence theory remains the foundation of US nuclear weapons
deployment and targeting policy. It postulates that the threat of massive
losses from nuclear retaliation deters nuclear conflict: "the more horrible
the prospect of war, the less likely it is to occur."[11] According to this theory,
living a life of complete comfort is assured because nuclear weapons are
devastating but inherently stabilizing.

As a logical extension of the neorealist perspective, classical deterrence
theory asserts that both competing states in a bipolar system must possess the
means to destroy one another to ensure stability in an anarchic world. The
balance of power is the true bulwark of peace, and nuclear proliferation is a
sound reinforcement that bolsters ultra-stable outcomes by raising the costs
of war to unacceptable levels. Consequently, conflict is least likely under a
nuclear balance—or "balance of terror." This argument was widely accepted
and justified the enormous buildup of nuclear arsenals during the Cold War.[12]

The theory of classical deterrence suggests that nuclear powers are unlikely
to fight in conditions of parity, and conversely, the disruption of the balance
of power provides the incentive for each of them to initiate a nuclear strike
against their rival. Figure 13.2 visually summarizes the theoretical prediction
of classical deterrence regarding the stability of deterrence affected by an interaction of each nation's killing capacity. The U-shaped valley with narrow
bottoms indicates ultra-stability under the MAD terror conditions, when both
nations' killing capacities equally reach the highest level (A), while an asymmetry of killing capacity can lead to a failure of deterrence (B or C) regardless
of who the challenger is.

The policy implication of the classical deterrence model is straightforward
and powerful. Most important of all, perhaps, a balance of terror is inherently
stable because the massive costs of conflict make any nuclear war unwinnable and unthinkable. The theory precludes any possibility of voluntary
nuclear exchange because rational actors facing an unacceptably high cost of
fighting an unwinnable war would never consider nuclear escalation a "desir-
able" outcome. The key finding of such analyses is that MAD will work as an
absolute stabilizer, regardless of the number and types of nuclear-armed actors present in the system. In brief, deterrence becomes much safer whenever
another nation acquires nuclear warheads with modernized delivery systems.

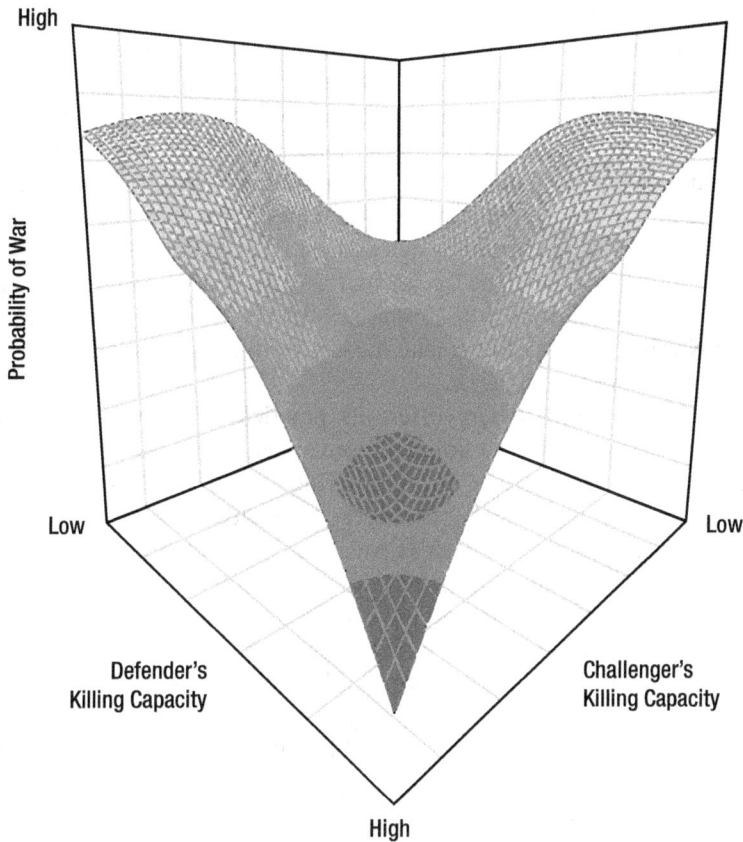

Figure 13.2.   Classical Deterrence Stability Assessment in Northeast Asia

To achieve the ultra-stable nuclear world, classical deterrence theorists advocate the virtue of spreading nuclear weapons in unstable regions. This idea of "*Deterrence/Proliferation optimism*" was the backbone of US national security during the Cold War and still continues to resonate with some prominent scholars of international relations. For instance, Mearsheimer[13] highlights the stabilizing effects of the US tactical nuclear weapons in Germany during the Cold War and the temporary retention by Ukraine of a nuclear force in the early post-Cold War era. Similarly, Kenneth Waltz,[14] a founder of the neo-realist school and prominent advocate of classical deterrence theory, recently argued that Iran should be allowed to develop and field nuclear weapons to balance those held by Israel. His notion is that a nuclear-armed Iran (possibly joined by Saudi Arabia and Turkey) would bring stability to the Middle East because war becomes "unthinkable" once nuclear weapons enter the picture.

In a more provocative vein, Mueller[15] claims that, if Iran and North Korea want the bomb, the United States should let them have it because, faced with an unacceptable loss, neither would initiate a nuclear conflict.

Classical deterrence suggests an ideal perspective that nuclear nondiscrimination will automatically induce further international stability by increasing the number of states that could retaliate against any potential nuclear user. Given the aforementioned arguments, the danger of major war in Northeast Asia would also be minimized by achieving a balance of terror. By mirroring the conditions that ensured peace during the Cold War, nuclear-armed Japan, South Korea, and Taiwan would bring stability to Northeast Asia because a nuclear North Korea would not take the risk of initiating disputes for fear of a retaliatory strike by the target.

Classical deterrence theory offers its practical prescription with some major advantages related to political convenience: it does not require that decision makers undertake an effort requiring great diplomatic skill or international cooperation to prevent the spread of nuclear weapons under conditions of prevailing distrust. That is particularly the case in Northeast Asia where regional rivals continue to argue over history and dispute territory. When all countries in the region are encouraged to build more devastating arsenals and increase stability by deterring each other, it would be a one-size-fits-all approach to responding to all those troubles without spending political resources.

Classical deterrence is quite compatible with another US grand strategy of "offshore balancing."[16] By promoting the voluntary arms race in Northeast Asia, the United States would not bear responsibility for subsidizing its allies' defense. Once regional powers can keep effective deterrents against potential rivals by developing and deploying nuclear weapons on their own, this "burden-shifting" strategy would enable the United States to husband its resources and concentrate on neglected domestic problems.[17]

If deterrence were easy, problems would already have been solved. Even practitioners step back from its logical implications. A most controversial implication of classical deterrence theory is that nuclear proliferation would induce automatic stability, and that stability would be further enhanced if the nuclear balance were secured in contested regions. Thus, a universal MAD is the optimal solution. Despite its logical elegance and parsimony, academics and practitioners alike have come to the realization that classical deterrence theory, based on the Cold War experience, is oversimplified, and many have rejected it in practice. Empirical shortcomings are manifest in three areas.

First, the US government does not fashion its policies on the basis of the theory of classical deterrence, specifically the notion that nuclear proliferation stabilizes contested environments. A central task of US nuclear policy has been not only to manage its stockpile of warheads but also to offset other countries' incentive to develop their own nuclear weapons program by an extended deterrence guarantee. Many other allied countries, including Japan and South Korea, all adhered to the terms of the Nuclear Non-Proliferation Treaty despite their significant latent capabilities to develop nuclear weapons immediately. They have never made a decision to develop them, however. US allies in Northeast Asia have refrained from developing nuclear weapons for political and not technical reasons.

Second, if MAD guarantees maximum stability, why is it current US policy to develop and deploy ballistic missile defenses (BMD) in Northeast Asia and Europe? Per classical deterrence theory, for deterrence to be stabilized, states should be defenseless against the second-strike capability from their enemies. Conversely, fielding shield defenses generates potential instability by undermining an opponent's retaliatory capability. Nevertheless, the historical evidence shows that US policy makers exhibit a general discomfort with the logic that MAD ensures stability. Rather, the Pentagon has sought to achieve a nuclear advantage rather than preserve MAD by developing BMD technology since the early 1980s.

The George W. Bush administration's withdrawal from the ABM Treaty in 2002 was the first US renunciation of an arms control treaty in the nation's nuclear history. After withdrawing from the treaty, the United States started to develop the layered BMD system that intercepts potential missile attack in all phases of flight. Most recently, US Missile Defense Agency Director James Syring testified that the agency's $7.5 billion budget request in fiscal year 2017 particularly address the concerns in response to escalating threats from North Korea and Iran.[18] In 2019, the United States recently confirmed an alliance decision to deploy the Terminal High Altitude Area Defense (THAAD) system to South Korea despite China's strong opposition.

Third, the global transfer of nuclear materials or other relevant equipment far beyond Northeast Asia is a growing international security concern. US government agencies have stated that North Korea supplied Syria with a nuclear reactor and that North Korea and Iran cooperate closely in ballistic missile programs.[19] The United States and Israel have at times expressed their concern regarding the triangular ballistic missile and nuclear cooperation of these three countries, which, they believe, could destabilize the Middle East.

In sum, in the minds of practitioners, nuclear weapons serve to both increase and decrease the likelihood of conflict, depending on the circumstances. Neorealist calculations may cause policy makers to be overly optimistic regarding the prospects of stable nuclear deterrence in the context of Northeast Asia. Classical deterrence correctly indicates that crises have not escalated to nuclear conflict since 1945 but incorrectly suggests that MAD insures absolute nuclear peace.

This line of criticism looks more troubling to policy makers in Northeast Asia because much of the existing literature on deterrence does not explicitly address anticipated challenges that may be generated in the twenty-first century by the acquisition of sophisticated nuclear capabilities by a new rising global competitor such as China or a rogue state such as North Korea. The next section examines an alternative scheme of deterrence that would bridge the chasm between such hardened polar positions.

TENUOUS NUCLEAR RELATIONSHIP: CONDITIONAL DETERRENCE IN NORTHEAST ASIA

Many scholars point out that the traditional understanding of classical deterrence based on the Cold War experience is selective, underspecified, and biased toward stability in light of an increasingly complex global and regional political setting.[20] Past nuclear stability does not guarantee that all future wars will be waged with conventional weapons.

Conditional deterrence, based on the principles of PTT, extends and generates a counterargument to the implications of classical deterrence.[21] This perspective posits that, as a risk-acceptant contender matches the killing capacity of the defender, deterrence may fail. Contrary to MAD, the preconditions for nuclear war are present as dissatisfaction with the status quo rises and as retaliation credibility declines. From this perspective, proliferation would be dangerous, particularly in a contested region.

Note that classical deterrence is tightly linked to the normative proposition that war never pays. It implies that the risky option of war is always to be considered inferior to the peaceful settlement of disputes because every rational decision maker presumably shares "zero" risk tolerance. Given that, common explanations for deterrence failure are "random" factors including accidental blunders, strategic mistakes, or cognitive bias.[22] A theoretical proposition cannot avoid errors. Blaming unpredictable events is a convenient but unacceptable explanation for potential deterrence failure. Conditional deterrence offers a systematic framework that focuses on the risk of deliberate nuclear exchange. This perspective assesses the conditionality of deterrence by incorporating more predictable regularities that account for the strategic decision process during a severe crisis.

Whereas others ask "what is the cost of war?" conditional deterrence asks the less apparent but equally significant question "what is the cost of maintaining the status quo?" States do not go to war because they believe that the cost is manageable. Rather, they sensibly compute the possibility of gain. War by definition is a risk-taking behavior because no party can be certain of the prospects for victory once the war starts.

   A critical realization is that maintaining the status quo involves less risk than launching a war, even though abiding by the status quo does not produce desired improvements. Instead, challenging the status quo, even when immensely risky, may produce positive returns. The historical record indicates that countries are at times willing to bear the risk of war in the hope of decisive victory, even when costs are great. Extreme risk-takers—like Hitler, Mao Zedong, or Bin Laden—seemingly viewed conflict as a reasonable chance to oppose the status quo under certain circumstances. Conditional deterrence implies that a dissatisfied and capable challenger would intentionally choose to take the opportunity associated with a potentially successful nuclear action when conditions are favorable. In other words, conditional deterrence proposes that war may not be an accident but rather be the outcome of goal-seeking behavior.

   The key elements of strategic war assessment include (i) relative capabilities to inflict mass casualties or damage on the other party, (ii) the risk propensity associated with the relative assessment of the status quo, and (iii) a credible counter-threat capability on the part of the defender. First, a shift in the distribution of capability is critical as it opens the window of opportunity for war. Consistent with previous findings,[23] conditional deterrence also argues that power parity, or the 50/50 condition, sets the timing for deterrence failure.

   Second, once the odds of winning and losing become approximately equal, a dissatisfied contender perceives a confrontation as an "opportunity" rather than as a "danger." This idea is consistent with the arguments of Kugler[24] and Kugler and Zagare,[25] who contend that dissatisfaction with the status quo drives individuals to adopt risk options.

   Third, the success of mutual deterrence depends on players' ability to project a credible threat. For deterrence to work, a potential opponent should believe in the resolute intention of the defender to inflict nuclear punishment or retaliation against a preceding nuclear strike.

   From a conditional deterrence perspective, figure 13.3 examines a specific case where contenders do not trust each other, while the challenger is risk-acceptant and dissatisfied. As shown in figure 13.2, figure 13.3 also illustrates the stability of deterrence on each nation's killing capacity but shows very different dynamics. Unlike the U-shaped representation of classical deterrence, conditional deterrence postulates the hill-shaped relationship with asymmetrical slopes.

   First, the satisfied defender's credible superiority leads to stable deterrence. Fully targeted threats do work effectively against a untrusting, risk-prone

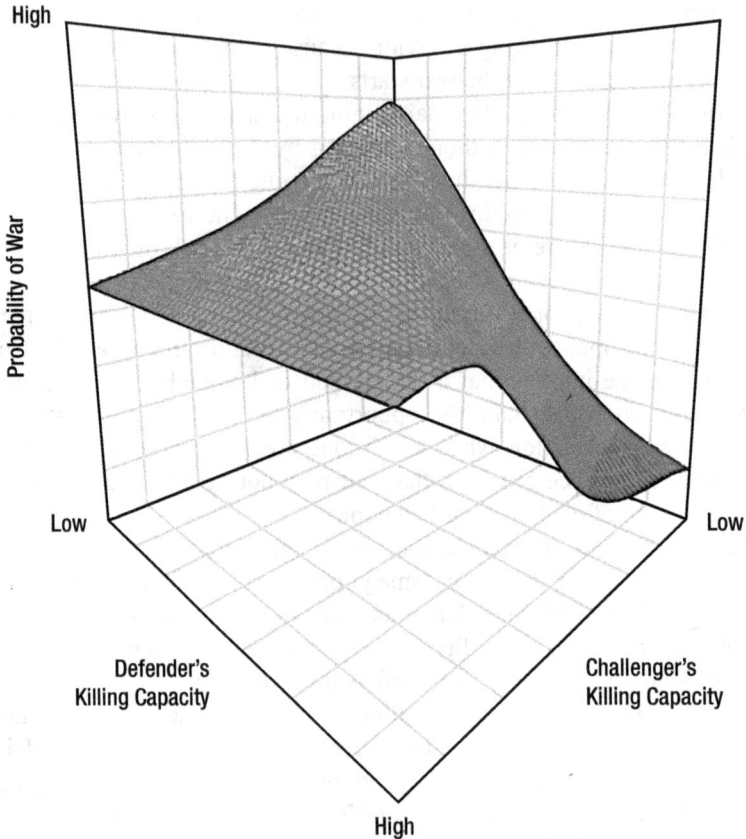

Figure 13.3. Conditional Deterrence Stability Assessment in Northeast Asia

potential nation as long as the defender maintains power preponderance. The US nuclear umbrella with its substantial military presence in South Korea and Japan has deterred North Korea from launching a nuclear strike. The US planned missile defense system would further enhance stability on the Korean Peninsula by increasing the credibility of US assurances to its allies. Regardless of a contender's evaluation of risk, deterrence would remain relatively stable between large and relatively small powers where conventional asymmetry is upheld by a credible threat. From this perspective, the Cold War remained stable between the 1960s and 1989 because the Union of Soviet Socialist Republics (USSR) and the Warsaw Pact could not conventionally defeat the United States and the North Atlantic Treaty Organization (NATO). As Zagare and Kilgour[26] correctly observed, "nuclear war has been avoided not because of nuclear weapons, but in spite of them."

Note that the United States faces a different set of threats from North Korea. North Korea's nuclear capability does not currently pose a direct threat to the United States, but it does constitute a serious indirect threat. And that flows from the possibility that North Korea could transfer nuclear technology and equipment to the Middle East and beyond. This represents a serious challenge to key US interests in various regions.

Second, dissatisfied and risk-acceptant states that reach conventional parity and possess nuclear arsenals may initiate all-out war. Contemplating the possibility of mutual annihilation may reduce the probability of reckless or inadvertent nuclear initiation. There is no clear reason, however, to believe that every potential opponent will desist from breaking the nuclear taboo if confronted with military disputes in which a first-strike option might be available. Under this circumstance, conditional deterrence directly contradicts classical deterrence because a risk-taking challenger may probe for advantages by waging a preemptive strike in accordance with a war-winning military doctrine.

The same judgment applies to the future of Northeast Asia regarding key questions frequently posed: "Under what conditions would China give up the potential satisfactory postwar world order when the use of weapons of mass destruction could reverse the outcome?" "Would Japan and South Korea resist using nuclear capabilities in potential confrontation with conventionally superior China?" Between the stark choice between fighting a nuclear war and surrendering, the conditions for an all-out war would likely emerge should the potential adversary be dissatisfied and risk-acceptant. As conventional and nuclear parity between the United States and China emerges in the long term, deterrence may then fail in Northeast Asia.

Third, deterrence will become most unstable under power parity, particularly when MAD is replaced by mutually assured protection with the proliferation of ballistic missiles (Condition C). Controlling for technical and budget constraints, the advantage of an effective missile defense system is clear if such a shield is in the hands of the preponderant status quo power. This conclusion will not be valid in the long run, however, as other countries join the game.

Conditional unlike classical deterrence anticipates serious threats to stability when the dissatisfied nations successfully gain access to sophisticated missile defense systems that nullify the credible threat of overwhelming nuclear retaliation from the defender. The recent report by the Federation of American Scientists shows that "Chinese development of strategic Ballistic Missile Defense (BMD) is ongoing . . . (as) an important hedging option against an uncertain and evolving future strategic environment."[27] Offensive missiles are no longer the ultimate option to secure peace.

In 2015, China decided to purchase Russia's S-400 missile defense systems anticipating their deployment in the first quarter of 2017.[28] Since then, Chinese and Russian military cooperation has increased dramatically. Modernizing offensive weapons and developing defensive shields figure as goal-oriented behavior aimed at achieving favorable cost-exchange ratios under conditions of mutual distrust. As in the case of the nuclear-dominant United States during the early Cold War, the unilateral deployment of US missile defense systems increased stability in the short term. However, its effect on China's status quo evaluation is disturbing as shown by the recent THAAD deployment that left China "deeply dissatisfied" and ready to take "necessary measures."[29] Given mutual distrust on security issues, the stability effects of BMD proliferation are not fundamentally different from those of nuclear proliferation in high-tech warfare. It is just a matter of weapon damage and efficiency.

Fourth, if the dissatisfied challenger has preponderant capability while the defender holds no deterrent, then the status quo will be revised. A confrontation would not escalate to nuclear strikes but instead end in the form of compellence (the opposite of deterrence). That is one of the major risks and dangers for Northeast Asia if the strategy of offshore balancing were implemented in practice as MAD no longer "balances" an aggressive stance. Japan, South Korea, and Taiwan would remain incapable of filling the void created by a withdrawal of US commitment to defend the regional status quo against a rising China. If the assurance of the US commitment were in question, the regional actors' incentive to pursue active nuclear programs for their own security would become a vital debate.

Although the fundamental logic of deterrence persists in the twenty-first century, it is dangerous to infer from the Cold War experience that previous grand strategies, morphed from massive retaliation to MAD, will ensure peace today and tomorrow. Nuclear war is indeed a rare event. Only once have nuclear weapons been used in conflict. A large number of crises that have involved nuclear threats have been settled without escalation.[30] However, given the proliferation of nuclear capabilities the fact that previous crises have not escalated to nuclear conflict since 1945 does not provide a guarantee that future crises and wars will remain conventional. Total severe wars that approximate anticipated nuclear costs are rare because structural conditions preceding previous ones have not been met since 1945.[31] Past results provide only partial solutions to specific problems that cannot be generalized.

FUTURE CONFLICT OR COOPERATION

The tentative argument advanced here is that regional stability exists only when a preponderant regional or global power has superior nuclear capabilities and is satisfied with existing norms.

The perspective of power transition contends that nuclear deterrence is conditional. This chapter argues that the size of nuclear arsenals does not generate stability monotonically. Conditional deterrence implies that nuclear initiation can be intentional and rational. The challenging implication is that to mitigate the risk of regional war, prescriptions that seek nuclear parity may enhance conflict, rather than reduce the likelihood of conflict. A strategy that preserves the preponderance of countries satisfied with the international order also stabilizes deterrence. In Northeast Asia a nuclear-free zone provides the best option for stability. At the global level, nuclear capabilities need to be retained, and as China overtakes the United States, stability is assured, assuming that the emerging dominant nation is motivated to accept the status quo.

A clear path toward stability has not yet been identified. Events in Northeast Asia show that the opportunity still exists to manage and potentially avoid conflict through cooperation and not confrontation. Without question, the development of North Korea's nuclear weapons makes regional reconciliation more difficult. A nuclear-free zone supported by a global power nuclear umbrella offering protection against any first use of nuclear weapons is the most stable option. Cooperative security emerges and is enhanced in the absence of threats. Indeed, Latin Americans achieved regional nuclear disarmament with the signing of the Treaty of Tlatelolco in 1967; in consequence, these actors no longer fear a regional nuclear war. Similar actions in the Korean peninsula enhanced by the United States and China could lead to regional stability in Northeast Asia. Any action that favors regional nuclear disarmament is better than inaction courting failure.

The task of sustaining stability and even moving to increasing cooperation is eased by the preponderance of Japan, an overt supporter of the status quo in this region. Japan's dominance prevents conventional conflict with either North or South Korea. Taiwan is an exception. China considers Taiwan a domestic rather than an international problem, and in this context, preponderance can lead to imposition. The policy that Taiwan and the United States adopt in the intermediate future will determine the resolution of this dispute.

Temporary stability in Northeast Asia can follow from the US and South Korea's recent decision to deploy an advanced defensive missile system since both support the status quo. North Korea would be less prone to seek new accommodation because it is currently incapable of fielding a defensive system. In the short term, the effective shield in the hands of the satisfied US alliance bolsters regional security. In the long term only a common commitment to international norms and values maintains peace.

NOTES

1. Global Map shows region contours. The hierarchy map shows the relative size of the top contenders in this region. Data are World Bank, "World Development Indicators," last modified March 27, 2016, http://documents.worldbank.org/curated/en/805371467990952829/World-development-indicators-2016.

2. Kristian S. Gleditsch, "Expanded Trade and GDP Data," *Journal of Conflict Resolution* 46, no. 5 (October 2002): 712–724. Forecast based on growth rates adapted from PWC 20250, "The World in 2050," last modified August 29, 2017, https://www.pwc.com/gx/en/issues/economy/the-world-in-2050.html.

3. Figure 13.1 source: Forecast based on growth rates adapted from PWC 20250, "The World in 2050," last modified August 29, 2017, https://www.pwc.com/gx/en/issues/economy/the-world-in-2050.html.

4. A discussion of regional deterrence could well have been the center of arguments in the chapter devoted to the Levant region, with its focus on Israel, or a central issue in the chapter on South Asia that covers India-Pakistan. Northeast Asia is chosen to discuss the implications of nuclear weapons on regional behavior because global deterrence policy, which was previously focused on Great Power confrontations, has been discussed extensively but the regional implications of nuclear proliferation are only now being directly addressed.

5. Hans M. Kristensen and Matt Korda, "Status of World Nuclear Forces," *The Federation of American Scientists Nuclear Notebook*, last modified May 2019, http://fas.org/issues/nuclear-weapons/status-world-nuclear-forces/.

6. Elbridge Colby and Michael Gerson, *Strategic Stability: Contending Interpretations* (Carlisle: Strategic Studies Institute and US Army War College Press, 2013).

7. Yoichi Funabashi, "Japan's Quiet Deterrence," *Japan Times*, December 17, 2015, http://www.japantimes.co.jp/opinion/2015/12/17/commentary/japan-commentary/japans-quiet-deterrence/#.V_f6yCQUzlc.

8. Scott Sagan, "The Case for No First Use," *Survival* 51, no. 3 (2009): 163–182; Scott Sagan, "Policy: A Call for Global Nuclear Disarmament," *Nature* 487, no. 7405 (2012): 30–33; Bruce Blair, Matt Brown, and Richard Burt, "Can Disarmament Work?" *Foreign Affairs* 90, no. 4 (July/August 2011): 173–178; George Perkovich and James Acton (eds.), *Abolishing Nuclear Weapons: A Debate* (Washington, DC: Carnegie Endowment for International Peace, 2009).

9. Richard K. Betts, "The Lost Logic of Deterrence," *Foreign Affairs* 92, no. 2 (2013): 87–99.

10. Bernard Brodie, *The Absolute Weapon: Atomic Power and World Order* (Manchester: Ayer Co Pub, 1946).

11. John J. Mearsheimer, "Back to the Future: Instability in Europe after the Cold War," *International Security* 15, no. 5 (1990): 56.

12. Brodie, *The Absolute Weapon*; Bernard Brodie, *Strategy in the Missile Age* (Princeton: Princeton University Press, 1959); Michael D. Intriligator and Dagobert L. Brito, "Can Arms Races Lead to the Outbreak of War?" *Journal of Conflict Resolution* 28, no. 1 (March 1984): 63–84.

13. Mearsheimer, "Back to the Future," 5–56; John J. Mearsheimer, "The Case for a Ukrainian Nuclear Deterrent," *Foreign Affairs* 72, no. 3 (Summer 1993): 50–66.

14. Kenneth N. Waltz, "Why Iran Should Get the Bomb: Nuclear Balancing Would Mean Stability," *Foreign Affairs* 91, no. 4 (July/August 2012): 2–5.

15. John Mueller, *Atomic Obsession: Nuclear Alarmism from Hiroshima to Al-Qaeda* (New York: Oxford University Press, 2009).

16. John J. Mearsheimer and Stephen M. Walt, "The Case for Offshore Balancing: A Superior U.S. Grand Strategy," *Foreign Affairs* 95, no. 4 (July/August 2016): 22.

17. Christopher Layne, "Offshore Balancing Revisited," *Washington Quarterly* 25, no. 2 (2002): 233–248.

18. Cheryl Pellerin, "Missile Defense Agency Budget Addresses Escalating North Korea, Iran Threats," *U.S. Department of Defense*, April 14, 2016, https://dod.defense.gov/News/Article/Article/721122/missile-defense-agency-budget-addresses-escalating-north-korea-iran-threats/.

19. Mark Manyin, Emma Chanlett-Avery, Dianne Rennack, Ian Rinehart, and John Rollins, "North Korea: Back on the State Sponsors of Terrorism Lists?" *Congressional Research Service*, no. 7-5700, January 21, 2015, https://www.fas.org/sgp/crs/row/R43865.pdf.

20. Alexander George and Richard Smoke, *Deterrence in American Foreign Policy: Theory and Practice* (New York: Columbia University Press, 1974); Jacek Kugler and Frank Zagare, *Exploring the Stability of Deterrence* (Boulder: Lynne Rienner Publishers, 1987); Paul Huth and Bruce Russett, "What Makes Deterrence Work? Cases from 1900–1980," *World Politics* 36, no. 4 (1984): 496–526; Frank C. Zagare and D. Marc Kilgour, *Perfect Deterrence* (Cambridge: Cambridge University Press, 2000); Carole Alsharabati and Jacek Kugler, "War Initiation in a Changing World," *International Interactions* 34, no. 4 (2008): 358–381.

21. A. F. K. Organski and Jacek Kugler, *The War Ledger* (Chicago: University of Chicago Press, 1980); Jacek Kugler, "Terror without Deterrence: Reassessing the Role of Nuclear Weapons," *Journal of Conflict Resolution* 28, no. 3 (1984): 470–506; Alsharabati and Kugler, "War Initiation"; Kyungkook Kang and Jacek Kugler, "Assessment of Deterrence and Missile Defense in East Asia: A Power Transition Perspective," *International Area Studies Review* 18, no. 3 (2015): 280–296.

22. James Fearon, "Rationalist Explanations for War," *International Organization* 49, no. 3 (1995): 379–414; Robert Powell, "Crisis Bargaining, Escalation, and MAD," *American Political Science Review* 81, no. 3 (1987): 717–735; Richard Lebow and Janice Gross Stein, "Rational Deterrence Theory: I Think, Therefore I Deter," *World Politics* 41, no. 2 (1989): 208–224.

23. Organski and Kugler, *The War Ledger*.

24. Kugler, "Terror without Deterrence," 470–506.

25. Jacek Kugler and Frank C. Zagare, *Exploring the Stability of Deterrence* (Boulder: Lynne Rienner Publishers, 1987).

26. Zagare and Kilgour, *Perfect Deterrence*.

27. Bruce W. MacDonald and Charles D. Ferguson, "Understanding the Dragon Shield: Likelihood and Implications of Chinese Strategic Ballistic Missile Defense," *The Federation of American Scientists Special Report* (2015), accessed on September 5, 2016, http://calhoun.nps.edu/handle/10945/46801.

28. Franz Stefan Gady, "China Makes Advance Payment for Russia's S-400 Missile Defense Systems," *The Diplomat*, March 22, 2016, http://thediplomat.com/2016/03/china-makes-advance-payment-for-russias-s-400-missile-defense-systems/.

29. Ian Armstrong, "Why the U.S.-South Korea Missile Shield Could Provoke China to Develop Advanced Weaponry," *The Huffington Post*, August 16, 2016, http://www.huffingtonpost.com/ian-armstrong/us-korea-missile_b_11532232.html.

30. Kugler, "Terror without Deterrence"; Huth and Russett, "What Makes Deterrence Work?"

31. Organski and Kugler, *The War Ledger*; Ron L. Tammen, Jacek Kugler, Douglas Lemke, Allan Stam, Carole Alsharabati, Mark Abdollahian, Brian Efird, and A. F. K. Organski, *Power Transitions: Strategies for the 21st Century* (New York: Chatham House, 2000).

Chapter Fourteen

Central Asia

Caught in the Middle

J. Patrick Rhamey, Jr.

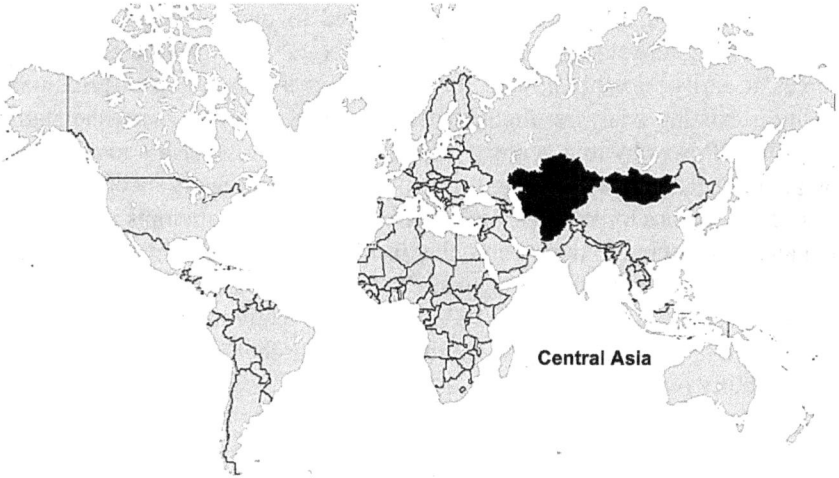

Central Asia

Central Asia Region

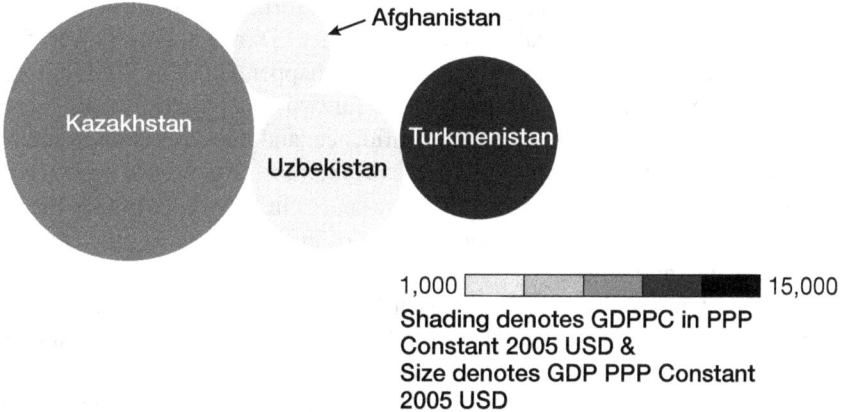

Afghanistan

Kazakhstan

Uzbekistan

Turkmenistan

1,000 ▭▨▨▨▨ 15,000
Shading denotes GDPPC in PPP
Constant 2005 USD &
Size denotes GDP PPP Constant
2005 USD

Central Asia Hierarchy

REGION UNDER STRESS

Given its geostrategic position, surrounded by the rising Asian giants most likely to challenge the US order in the twenty-first century, the Central Asia hierarchy presents an important case for evaluating regional stability.[1] As the economic and security interests of the United States, China, and Russia continue to rise in the region, so has recent analysis of their potentially conflictual impact.[2] The region has a long history as a space where major powers have attempted to extend their influence, often unsuccessfully, giving rise to violent conflicts, internal instability, and Great Power confrontation through proxy warfare and clandestine manipulation.

Little attention, however, has been granted to understanding better the potential for future stability or instability in Central Asia, given the emerging forces at parity. Notably absent, for example, is the inclusion of proximate India in existing analyses, though that country is likely to reach the status of a Great Power by mid-century.[3] Given the enormous outside interference by actors at parity, Central Asia is one of the most politically incoherent and disorderly regions today. Although there have been some attempts at developing an architecture of cooperation, that instability is likely to increase further as rising challengers struggle against existing US dominance. Much like the Middle East during the Cold War, Central Asia is likely to be a locus of volatility and rising competition for dominance among the Great Powers, as well as instability by mid-century.

THE ROLE OF GEOGRAPHY IN ADAPTING STATE BEHAVIOR

According to power transition theory (PTT), distance plays a significant role in modifying our understanding of capabilities, highlighting where states may or may not be capable of challenging one another.[4] During the Cold War, for example, Soviet confrontation of the US order happened not in Washington, but in those geographic spaces in between the two superpowers where there was some question about which state's influence, and thereby vision of international politics, would prevail. As a result, the most violent and protracted conflicts of the Cold War clustered in these spaces in between, visually forming a ring around the Soviet Union's sphere of influence: Berlin, the Middle East, Vietnam, and Korea.

Whether recounting the Peloponnesian War, the collapse of Rome, the expansion of the Abbasid Caliphate, or the demise of the Soviet Union, a similar pattern emerges where a dissatisfied rising challenger seeks to contest the pre-existing dominant order in those geographic spaces between the challenger and the dominant state. Challengers only challenge the dominant power in spaces where there exists some opportunity for success in altering the status quo. Absent that opportunity, they are constrained to diplomatic and economic cooperation and conflict within the context of the status quo if they wish to further their aims. Violent attempts by challenging states in geographic spaces where the strength of the dominant power is contested create what have been described, in various conceptual iterations, as shatterbelts,[5] security complexes,[6] or dominance vacuums,[7] wherein conflicts are routine because of the presence of balanced projected capabilities between the most powerful states projecting power into the region. In these spaces characterized by parity in the power projection of the most dominant states, conflicts are three times as likely as in spaces where a single state is dominant.[8] Combined with the finding that parity between actors within regions increases the probability of conflict,[9] regional spaces both without a regional power and with parity in the power projection of major powers are the most conflictual regions in the international system.[10]

As examples, the most violent battles of World War II, such as Stalingrad, occurred where the projected power of Germany and the Soviet Union or the United States intersected; the trench lines crossing Europe in World War I fell at the intersection of the projected power of France and Germany[11]; following enormous violence, the Siege of Port Arthur in the Russo-Japanese War ended with a Japanese victory, given the proximity of Japan and the great distance from the centers of Russian power in Europe, despite greater Russian military capability overall. However, perhaps one of the lengthiest historical epochs characterized by a regional space suffering repeated conflict as a battleground between a rising challenger and dominant power was Central Asia in the nineteenth century between Russia and the United Kingdom.

Not unlike the situation in the nineteenth century, the Central Asian space has once again found itself at the crossroads of external major power intervention. However, unlike the situation in the past, technological innovations have made the relative remoteness of the states and people in Central Asia less of a limiting condition, only further increasing the potential for challengers and powers to manipulate and contest one another within that geographic space. No other region has such an unfortunate position: Central Asia is central to the ongoing confrontations between the United States and Russia. In the future, India and China will play an increasing role in dictating the trajectory of this region as competition over control of the global arena tightens.

This chapter evaluates the present and future stability of Central Asia by examining the past. What can be learned about the impact of power parity from the historical precedents of the Great Game? Given the effects of the power projection of challengers and powers into the geographic space, how can one understand the contemporary cooperation and conflict? Finally, what does the future hold and how might the Central Asian region be managed to avoid instability?

CENTRAL ASIA'S PAST INTERACTIONS

Although the Great Game is typically described as a contest between Russia and the United Kingdom, it also emphasizes how in the past geography had a limiting impact on major powers' abilities to project their capabilities into remote spaces. Figure 14.1 illustrates dominance vacuums where the projected capabilities of Russia and the United Kingdom were contested in Central Asia.[12] In these spaces, either the two Great Powers were projecting an equivalent amount of power, or their capabilities were degraded so significantly that they no longer projected any meaningful power to a target destination.[13] Fearful of the proximity of a rival so near their borders, both powers sought to expand their influence to prevent gains in the relative influence of their opponent.

The Russians continued to expand into Central Asia throughout the nineteenth century, while the British sought to defend access to India by extending their influence into Afghanistan. Regionally, the distribution of capabilities between the two major powers was balanced. Indeed, measuring the projected capabilities of the two empires to Central Asia in a manner consistent with past attempts to evaluate power projected over distance[14] renders an outcome that appears to show that Britain and Russia were at relative parity around Kabul, albeit with quite limited capabilities as the First Anglo-Afghan War clearly demonstrated.

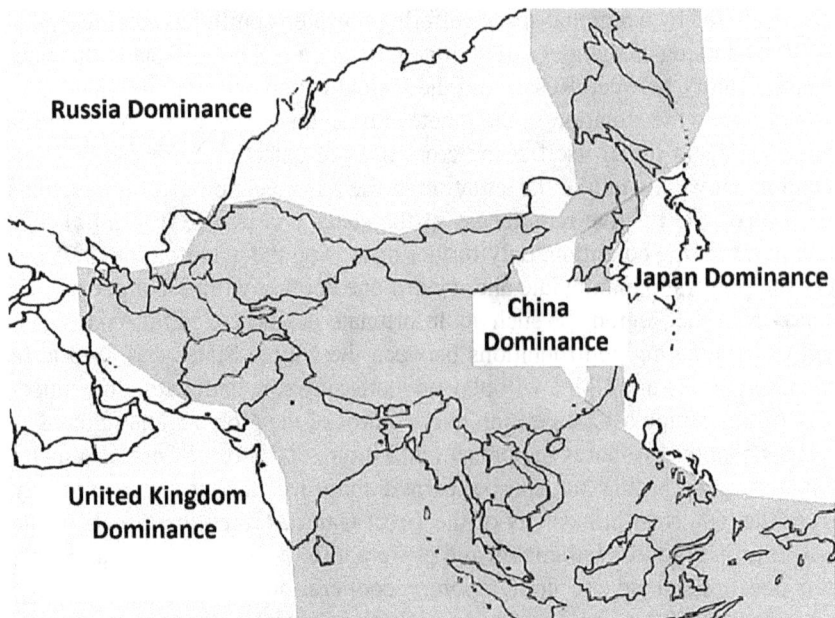

Figure 14.1. Nineteenth-Century Dominance Vacuums

Although neither empire desired war, both sides adopted policies consistent with modern realist prescriptions of offshore balancing, expanding their influence into Central Asia to counter each other's expanding influence. The results, however, were somewhat disastrous for both sides and contributed to violence and instability in the region. Initially, the British withdrawal at the conclusion of the First Anglo-Afghan War ended in significant defeat, as the two powers sought to rapidly fill the void left by the collapse of Mughal Empire in the eighteenth century. Given the relatively limited technological capabilities of the British empire in the early nineteenth century, projecting power to distant Kabul was difficult, resulting in the massacre of British soldiers in the 1842 retreat to Jalalabad, where, of the entire British army column, only British surgeon William Brydon returned. Afghanistan in this historical context operated as a buffer state assaulted on both sides by repeated, and somewhat poorly organized, influence and intervention on the part of the major powers who attempted to exert influence and control. Rather than that parity creating stability and peace, the result was relatively continuous periods of conflict and instability.

Britain's second military attempt was more successful, albeit still costly, in part because of the completion of the Suez Canal and the corresponding greater ease with which Britain could now project power to South Asia. Thousands died in fighting or by disease due to the Amir of Afghanistan accepting a Russian diplomatic mission but refusing to accept a British one. Trying to preserve the "balance" in Central Asia, not in terms of military or territorial control but simply diplomatic influence, not only failed to deter conflict and create a peaceful equilibrium but also sparked a war.

Although the two major players of the Great Game stopped short of direct war, that restraint was more a result of limitations in projecting power across difficult terrain than a result of the deterrence of bipolarity. Indeed, Russian advances into Uzbek territories led the British to support Pashtun conquest of Uzbek lands, resulting in significant violence and systematic discrimination against occupied peoples. Much like colonial influence elsewhere, the redrafting of borders, resettlement of peoples, and ethnic grievances the intervening major powers stirred up produced instability that continues to plague the region today. Contrary to the oversimplistic realist ideal of balance of power creating stability for the region, the balance in Central Asia created a space for recurring instability throughout the nineteenth century, with long-lasting impact. Furthermore, many of these same dynamics are emerging today as external powers seek to exert influence in the space much like the British and the Russians of the nineteenth century. As the Great Game wreaked havoc on the region, so too will the developing contests of the twenty-first century.

THE COLD WAR AND CENTRAL ASIA

During the Cold War, the contestation and parity that existed within the Central Asian region was reduced as the region, having been incorporated into the tsarist Russian empire in the latter half of the nineteenth century, fell squarely within the domain of the Soviet Union. Instead, the competition between the dominant power, the United States, and the challenger, the Soviet Union, played out in peripheral regions far from the Soviet heartland such as Southeast Asia and the Middle East.[15] Although some conflict did exist between the Soviet Union and China, those conflicts were limited to border disputes with China proper rather than contesting control over the region as, aside from Afghanistan, the region was part of the Soviet state. It was not until the Soviet-Afghan War of the 1980s that meaningful conflict in the geographic space reemerged, resulting in a conflict that did not subside until Soviet power began to wane, shifting attention to internal issues at the Cold War's end.

This decade of conflict in the 1980s, coinciding with a steady erosion in Soviet power, exhibits dynamics similar to the interfering major powers observed during the Great Game. Although the United States does not engage in a direct, overt manner, it supports local insurgents with assistance from proximate regimes (Pakistan) to destabilize the puppet regime of its primary competitor, much as the British did during the nineteenth century with their support of the Pashtuns.

This destabilization process continued until the Soviets eventually withdrew at the end of the 1980s. Following the collapse of the Soviet Union in 1991, as figure 14.2 shows, any residual contest that may have existed between the two major powers dissolved, leaving the United States as an unchallenged major power across almost the entire geographic space.[16] Although that dominance did not inherently produce internal stability in Afghanistan or in the successor states that emerged following the Soviet Union's demise, the negative impacts of external intervention caused by a parity in the power projection of the most powerful states was relatively absent.

Compared with both the 1980s and 2000s, the 1990s, particularly the latter half of the decade following the conclusion of the Tajik civil war, exhibited the greatest lack of balance of power within the region and were also far more stable, demonstrating a total failing of neorealist logic to accurately describe the politics at the regional level within the space. Note, however, that stability does not mean that the situation is either good or benevolent, as the stabilization that emerged coincided, for example, with the consolidation of power by the Taliban in Afghanistan, unchecked by US dominance. Other regimes in the region, furthermore, often had little respect for democracy, human rights, or liberal values.

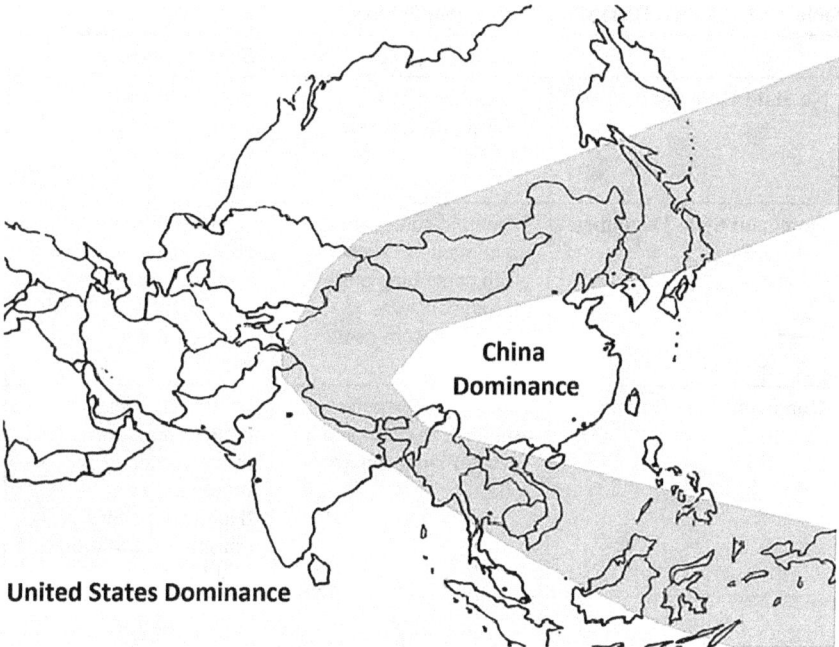

China
Dominance

United States Dominance

Figure 14.2.   Dominance Vacuums, 2015

More than simply exhibiting a relative absence in conflict, the region de-veloped a coherent pattern of behavior among its members in the late 1990s, and significant amounts of cooperation apart from intervention by external major powers.[17] However, following the terrorist attacks of September 11, 2001, and increased external involvement in the 2000s from China and Rus-sia, these cooperative patterns of behavior eroded. In a recent analysis of the region, one author finds that the Central Asian space has lacked coherence as actors are pulled in different directions from outside,[18] whereas others find that the Central Asian space as a politically relevant cluster of multilateral patterns of engagement existed briefly but then dissolved.[19] The fragmenting dynamics of the region that were characteristic during the nineteenth cen-tury, the end of the Cold War, and today were reduced during the 1990s, and so conflict was relatively less present. However, the increased capabilities of China and a resurgent Russia, alongside very direct engagement by the United States, have returned disorder to the region.

Confrontation, however, does not necessarily imply violence, as the Shanghai Cooperation Agreement and China's "One Belt, One Road" ini-tiative demonstrate. Inhibited by distance or the presence of an intervening major power, contesting states may employ cooperative means of increasing

Table 14.1. Parity, Distance, and Regional Politics

	Proximate Space	*Distant Space*
No State Dominant	Great Power War (World War I; World War II)	Proxy warfare (Arab-Israeli Wars, Russo-Afghan War, Vietnam War)
Dominant State Declining	Economic contestation, no immediate conflict given continuing presence of dominant state (Late-nineteenth-century Europe)	Low-level conflicts; cooperative architecture formation but failed implementation (Great Game; Central Asia today)
Dominant State Present	Effective cooperative architecture (Europe and Western Hemisphere today)	Limited diplomatic contestation, occasional military intervention by dominant state (Eighteenth-century coastal Asia; Middle East today)

their influence at less significant costs than entailed in conflict. Table 14.1 illustrates the expected relationship between distance and dominance for the behavior of major powers in a geographic space.

Moving forward, the Central Asian space is transitioning from one where a dominant state was engaged in the 2000s toward one where that geographic dominance, distant from US shores, is increasingly being challenged. However, although the US presence is still dominant, contesting states—China, Russia, and India—will likely engage in more subtle forms of competition than overt war to advance their goals. One such avenue is the formation of at least nominally cooperative architecture, but without an unchallenged dominant state to ensure the viability of cooperative institutions, their impact should be minimal.

An initial flurry of potential cooperation lay with the Shanghai Cooperation Organization (SCO), which declined into a forum representative of the region's fragmentation. Although the SCO initially appeared to be an attempt to offer the promise of cooperation, in the twenty-first century this institution had developed into a manifestation of the incongruent interests of two major powers of varying degrees of dissatisfaction. Russia being unable, given its limited capabilities, to provide meaningful cooperative architecture of its own supported the initiative yet later subverted attempts to provide stability that were incongruent with its own interests.[20] Institutional arrangements, security agreements, and economic engagement were often simply stopgap measures employed by Russia to prevent the further erosion of its power along its own border and within former Soviet territory.[21] China, likewise, has openly viewed the SCO as something of a forum to articulate its policy to the region, treating Russia as something of a participant no different from many of the nonmajor powers in the area.[22] With the addition of India and Pakistan to the organization, the "muddled" nature of the organization's agenda, and its limited practical effectiveness, only increased. To the extent that there are practical impacts of the SCO, it is not clear that these activities represent a clear alternative to the existing status quo. The United States, though not a member of the organization, still deeply influences most outcomes in Central Asia.

A second cooperative initiative emerges from the Chinese "One Belt, One Road" policy (see chapter 3). Although it is obvious that trade lanes allow China to penetrate new markets, perhaps followed by political and even military gains, the specific intent and operational details may be more difficult to orchestrate than China hopes. It is too early to assess the impact of this potentially massive initiative.

From a more competitive perspective, the United States, following its return to direct military intervention in the region after the terrorist attacks of September 11, views the Central Asian space as an opportunity to protect other external interests from the negative impact of violent nonstate actors. As a dissatisfied state in decline, Russia has sought to counter this US presence in low-level conflictual behavior, such as the ouster of the US military from the Kyrgyzstani base at Manas, whereas China has focused more on soft-power engagement.[23]

Given that the United States remains the dominant state globally, China has thus far engaged in somewhat passive, quiet methods of increasing its influence.[24] This quiet diplomacy and economic engagement of Chinese foreign policy closely mirrors the early nineteenth century behavior of Russia. When the Soviets began to contest the Central Asian space in the nineteenth century, similar tactics were used. Outmatched in capabilities by the dominant British, Russia at that time focused on diplomatic arrangements to expand its influence. However, Russian policies became the flash point for wars by dominant Britain. Thus, this relatively low level of dissatisfaction induced on the periphery by Russian acts expanded into larger regional conflicts. Similar patterns may emerge today as they did then.

Central Asian elites seek to extract gains today by playing external powers off against one another, notably by manipulating energy interests. Much like Dost Mohammad of Afghanistan in the early nineteenth century, who extracted gains for personal political advantage, exacerbating external divisions fed by parity to gain concessions, today leaders of Central Asian states engage in greedy behavior at odds with the desires of the United States and do so with impunity. For example, the highly antidemocratic behaviors of Turkmenistan and Uzbekistan, the corruption of the Afghan government, and the human-rights abuses in Tajikistan are all overlooked as the United States, facing direct competition from Russia and China, sets aside nonmaterial preferences to focus on the material advantages provided by the regional space.[25]

CENTRAL ASIA IN 2050

Looking forward, it would appear that the region is moving toward less clarity, rather than more, in the hierarchy of competing states, and those states seeking to govern the space are more proximate than they have been in the past. This trend will push Central Asia and Southeast Asia toward the upper left quadrant of figure 14.3. However, the topography of Central Asia is likely to minimize interdependence. This leaves Southeast Asia more susceptible to the staging of a possible global conflict. Figure 14.3 illustrates the distribution of contested versus uncontested spaces expected moving toward 2050.[26]

Given this distribution of capabilities, there are four simple predictions that can be made for the future of the region, based on demography, parity, and power transition logic as seen in figure 14.4. First, however, a brief

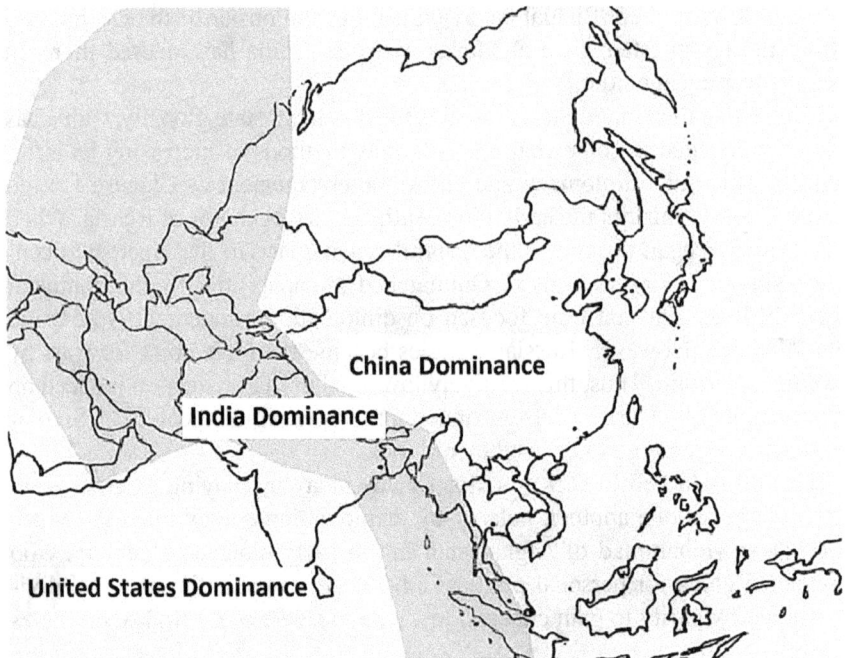

Figure 14.3.   Dominance Vacuums, 2050

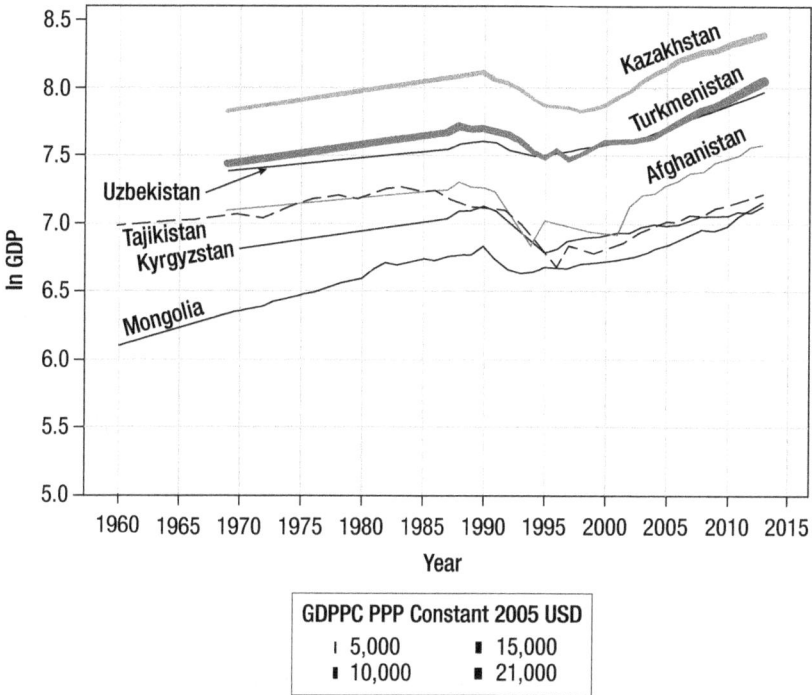

Figure 14.4. Power Projections in Central Asia

recounting of both historical and contemporary events thoroughly discredits the realist logic that suggests that a balance of power assures stability. Thinking about dominance versus parity on a continuum, those periods where the region has been dominated by a single power have had the greatest stability, whereas those with the greatest parity between competing actors led to increased conflictual behavior, whether in the nineteenth century, the 1980s, or unfortunately, possibly into the future. Despite preliminary attempts to create cooperative architecture, if the space lacks a dominant actor, Dushanbe and Tashkent are likely to suffer the fates of Sarajevo and Saigon. It should be noted, however, that the predictions that follow assume relative stability in the current demographic and economic trajectories of major powers.[27]

ROLE OF COMPETITORS

Russia

Although Russia has been active in the region over the past two decades, that activity has been motivated by decline rather than being an attempt at challenging the global or regional order imposed by the United States. It may continue to behave in ways that are incongruent with the desires of the United States, but given current capabilities Russia does not present a serious challenge to the status quo. Projecting into the future, despite its proximity, Russia's relevance will continue to diminish given its demographic character-istics: with a population of 144 million, it cannot hope to remain competitive with China's 1.4 billion or India's 1.3, particularly as those societies continue to develop economically. Russia's irredentist policies, as has been the case in Ukraine and Abkhazia, may continue, but in view of present Soviet capa-bilities, such policies are unlikely to succeed, with the exception of northern Kazakhstan. However, confronted with the likelihood of an overt military confrontation against more powerful states—the United States, China, or India—that would expose its relative weakness, Russia would likely hesitate. Indeed, by 2050, Russia may find itself effectively challenged by the United States and China even in its own backyard, subject to many of the same de-stabilizing effects of contemporary Central Asia.

India

Although existing literature typically overlooks India as not particularly engaged at present, demographics, proximity, and policy affinity with the United States are likely to make India a pivotal player. First, according to some estimates, India may attain Great Power status within the next few de-cades.[28] As a regional power, its greatest impediment lies in its rivalry with Pakistan, which may, however, decline in significance given the rising gap in capabilities between the two states. However, as China's relationship with Japan demonstrates, trouble with a neighbor is not sufficient to prevent extra-regional engagement, notably with neighboring Central Asia where they have had a history of involvement.

As a democratic state, India has preferences that may identify it as far more satisfied with the US system than China is. With the gap between the United States and others slowly diminishing, much like the British at the end of the nineteenth century, US attention may shift toward assessing which nations are satisfied or dissatisfied with the existing international system to promote the interests of one challenger over another. As the Brit-ish were confronted by a satisfied rising United States and a dissatisfied Germany, so too the United States, in its decline, may be confronted with a relatively satisfied India and a relatively dissatisfied China. The United States could, through India, manage a steady transition in the region to promote cooperation and avoid conflict.[29] However, should India play the role of liberal bulwark against illiberal China, the underlying groundwork for the next power transition, at the global level, is likely to play out in the Central Asian and Southeast Asian spaces between the two nations.

China

Although the SCO and other Chinese initiatives like "One Belt, One Road" represent a flurry of cooperative activity, it is not clear what policy will emerge from China's current economic thrust into Central Asia. In this region, civil wars, terrorism, and subterfuge have already characterized the region over the past decade, continuing patterns that were typical in the latter years of the Cold War and the Great Game. As parity mounts between China and the United States, intervention is likely to become more frequent as well. Furthermore, new avenues of engaging in unconventional conflict may occur, such as destabilization through cyberattacks between belligerents on targets relevant to the contested geographic space.

China has thus far not entered the security arena very vigorously. On the other hand, US foreign policy militarized these distant dominance vacuums and may simply exacerbate conflicts rather than deter them. Increased military presence in the region merely offers greater opportunity to engage in conflict, but given limitations imposed by the geographic space, and the contesting powers themselves, there will be more opportunities to suffer crushing defeats similar to the great retreat to Jalalabad by the lone British officer in the First Anglo-Afghan War. A US policy that overstretches the dominant state capabilities provides targets for rising challengers or an undeterred state or a nonstate actor seeking to exert influence in the fractured Central Asian region. China may choose this geographic space at parity to challenge the status quo supported by the dominant power.

FUTURE CONFLICT AND COOPERATION

Given issues of dissatisfaction, distance, and terrain, the Central Asia region is likely to continue what has been a historically consistent pattern of relatively limited conflict, but without the large-scale conflicts endemic to Europe. Although technology has made overcoming distance somewhat easier than it was when the British sought to project power to Kabul in the nineteenth century, constraints are still present. Confrontation is likely from external sources. The US reliance on air power has dramatically increased the ability of naval-based power to permeate the Central Asian space. The prospect of a conflict in Central Asia triggering larger confrontations could potentially loom large as China increasingly challenges the power of the United States.[30] Moreover, the fractionalization of Central Asia provides an opportunity for multiple disputes among the Great Powers over future distribution of regional resources. PTT considers such concerns to be unlikely. Note that during both the Great Game and the Cold War, Central Asia's multiple conflicts ran their course without escalating to a major power war, but—and this is important—in neither case did an actual power transition take place. Rather, Russia, the potential challenger, went into decline without ever reaching parity with the dominant states, Britain and later the United States.

The likely scenario, unless cooperation emerges, is that proxy wars, active attempts at destabilizing regimes in contested spaces, and other forms of limited conflict will proliferate. One cannot discount the possibility that, during the anticipated transition between a dominant state and a *dissatisfied* challenger, a major war could take place based on a conflict in Central Asia. Two such scenarios are likely. First, China is overtaking the United States, so the potential for conflict looms large in the near future.[31] Second, India may overtake China around the end of this century, providing a second opportunity for confrontation. Resolving differences in the status quo among these giants is not in the hands of Central Asian powers but may be a necessary prerequisite to sustain regional and global stability.

Cooperation is possible but at this point less likely. Regional conflict anticipated throughout this discussion is unlikely to subside within the region. China's "One Belt, One Road" initiative has such a potential (chapter 3). Yet, cooperative activity seldom flourishes in a region that is divided by conflict. In the Central Asian region, local leaders can seek to resolve disputes and establish institutions that reflect their views effectively. Initiatives such as the SCO, which restrict the forum to regional representatives and focus on reducing the fragmentation among them, could be a first step toward cooperation. A regional SCO-like initiative that excludes the global competitors could develop into a manifestation of the congruent interests of regional powers. The prospects for such actions are slim but not impossible. In the review of South America, we pointed to the completion of the Treaty of Tlatelolco that creates a nuclear-free zone in that region. Disagreements among Latin Americans persist and internal civil wars continue to be waged, but a modicum of stability emerged because internal or international conflicts are constrained. Central Asian states can also follow such a path that could eventually include further economic coordination. Cooperation can emerge, but in Central Asia this is admittedly a thorny road.

NOTES

1. Global Map shows region contours. The hierarchy map shows the relative size of the top contenders in this region. Data are World Bank, "World Development Indicators," last modified March 27, 2016, http://documents.worldbank.org/curated/en/805371467990952829/World-development-indicators-2016.

2. Alexander Cooley, *Great Games, Local Rules* (Oxford: Oxford University Press, 2012).

3. Thomas J. Volgy, Renato Corbetta, J. Patrick Rhamey, Jr., Keith A. Grant, and Ryan G. Baird, "Status Considerations in International Politics and the Rise of Regional Powers," in Deborah Larson, T. V. Paul, and William Wohlforth (eds.), *Status in World Politics* (Cambridge: Cambridge University Press, 2014).

4. Douglas Lemke, *Regions of War and Peace* (Cambridge: Cambridge University Press, 2002).

5. Paul R. Hensel and Paul F. Diehl, "Testing Empirical Propositions about Shatterbelts, 1945–1976," *Political Geography* 13, no. 1 (1994): 33–51.

6. Barry Buzan and Ole Wæver. *Regions and Powers: The Structure of International Security* (Cambridge: Cambridge University Press, 2003).

7. J. Patrick Rhamey, Jr., Michael O. Slobodchikoff, and Thomas J. Volgy, "Order and Disorder across Geopolitical Space: The Effect of Declining Dominance on Interstate Conflict," *Journal of International Relations and Development* 18, no. 4 (2015): 383–406.

8. Ibid.

9. Lemke, *Regions of War and Peace*.

10. Thomas J. Volgy, Paul Bezerra, J. Patrick Rhamey, Jr., and Jacob Cramer, "The Case for Comparative Regional Analysis," *International Studies Review* 19, no. 3 (2017): 452–480.

11. Rhamey et al., "Order and Disorder."

12. Figures 14.1 and 14.2 source: Figures illustrating dominance vacuums are created by using the work of Kenneth Boulding, *Conflict and Defense: A General Theory* (New York: Harper, 1962); loss of strength gradient, adjusted for terrain, for the global major powers, in a manner consistent with that done by Lemke, *Regions of War and Peace*. The formula for calculating the degradation of power across distance, where power is the proportion of capabilities possessed by a state of all global capabilities, is $P_{ij} = \text{Power}^{\log[(\text{miles})/(\text{milesperday})+(10\text{-}e)]}$.

13. For Lemke, this amount is less than 50 percent of the state's total capabilities.

14. For example, see the map of World War I power projection in Rhamey et al., "Order and Disorder," 392.

15. Rhamey et al., "Order and Disorder."

16. Mapping power projection in a manner consistent with Rhamey et al. using Boulding's loss of strength gradient shows that in 1991, the United States was dominant globally in all spaces except for the immediate geographic space surrounding Moscow and Beijing.

17. Patterns of behavior can be observed using network analysis to identify groups of actors (in this case states) that behave uniquely apart from the international system. Rhamey found that, during the 1990s, one such space existed for Central Asia, when looking at events data coded from news sources. See J. Patrick Rhamey, Jr., "Constrained to Cooperate: Domestic Political Capacity and Regional Order" (PhD diss., University of Arizona, 2012).

18. Leila Zakhirova, "Is There a Central Asia? State Visits and Empirical Delineation of the Region's Boundaries," *The Review of Regional Studies* 42, no. 1 (2012): 25–50.

19. Rhamey, "Constrained to Cooperate."

20. Roy Allison, "Regionalism, Regional Structures and Security Management in Central Asia," *International Affairs* 80, no. 3 (2004): 463–483.

21. S. Neil MacFarlane, "The 'R' in BRICs: Is Russia an Emerging Power?" *International Affairs* 82, no. 1 (2006): 41–57.

22. Boris Rumer, "The Powers in Central Asia," *Survival* 44, no. 3 (2002): 57–68.

23. Matteo Fumagalli, "Alignments and Realignments in Central Asia: The Rationale and Implications of Uzbekistan's Rapprochement with Russia," *International Political Science Review* 28, no. 3 (2007): 253–271.

24. David Shambaugh, "China Engages Asia: Reshaping the Regional Order," *International Security* 29, no. 3 (2004): 64–99.

25. Alexander Cooley, *Great Games, Local Rules* (Oxford: Oxford University Press, 2012).

26. Figure 14.3 source: Adapted from Boulding's (1962) loss of strength gradient, adjusted for terrain, consistent with that done by Lemke (2002).

27. Figure 14.4 source: World Bank, "World Development Indicators." Forecast based on growth rates adapted from PWC 20250, "The World in 2050," last modified August 29, 2017, https://www.pwc.com/gx/en/issues/economy/the-world-in-2050.html.

28. Volgy et al., "Status Considerations."

29. Zbigniew Brezezinksi, *The Grand Chessboard: American Primacy and Its Geostrategic Imperatives* (New York: Basic Books, 1997).

30. Sarajevo in World War I offers a prime example of diffusion. The somewhat remote events of Sarajevo were a direct result of proxy meddling in local ethno-nationalist dynamics by Great Powers, leading to an enormously destructive war that took place primarily not in the Balkans but the fields of France and Belgium.

31. Volgy et al., "Status Considerations."

Chapter Fifteen

Southeast Asia

Emerging Pacific Contenders

Marina Arbetman Rabinowitz and John Thomas

Southeast Asia Region

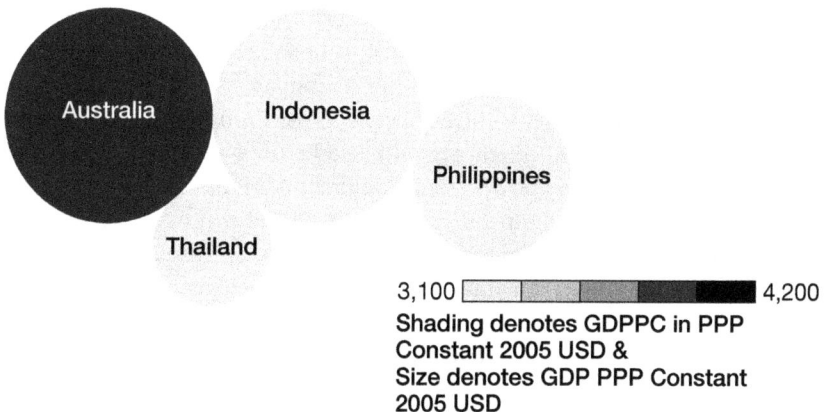

3,100 ▭▨▨▨▨▨■ 4,200
Shading denotes GDPPC in PPP
Constant 2005 USD &
Size denotes GDP PPP Constant
2005 USD

Southeast Asia Hierarchy

REGIONAL AND GLOBAL HIERARCHIES

Spanning multiple countries, cultures, and oceans makes this hierarchy unique.[1] To capture global effects but preserve the regional hierarchy perspective, this chapter proposes that effectively functioning regional hierarchies require relative independence from global powers. When global powers are focused on a region—such as the Middle East—the effects of regional hierarchies are distorted and minimized. When global powers are indifferent—as is the case in South America—the regional hierarchy effectively functions consistent with power transition principles.

The Southeast Asia region of concern here falls somewhere between these two extremes. Global powers compete and pay more attention to this region than they do to South America but are far less involved than in the case of the Middle East. Consequently, power transition logic applies to the Southeast Asia region.

SOUTHEAST ASIA CHARACTERISTICS

Southeast Asia is an unusual island and peninsular region whose members are greatly influenced by seas. This region includes countries surrounding the Arafura Sea, Coral Sea, the Philippine Sea, and the Tasman Sea. Southeast Asia is diverse economically, socially, and culturally. This region also includes many small countries. Our analysis focuses on Australia, New Zealand, Papua New Guinea, the Philippines, Indonesia, Singapore, Thailand, Cambodia, Vietnam, Laos, and Myanmar in the context of influences from the United States, India, and China.

All these states are linked by geography and have a diverse impact in the region. By any measure, Australia and Indonesia are the two dominant states in Southeast Asia. They operate in different spheres, although they occasionally overlap and have weathered serious diplomatic disagreements. Additional transitions within this hierarchy between the Philippines and Malaysia and between Thailand and Singapore will also be reviewed.

Figure 15.1 outlines the power transition preconditions for war or stability contingent on an overtaking in the process.[2] Indonesia will overtake Australia at the top of the regional hierarchy in the next decade. Based on current assessments of international interactions among these players, it is likely that both will move through this process as satisfied nations if residual nation-building issues are resolved.[3] If Indonesia manages to preserve the current status quo, Southeast Asia may become a modest counterweight to the growing challenge by China to dominate Asia.

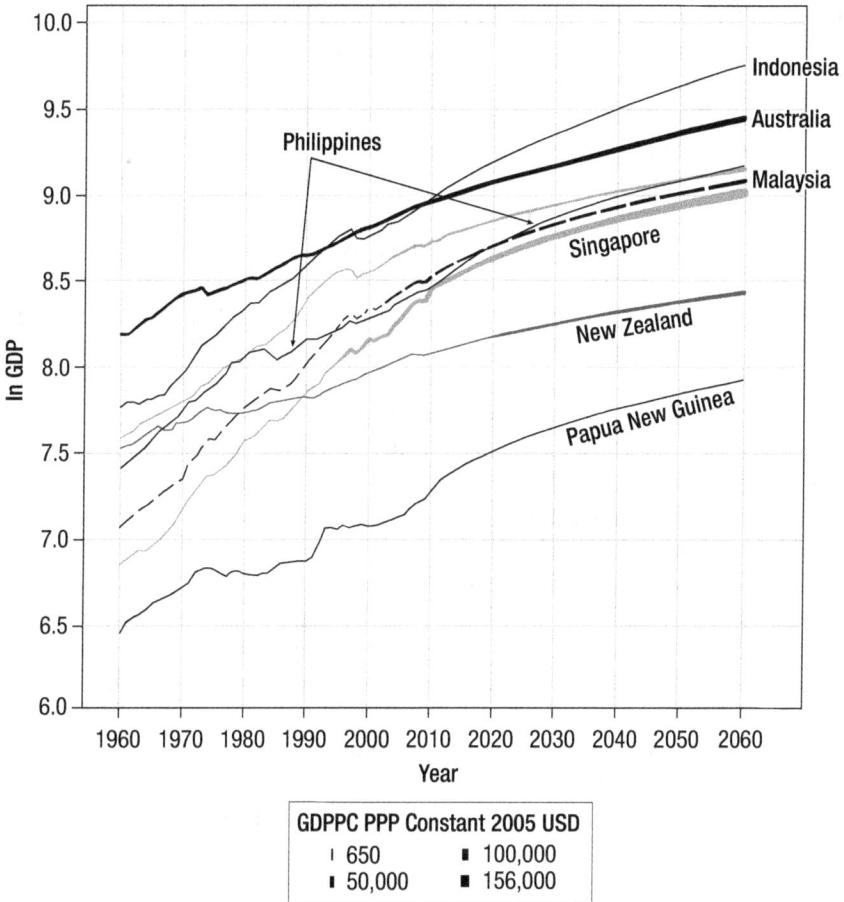

Figure 15.1. **Power Projections among Association of Southeastern Asian Nations+ (1960–2060)**

It is critical to look at this region because it contains many opportunities for transitions among states. Its members are forecast to enjoy higher economic growth rates than Western countries—which will generate regional imbalances. And the postcolonial effects are still vivid. The region encompasses states with large Muslim, Hindu, Christian, and Buddhist populations, creating an environment where neighbor states hold traditional or secular values.[4] Thus, the potential roots of regional dissatisfaction are deep. Driven by higher-than-average predicted economic growth and extremely diverse birth rates, transitions are bound to take place in the future.

One goal is to explore whether the forecast transitions set the preconditions for conflict among such diverse cultures. Is there a regional, satisfied dominant power in Southeast Asia that could foster stability? Will states in this expanding region seek bilateral regional or global arrangements? Given its proximity to Southeast Asia, will China's current modus operandi remain focused on economics or will it shift to more forceful security arrangements? What will be the role of India? What if any will be the response by the United States?

AUSTRALIA

Although not recognized regionally as such, since 1960 Australia has been the most powerful nation in Southeast Asia. Regional stability was sustained because Australia did not choose to challenge other members. The reason for this is that the focus of Australia is not regional. Although in general it has strengthened relations to Asia in lieu of Europe, Australia's primary focus remains global. At the global level, Australia has oscillated between the economic gains that Southeast Asia and China offer and the military security that the United States provides.[5]

Domestically Australia is weary of the political influence of China. Some journalists draw a parallel between Russia's influence in the US democratic system and China's impact on Australia's. However, at this point, China is seen as a seeker of financial opportunities while Australia is seen as a safe haven for Chinese investments. The reality is that China is the country's largest trading partner; with 28.8 percent of Australia's exports directed to China.[6] Australian export markets also include Japan, the United States, and South Korea; together, the four of them account for 55 percent of Australia's exports. Clearly the export focus is on the Great Powers rather than regional neighbors.

Population wise, Australia is becoming more Asian than European. The 2016 census data show that only half of its residents (50.7 percent) have two Australian-born parents. Of the 26 percent of the residents born overseas, the majority are from Asia, not Europe, and of those born overseas 8.2 percent were born in China.[7] China is also the second source of immigrants to Australia (India is the first). Both countries have enhanced their educational links; almost 160,000 Chinese students attend Australian universities, strengthening cultural ties with the large Chinese population in Australia.[8]

INDONESIA

The overtaking of Australia by Indonesia as indicated in figure 15.2 is anticipated within the next decade. For the first time this overtaking will alter regional dominance within Southeast Asia.[9]

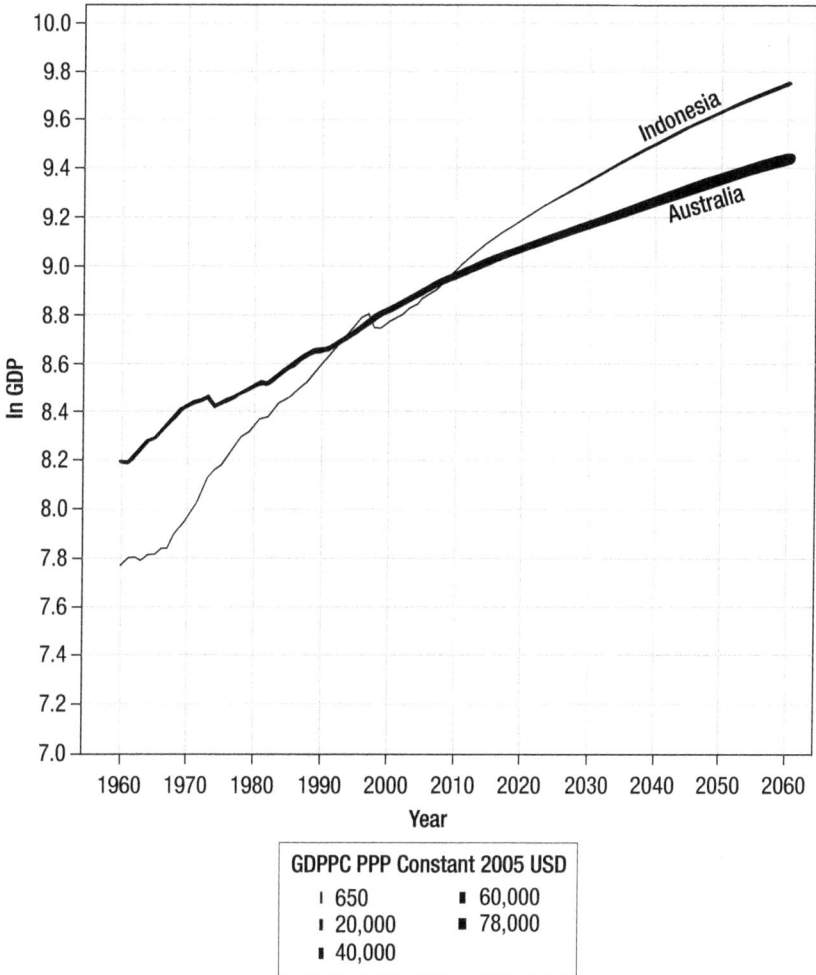

Figure 15.2. Transition between Australia and Indonesia

This upcoming event may alter both countries' regional perspective and involvement. Australia is not a member of the Association of Southeast Asian Nations (ASEAN), but it cooperates with other nations in the association. Indonesia, on the other hand, is a founder and active member of ASEAN.[10] Active since 1967, Indonesia, along with founding members Thailand, Malaysia, Singapore, and the Philippines, is a central actor. Indonesia's foreign and economic policy generally is consistent with ASEAN, but occasionally it diverges sharply. At times, Indonesia's foreign policy reflects that of an independent agent, willing to assert its regional position with minor competitors, but avoiding conflicts with major powers. On several occasions, Indonesia's relations with the global international community were tense. For example, in the mid-1970s Indonesia invaded and then annexed East Timor. A civil war ensued and continued until annexation was reversed by a referendum in 1999, which led to the eventual independence of East Timor.

Following decolonization, Indonesia's political views did not align with Australia's. Two factors prompted persistent disagreement: Sukarno's openness to the Indonesian Communist Party in the 1960s and the annexation in 1969 of Papua New Guinea (PNG). Australia maintained an anticommunist posture until Sukarno departed. Suharto, who ruled Indonesia from 1969 to 1998, likewise adopted an anticommunist position that closed part of the ideological divide with Australia.[11]

The annexation of PNG remains a point of dispute. Australia advocated a transition to independence for PNG after Dutch colonial rule ended[12] and opposed Indonesia's actions. West Papua is strongly pushing for independence, but as of September 2017 the United Nations (UN) decolonization committee has refused to take up the subject. The underlying concern is damage done to Western Papua New Guinea by the "Indonesianization" of the local population. Western Papua New Guinea and Australia oppose the migration flow from populous areas and the mining concessions granted by Indonesia to foreign companies.

The issues between Western Papua and Indonesia spill over to relations with the larger PNG.[13] Due to cultural and kinship communalities, Western Papua and PNG share a very porous 760 km border. This border is a source of concern to PNG and Australia, which see this as a potential security threat given the jihad presence in Indonesia.[14]

Indonesia had witnessed fewer terrorist incidents since the 2009 attack at the Jakarta Ritz Carlton Hotel, but the 2016 attack at a mall in Jakarta demonstrates the potential for additional terrorist operations in Indonesia despite effective counterterror capabilities by the government. For example, there is some presence of terrorist organizations operating in Central Sulawesi and in Aceh. Geographically Aceh and West Papua could not be more distant across the spread of the Indonesian Archipelago, but the local presence of Islamic State of Iraq and Syria (ISIS) sympathizers is undeniable.[15] Australia worries about the spillover of terrorists as well as the challenge of economic refugees. In both cases, Australia is an accessible target. Australian-PNG relations are complicated by an ongoing international dispute over refugees. There are more than six hundred asylum seekers in limbo that Australia refuses to accept. This four-year-old problem remains unresolved. PNG has issued a statement holding Australia financially and morally responsible for all asylum seekers and has been challenging them to find a long-term solution. As an overtaking approaches, if these concerns are not resolved, there is a possibility of local conflict.

On a more cooperative note, on balance, Indo-Australian relations have improved over the years. Indonesia benefits from Australia's technical and educational assistance to modernize its military. And in turn, Indonesia is trending toward a stronger democracy, with steady economic growth and a growing population. Indonesia has weathered many crises and reemerged effectively, thus creating the image of a strong dependable neighbor. Australia of course also has an established strong liberal democracy with an economy that is growing and an increasingly diverse population. Both competitors thus have sound reasons to engage in regional coordination. This bodes well for a relatively stable environment.

Beyond the competition for regional dominance in Southeast Asia, several transitions among smaller members loom large. Such transition would not be of significance if one dominant nation committed to stability in the region. The rise of Indonesia presents this opportunity, particularly if supported by Australia. Similar transitions among key regional members suggests the possibility that subregional confrontations may emerge independently beyond the influence of either regional or global powers.

SUBREGIONAL TRANSITIONS

Here are the most prominent transitions that loom large in this region.

The Philippines and Malaysia

As shown in figure 15.3, a transition between the Philippines and Malaysia is forecast to take place around 2040 or maybe earlier.[16]

On the positive side, these two countries are ethnically and culturally similar; they both speak Malayo-Polynesian languages (also English in the Philippines). Their common interests lie more in the political than in the economic arena. Politically, both countries seek to protect the Sulu Sea, which lies between the two countries, from piracy activities now run by the Islamic militant group Abu Sayyaf. A point of contention is the Malaysian claim of sovereignty over Sabah, which has very large maritime oil reserves and requires mediation to resolve peacefully.

Internally, the Philippines is dealing with insurgency in the southern part of the country, mainly from the Moro Islamic Liberation Front (MILF). The Mindanao insurgency consumes much of the Philippine government's effort and resources. But Malaysia is helping to broker a peace agreement.

Malaysian internal politics is marred by potential instability. The ruling coalition (BN) has been in power for six decades, though Najib Nazar's

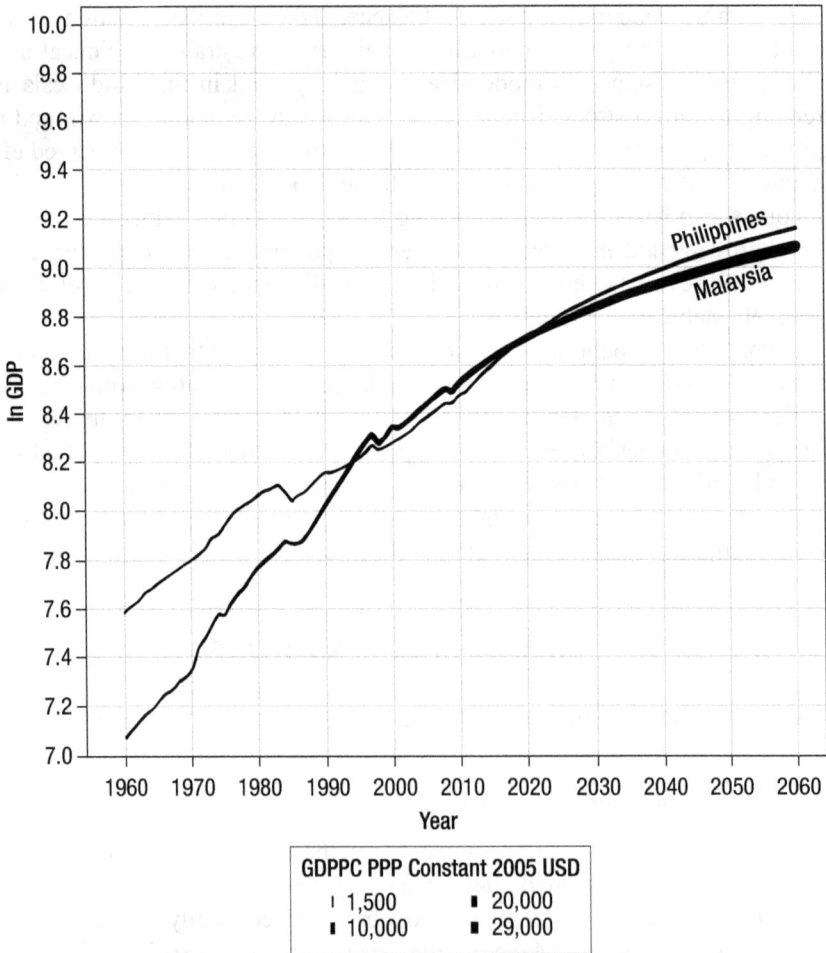

Figure 15.3. **Power Projections between the Philippines and Malaysia (1960–2060)**

ruling coalition, with its rural political base, has been losing the popular vote. However, because of gerrymandering, it still holds the majority of the parliamentary seats. With only 47 percent of the popular vote, the coalition appropriated 60 percent of the seats.[17]

The opposition coalition (People's Justice Party, Democratic Action Party, and Pan-Malaysian Islamic Party) has failed to present a united front and their internal fractures have allowed Prime Minister Nazar to capitalize on the discord among the different groups. Malaysia also has a domestic refugee problem, with 56,000 officially registered; an additional estimated 200,000 Rohingya people from Myanmar and Bangladesh are in Malaysia, lacking rights and resources. Being aware of the risk for radicalization of these refugees, Malaysia is actively cooperating with the Philippines.

Economic links are weak because these two countries are minor trading partners. Imports and exports from each other run between 2 and 5 percent. This is unlikely to change in the near future.[18] But Malaysia is a very important source of foreign investment for the Philippines. To cement this relationship and promote more opportunities, Malaysia opened a chamber of commerce in 2017. Its investments are mainly in banking, infrastructure, and manufacturing,[19] but the amounts are not significant.[20]

Population mobility is of some concern. Both countries host a large contingent of foreign workers. Malaysia, with a population of 30 million, has 2 million legal foreign workers and is host to 2.2 million illegal immigrants (amounting to 13 percent of the population). The projection is that by 2040, 24 percent of Malaysia's workforce will be made of foreign nationals, mostly unskilled labor. In the Philippines, the Commission on Overseas Filipino (COF) indicates that there are close to 800,000 Filipinos working and living in Malaysia (including an estimated 100,000 illegal Filipino workers). Illegal immigration is a point of contention with Malaysia. Differences in population size drive much of this concern. The Philippines has a much larger population, 103 million to Malaysia's 30 million. Thus, Filipino migrants constitute about 2 percent of Malaysia's population, whereas only 0.6 percent of Malaysians reside in the Philippines.

Despite frictions over population, no major contentious issue looms large, suggesting that as the Philippines transitions with Malaysia, no conflict will emerge. As in the case of Brazil and Argentina, the disparity in population size suggests that the smaller nation is likely to accept the larger nation's preponderance.

THE PHILIPPINES, THAILAND, AND SINGAPORE

In the Southeast Asia region, a second subtransition is forecast for the year 2060 as shown in figure 15.4. Thailand is predicted to be overtaken by the Philippines and, according to some estimates, also by Singapore.

The Thailand-Singapore transition should be peaceful. The bilateral relation between these two countries has always been cordial. In the security arena, Thailand and Singapore, along with Malaysia (also a close contender), jointly work on the suppression of terrorists in the Philippines. Moreover, in the economic arena, Singapore and Thailand have steady and substantive trade ties; Thailand's trade with Singapore accounts for about 4 percent of its total trade; while Singapore exports to Thailand account for around 4 percent

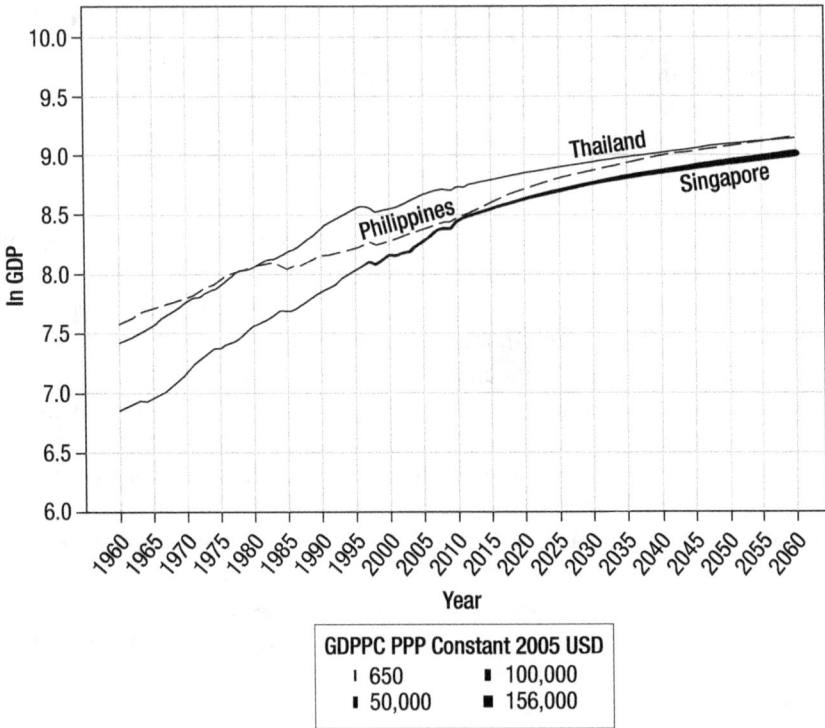

Figure 15.4. **Power Projections among the Philippines, Thailand, and Singapore (1960–2060)**

of its total exports, and close to 3 percent of its imports. Such a balanced relationship augurs well for further coordination.[21]

The Singapore-Thailand transition is likely to be peaceful because the population profile of these two countries is very dissimilar. Singapore's population is less than 10 percent of that of Thailand (5.5 vs. 67.4 million). The fertility rate of Thailand is twice that of Singapore (1.66 vs. 0.79). The gross domestic product (GDP) per capita is $58,000 compared with $9,000 for Thailand. The level of education shows that 38 percent of Singapore's population has attained a tertiary level, whereas in Thailand only 14 percent achieve this level. Given their profiles and the very long-term potential superiority of Thailand, this temporary shift in power will likely be more prone to cooperation than conflict. Both countries have more to gain from collaboration than from conflict. In sum, in the future Thailand will be the dominant partner in this dyad, driven by population differences. Our assessment suggests that the probabilities of a conflict-ridden transition are low. Neither the regional dominant states nor the global states currently have an incentive to intervene in this dyad.

As indicated, the Philippines is dealing with insurgency in the southern part of the country. This insurgency occupies much of the Philippine government's agenda and resources. But Singapore, and to a lesser degree, Thailand are helping to broker a peace agreement. It is far more difficult to assess the consequences of a transition between Thailand and the Philippines as both compete economically for similar markets. At the same time, both are long-term members of ASEAN. The direct influence of China on these two nations cannot be overlooked and may directly influence stability in the region. The Philippines is shifting away from the United States, whereas Thailand remains a solid ally. The future will tell if this transition is peaceful or confrontational.

THE IMPACT OF GLOBAL POWERS

Individually, the countries analyzed are more strongly related to global powers than to the regional dominant actors. So what role will Australia and Indonesia play in relation to the great external powers?

Indonesia and China have very close trade ties: 23 percent of Indonesia's imports come from China and 12 percent of their exports are shipped to China.[22] Indonesia has a very large trade surplus, although it has a trade deficit specifically with China. The amicable economic relations are not fully reflected in the domestic arena. Indonesia has more than three hundred distinct ethnic groups, but local Chinese, although comprising only 3 percent of the total population[23] and highly successful, are sometimes singled out for criticism.

China, the regional dominant power, has increased its penetration in virtually all the nations of Southeast Asia. For example, reversing its traditional suspicion about China, the Philippines now has accepted $24 billion in investments from China. And the Philippines has declared that it will not prevent China from building government or military facilities on the shoals of the South China/West Philippines Seas. This runs counter to US policy and could give China access to large oil and gas reserves in this area.

The deepening China-Philippines relationship can be seen also in rising trade figures. In 2016, exports from the Philippines to China and Hong Kong constituted 23 percent, to Japan 22 percent, and to the United States 16 percent. Top imports came from China and Hong Kong with 23 percent of the total, with the United States at a modest 9.5 percent. China is also increasing aid and arming the Philippines to fight the extremist Muslim groups. Public opinion is also shifting in favor of China over the United States.[24]

The China-Malaysia relationship also continues to strengthen. Continuing a trend begun under Prime Minister Mahathir Mohamad, Malaysia has looked to Russia for military and technical cooperation and has purchased naval vessels from China despite disagreements over the South China Sea.[25]

Singapore is China's ninth-largest trading partner and China is Singapore's third-largest trading partner. But Singapore maintains its independence with regard to Chinese actions and policies. For example, they have explicitly voiced their disagreement with China over the South China Sea dispute as well as in connection with some of China's policies in ASEAN.

Thailand, always sensitive to subtle and obvious changes in regional power distributions, purchased $1 billion of submarines from China in August 2017.[26] At the same time relations have cooled with Japan, which, since the Thai coup of 2014, has withdrawn its investments.[27] China is also investing in infrastructure projects at a fast pace, for example, the $5.2 billion high-speed railway from Bangkok to southern China. Cultural ties are also getting stronger. Chinese tourism was up by 12 percent in 2017, and many schools in Thailand are adopting Chinese as part of the curriculum.

In the past, the United States was an active leader in the region, providing military technology, being an arbiter for preserving peace and an active trade partner. Today, the political attitude has become similar to the South American strategy, which is to say that it is marked by political indifference.

FUTURE CONFLICT AND COOPERATION

Indonesia, the emerging dominant state in this region, and to a lesser extent Australia, will have much to say about future stability or instability. Stability between these two different countries will likely be maintained into the future. Indonesia, as an emerging regional power, will readjust its previous flexible policy and turn to ASEAN as a cooperative gesture. Such political flexibility augurs well for the region's contribution to stability.

At the subregional level, the Philippines overtaking Malaysia may well pass unnoticed because no large policy issues divide these two countries, and the disparity in the size of populations assures that the Philippines will emerge as a more powerful partner in this relationship. A similar story emerges from the Thailand-Singapore dyad.

Transitions within the region are not likely to be a source of conflict. The prospects for stability from a global perspective are less clear. The West is weakening in influence and in its presence in Southeast Asia. Australia, a bulwark of Western values, is changing its demographic and economic profile, looking more toward Asia than to Europe and the United States. Recent policy decisions suggest the United States is subtly withdrawing from this and other areas. The Trump administration has abandoned the negotiations on the Pacific Trade agreement, reversing the Obama shift with the pivot to Asia policy. Questions about the US role in the defense of Australia, Japan, and South Korea have arisen in Southeast Asia as a result of presidential comments. The on-off and highly unproductive negotiations with North Korea have weakened confidence in US leadership throughout Southeast Asia.

The US leadership role is diminishing in the Southeast Asia region while that of China rises; differences in their management styles are palpable. China is more pragmatic but exposes an ever more coercive style. The United States used to be focused on democratic values and individualism, but that now has shifted to trade, tariffs, and insults. These tactics may not persist, but some of the damage done will not be easily erased.

Previous chapters confirm that a global shift is underway. China will emerge by the middle of this century as the dominant global power.[28] The United States should respond to this by reinforcing existing partnerships in South and Southeast Asia and then linking these with tradition European alliances.

If on the other hand, the Western structures collapse, and US-NATO-EU interests continue to degrade from neglect or verbal hostility, the US ability to sustain stability in the region would be very much diminished. The greatest challenge is that nations in Southeast Asia will recognize the inevitable dominance of China and simply change allegiances.

NOTES

1. Global Map shows region contours. The hierarchy map shows the relative size of the top contenders in this region. Data are World Bank, "World Development Indicators," last modified March 27, 2016, http://documents.worldbank.org/curated/en/805371467990952829/World-development-indicators-2016.

2. Figure 15.1 source: Power estimations are based on GDP PPP Constant 2005 LCU that predicts transition to be in process, where GDP Constant 2005 USD implies transition around 2028.

3. World Bank, "World Development Indicators." Forecast based on growth rates adapted from PWC 20250, "The World in 2050," last modified August 29, 2017, https://www.pwc.com/gx/en/issues/economy/the-world-in-2050.html.

4. Artur Simon, "Southeast Asia: Musical Syncretism and Cultural Identity," *Fontes Artis Musicae* 57, no. 1 (January 2010): 23–34.

5. Ann Capling and John Ravenhill, "Symposium: Australia–US Economic Relations and the Regional Balance of Power," *Australian Journal of Political Science* 48, no. 2 (2013).

6. Gregory O'Brien, "Australia's Trade in figures," *Parliament of Australia*, https://www.aph.gov.au/About_Parliament/Parliamentary_Departments/Parliamentary_Library/pubs/BriefingBook45p/AustraliaTrade.

7. Statistical Language–Measures of Central Tendency, "2016 Census," last modified April 11, 2017, https://www.abs.gov.au/websitedbs/a3121120.nsf/home/statistical+language+-+measures+of+central+tendency.

8. IIE Home, "International Student Data 2018," accessed February 26, 2019, https://www.iie.org/Research-and-Insights/Open-Doors/Fact-Sheets-and-Infographics/Infographics/International-Student-Data.

9. Figure 15.2 source: World Bank, "World Development Indicators," last modified March 27, 2016, http://documents.worldbank.org/curated/en/805371467990952829/World-development-indicators-2016. Forecast based on growth rates adapted from PWC 20250, "The World in 2050," last modified August 29, 2017, https://www.pwc.com/gx/en/issues/economy/the-world-in-2050.html.

10. ASEAN members are Brunei, Cambodia, Indonesia, Laos, Malaysia, Myanmar, the Philippines, Singapore, Thailand, and Vietnam. Nonmember states are Australia, China, Japan, and South Korea.

11. Herbert Feith, "Suharto's Search for a Political Format," *Indonesia* 6 (1968): 88.

12. Indonesia declared its independence from the Netherlands in 1949, but West Papua was not included, remaining under Dutch rule, until 1963, when it was annexed by Indonesia. A controversial referendum was conducted in 1969 to settle the issue.

13. Harry Purwanto, "Border Security in Indonesia and Papua New Guinea," *South East Journal of Contemporary Business, Economics and Law* 12, no. 4 (2017), last accessed on July 8, 2019, http://seajbel.com/wp-content/uploads/2017/06/LAW-103.pdf.

14. Joseph Chinyong Liow, "ISIS in the Pacific: Assessing Terrorism in Southeast Asia and the Threat to the Homeland," *Brookings.edu* (10 May 2017), accessed on March 1, 2019, https://www.brookings.edu/testimonies/isis-in-the-pacific-assessing-terrorism-in-southeast-asia-and-the-threat-to-the-homeland/.

15. Especially since the Katibah Nusantara, a Southeast Asia ISIS formal group has been active in Syria. This group is a military entity that resides within Iraq/Levant. The group is made up of primarily Malay speaking people from Indonesia, Malaysia, the Philippines, and Singapore. This group is primarily identified with the 2016 Jakarta attacks.

16. Figure 15.3 source: A transition would take place earlier if the International Monetary Fund (2017) forecast rates of 6.6 percent are sustained, for the Philippines, compared to 5.4 percent for Malaysia; World Bank, "World Development Indicators," last modified March 27, 2016, http://documents.worldbank.org/curated/en/805371467990952829/World-development-indicators-2016. Forecast based on growth rates adapted from PWC 20250, "The World in 2050," last modified August 29, 2017, https://www.pwc.com/gx/en/issues/economy/the-world-in-2050.html.

17. Chin-Huat Wong, James Chin, and Norani Othman, "Malaysia—Towards a Topology of an Electoral One-party State," *Democratization* 17, no. 5 (2010).

18. Economic Planning Unit, Prime Minister's Department, "The Malaysian Economy in Figures," last modified in 2016, http://maddruid.com/wp/wp-content/uploads/2017/03/MEIF-2016.pdf; Republic of Philippines Statistical Authority, "Philippines Statistics Authority," accessed on February 2019, https://psa.gov.ph/.

19. "Malaysia-Philippines Trade to Grow with Newly Set up MCCIPI," *New Straits Times*, September 7, 2017, accessed on March 1, 2019, https://www.nst.com.my/business/2017/09/277229/malaysia-philippines-trade-grow-newly-set-mccipi.

20. "Total Approved Foreign Investments Reached P18.2 Billion in Q2 2017," *Philippine Statistics Authority*, September 15, 2017, accessed on March 1, 2019, https://psa.gov.ph/content/total-approved-foreign-investments-reached-p182-billion-q2-2017.

21. Figure 15.4 source: World Bank, "World Development Indicators." Forecast based on growth rates adapted from PWC 20250, "The World in 2050."

22. OEC—Brazil (BRA) Exports, Imports, and Trade Partners, "Indonesia," accessed March 1, 2019, https://atlas.media.mit.edu/en/profile/country/idn/.

23. Total Population by Country 2018, "Indonesia Population 2019," accessed on March 1, 2019, http://worldpopulationreview.com/countries/indonesia-population/.

24. Juliana Menasce Horowitz and Nikki Graf, "Pew Research Center," https://www.pewresearch.org/download-datasets/.

25. Bob Savic, "Is the US Losing East Asia to China?" *The Diplomat*, December 15, 2016, accessed on March 1, 2019, https://thediplomat.com/2016/12/is-the-us-losing-east-asia-to-china/.

26. Marwaan Macan-Markar, Asia Regional Correspondent, "Thailand and China: Brothers in Arms," *Nikkei Asian Review*, February 2, 2017, accessed on July 8, 2019, https://asia.nikkei.com/Politics/Thailand-and-China-Brothers-in-arms.

27. Adam Ramsey, "Thailand Is Finally Cozying Up to China. Why Now?" *OZY*, last accessed on July 8, 2019, https://www.ozy.com/fast-forward/thailand-is-finally-cozying-up-to-china-why-now/79740.

28. China's geopolitical and economic strategy is mixed. Although it now supports the Asia Bank that could provide needed resources to developing Asian nations such as Indonesia, the Philippines, or Thailand, and concurrently is building a land link to reestablish the Silk Road, China has adopted a confrontational posture in the China Sea of concern to Southeast Asia countries. This contradiction reinforces the security links between Australia and the United States, driven by fears that China may take a more aggressive posture particularly if the Philippines become a willing pawn in this competition. Established trade partners led by Japan, United States, and Australia are now in flux. Bilateral financial investments by China and the strategy of providing finished roads or infrastructure built by Chinese labor in the host countries have found some domestic resistance but also show the business acumen of China.

Chapter Sixteen

South Asia

India, the Emerging Global Giant

John Thomas and Fredrick Clarke

South Asia–India Region

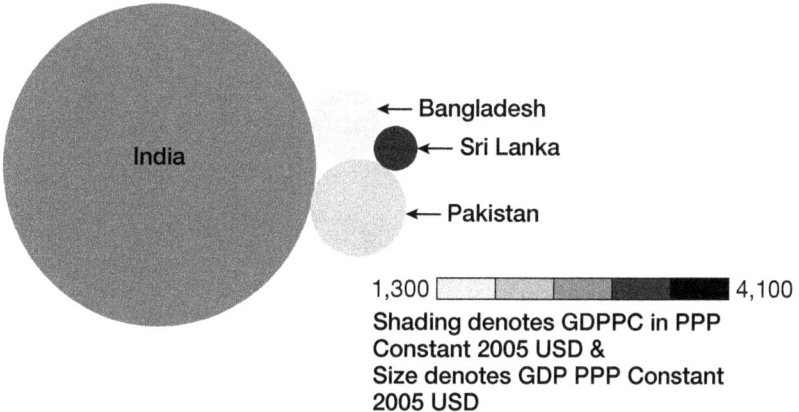

1,300 ▭▭▭▭▭ 4,100
Shading denotes GDPPC in PPP
Constant 2005 USD &
Size denotes GDP PPP Constant
2005 USD

South Asia–India Hierarchy

SOUTH ASIAN REGION

The South Asia hierarchy is dominated by India.[1] The growth of national power is influenced by population size, economic productivity, and political capacity. The focus here is on changes in population size and economic productivity, in particular, which can be used effectively to capture the dynamics evident within regional hierarchies. Variations in political capacity can disturb these estimates within a narrow range but will not determine them.[2]

With 75 percent of the region's entire population, India dominates South Asia. Birth rates for all members of this hierarchy are expected to decline.[3] This suggests that the population gap between India and the other nations in the region will not be bridged over the next fifty years. In fact, in light of its population, India has the potential to become a dominant nation within the *global* hierarchy as shown in figure 16.1. *Once India overtakes China in population size in the period 2025–2030, no further global demographic*

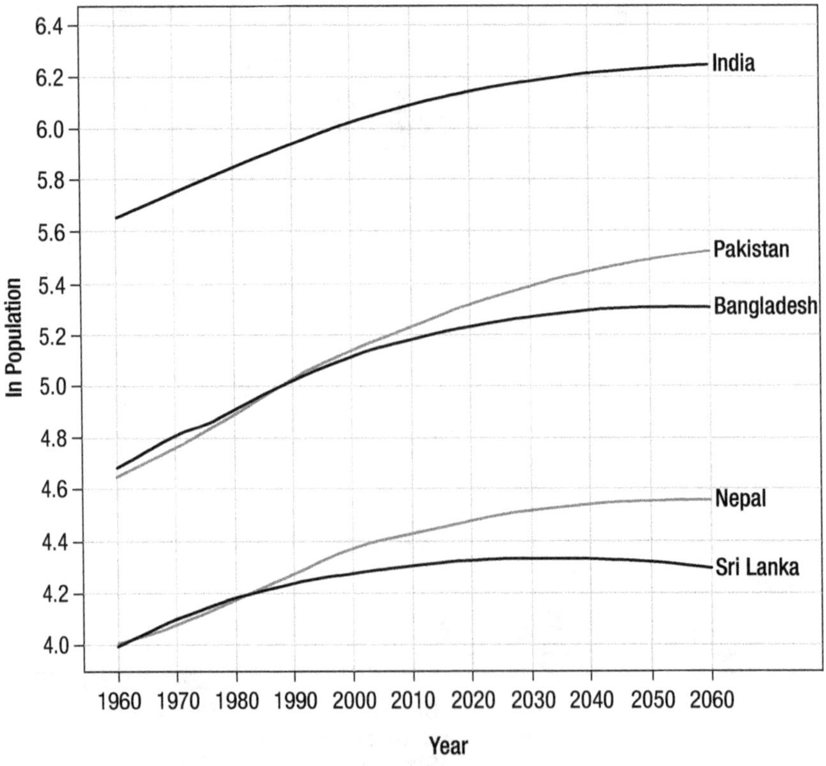

Figure 16.1. Demographic Dynamics (1960–2060)

shifts are likely to take place, with the result that the two powers could enjoy a long period of joint global dominance.[4]

Figure 16.2 shows the probable evolution of total output within the South Asian hierarchy.[5] Each line represents the corresponding country's relative share of economic output, and the thickness of each line indicates the corresponding country's per capita productivity. India towers over the other members of the South Asia hierarchy in economic output. Approximately

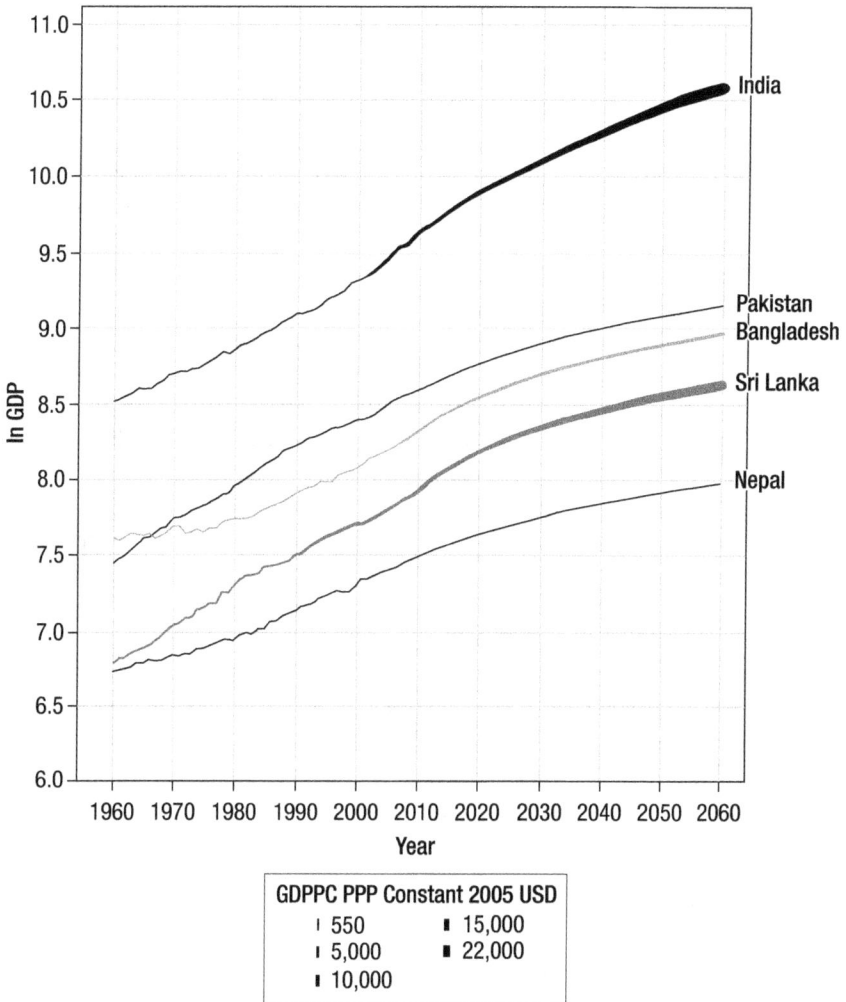

Figure 16.2. Shares of Total Output and per Capita Productivity in South Asia (1960–2060)

76 percent of the total resources within the hierarchy are located within India's borders. The substantial difference between India's gross domestic product (GDP) level and the levels of the other countries in the region is likely to be permanent. India will almost certainly maintain its economic superiority. Short of partition or internal turmoil, India will remain the dominant South Asian regional power during the next fifty years.[6]

Our forecasts obviously reflect a measure of uncertainty. Figure 16.2 assumes the validity of a low-growth scenario. But an alternative high-growth scenario might be realized. The implementation of economic reforms beginning in 1991 has helped India attain an annual growth rate in excess of 6 percent. Liberalization has also produced greater opportunities in sectors such as information technology and biotechnology. Successive governments have embraced the consensus view that deregulation and liberalization must continue and be deepened. It is possible for India to continue to experience sustained high growth—in the range of 8–10 percent—given a commitment to continued reforms.[7]

This fluid circumstance, with relatively stand-alone contenders, creates tensions and opportunities among the smaller officially unaligned countries in the region. Although India is the preponderant nation in South Asia, the other regional powers include dissatisfied Pakistan, a more conciliatory Bangladesh, and neutral Sri Lanka. These nations have some power resources, including nuclear weapons in Pakistan, but do not have the capacity to challenge India for dominance in the South Asian hierarchy.

The lowest rung of the hierarchy is occupied by Bhutan and Nepal. Both have few resources and limited influence and, thus, pose no direct threat to India's dominance in the South Asia hierarchy. Such small powers can, however, experience severe civil wars—as did Sri Lanka, for example—that drew the dominant nation into a regional war.

This chapter considers the dynamics within the local hierarchy among the top contenders whose actions mirror those in the global hierarchy—when regional hierarchies are *isolated* from major power interference. Regional hierarchies function in the same manner as the global hierarchy and operate under similar power rules. The regional status quo typically revolves around the definition of territorial boundaries, issues relating to river-water sharing, cross-border transit, and trade, among others.[8] Such issues affect relationships throughout Asia.

A country can belong to multiple hierarchies at the same time.[9] For example, India is one of the emerging Great Powers and belongs in the global hierarchy and also is a leader in the South Asian region.[10] Beyond a more defined hierarchy, India continues to be linked by colonial ties to England and increasingly cooperates with the United States, as Pakistan moves toward China. Yet, India still is largely focused on its immediate Southeast Asia neighbors.

INDIA

India has emerged as the undisputed dominant nation in South Asia, but it is currently dominated by China in the larger Asian region and by the United States at the global level. This dynamic can create the conditions for both cooperation and conflict, making this region, with its giant neighbors, the most potentially explosive by mid-century. India, as it rises, has the potential to join the United States, China, and the European Union (EU) as one of the Great Powers of the twenty-first century. This means that US and EU strategists must begin thinking now about how to influence and subtly persuade China and India to join the status quo in the collision stage.

In the decades following independence, India's foreign policy evolved in response to its "colonial sufferings"[11] with a strong emphasis on regional politics[12] marked by a consistent commitment, at least rhetorically, to several key principles: non-alignment, non-aggression, non-interference, equality, and peaceful coexistence.[13]

The commitment to non-alignment manifested itself in India's efforts to lead newly formed independent (postcolonial) states.[14] India's attempted leadership of the nonaligned movement persisted until the movement's raison d'être disappeared with the end of the Cold War. After the collapse of the Soviet Union, old benchmarks that had been employed to guide India's foreign policy began to crumble, and the country commenced a gradual tilt toward the West.[15]

Several factors help to illuminate the structural changes underlying India's reorientation toward the West and the new direction in Indian foreign policy. These include a shift in values, India's increasingly important role as a global power broker, and India's rejection of a Cold War mentality.

A change in values challenged the domestic status quo ante in India. This change involved the increasing abandonment of communalism and the embrace of modernity and market economics.[16] The statist and dirigisme ideals that had dominated the Indian political discourse for more than fifty years proved untenable. This opened new opportunities for trade, foreign direct investment, and participation in global decision making. Economic liberalization policies created rapid economic growth as regulations began to relax after 1991.[17] The new flow of capital and technology enabled Indian entrepreneurs, engineers, and software programmers to enter global markets. Instead of the foreign aid on which it had traditionally relied, India now was seeking foreign direct investment and export access to global markets.[18]

At the same time, India abandoned its traditional postindependence role as a leader of the Third World and became a global power broker. Indian political leaders seemed convinced of India's, and their own, greatness,[19] but very few leaders of other societies took India seriously because it lacked the economic capability to exert significant influence beyond its own borders. Liberalization invigorated the Indian economy. Observers became increasingly convinced, in light of China's example, that, if India sustained high growth rates, it had the capacity to emerge as a major regional and global power broker.[20] This perception became real when the World Bank projected that India's would be the fastest-growing large economy through at least 2021.[21] According to Ricardo Hausmann of Harvard University's Center for International Development, India can be expected to grow at an annual rate of 7 percent through 2024. Over time, such a growth rate could allow India to catch up with and overtake China around 2075.[22]

While these shifts were taking place, India also abandoned the traditionally anti-Western mode of thinking that had dominated its foreign policy during the Cold War. The end of the Cold War, and China's concomitant rise, prompted increased realism and greater alignment with the West on India's part. The shift in India's westward-leaning foreign policy was infused with new energy by Narendra Modi's landslide election in 2014.[23] Modi's "high-octane" diplomatic style, combined with a major increase in India's economic, military, and material capabilities, enabled the country to vault onto the global stage both as the dominant player in South Asia and as a pre-emergent power broker in the region.[24]

A closer examination of the ruling Bharatiya Janata Party's (BJP) 2014 election manifesto shows that India committed itself to ensuring that "a resurgent India" gained its "rightful place in the comity of nations and international institutions." The BJP expresses the resolve "to fundamentally reboot and reorient the foreign policy goals, content and process."[25] Modi has strategically left in place the basic foreign policy framework handed down by his predecessors while signaling a shift in India's foreign policy in a variety of ways, including vigorous regional engagement.[26] Modi has now traveled to forty-four countries since he first became Prime Minister in May 2014.

How does India see itself in the new world order, and what role does it hope to play in global politics? Will the change in its foreign policy affect the prospects for war and peace in Southeast Asia over the next fifty years? And how will Modi's strategic new foreign policy agenda affect India's neighbors, especially Pakistan and China?

INDIA AND CHINA

Only the two Asian giants, India and China, are potential contenders for regional dominance. Interestingly, neither has established formal alliances with other great Asian-Pacific nations such as Indonesia, Australia, or Japan; nor has either established subregional coalitions with smaller Asian-Pacific nations such as Thailand, the Philippines, or Vietnam. The dormant territorial dispute that led to the Sino-Indian War in 1962 continues to be a contentious issue between China and India.[27] Moreover, the two nations embrace alternate stances regarding Tibet that infrequently raise tensions between them. And the growth of India's population, which will overtake China's relatively soon (see figure 16.3), also suggests the likelihood of a power transition. Each of these issues can play a key role in facilitating cooperation or confrontation among potential regional leaders.

By mid-century and to some extent even now, the key contenders in the Asian hierarchy are India and China. Separated by the Himalayas, the two nations have engaged in long-standing territorial disputes related to the validity of the Johnson Line, between India and China, including the Aksai Chin area. The Sino-Indian War in 1962 took place in the wake of a series of violent border incidents that followed the 1959 Tibetan uprising and the failure of the parties to reach a political settlement along the Himalayan border, which spans 3,225 kilometers. Chinese troops captured Rezang La and Tawang. The

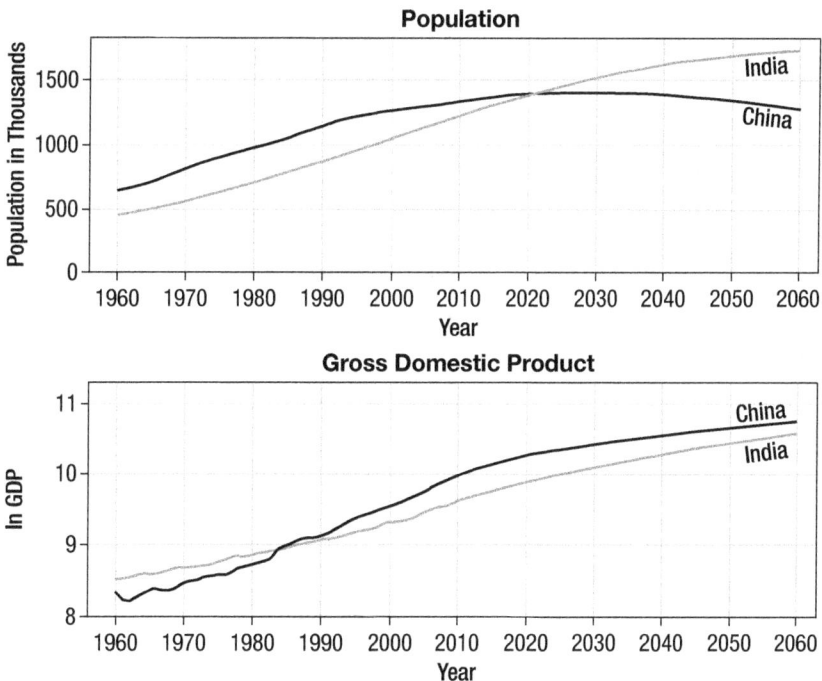

Population

Gross Domestic Product

Figure 16.3. Population and Gross Domestic Product Trends in India and China (1960–2060)

Indian military was unprepared to face this onslaught. The war ended when China declared a cease-fire on November 20, 1962, and withdrew from some of the areas it had entered. However, China did not vacate about fourteen thousand square miles of disputed territory.[28] This territory and others still occasion border negotiations and clashes. This and other Sino-Indo incidents have not led to full blown conflict because of the power differential between the two countries, but this dynamic is changing. Consider the trends over time in population and GDP; they indicate that India will easily overtake China in population, but India will continue to lag in total GDP.

Figure 16.3 shows that India and China underwent a peaceful power transition in the 1990s, and the shift in the demographic balance anticipated in 2020 foreshadows the possibility of a second transition by century's end.[29] Given the simmering territorial dispute and the relative dissatisfaction of both nations with the international system, the conditions could well develop for localized, regional, and even global conflict. But this is not predetermined and can be avoided by building satisfaction between the two potential adversaries.

A major difference is that China and India, based on population size coupled with productivity, will be the two dominant nations in the international system. Controlling for border changes, neither the EU nor the United States can approach the population size of China and India (more than 2 billion people). Their influence will depend in large part on the ability of China and India to sustain economic growth. If this is realized, these two Asian giants will have to choose between confrontation and cooperation. The first may lead to massive population losses; the second could produce an Asian regime similar to what the United States achieved following World War II. The choice between these alternate outcomes begins today.

Barring major changes in the economy of either country, the overall output of India will continue to lag behind that of China. Given the momentum generated by a much younger population, India's lead in population will continue, if not accelerate, for the foreseeable future. Although India's population will exceed China's, and even though it will be far more youthful, India's *productivity* will continue to lag behind that of its large neighbor. Unless India takes off economically or China's performance drops dramatically in the next two decades, the fact that China will continue to outperform India will preclude the occurrence of a transition by mid-century. However, this could change late in the century given that extrapolated data suggest that India may overtake China in GDP around 2075. Or it may change earlier if China's elderly population causes a drag on productivity prior to the same happening in India.

This signals an interesting regional dynamic. China will obtain sufficient power to challenge the United States well before India materializes as a threat to China. If the shift in the balance of power between China and the West is peaceful (such as the US-UK case), India and China most likely would be part of a satisfied coalition of countries. However, if the global hierarchy is unstable and both of the Great Powers in Asia remain deeply dissatisfied with the global status quo and feel threatened by each other, a severe regional or even global war could be triggered by a direct China-India conflict. The occurrence of a similar pattern preceded the outbreak of both previous world wars.

An alternative, peaceful path is also possible. China is currently planning to rebuild the Silk Road to encourage trade and development along its border with India. The reestablishment of the Silk Road, an ambitious project creating overland and maritime trade routes, could yield massive economic rewards for the region, accelerating growth in the least-developed portions of India and China. If the two countries choose to cooperate by settling border disputes and encouraging communication and economic exchanges across their border, a major expansion in both societies could well follow. Both are now members of the World Trade Organization (WTO). They share concerns related to the legacy of colonialism, restrictions imposed by patents, technology transfers, and investment flows. Such similarities do not eliminate the effects of entrenched differences in regime type and culture. Nonetheless, the possibility of accommodation is there, but only if China does not attempt to exploit its new economic reach by translating it into political and military leverage.

PAKISTAN

"Pakistan is not a state with an army but, rather, an army with a state."[30] To retain its power, prestige, and access to resources, the Pakistani Army has locked Pakistan into an enduring rivalry with India focused on Kashmir. Pakistan seems unlikely to self-correct because of the inherent strategic culture and bureaucratic power of the army.[31]

To achieve their goals of bureaucratic and political dominance, both the army and Pakistan's security establishment exploit civil unrest, religious dogma, and international politics. They sponsor and support non-Islamist insurgencies throughout India as well as a countrywide Islamist terror campaign that has brought the countries to the brink of war on several occasions. They have continued a proxy war in Kashmir since 1989, using Islamic militants. Despite Pakistan's efforts to coerce and terrorize India, it has achieved only minimal success.

Pakistan continues to see itself as India's equal and demands that the world do the same—despite the fact that India detached Bangladesh from Pakistan in 1971. Since the last war, and in spite of the two countries' nuclear capabilities, the differences in military power between the two counties have grown significantly. India is significantly stronger than Pakistan on all metrics and could overpower its neighbor should a protracted conflict occur, whether conventional or nuclear.

INDIA AND PAKISTAN

Territorial concerns, particularly those relating to Kashmir, have dominated relations between India and Pakistan. Disputes over water rights also affect relations among India, Pakistan, and Bangladesh. Furthermore, landlocked Nepal is dependent on India for trade and the security and openness of transportation routes.

No regional dispute in South Asia has been more severe than the conflict over Kashmir between India and Pakistan.[32] Despite three wars (1947, 1965, 1971) and continual skirmishes and confrontations, the massive structural changes that have taken place over the last decades have now created an insurmountable gap in capabilities between India and Pakistan. This makes it unlikely that Kashmir will precipitate a major regional war. Pakistan has little ability to challenge India successfully over Kashmir. India has taken the step of annexing Kashmir and thus altering the long-standing status quo. Prime Minister Modi is more hawkish than previous Indian leaders and has taken a tougher position on Pakistan.[33] He also has more flexibility to resolve disputes before escalation.

The current view of India's political leadership is that the problem of Kashmir is an internal matter that can be settled through the provision of greater autonomy to Kashmir or through elections that create a new small buffer state between Pakistan and India. The expectation is that crisis in Kashmir might linger but would not intensify beyond persistent guerrilla action.[34] Despite intensified troop mobilization, border conflict has not escalated to war.

The introduction of nuclear weapons into South Asia does not affect the calculus of war. Were Pakistan to invest heavily in the buildup of a larger nuclear arsenal, India could easily match and exceed Pakistan's investment (see the discussion of conditional deterrence in chapter 13). In the long run, Pakistan faces a potential confrontation with a far superior power. India cannot be deterred by the development of nuclear arsenals by smaller neighbors. In case of a serious dispute, India can choose to wage a conventional war that it could reasonably expect to win. Pakistan could threaten to use nuclear weapons, but the threat to do so would lack credibility because India could respond with its own nuclear weapons, imposing losses much greater than those that would result from a conventional conflict; there would be no hope for victory on the part of Pakistan in a nuclear exchange with India. India is thus likely to retain military dominance in South Asia, with the result that relative peace in the region can be expected to continue.[35]

FUTURE CONFLICT AND COOPERATION

India dominates the South Asian hierarchy, and this condition will likely persist over the next fifty years. During this time, India's actions will determine the future stability of the region. India could settle its dispute with Pakistan over Kashmir without war if Pakistan were to move aggressively to end cross-border terrorism. Unlike his immediate predecessors, Indian Prime Minister Narendra Modi is willing to bolster India's military strength to achieve his objectives in Kashmir.[36] Our analysis suggests that the protracted conflict within this hierarchy, between India and Pakistan over the status of Kashmir, is unlikely to become once more a severe war. Incursions in the Kashmir area are driven by small Pakistani factions whose members are dissatisfied but fundamentally unable to alter the status quo. The dominance of India suggests that the likelihood of escalation is minimal—unless it involves China directly.

Given the massive power asymmetry between these two nations, Kashmir is now an internal problem for India. This problem could be resolved through India's adoption, with respect to Kashmir, of national self-determination principles. A referendum could be held, allowing parties to decide whether to stay in India, join Pakistan, or create a small depoliticized buffer state between Pakistan and India that might integrate all of Kashmir. The choice was India's to make, and they did.

From a longer-term international perspective, the relevant structural conditions suggest that South Asia is likely to remain at peace for the next fifty years. Neither Bangladesh nor Sri Lanka can challenge India or each other. Nepal and Bhutan, on the fringe of this region, are more likely to be affected by domestic than international conflict.

Beyond the region, the shift in Indian power will influence prospects for war and peace in the larger Asian hierarchies. Today, bilateral relations with China provide India with both challenges and opportunities. Challenges arise from a disputed border, China's unwillingness to support India's quest for a permanent seat on the United Nations Security Council, China's relentless support of Pakistan's nuclear and missile programs, and competition for natural resources and influence in Africa. Opportunities involve a continued boom in trade that could render China—along with Japan, South Korea, Australia, and the United States—integral to India's export-driven economic development. Tensions may rise because interventions might impede productive trade relationships. Yet, cooperative solutions are at hand that could address trade differences and lead to mutual endorsement of the proposed Border Defense Cooperation Agreement.[37]

There is time for accommodation. India and China will not meet the necessary conditions for a power transition until late in this century. Because the potential turmoil resulting from China overtaking the United States and potentially challenging it for global dominance will occur before this time, it is difficult to anticipate the relative level of dissatisfaction on the part of the two Asian giants. A successful transition in the Sino-US dyad can provide the two Asian parties with a path to peace and the means to establish a stable hierarchy including both India and China—or a prescription for conflict the consequences of which would be enormous. Thus, depending on the outcome of the East-West interaction, the Asian hierarchy may face severe regional conflict, or alternatively, it might join a global hierarchy in which greater cooperation among constituents can lead to global integration. Under the leadership of India, China, the United States, and the EU, a lasting South Asian and global peace can result.

With strategic vision, India can have a dramatic effect on world politics. It will soon possess the power to make it an attractive partner in emerging global coalitions—perhaps the essential or swing voice for stability, which is entirely consistent with India's history and sense of self.

NOTES

1. Global Map shows region contours. The hierarchy map shows the relative size of the top contenders in this region. Data are World Bank, "World Development Indicators," last modified March 27, 2016, http://documents.worldbank.org/curated/en/805371467990952829/World-development-indicators-2016.

2. United Nations, "UN Population Projections," last modified 2019, https://population.un.org/wpp/.

3. Figure 16.1 source: Demographic data—mid-year population and birth rate per thousand—for all the countries in this study is taken from the International Database of the US Census Bureau, https://www.census.gov/programs-surveys/international-programs/about/idb.html.

4. Jacek Kugler, Ronald L. Tammen, and Siddharth Swaminathan, "Power Transitions and Alliances in the 21st Century," *Asian Perspective* 25, no. 3 (2001): 5–29.

5. Figure 16.2 source: Estimates of annual growth rates are taken from several sources. These estimates consist of both low- and high-growth scenarios. Low-growth scenarios for India are obtained from Angus Maddison, *The World Economy: A Millennial Perspective* (Danvers: OECD Publications, 2001). Low-growth estimates for India range from 3.5 to 5 percent growth. High-growth estimates for India are

drawn from Ajai Chopra, Charles Collyns, Richard Hemming, and Karen Parker with Woosik Chu and Oliver Fratzscher, *India: Economic Reform and Growth* (Washington, DC: International Monetary Fund Publication Services, 1995). These estimates range from 8 to 10 percent. The growth rates for Pakistan, Bangladesh, Bhutan, Nepal, and Sri Lanka range from 3 to 5 percent, which are currently seen as achievable objectives. World Bank, "The World Bank in Pakistan," last modified April 5, 2019, https://www.worldbank.org/en/country/pakistan.

6. World Bank, "World Development Indicators." Forecast based on growth rates adapted from PWC 20250, "The World in 2050," last modified August 29, 2017, https://www.pwc.com/gx/en/issues/economy/the-world-in-2050.html.

7. Among still-needed changes are the reduction of fiscal deficits and federal subsidies to agriculture, further reforms of the banking sector, large-scale disinvestments in the public sector, product de-reservation for small-scale industries, the elimination of price controls, and reform of the power sector. Successful reorientation of government spending toward such high-priority areas as health, education, and infrastructure development could also lead to higher rates of economic growth.

8. Douglas Lemke, *Regions of War and Peace* (Cambridge: Cambridge University Press, 2002).

9. Ibid.

10. Sri Lanka is lumped in the South Asia region, departing from Doug Lemke's regional classification as given in his *Regions of War and Peace*, 90–91.

11. Tajamul Rafi, Usha Shirvastava, and Nasreena Akhtar, "India's Foreign Policy—Retrospect and Prospects," *African Journal of Political Science and International Relations* 9, no. 6 (2015): 212–216.

12. Ibid.

13. *Civil Service Chronicle*, November 2009, 49, also known as the five principles or the Panchsheel. Made famous in 1954 when the Chinese signed the declaration of the five principles.

14. Usha Shrivastva, *India and the World* (Agra: Vikas Publications Company, 2003), 183.

15. W. P. S. Sidhu, *India's Foreign Policy Priorities and India-U.S. Relations, The Modi-Obama Summit: A Leadership Movement for India and the United States* (Washington, DC: Brookings Institution, 2014).

16. Raja C. Mohan, *India's New Foreign Policy Strategy*, draft presented at a Seminar in Beijing by China Reform Forum and the Carnegie Endowment for International Peace, Beijing, May 26, 2006.

17. Sumit Ganguly, *Indian Foreign Policy* (Oxford: Oxford University Press, 2015), 103.

18. Mohan, *India's New Foreign Policy Strategy*.

19. From Jawaharlal Nehru to Modi, most Indian leaders have felt they were destined to be global players.

20. Mohan, *India's New Foreign Policy Strategy.*

21. World Bank, "Darkening Prospects: Global Economy to Slow to 2.9 percent in 2019 as Trade, Investment Weaken," last modified 2017, https://www.worldbank.org/en/news/press-release/2019/01/08/darkening-prospects-global-economy-to-slow-to-29-percent-in-2019-as-trade-investment-weaken.

22. "India Will Be Fastest-Growing Economy for Coming Decade," *The Wall Street Journal*, last modified January 1, 2016, https://blogs.wsj.com/india-realtime/2016/01/01/india-will-be-fastest-growing-economy-for-coming-decade-harvard-researchers-predict/.

23. Raghupathy Anchala, Nanda K. Kannuri, Hira Pant, Hassan Khan, Oscar H. Franco, Emanuele Di Angelantonio, and Dorairaj Prabhakaran, "Hypertension in India," *Journal of Hypertension* 32, no. 6 (2014): 1170–1177.

24. Daniel Twining, "India's Foreign Policy toward East Asia and the Neighborhood under Modi: Implications for Europe," IFG Policy Paper no. 10 (2015).

25. The BJP believes a resurgent India must get its *rightful place* in the comity of nations and international institutions. The vision is to fundamentally *reboot and reorient the foreign policy* goals, content, and process in a manner that locates India's global strategic engagement in a new paradigm and on *a wider canvas*, that is not just limited to political diplomacy, but also includes our economic, scientific, cultural, political, and security interests, both regional and global, on the principles of equality and mutuality, so that it leads to an economically stronger India, and its voice is heard in the international fora.

26. Rajiv Bhatia, "A Review of Narendra Modi's Foreign Policy," *Newslaundry*, May 30, 2016.

27. This high-elevation border dispute consists of claims regarding the validity of the Johnson Line and along several points including Aksai Chin area.

28. Sumit Ganguly, "Sino-Indian Border Talks, 1981–1989: A View from New Delhi," *Asian Survey* 29, no. 12 (1989): 1123–1135.

29. Figure 16.3 source: World Bank, "World Development Indicators." Forecast based on growth rates adapted from PWC 20250, "The World in 2050."

30. Sarie M. Khalid, "An Army with a State: Pakistan's Serial Praetorians," *The McGill International Review*, May 25, 2016.

31. Christine Fair, "Fighting to the End: The Pakistan Army's Way of War," The School of Public Policy at Central European University, public lecture, March 27, 2015.

32. The origin of this conflict can be traced back to the partition of British India. Following the infiltration of Pathan tribesmen across the West Pakistan-Kashmir border in 1947, Maharaja Hari Singh of Kashmir signed the Instrument of Accession through which the government of India gained control over Kashmir. The introduction of Indian troops into the state of Jammu and Kashmir expanded the scope of the conflict leading to the First Kashmir War in 1947–1948. Since then, India and Pakistan waged a Second Kashmir War in 1965 and have had several major confrontations across the border. Sumit Ganguly, *Conflict Unending: India-Pakistan Tensions Since 1947* (New York: Columbia University Press, 2001). Ganguly provides a complete treatment of the major confrontations between India and Pakistan over the territorial issue of Kashmir in 1947–1948, 1965, and 1999 as well as the Bangladesh war of 1971.

33. Rahul Roy Chaudhury, "Modi's Approach to China and Pakistan," *What Does India Think?* European Council on Foreign Relations, 2016.

34. Jacek Kugler, Siddharth Swaminathan, Mark Abdollahian, and Steven Sboto. "The Crisis in Kashmir: An Expected Utility Analysis," paper presented at the annual meeting of the Peace Science Society (International), October 28–30, 2001, Atlanta, GA.

35. Of related interest is the border dispute between China and India that has simmered since 1962 over territories in the Himalayas. Forecasts indicate that China will be stronger than India until 2050. Only after 2050, assuming that India achieves a stable population and maintains high levels of sustained growth, will the conditions for a shift in relative power between India and China emerge. Even under these circumstances the shift will be a weak one because China and India will have equivalent base populations of more than 1 billion people each. In the next fifty years, therefore, there is ample opportunity to find a peaceful accommodation for existing territorial disputes. Hence, short of external intervention, the China-India dispute is unlikely to be revived in the first half of this century as China continues on its current path to establish its unchallenged dominance in Asia, and this status will be recognized by India in the first half of this century. On the other hand, if outstanding territorial issues are still unresolved after fifty years, China and India will enter parity and conditions for India to overtake China could once more focus their attention on their territorial dispute and could lead to conflict.

36. This is supported by his statements in a recent television interview. "Why do you think negative? If the country looks strong, then even its companions will change, neighbors will change, and the atmosphere will change," Ankit Panda, "Narendra Modi Clarifies Statements on Pakistan," *The Diplomat*, May 9, 2014.

37. Raghupathy Anchala, Nanda K. Kannuri, Hira Pant, Hassan Khan, Oscar H. Franco, Emanuele Di Angelantonio, and Dorairaj Prabhakaran, "Hypertension in India," *Journal of Hypertension* 32, no. 6 (2014): 1170–1177.

Chapter Seventeen

The Regional Setting for Trends in World Politics

Jacek Kugler and Ronald L. Tammen

Regions are currently the most important units in world politics. This is consistent with the power transition theory (PTT) approach but also with common sense. The factual argument is that developing nations, holding the majority of the global population, are slowly closing the gap with the developed world. Figure 17.1 tells us the long-term implication of the massive changes that take place over wide expanses of time in the global arena.

The relative population of large nations, normally associated with Great Powers, is shrinking rapidly in the developed world. From the first century to the start of the Industrial Revolution in 1820 the societies with the largest

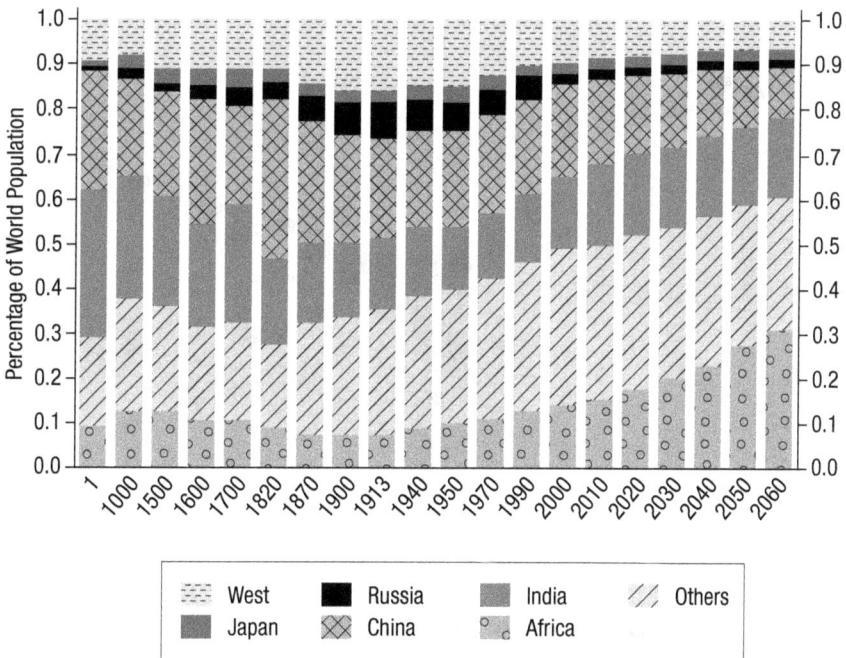

Figure 17.1. Share of World Population (1–2060)

Jacek Kugler and Ronald L. Tammen

populations had approximately equivalent productivity and held about 70 percent of the global population and output. China and India were the largest two societies, but major changes then took place. With increased productivity, the population of the great Western powers plus Japan shrank, but their productivity increased disproportionately. China and India still maintained their relative population size, but the Great Powers have shrunk overall to 40 percent of the world's population. Their proportion of the population will decline further to slightly more than 35 percent; yet, as figure 17.2 shows, these large nations account for most of the world's total output. Population growth is fastest in Africa, where it is expected to rise from less than 10 percent to about 30 percent of global population by 2060, but the relative impact of this change will be limited.[1]

Population is not a perfect indicator of the ability of nations to influence others in the international arena, or even a good one. A better indicator is total gross national output, and this perspective in figure 17.2 provides a far more familiar story.[2]

The reason for the disparity between population and power is relative productivity of the competing populations. Figure 17.2 shows that in the first century, all societies had equivalent levels of productivity. Thus, India and China dominated output simply because their populations were the largest.

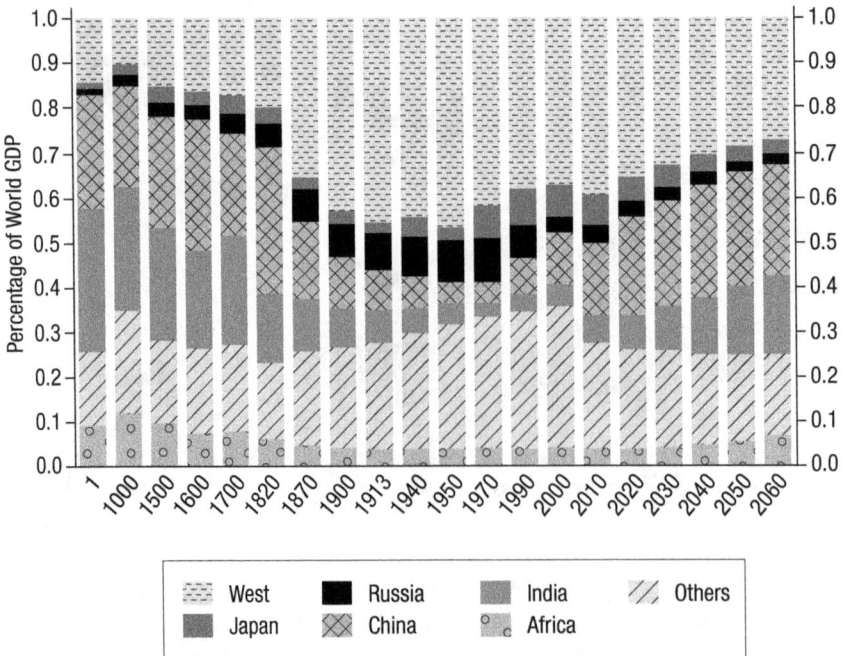

Figure 17.2. Share of World Gross Domestic Product (1–2060)

The West was relatively small, with the Roman Empire accounting for the majority of all output. By 1820, when the Industrial Revolution hit Europe, the picture changed dramatically.

China and India became mere shadows of their previous selves, with diminished political influence. Western nations led by Great Britain and the United States now dominated. Any student of international relations will understand that the unexpected dominance of the many by the few is directly linked with the technological advantage developed by Western societies.

Our forecasts indicate that the current period of US dominance is nearing its end. Even a unified West—now undermined by President Donald Trump's words and actions[3]—will not remain the global leader.

The Asian challenge is clear. China and India are the next international contenders whose zenith is likely to be achieved by the end of the century. Figure 17.3 shows in more detail how the convergence of gross domestic product (GDP) per capita among the Great Powers, for which data are available from the Maddison collection, is leading to the renaissance of Asian societies. As Tadeusz Kugler points out in chapter 6, population size is the core factor in power that materializes *when productivity is equalized.*[4]

As already indicated, from the first to the middle of the nineteenth century, per capita productivity among the Great Powers was relatively stable. Rome

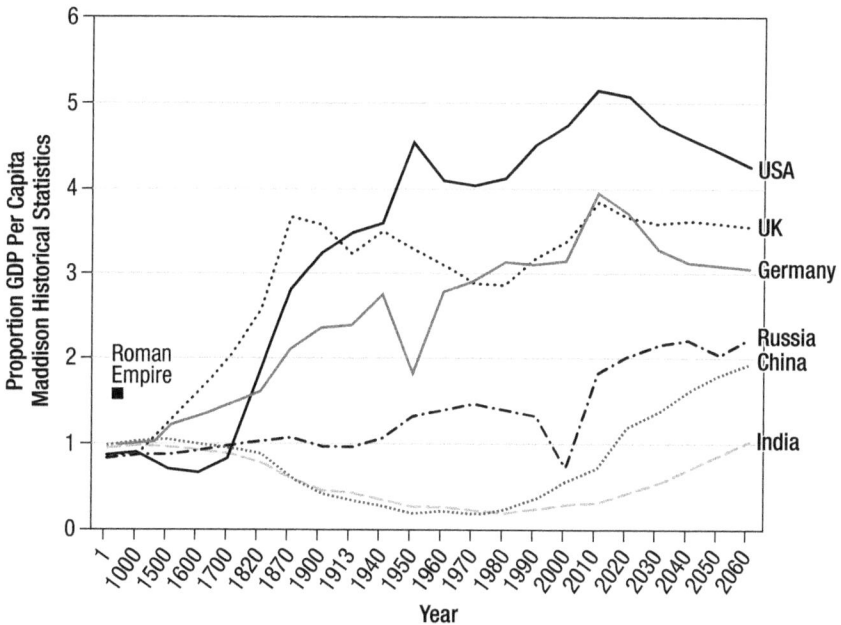

Figure 17.3.   Convergence of per Capita Gross Domestic Product among Great Powers (1–2016)

outdistanced competitors until 1500, when Great Britain emerged in the early 1900s, and then was only surpassed by the United States at the dawn of the twentieth century. Most of the Western Great Powers and Japan achieved production levels that tripled or even quadrupled that of their Asian competitors. Such trends are now reversing.

China has grown very fast since the death of Mao Zedong and is now overtaking the United States, whereas India, the weakest among developing competitors, is closing fast. The convergence in productivity is driven by the dispersion of technical know-how largely through the Internet and the increase in global trade that allows more direct competition among societies. These patterns are likely to persist and reinforce each other.

Previous figures demonstrate that the size of productive societies is associated with economic success. If, as anticipated, market effects provide substantial benefits to a larger political unit, then Brexit, as Birol Yesilada, Gaspare Genna, and Osman Tanrikulu indicate in chapter 5, will accelerate the decline of the United Kingdom within the international community. Similar effects should be felt by the United States if current policies weaken rather than strengthen United States–Mexico–Canada Agreement (USMCA) and trade agreements with Asia are not pursued.[5]

Note in figure 17.3 that a convergence of productivity is taking place. The reason is that doubling income at the $100,000 level is far more difficult than doubling a yearly income of $10,000. Simple technology transfers allow a farmer to double productivity by exchanging his burro for a tractor. Much more sophisticated technological breakthroughs and investment are required to achieve similar targets in an advanced society.

This book focuses mainly on the populations found within the developing world. The wars in Vietnam and Afghanistan have taught us that interventions by Great Powers into highly mobilized yet relatively small environments are not a viable strategy. The colonial era, when a handful of technically advanced invaders could control large, but far-less-advanced, societies, is over.[6] Small nations can defend their territory if the population is mobilized to do so. Mobilization is the key, providing the framework for increased productivity as well. Great Powers can alter outcomes, as in Syria, but can no longer determine the future of nations over a longer period without extraordinary investments. Expansion now depends on persuasion rather than force.

Even Western structures thought to be permanent are showing signs of decay. The North Atlantic Treaty Organization (NATO) has provided a security blanket for the European Union (EU) and more broadly the West. But this arrangement is fraying as commitments to the status quo and established norms are challenged by an untraditional US president.

Some will celebrate the fact that, if NATO falters, the EU will likely create a European force led by France and Germany that would be capable of defending Europe against Russia. But a nuclear buildup could follow to replace the US nuclear umbrella. At that point, this new independent Europe could pick and choose what country or coalition to join in a future confrontation. It would no longer be assured that the choice would be its old partner in the Atlantic Alliance. It could, for example, remain neutral. A balance of power based on need and not dependent on common norms could emerge. That would not bode well for world politics where shared norms are an important value.

In chapter 13, Kyungkook Kang shows that conditional deterrence derived from PTT indicates that realist-endorsed developments would generate the necessary but not sufficient conditions for regional or global nuclear war. On the other hand, Kang also reminds us of the importance of nuclear-free zones. Such security arrangements, pioneered by the Latin Americans in the Treaty of Tlatelolco, have now been extended with variations over much of the developing world.

A few nuclear powers can assure regional nuclear stability by extending retaliation guarantees for all participants in nuclear-free zones. But Kang shows that the nuclear-free world that many idealists seek is no longer practical. And he demonstrates that mutually assured destruction (MAD) is tenuous. To avoid nuclear war among nuclear powers, one needs to assure those that choose *not* to develop such capabilities that their future is secure with guarantees.[7]

This book argues that the rise of regions results from the relative decline of Great Powers. Where their power or interest wanes, regionally dominant nations take over. These events occur during and after shifts in relative capabilities. Figure 17.1 shows that the Great Powers no longer hold most of the global population, even though figure 17.2 indicates that their hold on output has not changed. Note further that fertility patterns in the more advanced nations are leading to a decline of populations, and in the least-advanced parts of the globe, local populations continue to increase. Given the convergence in per capita output, portions of the world that had only a marginal impact on global matters will become increasingly important and independent.

In chapter 14, Patrick Rhamey confirms that the strong reach of Great Powers is shrinking, and as their influence declines, regional powers emerge. His review of countries "in the middle" provides a new context for understanding the push and pull of regional politics. Analysis of South America in chapter 12 by Marina Arbetman-Rabinowitz and Ayesha Umar Wahedi indicates that societies are now far more willing than previously to trade with China and are more independent. Brazil remains a reluctant leader. Intervention by Europe and the United States is no longer. The integration process of Mercosur has faltered not because external powers prevented such developments but because Latin American nations have not found a common economic path.

In South Asia, discussed in chapter 16, John Thomas and Fredrick Clarke argue that India is the dominant power in the region whose actions are independent of all other countries. China, the dominant power in East Asia, is attempting to create in the South China Sea what the United States achieved in the Caribbean. It is involving neighbors through the new Silk Road system and seeks to expand economically into Europe, South America, and Africa. This provides a direct overlap between a South Asia dominated by India and a Southeast Asia where China has influence but Indonesia will play a significant role. Vietnam also plays an important regional role in Southeast Asia by engaging with the United States in economic activity and even in mutual national security matters.

Building a trade road will extend China's influence into neighboring countries. Trade-road developments can lead in either of two directions, according to Ronald L. Tammen and Ayesha Umar Wahedi in chapter 2: to an agreement in which the two Asian giants share control and ultimately emerge as the global dominant coalition or to a conflict between them. In chapter 3, Yi Feng, Zhijun Gao, and Zining Yang also provide insights and context about that strategic development, which provides leverage for China and perhaps other associated nations.

From a global perspective, developments in these two regions have the most profound implications for global stability. What happens in the relationship between India and China will determine future global stability in the last half of the twenty-first century just as the relationship between the Union of Soviet Socialist Republics (USSR) and the United States determined stability in the latter half of the twentieth century. In chapter 15, Arbetman-Rabinowitz and Thomas show that the Southeast Asian region is emerging from the shadows of Western control even as Indonesia and Australia seek to find new footing in the global economy and as countries in Southeast Asia pick and choose which superpower to follow, be it China, India, or the United States.

Staying with the global perspective, Eurasia is a region of paramount concern. Kristina Khederlarian, Allison Hamlin, and Jacek Kugler remind us in chapter 7 that all severe global conflicts emerged from confrontations over control of Eurasia. The regional conflict between Russia and Ukraine has global implications. Guarantees of sovereignty provided by Western nuclear powers were violated when Russia, with the support of China, annexed Crimea. The credibility of the Memorandum of Security (MOS) that guaranteed the integrity of Ukraine, essential to persuade non-nuclear nations not to proliferate or acquire nuclear arsenals, was abandoned to prevent a confrontation between NATO and the Russia-China team. Because China chose to align with Russia on this question, this creates anxiety about China's future role.

The conflict in Ukraine continues to simmer. Unlike conflicts in the Middle East, in Afghanistan, or in past wars in Vietnam, this regional confrontation (along with China's demands over the South China Sea) could prompt a regional conflict that could rapidly escalate. Although disputes involving North Korea or Taiwan also have escalatory potential, only the Ukrainian crisis lies at the heartland of Eurasia where the interests of Europe, Russia, and the United States collide. Any attempt to create a global coalition that seeks to preserve peace must start with a resolution of this problem. Scholars who dismiss the Russian invasion of Crimea and the incursion into Ukraine as past events that can be accommodated are failing to think strategically about the locus of war.

In Africa, while colonial rulers have departed, nation building has not been completed. Like South America, Africa is emerging from European influence as a fractured and divided continent. Sudan, the largest territorial entity in Africa, has split into South and North. No dominant state capable of unifying large portions of the continent is at hand. Competition over basic resources is further dividing countries into spheres of US, European, Chinese, and Indian influence. Africa, along with the Middle East, remains the least-independent region. In chapter 11, Nicholas Coulombe and Kristin Johnson recognize that internal concerns dictate most political decisions within large African nations and that they are more focused on civil stability than international goals. Given Africa's potential role in world politics in the future, this is a significant observation.

In chapter 9, Ali Fisunoglu argues that the contest in the Middle East region has shifted from being centered on Israel to a focus on Iran, Turkey, and Saudi Arabia. This should be of high interest to the policy community, which often seems frozen on "the next move." In chapter 8, Marina Arbetman Rabinowitz and Zeyad Kelani show that competition in the Middle East is leading to the formation of unanticipated coalitions as power transitions among contenders are fueled by religious differences. That analysis indicates that prospects for stable interactions in the African and Middle East regions are low. The prospects for civil wars morphing into international interventions are very high. Trust and a common set of norms that sustain stability could be built, but they are not in place or even in sight in some cases.

Finally, North America emerges, in chapter 4 by Patrick James and Athanasios Hristoulas, not unexpectedly, as a region of stability. A major reason is the presence of the United States, which towers economically, politically, and, of course, militarily over both Mexico and Canada. Although prospects for the further integration of USMCA in the mold of the EU seem to be fading, the likelihood of security breaches in the region are remote. The North American region is expected to remain a stable zone within a more challenged global environment.

COMPARING REGIONAL HIERARCHIES

The global system is fundamentally asymmetric. China leads in East Asia, the United States is preponderant in North America, and India towers above all others in South Asia as shown in figure 17.4. These are the main players in the future global hierarchy. The EU is also a member of the global hierarchy despite not having overwhelmingly dominant power.[8]

The top powers that compete over control of the global system affect decisions in all hierarchies. The preponderant nations of the smaller regional hierarchies seldom affect overall changes at the global level. To the degree that attention is centered on a smaller region, such as the Levant, regional outcomes are distorted by the intervention of members of the global hierarchy. The Vietnam War, the wars in Iran and Afghanistan, the interventions in Libya, and the Syrian conflict all provide a ledger of recent events affected by global power intervention in regional affairs.

The reverse is not so evident. Despite visibility attached to the Russian intervention in Syria that tilted the balance in favor of the Assad regime, Russia no longer vies for global leadership. Russia's intervention in Ukraine is a regional Eurasian phenomenon with global implications. Saudi Arabia's actions in Yemen are restricted to the Levant. Regional conflicts even of the magnitude of the Iran-Iraq War of 1980–1988 did not spread to the remaining hierarchies. On the other hand, global power confrontations, like the budding dispute over control of the South China Sea, have the potential to diffuse more broadly.

DOMINANT POWERS IN REGIONAL HIERARCHIES

Figure 17.5 shows the relative capabilities of hierarchies along with the size of the dominant powers within each of these aggregates.[9] Three distinct levels emerge. The North American, East Asian, European, and South Asian hierarchies lead the pack by a large margin. Each of these hierarchies except the European is led by a dominant nation that faces no serious challenges from within its own region. This preponderance assures internal stability. As

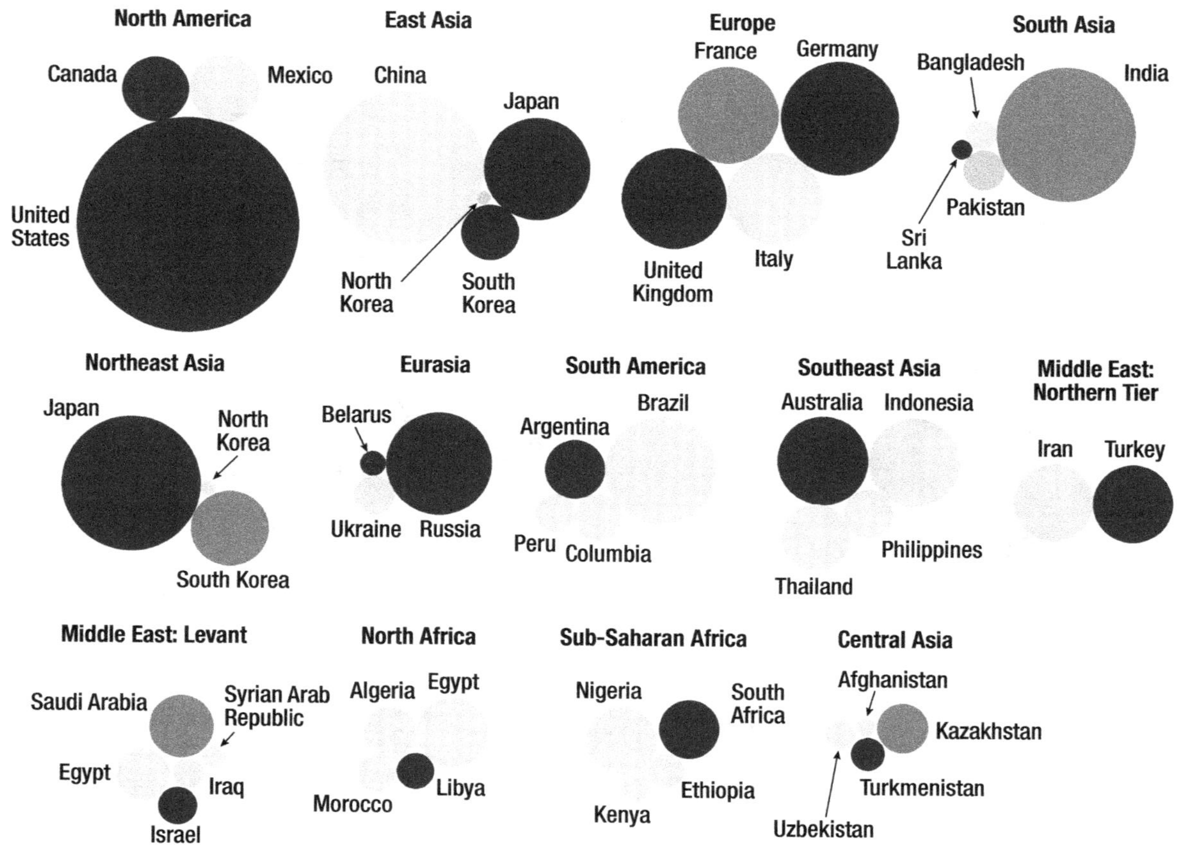

Figure 17.4.   Relative Size of Regional Hierarchies

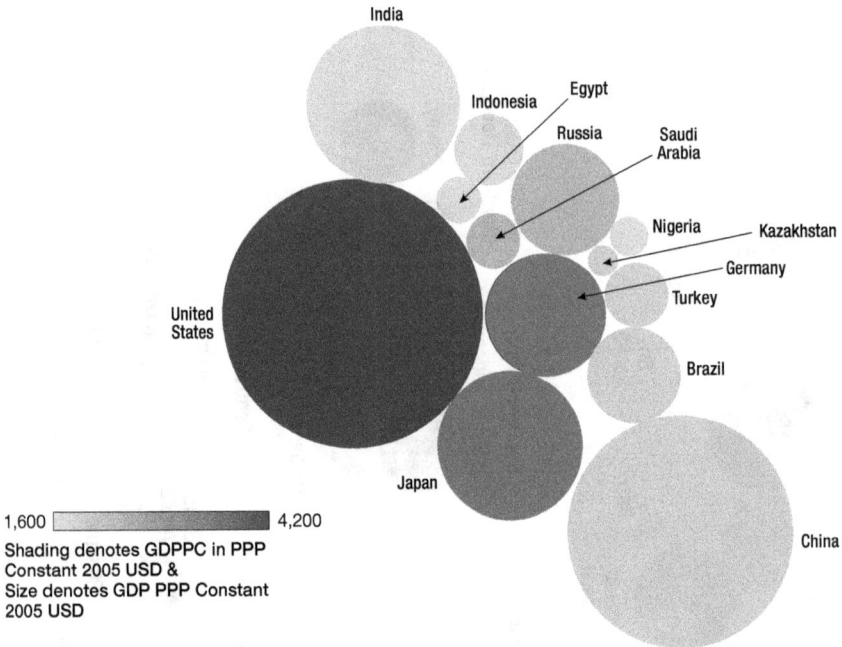

Figure 17.5.   Dominant Powers in Regional Hierarchies

for Europe, this sector remains stable because it operates as a largely unified system under the banner of the EU. This integration process is still a coherent grouping because of the reduction of economic tensions and almost universal participation in NATO.

The second group of hierarchies contains important dominant nations that can directly influence their own respective regions but not the global hierarchy.

Northeast Asia, dominated by Japan, has preserved a tenuous intraregional stability following the Korean War of 1950–1953. Only North Korea is explicitly dissatisfied and fundamentally opposed to the global norms. The remaining states in the region have sided with the United States and are covered by alliances and a nuclear umbrella. The exception, North Korea, does not have the capacity to alter the regional status quo by conventional means. Today, South Korea is a far more powerful nation. The costs of a conventional or nuclear war with the North would be staggering for the South, but the cost for North Korea would be the complete destruction of the ruling family and its military allies and a likely takeover of the North by China.

Eurasia is effectively dominated by Russia. The predecessor state that collapsed in 1991 was a certified member of the global hierarchy, but Russia no longer holds this rank. It has lost a significant portion of its population, spends a disproportionately large percentage of its gross domestic product

(GDP) on its military,[10] and suffers from a shrinking and increasingly medically at-risk population.

MID-SIZED AND SMALLER HIERARCHIES

The South American region is dominated by Brazil, which overtook the much-richer Argentina in the nineteenth century. In agreement with the work of Lemke, South America is a relatively stable region dominated by Brazil. Nations there took the lead by agreeing in the Treaty of Tlatelolco to form a nuclear-free zone. This happened despite the fact that Argentina and Brazil and to a lesser degree Mexico had substantial investments in the early research on and development of nuclear weapons. This region has been relatively isolated from global interventions largely because the United States, the global dominant power, treated South America as a very secondary region of interest.

Recent economic involvement by China and residual interest by Russia in Venezuela following Moscow's failed involvement in Cuba suggest a rising interest in the region. However, because the center of competition among the global powers focuses on the Eurasian and Asian regions, it is unlikely that South America will become a central focus of competition in the future. Analysis suggests that the preconditions for interstate war are absent but intrastate conflicts are likely to continue to be driven by the relatively low level of economic success and weak political performance of South American societies.

Australia and Indonesia play separate roles in Southeast Asia. Australia, having the larger economy of the two for the time being, has focused on the United Kingdom, the United States, and China. It has engaged in regional affairs only on a limited basis. The emerging dominant nation is Indonesia. Its participation in the Association of Southeast Asian Nations (ASEAN) may change the direction of policy there and generate increased competition among nations in the region. The transition with Australia is likely to be peaceful because the main differences that appeared early on have largely dissipated. Located close to China, members of this region may be pressed to make territorial concessions in the South China Sea. They also may be pressured to take a side if the future US-China transition becomes confrontational.

The last hierarchy in the middle group is the Middle East Northern Tier. Here Iran and Turkey are potential competitors. Each seeks to become the leader of the extended Middle East. Both face a common challenge from the Kurdish minority distributed within their borders and those of Iraq. Each houses the largest concentrations of Shia and Sunni denominations of Islam, and both have forcefully attempted to impose their will on Syria.

Turkey is dissatisfied because of the rejection of its application to join the EU and has moved to reconcile with Russia and other Middle East nations instead of focusing on Europe, where its economic interests overwhelmingly reside. Iran has managed to establish an inroad into the EU, but treaty limitations on the development of nuclear warheads have been rejected by the United States and the associated embargoes have imposed significant financial penalties. Given these factors, it is likely that Turkey will turn toward China and its new Silk Road.

The transition between Turkey and Iran, coupled with their dissatisfaction with regional and global norms, indicates a serious possibility of conflict. Domestic instability is unlikely in the immediate future, but both Turkey and Iran have authoritarian leaders who, although in full control of the population, have not assured effective economic rewards.

The smallest hierarchies, Middle East-Levant, North Africa, sub-Saharan Africa and Central Asia, are not major players in global politics but are directly affected by the interests of the global powers. Regional actors emerge undisturbed when external actors are not directly concerned with the outcomes. This is particularly true of sub-Saharan Africa. Global powers affect events in Central Asia modestly, a bit more directly in North Africa, and are deeply involved in the Middle East-Levant.

The sub-Saharan region is large and diverse. As Lemke indicated, the surprising element is that so few interstate wars have been waged since the postcolonial period. The two dominant nations are Nigeria and South Africa, but, despite a recent transition, they interact infrequently and have few competitive issues. Within their localized neighborhoods, both help to assure subregional stability.

Ethiopia is undergoing a transition with Kenya, but the postcolonial conflicts are dissipating and the moderating influence of the African Union in Addis Ababa supports resolution of disputes and confidence building. The prospects for a continuing peaceful transition are in place. As throughout most of Africa, the major prospects for disruption are found in subnational conflicts created by nonstate actors. Despite evidence of cross-national cooperation, one needs look no further than South Sudan to identify and understand the long-term influence of enduring internal divisions that frequently generate civil war in this region.

In Central Asia, the dominant nation is Kazakhstan, as influenced by Russia and to some degree China and the United States. Despite the potential for border disputes, this has been a relatively quiet neighborhood, but given religious tensions along the Chinese border and resource exploitation, there are always localized points of tension. Conflicts involving the United States in Afghanistan and Russia in Chechnya have attracted the attention of global players but because of the distribution of resources, it is unlikely that either of these interventions could spark regional war.

North Africa is dominated in the East by Egypt and in the West by Algeria. Egypt sits at the crossroads of these regions. In the Levant, Israel dominates the neighborhood and Saudi Arabia provides the economic backing needed to accelerate lagging growth. In the South, Sudan's partition provided an important if unsuccessful distraction. To the West, Libya posed some international challenges that were resolved with the collapse of Muammar al-Qadhafi's regime. All members except for Morocco were directly affected by the civil disturbances of the Arab Spring. Egypt, Tunisia, and Libya changed regimes and are still finding their footing. Algeria avoided leadership replacement in the short term but is now facing this challenge. Structural conditions indicated that the region is unlikely to meet the transition preconditions required for an international conflict. The involvement of global actors is diminishing, suggesting intrastate stability. However, the lack of development coupled with dissatisfaction ensures that the protracted civil war in Libya will continue, challenges to the regime in Algeria are imminent, and Egypt may face a second Arab Spring unless economic growth substantially increases. Morocco and Tunisia are the two societies likely to preserve domestic stability.

Finally, the Middle East-Levant is and will continue to be a most volatile region. The regional and cross-regional conflicts that have devastated this region have produced the largest proportional casualties since World War II. The cross-regional conflict between Iran and Iraq following the revolution that overthrew the Shah was a violent and protracted event. The succession of interventions by the United States in Iraq destroyed a major power in the region and directly contributed to an intense civil war that diffused to Syria and Yemen. Saudi Arabia has emerged as the dominant state in this region, overtaking Israel, which, despite its small size, took advantage of advanced productivity to hold off larger, less-developed Arab states. Intrastate stability in this region could be ensured were Saudi Arabia, Egypt, and Israel to join a coalition aimed at preserving stability in the Levant in the face of potential challenges from Iran or Turkey, who aspire to control the extended Middle East region.

Regions differ. Arguments that account for global patterns sometimes completely miss behavior within regions. Transitions combined with common norms consistently lead to stability within regions and at the global level. On the other hand, confrontational policies under transition conditions lead to war, locally and globally.

Regions are becoming increasingly independent. The centralized global structures that were built by Western nations are fraying because of the rise of the Asian giants and the expansion of populations in regions no longer controlled by Western powers. The new world will be far more decentralized than the one we are used to. Not only will the center of politics shift from

Europe and the United States to Asia, but within the developing world, new centers of power in South America, South Asia, and perhaps even Africa, will emerge from the shadows.

Britain, Japan, and even Russia—the Great Powers of the nineteenth and twentieth centuries—will leave the world stage to be replaced by Brazil, Indonesia, Pakistan, Nigeria, and Bangladesh—all with future large productive populations based on current trends. The powerful effects of large productive populations will soon be the new coin of the realm, the new elixir of power.

To understand the future, it is essential to comprehend the underlying structural shifts underway today. This book outlines that structure and analyzes the likely outcomes of the world that will exist from now to mid-century when the twin giants, China and India, seize center stage.

NOTES

1. Figure 17.1 source: Maddison Historical Statistics, Jutta Bolt, and Jan Luiten van Zanden, "The Maddison Project: Collaborative Research on Historical National Accounts," *The Economic History Review* 67, no. 3 (2014): 627–651.

2. Figure 17.2 source: Maddison Historical Statistics, Jutta Bolt, and Jan Luiten van Zanden, "The Maddison Project: Collaborative Research on Historical National Accounts," *The Economic History Review* 67, no. 3 (2014): 627–651.

3. If President Trump, following realist insights, succeeds in destroying NATO, the decline of the West will be accelerated. China will be the next dominant power; Russia and the United Kingdom alone can no longer be counted among the great powers. The European Union, the United States, China, and India will dominate until the potential growth and possible unification of Africa or an expansion of Mercosur allows Brazil to lead the emergence of Latin America among the Great Powers and provides the international community with a new global power.

4. Figure 17.3 source: Maddison Historical Statistics, Jutta Bolt, and Jan Luiten van Zanden, "The Maddison Project: Collaborative Research on Historical National Accounts," *The Economic History Review* 67, no. 3 (2014): 627–651.

5. Contrary to the realist self-reliance arguments, the recently signed agreement among the EU, Japan, and Canada should have positive economic consequences, whereas the withdrawal of the United States from the Pacific Partnership should have long-term negative implications.

6. Cortez conquered the Aztec empire of several million people with fewer than four hundred isolated Spanish soldiers and a few horses. Pizzaro did likewise in Peru, destroying the Inca empire with fewer than two hundred conquistadors. Casualties in these encounters were enormous. How could so few kill so many and then control them? The answer is now known. The Spanish conquistadors created alliances with the dissatisfied population of the Inca and Aztec empires and used them to defeat the previous rulers. Graveyards in Peru show that 85 percent of all casualties in the

decisive battle for Cuzco were killed by stone axes and arrows. The Spaniards did not use such weapons. The story of British successes in India follows a similar path.

7. Kang and Kugler (forthcoming) formally show that MAD is unstable under the following conditions: (i) when conventional capabilities are at parity—China and the United States will face these conditions in the near future; (ii) when a nuclear nation threatened by a larger conventional power may act to avert defeat—Israel and Iran may soon face this condition; or (iii) when dissatisfied nonstate actors that may acquire primitive nuclear devices use them to avoid exposure. To limit this danger, Kang and Kugler urge that the number of nuclear nations be reduced only to those that have global reach (United States, Russia, India, China, the EU). Further proliferation will defeat all attempts at preventing a nuclear war.

8. Figure 17.4 source: World Bank, "World Development Indicators," last modified March 27, 2016, http://documents.worldbank.org/curated/en/805371467990952829/ World-development-indicators-2016.

9. Figure 17.5 source: World Bank, "World Development Indicators," last modified March 27, 2016, http://documents.worldbank.org/curated/en/805371467990952829/ World-development-indicators-2016.

10. In 1918 in US billion dollars, the defense budget of the United States was $643, NATO Europe $264, China $168, and Russia $63.

Index

Page numbers in italics indicate figures and tables.

nationalistic parties of Europe, inspiring, 107; South America as learning from, 202; as a still-evolving process, 79; as the tip of the iceberg, 196; Turkish petition for EU membership, affecting, 93, 148

Britain. *See* United Kingdom

Brodie, Bernard, 210

Brydon, William, 227

Budapest Memorandum of Security Assurances, 119

Buhari, Muhammadu, 178

Bulgaria, *95*, 122

Burma, 23

Bush, George W., 63, 71, 213

Cambodia, 50, 52n5, 240, 252n10

Cameroon, 178, 180

Canada: in Comparative Military Power table, *90*; Mexico-Canada relations, 56, 67–68; in North American region, *55*, 56, *59*, 122, 278, *279*; trilateral relations with US and Mexico, 56, 68–72, 74–75, 116, 122, 274, 277–78; United States-Canada relations, 60, 61–65, 72–73; Western Coalition, as a member of, 6

Canada-United States Free Trade Agreement (FTA), 63, 68–70, 73

Caribbean, 15, 56, 75n2, 106, 199, 276

Castañeda, Jorge, 67–68, 71, 72

Central African Republic (CAR), *173*, 176–77, 182–84

Central America, 15, 56, 75

Central Asia: in the Cold War era, 228–32, 235; color revolution, US encouraging, 47; former provinces of the USSR, made up of, 14, 118; the Great Game, played in, 226–27; New Silk Road route, 23; productivity of, 46; Russian influence in, 48, 224, 225, 229–31, 233–34, 236, 282; Silk Road Economic Belt, northern route passing through, 38; Turkey and

Iran, increasing their influence in, 145; US presence in region, 224–25, 227–31, 282

Chad, 114n2, 178, 180

Chechnya, 118, 282

Chile, 66, 73, 195, 197, *198*, 201

China: African interests in, 15, 30, 50, 187, 188–89, 190, 275, 277; Australia-China relations, 32, 242, 253n28, 260–61; camouflaged Chinese senior official, 33–34; Central Asia, Chinese presence in, 47, 224, 225, 229, 230, 235; China-Pakistan economic corridor, 38, 45–46, 48; in Comparative Military Power table, *90*; Cultural Revolution, 20, 25, 33; democracy level score, 49–50; dominance of, 6, 11, 14, 31, 251, 259, 284; East Asia, presence in, 218, 276, 278; economy, opening of, 21, 44–45; as a global power, 11, 23, 27, 29, 30–31, 78, 119; growth of, 20–22, 41–42, 104, 182, 273; India-China relations, 9, 30, 32, 234, 236, 256–57, 260–63, 265, 276; Iran, Chinese interest in, 141, 142; Kazakhstan, influence on, 282; the Levant, investments in, 133; Mexico-China relations, 73; Middle East, Chinese interest in, 30, 139, 141; natural gas, as top importer of, 122; the new China, 22, 23, 27, 28, 41–42, 43; Northeast Asia, influence on, 15, 206–207; North Korea, possible takeover of, 280; as a nuclear power, 208, 214, 217, 219, 285n7; One Belt, One Road policy, 229, 231, 235, 236; Pakistan-China relations, 23, 38, 45, 48, 258; Philippines-China relations, 41, 249, 253n28, 261; population size, 20–21, 104, 112, 234, 256, 262, 271–72; productivity of, 117, 124n15, 174, 203; rise of, 15, 27, 31, 38, 39, 260; Russia-China alliance, 6, 9, 27–28, 30–31, 113, 119–20,

Indian Ocean, 13, *40*, 45, 46, 47, 48

Indonesia: ASEAN, as a member of, 52n5, 243, 250, 281; Australia-Indonesia relations, 15, 244; in Comparative Military Power table, *91*; economic output, 174; Indonesia-China relations, 32, 249, 253n28, 260–61; rise of, 2, 15, 245, 250, 281; Southeast Asia, as a part of, 50, 240, 242–45, 276, 281; Straits of Malacca, surrounding, 30

Industrial Revolution, 11, 78, 104, 271, 273

Inglehart, Robert, 93–94

Integrated Cross Border Maritime Law Enforcement Operations. *See* Shiprider program

Inter-American Treaty of Reciprocal Assistance (ITRA), 65, 73

International Atomic Energy Agency (IAEA), 199

International Energy Agency (IEA), 122

International Monetary Fund (IMF), 200, 201

Iran: in Comparative Military Power table, *91*; growth rate, 120, 142, 145, 150nn8–10; Levant, as a part of, 126–27, 133; in Middle East region, 133, 138–39, 283; New Silk Road, meant to deter, 47; nuclear capabilities, 142, 145, 147, 211, 213, 217, 285n7; Syrian conflict, involvement in, 131, 135n17, 281; Turkey-Iran relations, 133, 139–41, 143–46, 148, 149n4, 282; Yemen, interfering in, 129

Iranian Revolution (1979), 140, 144, 283

Iran-Iraq War (1980–88), 138, 140, 149n3, 278

Iraq: disorderliness of Middle East, as causing, 142; Iran, destabilizing recovery of, 144; Iraq-Turkey dyad, 145; Iraq War, Canadian opposition to, 64, 73; Kurdish minority in, 139,

281; the Levant, as part of, 183; in Middle East region, 120; power status, 140, 141, 148; Syrian Army, assisting, 131; US interventions in, 88, 139, 283

Islamic State of Iraq and Syria (ISIS), 142, 143, 157, 159, 166, 168, *169*, 244

Israel: Arab-Israeli Wars, 140, *230*; in Comparative Military Power table, *90*; Egypt-Israel relations, 126, 128, 130, 133, 138, 155, 170; Iran, concern over its nuclear capabilities, 147, 214; as a nuclear power, 133, 139, 145, 211, 217, 285n7; political capacity of, 128–29; regional relevance, loss of, 127, 130–31, 133, 138, 140, 146, 148, 277; Saudi/Egypt/Israel coalition, 130, 133, 148, 283; Turkey, relations with, 144; US military aid, receiving, 132

Italy: Chinese influence in, 15; CFSP, likeliness for rejecting, 98; democratization of, 78; economic status, 79, 84; population decline, 112; power status, 6, 104; Tunisian diaspora in, 165; value preferences, 94, *95*

James, Patrick, 277

Japan: as an Asian-Pacific nation, 261; Asian Development Bank, influence over, 47; Australia, trade with, 242; China-Japan relations, 23, 25, 26, 27, 32, 33, 217, 234, 253n28; in classical deterrence theory, 212; in Comparative Military Power table, *90*; economic productivity, 35n18, 78, 174, 271–72, 274; Great Power status, loss of, 32, 284; India, trade with, 265; in Northeast Asia region, 15, 206, 207, 280; Nuclear Non-Proliferation Treaty, adhering to, 213; Pearl Harbor, decision to bomb, 10; Philippines, trade with, 249;

Union of South American Nations
(UNASUR), 199, 201
Union of Soviet Socialist Republics
(USSR): Canada, monitoring Soviet
activity over, 62; Chinese-Soviet
relations, 25; collapse of, 2, 11,
32, 78, 79, 96, 106, 228, 259, 280;
EU, posing common threat to, 72;
European states, effect of Russia's
rise on, 104; former provinces
of, 13, 14, 78, 116–17; military
expenditures, *92*; as a nuclear power,
216; Russian Federation, decline of,
117–18; Soviet-US relations, 276;
US preponderance over, 9, 11, 216.
See also Russia
United Arab Emirates (UAE), 129–30,
134n2, 157
United Kingdom: Afghanistan, British
influence in, 226–27; Anglo
American alliance, 8, 81; Australia,
relations with, 281; Canada,
declining to support, 56; Central
Asia, presence in, 235–36; China,
relations with, 33; in Comparative
Military Power table, *90*; conflict
with EU as unlikely, 97; decline of,
35n18, 62, 104, 274, 283, 284n3;
dominance of, 231, 273; EU, quest
for membership in, 79; Germany-
UK relations, 82–83; immigration,
effect on, 105, 110, 112; India,
continued colonial ties to England,
258; Iran nuclear deal, attempts to
restore, 142; NATO membership, 78,
89; Pashtuns, early British support
for, 227; population of, 106, 107,
109–11, 111–13; SDF, supporting,
131; Turkey-UK relations, 93;
Ukraine, agreeing to protect, 119;
value preferences, *95*; in War of
1812, 59, 76n7; Western coalition, as
a member of, 6. *See also* Brexit
United Kingdom Independence Party
(UKIP), 105, 107

United Nations (UN), 31, 64, 168, 170,
177, 183, 244
United Nations Security Council
(UNSC), 64, 145, 265
United States: Africa, interests in,
188; Alien Exclusion Acts, effect
on immigration, 106; America
First orientation, 45, 46–47; Asia,
as overtaken by, 3, 284; B&R
Initiative, interests in, 41; Canada-
US relations, 59–60, 61–65, 68,
72–73; Central Asia, presence in,
224–25, 228–31, 282; China, as
overtaken by, 41, 74, 120, 266,
273; China, competing with, 23,
74, 120, 148, 190, 196, 232, 235,
262; classical deterrence theory,
supporting, 210, 212–14; in Cold
War, 9–10, 211; in Comparative
Military Power table, *90*; East Asia,
nuclear defense of, 209, 217–19;
European decline in relation to,
104; Europe-US alliance, 113, 123,
275; global dominance of, 6, 104,
259, 273; Great Power status, 107;
halo effect on Northeast Asia, 15;
India-US relations, 11, 234, 258,
266; Iran, concern over nuclear
status of, 142, 145, 211, 282; Iraq,
interventions in, 88, 139, 283;
Israel, supporting, 130–31, 132;
Japan-US relations, 41, 208, 218;
Levant and, 126, 133; Mexico-US
relations, 60–61, 65–67, 73, 75;
Middle East, influence in, 132,
139, 143, 146; North America,
as dominating, 56, 74, 277–78;
Northeast Asia, US involvement in,
207, 280; productivity of, 78, 79,
118, 174, 197; Russia-US relations,
119, 121, 208, 233–34, 242; South
America, interest in, 194, 195, 196,
203, 276, 281; Southeast Asia, US
influence as weakened in, 251;
Taiwan, US protection of, 206;

About the Contributors

Amir Bagherpour is Non-Resident Fellow at Federation of American Scientists (FAS) focused on application of advanced analytics to detect and prevent global catastrophic events. He is also a Senior Manager at Accenture's federal Applied Intelligence practice where he consults for numerous government agencies. Prior to Accenture, Bagherpour was a partner and Chief Analytics Officer of giStrat, where he built cloud-based technologies focused on modeling complex geopolitical problems. Prior to his commercial experience, Bagherpour was the Director of Data Analytics in the Office of the Secretary of State. He was also the senior analyst and team lead for the Advanced Analytics Unit at the Bureau of Conflict & Stabilization Operations. Bagherpour served at Voice of America's Persian Service and in the US Army as an Armor Officer and is a graduate of West Point. He has a PhD in Political Science with a focus on quantitative methods from Claremont Graduate University and an MBA specializing in market research and macroeconomics from the University of California, Irvine. He is fluent in both Farsi and Dari.

Fredrick Clarke is an Associate Professor of Economics at the Zapara School of Business, at La Sierra University. His research interests include political economy, game theory, and microeconomics.

Nicholas M. Coulombe is a PhD student specializing in International Relations at Rice University. While earning his MA at the University of Rhode Island, he conducted research on subnational structural influences on conflict. This research extended to a collaborative project on localized political violence in Nigeria. His current research focuses on the design of military alliances and the implications varying alliance commitments have for conflict and cooperation. Through this line of inquiry, he continues to examine the role of differing levels of state capacity and its relationship to interstate conflict processes.

Yi Feng is the Luther Lee Memorial Professor and Chair of the Department of International Studies at Claremont Graduate University. Feng's research focuses on political and economic development. He has published extensively on topics such as economic growth, investment, human capital, international trade and foreign direct investment, demographic transition, and political regime transitions in various economics and political science peer-reviewed journals. His works on regional development focus on political and economic issues in Latin America, Pacific Asia, and sub-Saharan Africa. He has also published on China's financial markets, labor and human capital, economic growth, state enterprises, foreign direct investment, and trade policy.

Ali Fisunoglu is a research fellow at the Carlos III Juan March Institute of Social Sciences, Madrid, Spain. He was previously an Assistant Professor of International Relations at Ozyegin University, Istanbul, Turkey. Fisunoglu received his BA in Economics from Koç University in 2009, MA in International Political Economy from Claremont Graduate University in 2012, and PhD in Political Science and Economics from Claremont Graduate University in 2014. His research interests include political economy of growth and development, peace and conflict studies, political demography, international political economy, econometrics, game theory, and computational analysis. In addition, Fisunoglu was awarded the Fulbright scholarship and fellowships from Vehbi Koç Foundation and Claremont Graduate University. He is a Research Associate at the TransResearch Consortium.

Zhijun Gao is an interfield PhD student in political science and economics at the Department of International Studies, Claremont Graduate University. His research focuses on international political economy, international finance, development economics, globalization, and the political economy of China.

Gaspare M. Genna is Professor of Political Science and Director of the North American Studies Program at the University of Texas at El Paso. His research explores the development and impact of regional integration around the world both economically and politically. His work appears in *European Union Politics, Review of International Political Economy, International Interactions, Latin American Perspectives, Comparative European Politics, International Politics, Journal of International Relations and Development,* and *Journal of European Integration,* among others. Genna is the coauthor of *Regional Integration and Democratic Conditionality: How Democracy Clauses Help Democratic Consolidation and Deepening, Efectos Regionales del Libre Comercio: El Caso del Noreste de México,* as well as coeditor of *North American Integration: An Institutional Void in Migration, Security and*

Development, and *Jürgen Habermas and the European Economic Crisis: Cosmopolitanism Reconsidered.*

Allison Hamlin is completing her dissertation at Claremont Graduate University analyzing the North American Free Trade Agreement (NAFTA)–United States Mexico Canada (USMCA) negotiations. After completing her ABD, Allision joined the Washington community and is currently a senior member of Accenture Consulting in Washington, DC. Her interests range from decision-making applications to policy to structural assessments of the likelihood of civil and international conflict. She is a member of and active participant in the International Studies Association and the Peace Science Society.

Athanasios Hristoulas has been a Professor of International Relations at the Instituto Tecnologico Autonomo de Mexico since 1996. He also serves as Director of the National Security program at the same institution. He received his PhD in Political Science from McGill University in 1995. Before relocating to Mexico, he was the Military and Strategic Post-Doctoral Fellow at the Norman Paterson School of International Affairs at Carleton University. He is a member of the editorial committee of *Foreign Affairs en español,* and founding member of the Mexican think-tank Committee for the Analysis of Security and Democracy (CASEDE). Hristoulas is a member of the prestigious National System of Researchers, Level II, and is invited by the Mexican Senate, Mexican Navy, Mexican Army, and Mexican intelligence service as a consultant and guest speaker. His principal research interests include Mexican national security and North American security cooperation.

Patrick James is Dornsife Dean's Professor of International Relations at the University of Southern California (PhD, University of Maryland, College Park). James specializes in comparative and international politics. His interests at the international level include the causes, processes, and consequences of conflict, crisis, and war. Regarding domestic politics, his interests focus on Canada and, most notably, with respect to the constitutional dilemma. James is the author or editor of twenty-five books, and more than 130 articles and book chapters. He is a past president of the International Studies Association (ISA; Midwest) and the Iowa Conference of Political Scientists. James has been Distinguished Scholar in Foreign Policy Analysis for the ISA, 2006–2007 and a Distinguished Scholar in Ethnicity, Nationalism and Migration for ISA, 2009–2010. He served as President, 2007–2009, of the Association for Canadian Studies in the United States and President of the International Council for Canadian Studies, 2011–2013. James also served a five-year term as editor of *International Studies Quarterly.* He is the immediate past president of the Peace Science Society, 2016–2017, and served as president of the ISA, 2018–2019.

Kristin Johnson is an Associate Professor in the Political Science Department at the University of Rhode Island where she teaches courses on political violence, international development, and African Politics. Her published work includes examinations of the influence of political capacity on individual attitudes, including political and social trust, political violence, and human development. Johnson's current research is predominantly subnationally oriented, with current projects focusing on conflicts in Nigeria and Mexico. Recent publications include work appearing in *The Journal of Peace Research*, *Public Opinion Quarterly*, *The Lancet: Planetary Health*, and the *Handbook of Political Trust*. She received her PhD in 2007 from Claremont Graduate University and serves on the board of the TransResearch Consortium.

Kyungkook Kang is an Assistant Professor in the Department of Political Science at the University of Central Florida (UCF) and a senior fellow at TransResearch Consortium. Areas of specialization include: international relations, positive political economy, and formal and computational modeling. He is especially interested in theories of interstate conflict initiation and deterrence. Before teaching at UCF, he taught various courses on security studies at Claremont Graduate University, the University of Southern California, and La Sierra University. His academic works appeared in *International Studies Quarterly*, *International Interactions*, *International Area Studies Review*, and several book chapters. He earned his BA in Political Science and International Studies from Yonsei University, Seoul, Korea, and his MA in Economics and PhD in Political Science and Economics from Claremont Graduate University.

Zeyad Kelani is a world politics and computational analytics PhD student at Claremont Graduate University. He taught comparative politics and political methodology within political science departments at Cairo University and AMIDEAST. Currently, his research highlights the role of values in international relations using machine learning models handling structured and unstructured data. He served as a former 2016 UNAOC fellow, was honored as the 2015 ambassador for the Shafik Gabr foundation, and is an advocate for research transparency through the University of California, Berkeley Initiative for Research Transparency. Zeyad completed his undergraduate degree in political science and public administration at Cairo University, a joint MA degree at the American University in Cairo and Tubingen University in Germany, and studied abroad at Columbia University and Moscow State Institute of International Relations.

Kristina Khederlarian is currently a manager in the Division of Finance and Administration at the University of California Irvine. She also serves as a Board Member for TRC and holds two Masters Degrees in both International Relations and Business. Kristina is presently finishing her doctorate degree at Claremont Graduate University. Prior to coming to UCI, Kristina served the Claremont Colleges as Pomona College's Business Analyst, and the Project Manager of the Digital Innovation and Text Analysis Lab. Kristina is also an active member of the International Studies Association. Prior to entering higher education, Kristina served as a Project Manager and International Business Consultant to companies in the United States, Canada, and Europe.

Jacek Kugler is the Elisabeth Helm Rosecrans Professor of World Politics at Claremont Graduate University (PhD, University of Michigan). His interests in world politics range from economic growth, conflict, formal models, and decision making to political demography. He pioneered the development of power transition theory, political performance measures, and the development of formal agent-based models of decision making and deterrence. As a writer, he has authored or edited seven books and numerous articles. The topics covered range from international and civil war to deterrence and integration, applying techniques ranging from structural assessments to detailed formal analysis of individual decisions. Kugler is the former president of the Peace Science Society and the International Studies Association. He started the Political Demography and Geography Section at ISA that seeks to understand the interaction between individuals and society and is the past editor of *International Interactions* with editing credits spanning a number of special volumes for key journals in the field. He is the cofounder of several policy consulting firms, most recently Sentia and Acertas, dedicated to the impartial and systematic analysis of policy decisions. In addition, he is the cofounder of the TransResearch Consortium dedicated to the advancement of promising young academics and the collection of systematic indicators of politics. His lecturing and teaching positions have included universities in the United States, China, Russia, Ethiopia, the European Union, and much of Latin America. Most recently he received a Fulbright Grant at the Nobel Institute in Norway.

Tadeusz Kugler is an Associate Professor of Political Science at Roger Williams University. He received his PhD in Economics and Politics at Claremont Graduate University. His publications can be found both in edited volumes and journals with a focus on the economic and demographic foundations of growth and their connection to international power and the dynamics of recovery after war. Future projects include exploring how foreign aid undermines domestic political institutions, differentiating recovery after genocides from wars, and the finalization of a book project concerning the long-term consequences of political choices on the underlying demography of nations. His recent publications include *Demographic and Economic Consequences of Conflict* (2013) and *Political Consequences of Population Dynamics* and *Power, Space and Time*, both published in 2020.

Marina Arbetman Rabinowitz holds a MA in Economics from Universidad de Buenos Aires and a PhD in Political Science from Vanderbilt University. At present, she is an evaluator and consultant in New Mexico. She taught at the Facultad de Economía in Argentina, University of Missouri-Columbia, Tulane University, Brooklyn College, and University of New Mexico. She has had a career as an economic and political consultant, both overseas and in the United States, working for Technologica, BHF, Tasmanian Institute, Sentia Group, the World Bank, United Nations, the US State Department, and a number of private businesses. She is a Research Professor at Claremont Graduate University and a board member of the TransResearch Consortium and of the Southwest Women Law Center. Her research focus is on political and economic development, as well as forecasting and strategic planning using statistical modeling. Rabinowitz's expertise is in empirical modeling, data analysis, and measurement, and her publications include *Political Capacity and Economic Behavior*, as well several articles on government effectiveness, economic costs of war, vital rates, hegemony, and black-market exchange rates fluctuations.

J. Patrick Rhamey, Jr., is Associate Professor in the Department of International Studies and Political Science at the Virginia Military Institute, where he teaches courses on international politics, conflict processes, and political demography. He received his PhD in Political Science from the University of Arizona. His publications include work on behaviors of major and regional powers, comparative regionalism, and the international politics of sporting competitions. Across research areas, he is interested in how hierarchy conditions state behaviors and how states recognize one another's strength and authority. In addition to his research, Rhamey serves on the board of the TransResearch Consortium, is an elected member of the Lexington City Council, and serves as program chair for the Political Demography and Geography Section of the International Studies Association.

Ashraf Singer is an Associate Professor, Department Chair of Political Science in Port Said University, Egypt, and a member of the Egyptian Council for Foreign Affairs. He received his PhD in Political Science from Claremont Graduate University in 2008. He is a Research Fellow for TransResearch Consortium. Previously Singer was a Fulbright Scholar in Residence; he is also a political analyst and commentator for various Egyptian channels, newspapers, and Egypt's public radio network. Singer is an expert in Middle East politics. He taught at Claremont Graduate University; American University in Cairo, Egypt; and University of California in Irvine.

Ronald L. Tammen is President of the TransResearch Consortium—a community of world politics scholars. He is Professor Emeritus at the Mark O. Hatfield School of Government at Portland State University and a Research Fellow at Claremont Graduate University. From 2000 to 2015 he served as the founding director of the Hatfield School. In prior positions he was department chair and associate dean at the National War College in Washington, DC, and chief of staff for Senator William Proxmire of Wisconsin. His research interests center on world politics with an emphasis on the emergence of China and India as world powers. He is the author or coauthor of several books dealing with national security issues, including *The Performance of Nations*, *Power Transitions: Strategies for the 21st Century*, *MIRV and the Arms Race*, and *The Economics of Defense Spending*. He received his PhD in World Politics from the University of Michigan.

Osman Goktug Tanrikulu is a political economist with a research focus on international relations and behavioral sciences. He is currently a PhD candidate at the Public Affairs and Policy Program at Portland State University (PSU). Tanrikulu works as the coordinator and senior research assistant of the Center for Turkish Studies at PSU, where he also teaches a course in the political development of modern Turkey. He has been a research fellow at the TransResearch Consortium since 2016 and was a graduate fellow at the Ashburn Institute in 2017–2018. His research focuses on regional integration models, military alliances and cooperation, human development dynamics, and modeling human behavior via agent-based modeling and computer simulation. Osman Tanrikulu's publications are related to European Union integration, Turkey's political development, and modeling rational behavior.

John Thomas is Dean of the Zapara School of Business and Bashir Hasso Professor of Entrepreneurship and Political Economy at La Sierra University in Riverside, California. A creative thinker committed to integrity, compassion, and entrepreneurship, Thomas has led the La Sierra University Zapara School of Business in radically redefining its mission to incorporate a focus on global service and entrepreneurial creativity and identifying distinctive market niches ideally suited to its traditions, commitments, and capacities. Thomas holds a PhD in political economy from Claremont Graduate University, and MAs in marketing, finance, and international political economy.

Ayesha Umar Wahedi specializes in macroeconomic policy analysis, with focus on emerging markets. She has a keen interest in financial sector reform in emerging markets, the role of capital flows in development, links between corruption and foreign investments, impacts of foreign capital on income and gender inequality, the role of institutions in development, financing sustainable development, foreign aid, security, and general issues in international political economy. Wahedi is an Adjunct Professor of Political Science at Portland State University and teaches courses in multinational corporations in world politics, political and economic reform in emerging markets, and international political economy. She has also taught economics for business as part of the MBA faculty at Presidio Graduate School. Wahedi has broad experience in all aspects of macroeconomic data handling including data collection, data analysis, time-series analysis, and forecasting. She received her PhD in the field of Political Economy from Portland State University, her MS in Economics from Oregon State University, a BA in Economics, and a BS in Mathematics and Statistics from Kinnaird College, Pakistan.

Zining Yang received her PhD in Political Economy and Computational and Applied Mathematics from Claremont Graduate University in 2015, an MA in International Studies from Claremont Graduate University in 2011, and LLB in International Politics from Beijing International Studies University in 2009. Her research interests include political economy, predictive analytics, and computational modeling and simulation. She has numerous publications in the fields of agent-based modeling, complex adaptive systems, network analysis, human social-cultural-behavioral modeling, and international political economy. Her recent research is indexed by Springer Advances in Complex Adaptive Systems Modeling, Lecture Notes in Computer Science, and New Political Economy.

Birol Yesilada is the Director of the Mark O. Hatfield School of Government and Contemporary Turkish Studies and holds an endowed chair in Political Science and International Studies at Portland State University. He is also a principal investigator of the World Values Survey project in Cyprus. Yesilada received his PhD in Political Science from the University of Michigan, and his recent publications include *Global Power Transition and the Future of the European Union* (with Jacek Kugler, Gaspare M. Genna, and Osman Goktug Tanrikulu, 2017), *EU-Turkey Relations in the 21st Century* (2014), and *Islamization of Turkey Under the AKP Government* (edited with Barry Rubin, 2010).